THE NATIVE AMERICAN CHRISTIAN COMMUNITY:

A Directory of Indian, Aleut, and Eskimo Churches

THE NATIVE AMERICAN CHRISTIAN COMMUNITY:

A Directory of Indian, Aleut, and Eskimo Churches

Dr. R. Pierce Beaver, Editor

MARC

919 West Huntington Drive, Monrovia, California 91016
A Division of World Vision International

Library of Congress Number 78-70999

Copyright © 1979 by
MISSIONS ADVANCED RESEARCH AND
COMMUNICATION CENTER
A Division of World Vision International

All Rights Reserved

ISBN 0-912552-25-5

Printed in the United States of America

CONTENTS

64575

I
INTRODUCTION

I
INTRODUCTION

EARLIER SURVEYS AND ESTIMATES

A series of Atlases and Statistics of Protestant World Missions was published between 1901 and 1925.* Missions to Native Americans were included since they were cross-cultural missions to persons of other religions. The Century opened with 13,495 communicant or strictly defined members in 195 stations and out-stations and probably with more local churches than that number. By the end of the first decade they had increased to 28,406 members in 534 churches with a total Protestant constituency of 68,143. There had evidently been ten years of effective evangelism and Christian nurture. See TABLES I and II. Less than 1,000 communicants were added during the next five years, but the total Protestant community including baptized and those under

* Beach, Harlan P., *A Geography and Atlas of Protestant Missions*. 2 v. NY: Student Volunteer Movement for Foreign Missions, 1901-03.

Dennis, James A., Harlan P. Beach, and Charles H. Fahs, eds. *World Atlas of Christian Missions*. NY: Student Volunteer Movement for Foreign Missions, 1911.

Beach, Harlan P., and Barton St. John. *World Statistics of Christian Missions*. NY: Committee of Reference and Counsel of the Foreign Missions Conference of N.A., 1916.

Beach, Harlan P., and Charles H. Fahs, eds. *World Missionary Atlas*. NY: Institute of Social and Religious Research, 1925.

instruction was reported at 47,168. See TABLE III. At the end of
the first quarter-century communicants were said to be 32,465 in
514 churches, with a total constituency of 36,174. TABLE IV. Why
had the same mission statisticians discovered that in almost a
decade membership had increased only some 3,000 and the
constituency had shrunk by 10,000? Those last were really 1923
figures, and in that year Dr. G. E. E. Lindquist published his
Red Man in the United States. [NY: Doran, 1923] with statistics
which he had given to the Home Missions Council in 1922.
(pp 428-429) See TABLE V. He states that there were 32,164
Protestant members in 597 churches which closely corresponds to
Beach and Fahs.

The next statistical survey was made by G. E. E. Lindquist and
E. Russell Carter in 1951. [*Indians in Transition,* NY: National
Council of Churches, Division of Home Missions, 1951] They found
the communicant membership to be 39,200 and the constituency
some 140,000. There had been a meager growth in hard core membership of only 7,000 in 25 years, but the constituency had increased
by 72,000 and was 3.57 times larger than the basic membership.
That points either to a very large number of persons under
instruction, many baptized but unconfirmed children, or much
nominalism.

The surveys reveal further that the Protestant churches had 224
native workers of both sexes, ordained and unordained, in 1901,
while there were 158 ordained men and 312 lay workers in 1911.
Strangely the number of ordained pastors dropped to 124 in 1916,
with 328 lay workers. The 1925 statistics indicated 263 ordained
Native American men along with 457 lay men and 22 lay women
workers. Dr. Lindquist in 1923, however, gave slightly different
figures: 268 ordained men and 550 "native helpers."

The white staff was reported as follows:

YEAR	Ordained Men	Unordained Men	Missionary Wives	Other Missionary Women
1901	176	49	76	183
1911	173	47	125	147
1916	210	75	168	253
1925	263			
Lindquist	160			

SCHOOLS: Schools in 1901 were day schools 65 with 2,315 pupils;
1911, 30 boarding and high schools with 1,784 students, 41
elementary schools with 1,046 pupils; and in 1916, 49 elementary
schools with 2,981 pupils, 8 secondary schools with 538 students,
one college with 44 students, and 3 seminaries or Bible schools.
The 1925 figures are 45 lower schools 2,284 pupils, and 12 high

schools with 611 students. Lindquist in 1923 reported 38 schools of all types with 2,262 students. Lindquist and Carter in 1951 reported on 21 institutions, 6 of which were homes that sent their children to neighboring schools, and they had received data from 16, in which the pupils and students totaled 1,767.

MEDICAL SERVICE was never great: 5 hospitals or dispensaries with 10 physicians in 1901; 6 hospitals and 7 dispensaries in 1911; 11 hospitals, 14 dispensaries, 12 doctors and 8 nurses in 1916; and 12 hospitals, 13 dispensaries, 7 doctors and 13 nurses in 1925.

The sources of Roman Catholic information is the Bureau of Catholic Indian Missions and its twin organization, the Commission for Catholic Missions among the Colored People and the Indians. The Bureau published an *Annual Report* for some years and the annual statistics were printed in an annual magazine entitled *Our Negro and Indian Missions,* last issued in 1976. The statistics 50 years before the last tabulation, in 1927 were: Catholics 90,766; churches 321; priests 182; infant baptisms 2,851; adult baptisms 798; schools 81; pupils 7,013. The figures rise very gradually until in 1944 there were 94,085 Catholics in 395 churches, with 206 priests. Infant baptisms were 3,822 and adult baptisms 580. 64 schools had 6,640 pupils. Then 26 years are lacking. The Bureau reported in 1970, 141,573 Catholics in 397 churches, with 257 priests. Infant baptisms that year were 4,917 and adults 1,038. 46 schools enrolled 7,852 pupils. There was a gradual rise in members to 156,728 in 1976, when there were 397 churches and 271 priests. Infant baptisms were 3,772 and adults 721. Schools were now 37 with 5,947 pupils.

The evangelistic drive which was sustained during the long period when Stephan and Ketcham were directors of the Bureau waned, and the number of local parish churches averaged slightly under 400 for 50 years. Yet the community grew steadily because there was faithful pastoral care and nurture and infant baptisms averaged nearly 4,000 per year. The increase came mostly out of the births in Catholic families. Adult baptisms averaged about 800 per year, and that is evidence that there was parochial evangelism, if not the founding of new churches.

THE PRESENT SURVEY AND DIRECTORY

The several sources of information mentioned above are now very scarce, and few persons are aware of their existence. Information about the contemporary Native American Community has been even more difficult to obtain. Central denominational offices can seldom provide a list of their Indian/Eskimo churches and pastors. Yearbooks do not distinguish between Native American and other churches unless the term Indian is in the title. Some yearbooks

omit nearly all Indian ministers and churches, while it is
impossible to note an Indian in a clergy list if he has an Anglo
name. No one has ever attempted to compass the boundaries of the
entire Native American community -- Orthodox, Roman Catholic,
Protestant -- and many Native Americans have asked the writer
questions which he could not answer. Moreover, he is writing a
history of the four centuries of the missions and the development
of the churches, and it seemed imperative at this point to
discover what the total product of those centuries might be.
Consequently the survey was undertaken and this directory has
issued from it. The project has required two years and four
months and has been exceedingly frustrating, -- far more difficult
than any overseas mission survey which the author ever undertook.
And now when it is published it is already out-of-date. Neverthe-
less, this book permits the dimensions of the Native American
Christian community to be readily discerned, and it will provide
the community with facts that may aid in the study, discussion,
planning, and action now in progress. I hope, too, that it will
assist Indian/Aleut/Eskimo Christians in getting acquainted.

METHODOLOGY

Two six-page questionnaires were prepared, one for Roman
Catholics and one for Protestants. A few questions about organization and jurisdiction were asked, and a few about history. If
the church or mission has an official statement of policy on
Indian/Eskimo ministry a copy was requested. Questions were asked
on integration or segregation, on policy and program for
recruiting and training the clergy, and the actual extent of
education of present pastors. There was inquiry about pastors'
finances, i.e., the salary range, self-support, and the like.
Other questions were asked on the official attitude towards Native
American culture and religion and the use of the indigenous
heritage in Christian life and worship. Similar questions were
put about the attitudes of pastors and missionaries. Inquiry was
made whether there were two or three pastors or laymen who could
discuss with real understanding the questions of relationship of
the traditional religion and culture to the gospel and of
acculturation and accommodation. Which local churches might be
considered truly indigenous? Further questions were asked about
schools and other programs, about cooperation with other churches
and missions, with interchurch agencies, with public agencies,
especially in the realm of service and advocacy. Does the church
or mission engage in support of Native American rights and in
advocacy of the same? In what manner? What is the attitude
toward the several Indian activist organizations? Where are the
records and archives? What are the publications? Finally there
was a double-page form for a statistical report: names and
addresses of churches and missions, tribe served, number of
churches and chapels, communicant members, total community,

conversions, adult and infant baptisms, Sunday or church schools, societies, vacation Bible schools, other programs. These questionnaires were sent to executive secretaries of Protestant home mission boards, to the executives of denominations, to Roman Catholic bishops and to provincials or mission directors of missionary orders, as well as to a variety of individuals thought to be responsible for these ministries over large areas. The response was varied, but on the whole poor. The questionnaires came back largely with questions answered but without the statistical information.

Originally it was the intention to survey the Native Canadian also, but it soon became evident that the obstacles to that were even greater than in the United States, and that objective was surrendered. It was soon apparent, also, that the desired information for the United States could be obtained only on a careful state by state, region by region, diocese by diocese, synod by synod, conference by conference search. The questionnaires with letters were sent again to the Roman Catholic bishops, and now to Episcopal and Methodist bishops, to many others. Letters of inquiry were directed to the executive officers of synods and presbyteries, district conferences, associations, and to the executives of state and local councils of churches, along with those of the national service agencies. Trips were made across the country to ferret out information. The *Official Catholic Directory* and national and regional yearbooks and annuals were searched. As names and addresses of pastors and churches were discovered one-page questionnaires were sent to them. Other one-page question sheets were sent to missionaries, to schools, and to other institutions. Return postage was always included. Hundreds of follow-up letters were written. Altogether, some 1,425 letters or communications were sent. The greatest single source of information was the Bureau of Catholic Indian Missions. Msgr. Paul A. Lenz placed at my use all the reports submitted in the autumn of 1977 by the Archbishops and Bishops, and the staff of the Bureau were most gracious and helpful. Why some denominational officials were not more helpful and why some Anglo pastors did not respond, I do not know. I did learn that many Indian pastors did not respond because they are suspicious of any questionnaires and inquiries. They say that they have been questioned to weariness by investigators and exploited by anthropologists and sociologists. Some supposed that my surname Beaver indicated that I am Indian and welcomed a brother seeking such information. Some churches and pastors will not even report to the state convention. Out of one group of 121 Indian pastors only nine replied. Yet others commended my effort and looked forward to the directory coming into their hands.

STATISTICS

The statistics are problematical and highly suspect in many cases. Churches define membership in widely varying terms, and some actually have no membership, and only record attenders or participants in the fellowship. It depends on the ecclesiology of the denomination or local church. Roman Catholics count every person baptized a member all his life, and their membership figures are always the total number of baptized. They seldom have data on currently communicating and regularly attending persons. Episcopalians, Lutherans, and a few others always know the baptized, the confirmed, the communicating, and often the fringe community. Some of the churches which baptize none but adult believers count only such persons members, but they may know how many children of members there are in the church family. It is necessary to have Protestant equivalant to the Roman Catholic membership figure. Therefore, I asked for the total number in the "Baptist community," "Methodist community," or the like. This statistic has been employed in overseas missions for 80 years or more. It includes all baptized, active participants, unbaptized children of members, enquirers, and those who would say that they "belong" and are not participants elsewhere. When only hard core membership figures were given, I studied the pattern of the churches of the denomination and area, the statistics for conversions, baptisms, Sunday School, and the various programs and tried to arrive at a reasonable "community" figure. The number of those who would call themselves Christians is larger even that the community figure, since where there is only 1 church in a village or isolated district all the inhabitants may think of themselves as "belonging." Thus in a certain Chippewa village in Michigan the whole populace think of themselves as Methodists, but the church reports only 23 active members.

The entire Native American Christian community numbers about 320,00. In summary:

CHURCH STATISTICS

Churches and Societies	Churches Chapels	Communicants Regular Attenders	Baptized Members Total Community
Orthodox Church	83	20,000	22,000
Protestant			
Denominations	1,280	79,279	109,748
Societies	67	1,937	2,800
Independent churches	164	6,950	8,000
Protestant Totals	1,511	88,166	120,548
Roman Catholic Church	454	---	177,651
GRANT TOTALS	2,048		320,199

For details of the statistics see the TABLES following this
Introduction

ACKNOWLEDGEMENTS

The compiler gratefully acknowledges grants and funds towards
the expenses of this project given by World Vision International
and the Mennonite Central Committee.

The kindness and assistance of Msgr. Paul A. Lenz, Executive
Director of the Bureau of Catholic Indian Missions, and of his
staff are gratefully acknowledged. My gratitude is expressed to
the numerous Archbishops, Bishops, Presidents, Executive
Ministers, Directors and Secretaries of denominations, dioceses,
synods, conferences, presbyteries, associations, and districts
who gave me information. Thanks are extended to Directors of
state and city councils of churches, to the Executives of
numerous agencies, to scores of pastors and missionaries, and to
others who helped. At the risk of too many omissions a few
persons must be singled out for mention: Dr. B. Frank Belvin of
Okmulgee, Oklahoma; Dr. Coy E. Lee, Executive Minister of Eastern
Oklahoma Presbytery; Rev. Robert Pinezaddleby and Mrs. Daisy Ross
of the Oklahoma Indian Ministries; Dr. Chester B. O'Brien,
Executive Director of the Baptist General Convention of New
Mexico and Mrs. O'Brien; Dr. Robert Haskins, Director of Language
Ministries of the Baptist General Convention of Oklahoma; Dr.
Cecil Corbett and Rev. Gary Kush of the Cook Christian Training
School; The Rt. Rev. Walter H. Jones of the Diocese of South
Dakota, especially for checking the large section of the directory
applying to his diocese; the Rev. J. R. Stogsdill, general
missionary to the Cherokee Baptist Association; Dr. Charles
Chaney, Illinois Baptist Convention, who made important contacts
for me; Dr. James N. Lewis, Jr., Associate Director of the
Department of Language Missions, Home Mission Board of the
Southern Baptist Convention. Others who helped: Rev. E. R.
Isbell of Citronelle, Alabama; Dr. Delbert D. Fann of Phoenix;
Rev. Tom E. Brewington of Pembroke, North Caroline; the Rev. Don
R. Ramsey of the American Indian Bible Institute; and Mrs. Frances
J. Rhodes of Oscoda, Michigan.

I am grateful to the several Indian executives of the mission
agencies who gave aid: Mr. Eugene Begay of the Program Agency of
the United Presbyterian Church U.S.A.; Miss Billie Nowabbi of the
Division of Home Missions of the United Methodist Church; and
others; to Rev. Raymond A. Baines, now directing the self-study
of the Methodist Native American churches, for sharing his
knowledge and insights. Sister Maria Branigan of the Sisters of
the Blessed Sacrament provided a great sheaf of material. Father
Ed Schultz of St. Nicholas Center in Tucson was very helpful. So
were Rev. Tom Dolaghan of the Navajo Gospel Mission and Rev.

David Scates of the Christian Mission, and I especially
acknowledge their generosity in permitting me to draw on and
cite their recent book, *The Navajos Are Coming To Jesus*. Above
all, thanks to Miss Carol Lichti, a Mennonite Service Volunteer
of the Tucson Unit, who did all the typing involved in the
correspondence and the preparation of the manuscript.

PLEASE HELP MAINTAIN AN INFORMATION BANK!

This directory is out-dated as soon as published, but it
provides the basis for an information bank on the Native American
Christian community. Please report omissions. Please report
changes. Please report major new organizations and developments.
Your help is needed.

Send corrections and further information to:

MARC/WORLD VISION INTERNATIONAL
919 West Huntington Drive
Monrovia, California   91016

MARC is the Research and Information arm of World Vision.
It publishes the comprehensive and authoritative *Mission Handbook:
North American Ministries Overseas*. The MARC staff will receive,
file, and keep available current information on the Native
American churches, missions and ministries.

STATISTICAL TABLES

TABLE I   1901 – 1903

Countries and Societies	Year included in the report	Year of its first work in this field	Foreign missionaries, including physicians					Stations		Native constituency		Educational				Medical			
			Ordained, men	Unordained, men	Missionaries' wives	Other missionary women	Native workers, both sexes	Where missionaries reside	Outstations, or substations	Communicants	Adherents, not communicants	Day-schools	Pupils in same	Higher institutions	Students in same	Foreign male physicians	Foreign women physicians	Hospitals, or dispensaries	Patients during year reported
II. ALASKA																			
American Societies																			
American Friends' Board of Foreign Missions......	1900	1887	3		3	3	15	3	4	235	620	3	144						
American Missionary Association...........	1900	1890			1	16[a]	2	1	1			2	100						
Board of Home Missions of the Presb. Church, North[b]	'00-'01	1877	1[a]	10[a]		7	11	9	5	868		4	151						
Domestic and Foreign M. S., Prot. Episcopal Church[b]	'00-'01	1897	9	1	3		5	11		405						1		1	1930
Missionary Society of the Methodist Episcopal Church	1895	1895	11	1	1	6	1	3		63						1		3	
Peniel Missionary Society........	1895	1887	4		3		1	3											
Swedish Evangelical Mission Covenant of America...	1900	1900			1	4		1											
Synod for the Norwegian Evangelical Lutherans....	1900	1893	6		2		3	3	1	186		3	136						
Woman's American Baptist H. M. Society (Boston)	1900	1900	1		1	2		1		10		1							
Women's National Indian Association...........	1900	1900	2	1				1	2										
Totals, 10 American Societies			**37**	**12**	**15**	**38**	**37**	**33**	**13**	**1,767**	**620**	**13**	**531**			**3**		**4**	**1930**
International Society																			
Mission der Brüdergemeine...........	1899	1885	6	1	7	2		3	4	282	657	2	51			1			
**Grand Total, 11 Societies....... **			**43**	**13**	**22**	**40**	**37**	**36**	**17**	**2,049**	**1,277**	**15**	**582**			**4**		**4**	**1930**
IV. INDIANS IN THE UNITED STATES																			
American Societies																			
American Baptist Home Mission Society...........	1900	1879	8[e]		4	18[e]		4		67		5		6					
American Friends' Associated Com. Indian Missions	1900	1870	9[f]		9[t]	4[f]		10	3	384		25	211	1					
American Missionary Association...........	1900	1846	9	7[r]	13[t]	20	42	11	34	1,303		3	1,300	1					
Board of Home Miss. of the Presb. Church, North[b]	'00-'01	1802	65[t]	23[t]		63[t]	42	77	20	4,312[s]					201				1530
Board of Missions and Church Erection, Cumb. Prb.	1900	1860	1[g]		8			1											
Domestic and Foreign M. S., Prot. Episcopal Church	'00-'01	1889	9[h]	2		2	72	11	76	3,282		6		8		1	2		
General Assembly's Home Missions, Southern....	1900	1896			1	5	10	7											
Gospel Missionary Union	1900	1880	2	2	4	2		1											
Mennonite General Conference of North America	1900	1880	6			2		7		30		1							
Missionary Society of the Methodist Episcopal Church	1900	1814	15		1		11	15		1,920		1	45			2	1	1	
Philadelphia Yearly Meeting of Friends...	1900	1798	2	2	2			1				1		1					
Synod of Reformed Presb. Church in N. America[b].	1900	1889	1			3		1				1							
Synod for the Norwegian Evangelical Lutherans	1900		1	2	3	2	2	1				1	63						
Woman's F. M. Society, Methodist Church, South.	1900				3			1											
Women's Baptist Home Mission Society...........	'99-'00	1878			1	12		8	1			7	114	1					
Women's General M. S., United Presbyterian[i]	'99-'00							2											
Totals, 16 American Societies			**128**	**36**	**49**	**143**	**171**	**156**	**134**	**11,308**		**50**	**1733**	**18**	**201**	**3**	**3**	**1**	**1530**
International Society																			
Mission der Brüdergemeine...........	1899	1890	5		5		16	3		135	136								
**Grand Total, 17 Societies....... **			**133**	**36**	**54**	**143**	**187**	**159**	**134**	**11,443**	**136**	**50**	**1733**	**18**	**201**	**3**	**3**	**1**	**1530**

TABLE II   1911

COUNTRIES AND SOCIETIES	Year of First Work in this Field	Ordained Missionaries	Physicians Men	Physicians Women	Lay Missionaries (Men) not Physicians	Married Women not Physicians	Unmarried Women not Physicians	Total of Foreign Missionaries	Ordained Natives	Unordained Natives, Preachers, Teachers, Bible-women, and Other Workers	Total of Ordained and Unordained Native Workers	Principal Stations	All Other Sub-Stations	Church Organizations	Communicants Added During the Last Year	Total Number of Communicants	Tot'l Number of Baptized Christians	Total of Native Christian Adherents, incl. Baptized and Unbaptized, All Ages	Sunday Schools	Total Sunday School Membership, Including Teachers and Pupils	Total of Native Contrib'butions in U.S. Gold
UNITED STATES OF AMERICA, INCLUDING ALASKA (Indians and Eskimos) **American Societies**																					$
American Baptist Home Mission Society	1865	13				9	1	22	37		37	13		102	106	4 269	4 269	8 156	68	2 832	464
American Friends' Board of Foreign Missions	1886	2			1	5	1	12	7	5	6	6	4	6		1 350	1 350	1 650	7	150	154
American Missionary Association	1852	9		1		1	3	14	2	23	25	7	45	21	45	°1 492	1 492	3 000	20	1 452	
Associated Executive Com. of Friends on Indian Miss.	1869	a9	1	1		10	3	23		4	6	10	5	9		550	550	2 250	10	769	30
Board of For. Miss., General Conference Mennonites	1880	b10		2	1	8	6	13		3	3	7	3	5	38	162	162	1 362	2	200	
Board of Heathen Miss., Christian Reformed Church	1884	8		1		3	11	19		3	3	3		1		75	°550	1 000	3	200	
Board of Home Missions, Methodist Episcopal Church	1814	25		2	17	9	55	13	10	3	3	35	114	42		2 112	2 112	5 000	44	1 597	
Board of Home Missions, Presbyterian Ch. in U.S.A.	1865	39				37	4	151	34	50	84	47		114		7 548	7 548	18 108	485	6 431	
Central B'd of Miss., Reformed Presbyterian Church		1		1				5	30			1		1		104	¹104	350	3	60	
Dom. and For. Miss. Soc., Protestant Episcopal Church		17		2	4	4	25	51	8	64	98	17	94	105	390	⁴559	⁴559	12 900	13	585	872
Executive Com. of Home Miss., Presby. Ch. (South).	1861	4						4	8		8	4	9	20	47	655	700	1 130			
Gospel Missionary Union		1		3		2						1		2							
Home Mission Board, Southern Baptist Convention		3		7		2	3	9		2	2	3	14	2		107	107	500	3	160	54
Joint Lutheran Synod of Wis., and other States	1894	4				2		8		3	3	1		1		14	²28	744	2	380	
Metlakahtla Christian Mission	1887	1				2		7				3		1		150	150	500	2	*100	
National Indian Association		1						1		20	20	1	14					176		50	
Seventh-Day Adventist Mission Board				1						1	1	6		1		43	43	*172			
American Societies—Concluded																					
Sheboygan Classis, Reformed Church in U.S.	1878	1						1				1	1	1		64	⁴64	106	1	32	$
Swedish Evangelical Mission Covenant of America	1889	2				3	1	7				3	3	3	92	600	⁴600	*2 400			
Synod for Norwegian Evangelical Lutheran Church	1889	2				2	2	6				3	2			100	100				
United Danish Evangelical Lutheran Church		2				1	1	5		1	1	2	1	2		9	19	744	3	380	
United German Synod (Lutheran)		4						1				1	1								
Woman's American Baptist Home Mission Society	1885	4				4	12	18		32	133	11		6	6	588	⁵588	1 200	5	472	380
Woman's Ex. Com., B'd of Dom. Miss., Ref.Ch.(Dutch)	1894	5				3	4	14				4	1		83	3 310	³310	5 000	28	684	
Woman's For. Miss. Soc., M. E. Church, South.		3				3	4	17				2	4		7	75	75	280		97	
Woman's Gen. Miss. Soc., United Presbyterian Church		3				1	2	1		1	1	1	2	1	725	27 936	²3 012	66 928	303	10 631	1 588
Totals, 26 American Societies		**163**	**6**		**1**	**36**	**114**	**145**	**464**	**155**	**101**	**300**	**190**	**301**	**528**	**725**	**27 936**	**28 012**	**66 928**	**303**	**10 631**	**1 588**
International Societies																					
Mission der Brüdergemeine	1885	10				3	10	1	23		12	12	6	25	6	68	470	470	848	6	366	154
Salvation Army		10				3	11	2	5	3	12	12	8	6	6	68	470	470	848	6	366	154
Totals, 2 International Societies		**10**					**10**	**2**	**28**	**3**	**12**	**12**	**8**	**31**			**470**	**470**	**848**	**6**	**366**	**154**
Grand Totals, 28 Societies		**173**	**6**		**1**	**41**	**125**	**147**	**492**	**158**	**312**	**470**	**198**	**332**	**534**	**793**	**28 406**	**28 860**	**68 143**	**309**	**16 997**	**1 740**

TABLE III   1916

AREAS AND SOCIETIES	Year of First Work in This Field	FOREIGN STAFF							NATIVE STAFF				CHURCH							
		Total Foreign Staff	Ordained Men	Unordained Men	Wives	Unmarried Women and Widows	Short Term Workers Included in Foregoing	Residence Stations ‡	Total Native Staff	Ordained Men	Unordained Men	Women	Organized Churches	Other Places Having Regular Services	Communicants	Baptized Non-Communicant Adults and Children	Others under Christian Instruction	Sunday Schools	Teachers and Pupils	Contributions for Church Work
UNITED STATES, INCLUDING ALASKA (North American Indians and Eskimos)																				
Grand Totals, 24 Societies	—	686	210	75	168	233	4	238	452	124	272	56	323	461	29 252	*2 243	15 673	*514	*19 289	*348 619
American Societies																				
Totals, 23 American Societies	—	667	201	73	160	233	4	233	442	124	263	55	318	424	28 331	*1 501	15 643	508	19 041	48 524
American Baptist Home Mission Society	1865	34	9	10	14	17	—	10	3	3	3	—	20	14	1 495	*	—	29	1 220	4 312
American Missionary Association	1832	36	6	7	6	17	—	17	24	3	21	—	25	14	1 488	—	600	11	605	1 798
Associated Exec. Com. of Friends on Indian Affairs	1869	17	8	—	8	1	—	8	5	—	3	2	7	5	550	—	210	8	400	349
Board of For. Miss., General Conference, Mennonites	1880	26	8	4	11	13	—	9	7	—	4	3	8	2	260	—	600	8	288	—
Board of Heathen Miss., Christian Reformed Church	1897	27	1	—	6	13	—	5	25	10	15	—	2	5	90	—	3 517	3	300	—
Board of Home Miss., Methodist Episcopal Church	1814	38	6	—	69	71	—	71	177	41	94	42	50	48	2 583	†1 000	16 000	50	2 179	*3 778
Board of Home Miss., Presbyterian Church in the U.S.A.	1865	226	61	25	2	2	—	3	8	9	6	2	150	118	9 337	*	—	141	7 496	15 904
Board of Missions, Friends' Church of California	1886	6	2	—	—	—	—	5	32	32	—	—	5	3	484	*	—	4	—	—
Board of Miss., Methodist Episcopal Church, South[a]	—	5	5	2	6	2	—	3	—	—	—	1	15	80	875	—	—	38	766	—
Central Board of Miss., Reformed Presbyterian Church[a]	—	3	1	5	9	39	—	5	122	29	92	1	1	17	74	—	—	3	175	—
Dom. and For. Miss. Soc., Protestant Episcopal Church	—	84	30	2	9	13	—	47	11	8	3	—	20	139	*6 982	—	3 118	*84	*1 500	*18 736
Exec. Com. of Home Miss., Presby. Church (South)	1861	31	5	4	4	—	—	24	4	—	4	1	1	—	600	—	1 200	10	525	1 618
For. Miss. Conference of the Mennonite Brethren	1900	4	2	—	2	6	—	3	2	—	1	1	2	2	75	—	—	1	45	—
Indian Commission, Gen. Synod of Wis., Minn., etc.[a]	1894	10	4	2	1	1	—	1	7	1	7	—	1	2	120	—	—	4	500	200
International Committee, Y.M.C.A.	1911	6	1	—	2	3	—	2	2	—	2	—	—	—	—	—	—	100	2 200	75
Miss. Board, United Danish Evan. Lutheran Church	—	5	3	1	1	1	—	1	7	1	7	—	1	4	50	63	250	4	80	—
National Indian Association	1879	9	1	2	—	27	—	2	2	—	2	—	1	—	16	—	40	1	100	—
Sheboygan Classis, Reformed Church, U.S.	1878	9	3	1	3	3	—	1	1	—	1	—	1	—	44	—	108	1	30	—
Swedish Evangelical Mission Covenant of America[a]	1887	9	1	—	8	8	—	3	1	—	1	—	1	—	300	415	—	—	42	—
Synod for Norwegian Evangelical Lutheran Church	1889	8	3	3	7	5	—	9	5	—	6	—	—	—	—	—	—	—	—	—
Woman's American Baptist Home Mission Society	1896	29	6	4	—	—	—	5	6	1	—	4	—	2	908	23	—	6	590	1 754
Woman's Home Miss. Soc., Methodist Episcopal Church	—	25	8	—	—	—	‡2	—	—	—	—	—	7	—	—	—	—	—	—	—
Woman's Board of Dom. Miss., Reformed Church (Dutch)	1891	24	8	2	—	—	—	—	—	—	—	—	—	—	—	—	—	—	—	—
International Society																				
Moravian Church	1890	19	9	2	8	—	—	5	10	—	9	1	5	37	921	742	30	6	248	95

TABLE IV   1925

Areas and Societies	Native Staff — Total	Ordained Men	Unordained Men	Women	Organized Churches	Self-Supporting Churches Included in Col. 5	Other Places Having Regular Services	Communicants Added During the Year	Christian Community—Totals of Cols. 10, 11 and 13	Communicants	Baptized Non-Communicants	Total Baptized—Total of Cols. 10 and 11	Others Under Christian Instruction	Sunday Schools	Sunday School Teachers and Pupils	Contributions for Church Work—U.S. Dollars
ALASKA																
American Societies																
Totals, 5 American Societies	8	0	6	2	31	0	2	25	1,000	533	7	540	460	14	927	500
American Baptist Home Mission Society	0	0	0	0	1	0	0	25	22	22	0	22	—	1	—	—
Friends Church of California, Board of Missions	0	0	0	0	5	0	0	—	—	—	—	—	—	1	—	—
Lutheran Missions in Russia Society	—	—	—	—	0	0	0	—	7	0	7	7	—	—	—	0
Presbyterian Church in U.S.A., Bd. of Home Missions	3	0	1	2	22	0	2	—	819	467	0	467	352	8	†752	500
Svenska Evangeliska Missionsforbundet in America	5	0	5	0	3	0	—	0	152	44	0	44	108	4	175	—
UNITED STATES (American Indians)																
American Societies																
Totals, 21 American Societies	734	263	451	20	483	10	163	570	35,174	31,932	2,290	34,192	982	319	15,514	25,228
American Baptist Home Mission Society	4	3	1	—	32	—	—	78	2,373	2,373	0	2,373	500	23	1,597	9,700
American Missionary Association	25	4	21	—	21	—	7	†46	1,996	996	500	1,496	—	7	250	—
Christian Reformed Ch., Bd. of Heathen Missions	0	0	—	—	1	—	5	13	193	193	0	193	—	7	962	—
Evangelical Luth. Syn. of Mo., Bd. of Indian Miss.	0	0	—	—	—	0	—	—	75	75	—	75	—	—	—	—
Friends, Assoc. Exec. Com., Indian Affairs	4	0	4	—	3	0	6	—	30	30	—	30	100	5	150	—
Indian Committee, Gen. Synod of Wisconsin	5	0	—	—	2	0	13	*90	700	300	300	600	—	7	600	—
Mennonite General Conf., Bd. of For. Missions	44	15	14	15	8	0	1	—	480	480	0	480	*180	35	1,519	28
Methodist Episcopal Church, Board of Home Miss.	102	36	66	—	30	—	—	*0	2,266	1,986	*100	*2,086	—	45	1,278	—
Methodist Episcopal Church, South, Bd. of Missions	1	—	—	—	78	10	—	62	2,388	2,388	0	2,388	45	1	27	*15,000
National Indian Association	14	7	5	2	—	0	110	—	45	*0	—	—	—	—	623	0
Presbyterian Ch. in U.S., Exec. Com. of Home Miss.	218	75	143	2	20	—	1	—	636	636	0	636	—	73	4,235	—
Presbyterian Ch. in U.S.A., Bd. of Home Missions	93	36	57	0	125	—	—	110	6,594	6,594	0	6,594	—	18	814	—
Protestant Episcopal Ch., Dom. and For. Miss. Soc.	8	0	8	—	29	—	—	—	9,526	9,526	0	9,526	35	5	581	—
Reformed Ch. in America, Women's Bd. of Dom. Miss.	3	0	3	1	7	—	20	1	918	883	0	883	—	1	88	—
Reformed Church in U.S., Tri-Synodic Boards	4	0	2	2	1	0	—	6	144	64	15	79	—	1	50	—
Reformed Presbyterian Church, Central Bd. of Miss.	—	—	—	—	1	0	—	—	72	72	0	72	57	1	2,175	—
Seventh-Day Adventist Denom., General Conference	189	86	103	0	1	1	—	219	4,176	4,176	0	4,176	—	80	451	400
Southern Baptist Convention, Home Mission Board	11	1	10	0	114	—	—	56	2,322	1,039	1,226	2,265	—	8	80	—
United Brethren in Christ, Prop. Gospel (Moravians)	2	0	0	0	8	1	—	—	175	56	119	175	—	1	44	—
United Danish Evangelical Lutheran Ch., Miss. Bd.	—	0	2	—	1	0	—	—	65	65	0	65	—	1	—	100
Wesleyan Methodist Connection of America	—	—	—	—	1	0	—	—	—	—	—	—	—	—	—	—

TABLE V   LINDQUIST 1923

Denomination or Society	No. Tribes Served	No. Churches[2]	Ordained Ministers — White	Ordained Ministers — Native	Native Helpers	Material Equipment — Value of Church Buildings	Material Equipment — Value of Parsonages	Material Equipment — Value of Other Buildings	Finances[3] — Annual Appropriations	Membership[4] — Total on Roll	Sunday Schools — No.	Sunday Schools — Enrollment	Young People's Societies — No.	Young People's Societies — Enrollment	Women's Societies — No.	Women's Societies — Enrollment	Mission Schools — No.	Mission Schools — Enrollment
Adventists (Seventh Day)	1	1	1	...	4	...	...	$12,000	No Report	...	...	...	...	...	...	...	...	...
Baptist (Northern Convention)	20	32	18	5	34	$56,850	$22,800	11,350	$48,856.63	2,810	23	1,597	9	246	14	311	3	320
Baptist (Southern Convention)	14	114	8	86	103	83,250	19,350	18,555	12,294.38	4,176	80	2,175	42	713	64	686	2	225
Congregational	5	17	4	11	17	34,300	12,500	11,100	38,021.50	1,178	3	346	5	118	21	444	...	...
Disciples of Christ[5]	1	8	6	...	...	3,600	4,200	10,000	23,166.66	107	...	...	1	9	1	12	...	...
Friends	9	8	1	2	3	1,500	...	4,000	6,250.00	No Report	5	299	...	...	...	...	...	...
Gospel Union[2]	1	...	8	...	...	...	...	...	No Report	...	...	...	...	...	...	...	...	...
Lutheran	4	8	11	...	14	15,000	5,000	500	4,137.50[7]	473	3	540	2	24	1	8	1	56
Mennonites (Two bodies)	4	12	26	...	49	12,800	24,900	9,750	23,021.00	485	6	979	...	...	...	...	6	360
Methodist Episcopal (North)	25	43	1	15	14	68,000	37,300	7,620	65,017.00	1,986	35	1,519	6	151	6	111	2	75
Wesleyan Methodist	1	1	...	...	2	2,000	1,500	...	575.00	65	1	44	1	35	1	...	...	...
Methodist Episcopal (South)[6]	...	...	2	36	...	...	...	...	50,000.00	2,388	45	1,278	16	201	26	363	1	50
Moravian[5]	8	78	3	...	66	47,800	6,200	49,840	3,227.43	2,154	1	38	...	...	1	11	...	...
Plymouth Brethren[2]	3	3	3	...	3	3,200	2,700	1,400	No Report	13	1	77	...	...	...	...	...	...
Presbyterian, U.S.A.	43	125	37	75	143	188,400	67,535	56,025	209,532.00	6,594	73	4,235	29	722	36	807	7	401
Presbyterian, U.S.[6]	4	20	2	11	21	8,350	8,030	5,500	5,009.00	656	13	508	1	46	10	114	2	137
United Presbyterian[2]	2	4	3	...	3	9,000	4,500	...	4,000.00	137	...	...	2	40	1	40	...	...
Reformed Presbyterian	2	1	1	...	...	...	...	...	...	94	3	121	...	...	...	...	...	...
Cumberland Presbyterian	...	15	...	13	2	5,000	5,000	5,000	6,400.00	189	10	50	5	51	7	62	...	...
Protestant Episcopal[6]	13	93	14	14	10	7,700	1,100	1,750	No Report	9,526	18	149	...	...	...	...	...	...
Reformed in America[2]	7	7	5	...	43	152,870	59,575	153,400	112,695.00	883	5	814	9	279	59	1,411	7	270
Christian Reformed[2]	2	5	5	...	8	10,500	14,500	12,200	57,526.42	193	4	581	5	79	4	39	2	122
Reformed in United States[2]	1	2	1	...	5	10,000	13,000	6,000	65,433.00	57	1	424	3	43	...	...	2	136
National Indian Association[2]	1	1	1	...	1	200	1,500	12,000	7,740.00	...	1	67	1	12	2	...	2	90
American Tract Society[8]	...	...	...	...	...	1,000	1,000	...	No Report	...	...	...	...	...	...	...	...	...
Independent	...	...	...	...	...	...	...	...	1,800.00	...	1	27	...	...	...	...	1	20
TOTALS	175	597	160	268	550	729,820	309,990	387,990	744,702.52	34,164	332	15,868	137	2,740	251	4,419	38	2,262

[1] Statistics given herewith are based on reports from the field, but in two or three instances confirmation has been received from denominational headquarters.

[2] Unorganized churches, where services are held with fair degree of regularity, included.

[3] Taken from the figures furnished to the Home Missions Council, 1922. Educational missions included.

[4] Includes communicants but not adherents. The latter figure varies according as one or more denominations are at work in a given field. Usually where there is no Roman Catholic work the entire Indian population is considered the Protestant constituency. The estimated number of Protestant adherents is 80,000.

[5] No station. Community work only. See under Washington Indians, Ch. XIV, § III.

[6] Partial report only.

[7] Partial report only. See also statistics for Five Tribes, given below.

[8] Distribution of literature only.

TABLE VI

ROMAN CATHOLIC INDIAN MISSION STATISTICS

Year	Catholics	Churches	Priests	Baptisms Infant	Adult	Schools	Pupils
1927	90,776	321	182	2,851	298	81	7,013
1931	85,568	390	197	2,771	514	88	7,557
1934	76,575	412	215	3,393	751	76	7,596
1936	79,982	413	204	4,245	1,372	72	6,988
1937	82,292	407	201	3,712	619	71	6.938
1938	87,844	401	199	3,966	658	71	6,868
1940	90,353	398	199	3,778	710	68	6,944
1941	90,404	385	200	4,247	808	67	7,235
1943	91,604	388	198	4,014	620	68	6.961
1944	94,085	395	206	3,822	580	64	6,640
1970	141,573	397	257	4,917	1,038	46	7,852
1971	143,122	391	264	4,674	859	47	7,603
1972	146,980	409	250	4,630	732	45	7,407
1973	149,317	388	258	4,470	801	44	7,413
1974	152,670	397	259	4,459	609	40	7,049
1975	155,660	398	265	3,680	747	39	6,538
1976	156,728	397	271	3,772	721	37	5,947

II
THE NATIVE
CHRISTIAN
COMMUNITY IN
THE 1970s

II
THE NATIVE CHRISTIAN
COMMUNITY IN THE 1970s

HISTORICAL FACTORS

Many features and aspects of the contemporary Native Christian
community are determined by past history. It has been fashioned
by four hundred years of missionary endeavor. That mission was
undertaken by Europeans who never questioned the identification
of the Gospel with European culture and with their denominational
forms of Christianity. Whether Spanish, English, Russian, or
German, whether Protestant, Orthodox or Roman Catholic, the
missionaries sought simultaneously to evangelize and "civilize"
the Indian, conforming him to the white man's cultural and
ecclesiastical pattern. Successive generations of white Americans continued the effort to attain the same goals. It has been
a colonial enterprise down to this day, and the Native Americans
have been a subject people under colonial powers politically,
culturally, militarily and religiously. Their colonial status
did not end when the Indians and Eskimos became United States
citizens in 1934, but at last in the 1970's the beginning of the
end appears. A new day of self-determination dawns.

The denominations are distributed as they are because of
evangelization by mainline churches in the free competition,
religious liberty, and voluntaryism that marked American
Protestantism before the Civil War and by the government's
assignment of Indian reservations to specific denominational
mission boards under General Grant's "Peace Plan." The opening
of all reservations to all churches in 1881 allowed subsequent
duplication. The newer missions of the several conservative
Evangelical denominations and nondenominational missionary

societies are part of the expansion of such churches in the last 50 years and are evidence of their economic development. Before 1870 the few Roman Catholic Indian missions were almost entirely a foreign mission of Europeans, and then the vigorous direction of the work by the new Bureau of Catholic Indian Missions made it the mission of the American Church. It began with reservations alloted under the Grant Peace Plan and quickly expanded, with special effort to revive or renew the long abandoned or dormant Spanish missions of the southwest. There are practically no Catholic Indian churches east of the Mississippi River excepting in the Old Northwest where there was development out of the French missions and among the Houma in Louisiana, also a legacy from the French. The Orthodox Church is confined to Alaska, where it continues to work among Aleut, Athabascan and Eskimo peoples begun by the Russian Orthodox Church in 1792.

SIZE AND DISTRIBUTION

There are 2,048 local churches, congregations, or missions belonging to 42 denominations and 13 nondenominational societies, and including 164 independent churches. The Protestant churches have a communicant or regularly attending membership of 79,279 in the denominations, ·1,937 in the society churches and 6,950 in the independent congregations, or a total "hard core" active membership of 88,166. The Orthodox Church has 20,000 such members. It is not possible to state the communicant membership of the Roman Catholic Church, but that church reports a baptized membership of 177,651. Total community figures of 22,000 for the Orthodox Church and of 120,548 Protestants may be placed alongside the Roman Catholic membership figure. The total Native Christian community is therefore about 320,199. This is about 43% of the total Native American population of 763,594 according to the U.S. Census of 1970.

The denominations with more than 1,000 communicant members or regular attenders are:

DENOMINATION	HARD CORE OR COMMUNICANTS	TOTAL COMMUNITY
American Baptist Churches	1,000	1,200
Assemblies of God	2,980	3,330
Church of the Nazarene	1,557	2,652
Episcopal Church	10,364	19,674
American Lutheran Church	1,758	2,603
Wisconsin Ev. Lutheran Synod	1,160	3,095
Orthodox Church of America	20,000	22,000
Pentecostal Church of God	1,980	2,200
Roman Catholic Church	---	177,651
Southern Baptist Convention	28,577	36,000
United Church of Christ	1,083	1,350

The Native Christian Community in the 1970's

DENOMINATION	HARD CORE OR COMMUNICANTS	TOTAL COMMUNITY
United Methodist Church	11,969	14,360
United Presbyterian Church	6,826	8,190

The churches are relatively small among the Protestant denominations: 71.5 in the denominations, 26.15 in the societies, and 42.37 in the independent churches. The size of the average church in some denominations is: Assemblies of God 60.4, Christian and Missionary Alliance 38, Christian Reformed 59.33, Church of God 47.5, Nazarene 48.65, Episcopal 62, California Friends 60.4, Lutheran Church – Missouri Synod 64, Wisconsin Lutheran 72.5, Mennonite Church 26, Mennonite General Conference 40.45, Moravian Church 120.86, Orthodox 240, Mennonite Brethren 60, Pentecostal Church of God 56, Presbyterian U.S. 65, Reformed Church 74, Southern Baptist Convention 95.6 (would probably be smaller were all statistics in hand), United Church of Christ 62.5, United Methodist Church 73.4, United Presbyterian Church 66.3.

The Southern Baptist Convention has 63 churches with membership between 100-199, 11 between 200-299, 4 between 300-399, and 2 between 400-499, none larger. The United Methodist Church has 18 congregations between 100-199, 5 between 200-299, 2 between 300-399, and 1 between 400-499. The second largest Protestant Indian church in the United States is a Lumbee Methodist Church in Maxton, North Carolina with a membership of 670. The third largest is a United Presbyterian Eskimo Church at Barrow, Alaska with 628 members. The United Presbyterian Church has 9 parishes between 100-199 members, 1 between 200-299 and 1 between 300-399. The largest Protestant church reported is Holy Apostles Episcopal Church of the Oneida Nation with 800 communicants at Oneida, Wisconsin. The Episcopal Church has 6 parish churches with between 100-199 communicants, 1 between 200-299, 1 between 300-399 and 1 over 500; while 15 churches have 100-199 baptized members, 3 have between 200-299, 1 each in each of the next century brackets and 1 over 500.

Roman Catholic churches tend to run larger than Protestant even when communicants are reported. Churches in the Diocese of Fairbanks, Alaska are reported at 250,650, communicants 500 and total 750, 250, 450, 260, 120, 160. In the city of Tucson, Arizona the statistics for communicant and baptized or total members are 200 and 300, 200 and 350, 150 and 600, 250 and 300, 200 and 400, 200 and 400, 80 and 240 and at San Xavier Mission 900 and 900. There are 13 churches on Rosebud Reservation in South Dakota with 5,500 communicants and 8,100 total members or 423 communicants and 623 members per church. 2 Menominee churches in Wisconsin have respectively 250 communicants and 800 baptized members and 300 and 1,000. These are instances taken at random when both sets of membership figures are given. Several missionaries with whom I am acquainted told me that communicants run about 10% of the baptized total. The estimate seems too extreme for general application, but it would be true in the huge Pueblo parishes of New Mexico where after the reconquest in 1692-1696 there has been a general acceptance of nominal baptism but firm practice of the traditional religion. The pastor at one of the ancient Pueblos reports that all persons have been baptized and only a handful joined the Protestants, but while there are 2,000 baptized members, there are only about 200 participating Catholics. Yet even that figure would be a fair parish of Indians.

The disparity between the communicants or attenders and the baptized total or the large community makes it appear that there is most everywhere a huge task of internal evangelism to be done - the winning of the inactive persons to full commitment and discipleship. It is a primary task of the believing disciples to seek to bring these persons back to living faith. Pope Paul VI called attention to this special sphere of evangelization in Section 56 of his Apostolic Exhortation *On the Evangelization of the Modern World*. The transplanted urban Native Americans having so few local churches to care for them are in constant danger of lapsing into nominalism. The leadership of the churches need to wrestle with this giant task of internal evangelization as well as with the primary call of communicating the gospel to the 57% of their brothers and sisters who are not believers.

There is considerable duplication of churches on some reservations and in some traditional tracts, and generally there are both Roman Catholic and Protestant churches present. Historically duplicating missions have been forces of social disruption in the life of a tribe. Where there is duplication the joint belonging to Christ needs to be publically demonstrated and the unity given in him by God be shown in fellowship, mutal support, common ministry and common worship.

Roman Catholic local churches, being on the whole larger than Protestant congregations, should have a stronger economic base. Since the great majority of the latter are under 100 in membership the financial support and the personnel resources for leadership and teaching are restricted. Sharing between churches and use of the now available means of training for ministry can offset that fact. It would be useful to know the financial status of the churches, but the information could not be gathered in sufficient detail at this time.

Geographic distribution is due chiefly to U.S. government policy and action in removing and locating the tribes, to accidents of church history, and to past missionary endeavors. The largest numbers of Christians are to be found naturally in the states with the largest number of Native Americans.

STATE	1970 CENSUS	BIA POPULATION	CHRISTIANS
Oklahoma	96,803	85,228	31,350
Arizona	94,310	114,178	45,591
New Mexico	71,582	92,963	30,426
Alaska	61,080	61,028	43,440
South Dakota	31,043	31,570	26,804
Washington	30,824	17,708	8,553
Montana	26,385	25,922	16,511
Minnesota	22,322	11,273	14,303
North Dakota	13,565	14,881	20,847

An exception to this generalization is California where the 1970 Census reported 88,263 Ind. and the 1973 BIA resident registration is 37,582. There the Christian population is 7,460 or 19.85%.

States where over 50% of the registered BIA resident population are Christian are: Alaska 71%, Colorado 154.75%, Iowa 78%, Kansas 549%, Maine 216% (census figure), Michigan 319.53%, Minnesota 126.88%, Mississippi 115%, Montana 63.69%, North Dakota 140%, South Dakota 84.88%, Wisconsin 109%, Wyoming 58.39%. How does one account for the eight states where the church membership is reported as larger than the BIA registered resident population in 1973? It may be that numerous Indians moved from out of state into cities and joined churches, or it may be that the churches have simply claimed too many members.

SOME REGIONAL CHURCHES

A very substantial regional Christian community, of which this writer had no knowledge until the last three years, is that of the Lumbees, mostly in Robeson County, North Carolina. The Lumbee population is from 26,000 to 30,000. This people has only in very recent years been recognized by the Federal government. The largest church is the Southern Baptist Convention. 48 congregations belong to the Burnt Swamp Baptist Association. There belong to that Association also 57 ordained ministers and 52 licensed ministers, all Lumbees. The churches average 121.6 resident members, an Association total of 5,498 members, and an average total membership of 132 per church — an Association total of 5,968. These are adult-believer-baptism practitioners, and there are no children in membership and no other family members and occasional church attenders are included. 262 baptisms (adults) were reported in a year. Every church has a substantial Sunday school and vacation Bible school. There are Women's Missionary Unions and Brotherhoods. Youth societies are on the small side. There are 10 United Methodist churches with a total of 1,785 active members and an average of 178.5 per congregation.

The Native American Christian Community

The largest is Prospect U. M. Church at Maxton with 670 members. 10 Sunday Schools average 131.5, and all parishes have vacation schools. There are activities for women and others. There is one ordained white pastor and two white lay pastors, but two ordained Indian pastors, two Indian deacons and one Indian seminarian serving as pastor. There is one small Assembly of God with 20 members and a white ordained pastor, a small Seventh Day Adventist group and a solid Christian and Missionary Alliance Church with 125 members and a community of 160 under an ordained Indian pastor. Since most churches among the Lumbees are believers' baptism practitioners, there are at least 7,428 adult practicing members. Add the non-member spouses, the unbaptized children and other family members and those who feel that they "belong" and it would appear that nearly every Lumbee is a Christian of some sort.

The "Five Civilized Tribes" in Oklahoma and those kindred bands still remaining in the lands of the forefathers in the southeast still form the largest block of Christians. These are the Cherokees, Choctaws, Chickasaws, Creeks and Seminoles. The first four at least were almost totally Christian and assimilated before crossing the Mississippi to Indian Territory. They are actually in a post-Christian Era, but there are more Christians and more ministers among them than any other Indian Nation. The Eastern Cherokees have 12 churches and 1,406 communicants, and the Oklahoma Nation 58 churches and 5,330 communicants. There are 46 Chickasaw churches with 2,160 members. Choctaws count 46 churches and 2,160 members in the eastern bands and 143 churches with 4,202 communicants in Oklahoma. Creeks are 11 churches with 1,286 members in Alabama (if those in the Citronelle area are Creeks), and 85 churches with 4,664 communicants in Oklahoma. The Seminoles are 11 churches and 615 members in Florida and 72 churches with 4,435 members in Oklahoma. Therefore, there are 427 churches with 24,088 communicant or participating members.

Considering the nominal Christians along with the active ones, the Five Civilized Tribes must account for at least 75,000 persons who call themselves Christian in some sense.

Oklahoma Native American Christians are more varied in origin and character than those of any other state. Some small remnant, at least, of every tribe removed from the East is incorporated into some church in Oklahoma. Thus there are Stockbridges of the Housatonic Valley of Massachusetts, Puritan Congregationalist in origin, who are members of Southern Baptist churches; and Delawares of the Hudson and Delaware Valleys are Oklahoma Southern Baptists and United Methodists. Arapahoes are American Baptists, Mennonites, Pentecostals, Roman Catholics and United Methodists, while Caddos are Methodists and Southern Baptists. Cayugas and Seneca of New York are Friends in Oklahoma. The Southern

Cheyennes remain closer to their homeland then most, as do the
Comanches. Geronimo's Chiricahua Apaches are Reformed, American
Baptist and Pentecostal. The Eucha and a few Omaha are United
Methodists. The Southern Baptist Convention embraces the Quapaw
and the Shawnee. The Kickapoo are Friends, Catholics and United
Methodists, while the Kiowas are American Baptists, Pentecostals
and United Methodists. The Osages are Friends, Catholics and
Southern Baptists. The Otoe-Missouria find a spiritual home in
the Pentecostal Church of God and the Southern Baptist Convention.
The Pawnees belong to the Catholic and Methodist churches, and the
Poncas to the latter and the Church of the Nazarene. Potawatomies
are Catholics and Methodists. The Wichita are mostly Southern
Baptists along with one American Baptist Church and one United
Methodist. The Wyandots are Friends. What a roster of tribes
and denominations! It is a noble heritage, but it demands
constant effort to manifest the unity of the Spirit in the bond
of Jesus Christ. Oklahoma Indian Ministries, Inc. is one means
of doing that.

The Apaches, once the destroyers of the settlements and of the
older mission churches, have Christian fellowship of note. They
are developing their resources and their leadership. The White
Mountain Apaches of the Fort Apache Reservation in Arizona have
13 churches with about 1,000 members, and their neighbors of the
San Carlos Reservation have seven congregations with more than
725 communicants. The Lutheran Wisconsin Synod is the strongest
group. The Chiricahuas have only three small churches in
Oklahoma, with a similar number among the Prairie Apache or Kiowa-
Apache. The Jicarilla Apaches in New Mexico have three churches
with only a few more than 100 members and the other New Mexico
Apaches, the Mescalero, have also three churches with 189 members.
The Christians, then, are relatively few, and they are faced with
a mighty task in communicating the gospel to their fellows who
generally remain resistant.

One of the oldest, largest, and strangest blocks of Christian
parishes lies between the Oklahomans and Navajoland. These
people are the Pueblo Indians, originally coercively converted by
the Spanish Conquerors. By 1630 there were reported to be 60,000
converts, but the serfdom and enforced Christian profession were
intolerable, and the Pueblos revolted in 1680. They drove out
the Spanish and abjured their imposed faith. After Diego de
Vargas reconquered the region in 1690-1696 the conquered ones and
their overlords formed a *modus vivendi*. Each Pueblo accepted a
patron saint and children have been presented for baptism and
christening, but the people generally have followed the traditional religion. The Northern Pueblos of Nambe, Picuris,
Pojoaque, San Ildenfonso, San Juan, Santa Clara, Taos and Tesuque
with a total population of about 5,000 are solidly Roman Catholic
parishes in name. The Southern Pueblos are much larger parishes:

The Native American Christian Community

Acoma with 3,000 baptized; Cochiti with 488; Isleta with 3,000; Laguna with 4,000; Sandia with 216, San Felipe with 1,645; Santa Anna with 392; Santo Domingo with 2,349; Zia with 508. Zuni is least Catholic with 30% baptized members. There has usually been a working alliance between the priests of the traditional religion and the Roman Catholic pastors to keep out Protestants. Consequently Protestant church membership is very small. Picuris has a tiny Pentecostal church. There are Southern Baptist churches at Santa Clara, Taos, Acoma, Isleta, Jemez and Laguna with a total of 291 members. Two Presbyterian churches have 89 members together. There is a tiny Assembly of God and one small Christian Reformed Church. There is an enormous task of internal evangelism and nurture and there is a tremendous challenge in attempting to bring the traditional culture and religion to Christ and his Church.

The Hopis in northern Arizona have been impervious to even a veneer of Christianity, but the Navajos, who surround them entirely have since 1960 shown receptivity towards the Christian faith. The largest Nation on the largest reservation exerts a great power of attraction on missionaries and evangelists, but Navajo ministers have appeared in abundance. The Franciscan Friars of St. John the Baptist Province approached the Navajos first in 1873 making their base at St. Michael's, near Window Rock, the Navajo Capital. Father Anselm Weber was their most famous pioneer. They estimate that during the course of the next century they baptized 30,000 persons and that there are 18,000 baptized Navajos today. (United) Presbyterian and (United) Methodist missions began just a little earlier and the Southern Baptists soon after 1900. Now 24 denominational mission boards and nondenominational societies have founded local churches. Moreover, there are 151 independent churches founded by white missionaries and "prophet" type ministers-evangelists-pastors who have arisen spontaneously among the people. An intense charismatic movement is taking place. Navajo leaders are arising in the camps and forging the kinship groups into small close-knit churches. Rev. Thomas A. Dolaghan and Rev. David Scates have made a personal canvass of the reservation interviewing pastors and people. Their survey, reported in *The Navajos Are Coming To Jesus* [Pasadena: William Carey Library, 1978] reports that Protestant Sunday church attendance on the reservation has increased from just a few hundred 25 years ago to 12,395 on any given Sunday in 343 churches under 203 Navajo pastors and 121 Anglo pastors. The average size church is 35.1 members, and the very largest is a Christian Reformed Church of 220 attenders. The diversity is so extreme that it is not easy to find the common characteristics. Unfortunately there is divisiveness in the diversity, and certain pastors, missionaries and people will not associate with others. The Navajo Nation is rapidly developing in political power and economic resources. The people are

becoming financially able to support such ministries as they want.
They are beginning also to do some cultural adaptation to
Christian worship, life and practice.

The Pimas and Papagos of Arizona are two large tribes predominantly Presbyterian and Roman Catholic respectively, engaged in
a three-sided adjustment, - indigenous, Anglo, and Hispanic. The
Northwest tribal churches have declined from their early state of
promise. Among the northern tribes the Chippewas are scattered
across Michigan, Wisconsin and Minnesota in five denominations,
and have too little chance for achieving a sense of unity and
self-identity. The Crows of Montana are a fairly small community
of Christians, and the Gros Ventre of that state are almost all
Roman Catholics. See page 355 and following.

The Dakotas or Sioux separated on their numerous reservations
are the large Christian people of the Northern Plains. They are
mostly in the South and North Dakotas, with some in Minnesota,
Montana, Santee Reservation in Nebraska, and one big church in
Iowa. They are dispersed among more than 10 denominations. The
largest portion are 20,000 Catholics in 56 churches. The
Episcopal Church counts 9,128 baptized members in 113 churches,
the United Presbyterians about 1,000 communicant members in 20
churches, and the United Church of Christ 346 members in six
churches. The Southern Baptists have recently established 14
churches with 500 members. Again the reality and demonstration
of unity are urgent, but the Dakota ministers and the Anglo
missionaries of the three long-established Protestant churches
and the Roman Catholic church appear to be friendly and cooperative. There has been loss and weakness in the older bodies.

Mention must still be made of the Native Alaskan churches.
Their people are distinctly different than most of the people of
the lower 48 states. The Aleuts and Eskimos are not Indians.
The several Athabascan peoples - Tlingits, Haida, Tsimsian - are
Indians, but very different culturally from the lower mainlanders.
The Alaskans were not displaced from their land and sea holdings.
They early established an economic base in fishing, fish canning,
and lumbering. The Alaskan Native Brotherhood has given them
political clout. The Orthodox Church in America is the "national
church" of the Aleuts and is strong among the Eskimo. It is said
to be lessening its hold on the Tlingit and Haida. Due to the
original comity agreement the United Presbyterian Church has
substantial churches among the Tlingit, Haida, and the Eskimos of
the Yukon. The Jesuit Mission and the Episcopal Mission, both
based in Fairbanks, have established strong communities among the
Eskimos and some Athabascans. The American Lutheran Church,
Evangelical Covenant, and the California Friends have old and
strong Eskimo churches, as do the Moravians. 11 churches and
societies which work among Eskimos have 127 churches with some

20,000 inclusive membership, half Catholic, half Protestant, in addition to the Orthodox, who cannot now be estimated. Eight or nine agencies work with the several Athabascan peoples in 67 churches and local units and a few thousand members. Three nondenominational missionary societies work in Alaska: The Arctic Mission, Central Alaska Mission, and the Slavic Gospel Association. This is an area where the Salvation Army builds up Native Corps or congregational equivalents.

THE NONDENOMINATIONAL MISSIONARY SOCIETIES

The nondenominational societies, often called interdenominational, came into being as agencies of world mission or overseas mission primarily to push the missionaries into the "Regions Beyond." The China Inland Mission is their great prototype. The Women's Union Missionary Society of New York was the first American such society. Now there are scores of them. They draw their personnel and support from congregations and persons in several denominations and independent churches and depend in faith on the Lord to provide all needs. Thus they are called "faith missions." They are theologically conservative and almost entirely stress evangelization and church planting. They give a large place to education. They tend to have warm fellowship with others of a similar viewpoint, but often shun those who do not fit the pattern. There are three which operate in Alaska, one in Texas and Oklahoma, and nine among the Navajos. The World Gospel Mission maintains Southwest Indian School in Peoria, Arizona. CHIEF is a service agency. The Wycliffe Bible Translators/ Summer School of Linquistics is running numerous linquistic projects translating the Scriptures into vernacular languages. These societies together have 67 local churches with 1,937 members and total communities of about 2,800. See page 273 and following.

THE INDEPENDENT CHURCHES

The independent church is overwhelmingly a phenomenon of Navajoland. Five are urban churches. Five are among the Haliwa people in North Caroline, four are independent Baptist churches among the Seminoles in Florida, and a few are among the Alabama-Coushatta in Texas. The Mohegan Congregational Church at Uncasville, Connecticut became independent simply because its pastor wanted it to withdraw from the United Church of Christ. 151 are Navajoland churches. In the past they were mostly the products of evangelization by independent Anglo ministers. Now during the last few years they have been multiplying as indigenous camp churches form around a charismatic minister who is usually a kinsman of the group. The Navajo may be developing a style of ministry congenial to their culture, but there are tremendous limitations involved in such a system.

STATE OF THE MINISTRY

The English Puritan missionaries of New England in the 17th century set as one of the chief goals of mission the recruiting, training, and deploying of indigenous ministers, who alone and not the whites, could effectively evangelize and provide pastoral care. There were 37 by 1700. Unhappily, a full supply of ordained Indian clergy could not be attained because of the constant pressures of the forces of destruction and the repeated removal of the peoples. Three of the denominations which early in the 20th century had a considerable number of ordained men saw that number dwindle steadily. When Dr. B. Frank Belvin made a survey of Protestant ministers in 1948 he found a critical situation with generally an inadequate number, poor preparation, meager support, and tending to be over-aged. The crisis continued to deepen. The staff of the Cook Christian Training School in 1974 made a survey of ministry in the seven denominations directly related to that School. It is entitled *Mending the Hoop*. It revealed that the 452 Native American parishes of those churches had only 68 ordained ministers and priests and that only four students were in the Theological Seminaries that year. Actually in all the Protestant churches there are 520 ordained men and 12 women; but that is a very small number for 1,511 churches. Moreover 249 of them are ministers of the Southern Baptist Convention, and 156 of them are in Oklahoma and 57 in the Lumbee's Burnt Swamp Association in North Carolina. Less than 10 of all these Baptist ministers have graduated from a Theological Seminary and only three or four candidates are now students in Seminaries. While the United Methodist Church has 79 ordained ministers 72 are in the Oklahoma Indian Missionary Conference — 39 having full connectional membership, 28 associate, and five probationary. Their ordination is, however, not acceptable for membership in other United Methodist Conferences. The ordained ministers in the several conservative Evangelical denominations and the nondenominational societies have been prepared in their own Bible schools, not Theological Seminaries. Only five Indian pastors of independent churches can be clearly discerned to be ordained. Ordination in independent churches can not have the standards, safeguards, and requirements that are usually expected in denominations.

The Orthodox Church in America had to undergo a struggle for some years after the Communist revolution in Russia and until it became thoroughly domesticated with the other Russian congregations in the United States. It established St. Herman's Theological Seminary at Kodiak in order to facilitate the education of Alaskan clergy and to train lay readers, choir directors, and teachers so that the services may be maintained in villages where there is no priest. There are at least 10 Alaskan Native priests, some deacons and subdeacons, and large numbers of readers. Since Aleuts have taken Russian surnames and some Athabascans have American surnames, the ethnic identity of the Orthodox personnel is difficult to identify.

The Roman Catholic Church is the most colonial-minded of the churches and has done next to nothing to raise up Native American clergy and religious. The European mentality long delayed an emphasis on indigenous clergy in the overseas mission after the defeat of the Jesuits in the disasterous Rites Controversy, except for the great feats of the Foreign Mission Society of Paris in Vietnam and Korea. However, the exhortations of the succession of Popes, beginning with Benedict XV and his encyclical, *Maximum Illud* of November 30, 1919 slowly brought some progress and there is now steady multiplication of the number of indigenous priests. American churchmen have not appeared to think this policy applied to this land. The Bishops in their reports do not usually distinguish between Native American and other priests and religious, so that it is difficult to be certain about numbers. Only 11 priests have been noted in the reports along with one brother. Only nine Sisters were discovered, but I have learned that there are 52. However, 46 deacons have been noted and this is a new development, the consequence of the authorization of the ordination of permanent deacons which came about as a result of Vatican Council II. Almost all of these deacons have been trained in the Jesuit's program and employed in their Alaska mission. There is a Diaconate Training program at St. Paul's Mission at Marty, South Dakota, and one at Sioux Spiritual Center at Plainview, S.D.

The Episcopal Church in Alaska has attempted a step halfway between the diaconate and full priesthood, namely, the office of sacramentalist. The minister is much like the village Mass priest of the Middle Ages, and the person educated and then ordained performs the sacraments and rites. 13 men and two women have been ordained. The experiment has not been fully satisfactory. Elsewhere there has been training of a few men and women for the priestly office under Canon 8, which makes special provision for ethnic minorities and mature persons who go from a profession to ministry at a late date. The diaconate is only a transitional step in this process.

It is only by the large scale use of laymen in pastoral ministry that the churches have been sustained. By and large not a great deal of distinction has been made between licensed ministers and lay pastors. 89 men and 7 women are licensed as pastors in the denominational churches and one man in a society church. Lay pastors, male, number 101 in the denominations and societies and 61 in the independent churches. There are 7 women lay pastors. Lay and licensed pastors total 265. The pastors are joined by 239 Native American lay workers. The Roman Catholic

Church has its host of faithful lay workers, some 624 have been noted. And, it must ever be renumbered, Sisters carry much of the responsibility for parish ministry and there are 52 Native American Sisters.

The white or Anglo staff remains extensive: 339 Roman Catholic priests, 38 brothers and 480 Sisters; Orthodox priests, at least 10 and a bishop; Protestant churches, societies, and independent churches 349 ordained men, 15 ordained women, 21 licensed men, 172 male lay pastors, 57 women lay pastors and 380 lay workers of both sexes, and about 275 teachers and service persons.

EDUCATION FOR MINISTRY

The diaconate and sacramentalist training programs mentioned are part of a new approach to training for the ministry. Less conventional methods following other than the usual curriculum for white Americans for service in white churches. Moreover, it is recognized that, just as in the Third World churches, more parish ministry, service, and evangelism will of necessity have to be done by lay persons than by ordained clergy, and training is for a wide range of ministries.

The staff of Cook Christian Training School, associated with denominational agencies, took the lead in creative study and experimentation. The method of Theological Education by Extension now so widely used among Third World churches was adapted to the Native American churches. Cook School reduced its campus instruction program to develop new extension work. It educates men and women through extension materials and the guidance of leaders in extension centers, leaving them in their homes, churches and jobs. Some hundred of individuals have already participated in programs set up in 19 states and Canadian provinces. Following this model and in cooperation with Cook School the Episcopal Church Dioceses of South and North Dakota established the Dakota Leadership Program at Mobridge, South Dakota. The Christian and Missionary Alliance has set up Alliance Theological Centers with a number of regional TEE centers.

Further leadership by the Cook School staff led to the foundation of NATA, The Native American Theological Association. It is a consortium of theological seminaries, colleges, training schools, and church agencies which provides three tracks of curricula for ministerial work at all levels in combinations of TEE and residential study. Track III, which requires five years of reisdence in college and seminary, leads to a Master of Ministry degree. The curricula are intended to be more realistically aimed at the concrete reality of the Native American churches and not be unduly molded by the European-American, white theological educational tradition.

GENERAL AND RELIGIOUS EDUCATION

Until the 20th century all education for Native Americans was provided by the missions with financial support by the federal government. Since the dissolution of that partnership the number of church schools has steadily declined, justified by the improvement in BIA schools and the increasing availability of public schools. Today schools are closing because of rising expenses and the decrease in the number of Sisters available as teachers. Protestant mission schools in 1922 numbered 38 with 2,262 students. Today there are but half that, 20 schools with 1,165 pupils and students. 50 years ago the Roman Catholic missions operated 81 schools with 7,013 children and youths, while today there are 38 schools with 4,945 pupils and students.

As parochial and mission schools for Indians and Eskimos decrease, there is an ever greater emphasis by all on week day religious education. With the passing of the Office of Indian Affairs of the National Council of Churches the central administration of religious instruction in the BIA boarding schools ceased, and where a coordinator still serves under mission board appointment it appears to be by general consent and in accord with the tradition of the school. Roman Catholic and Protestant chaplains and teachers are found at the major schools. Many of the missions send teachers into both boarding and day schools where permitted, but others provide released time instruction near at hand, some even erecting buildings primarily for that purpose. The conservative Evangelical missions are particularly zealous. The Roman Catholic Dioceses have strong C.D.C., catechetical and week day programs, usually conducted by Sisters, and 76 such programs have been noted.

URBAN MINISTRIES AND SERVICE MINISTRIES

World War II drove thousands of Native Americans into the cities seeking employment and urban life, and returning Vetrans of that war, Korea and Vietnam, often preferred the city to the reservation. The government's Termination Policy speeded the migration. While many returned home, other continued to make the change to urban living. The Census of 1970 revealed that almost half the Native American population dwelt in the cities, namely, 340,367 out of 763,594. Anne Lively found through a survey for the National Council of Churches in 1958 that 14% of missionaries and workers were in the cities, but that development has not greatly accelerated. A union Protestant Urban Indian Center was established in Rapid City as a pilot project, but it has not continued until this day. A large-scale ministry in St. Paul and Minneapolis does continue and has been extended state-wide. By

and large Roman Catholics and Protestants preferred to help
Indians set up public centers and publically fund them. Church
ministries usually remain in fairly close relationship to such
centers. Gradually state and regional councils of churches and
ad hoc consortia began organizing both for advocacy of Native
American rights and for service. .Other churches acted directly.
There are about 50 local service ministries which provide a
variety of services: aid in transition, settlement, housing,
food, clothing, health service, financial assistance, counseling,
alcoholism treatment, transportation, recreation and referrals.
See page 319 and following.

CHILD CARE is a more traditional kind of ministry which still
continues but on a small scale. There are 14 homes and care
centers, two of them Roman Catholic. It is puzzling why what has
been so important a part of Roman Catholic mission action in
Third World countries has had so little attention in the mission
to Native Americans. See page 326 and following.

The churches apparently have not followed their people into the
cities with church fellowship, worship, pastoral care, and
Christian nurture as well as with material services. This
compiler has discovered only 67 Native American churches and 19
partial ones where there are large Indian minorities in 32 cities
with more than 30,000 population. See section V. The cities cry
for evangelization and church planting because the White, Black,
and Hispanic churches will not draw and satisfy the Native
Americans.

CHURCHES, GOVERNMENT AND THE PUBLIC

Although the intimate partnership of the churches with the
United States government ended in 1899, relationships generally
remained cordial except when John Collier was Commissioner of
Indian Affairs. It was believed that his attitude and policies
threatened all that the church had striven for ever since the
establishment of the nation, both in evangelization and
civilization. As long as the Committee on Indian Affairs of the
Home Missions Council and then of the National Council of Church
Churches was in existence it vigorously intervened to protect
Native American rights. The Native American Task Force of JSAC
has now taken over the functions of the older office. The
Bureau of Catholic Indian Missions intervened with government in
its active days, and may now again be expected to exert influence
with government agencies and officers. The United States
Catholic Conference on May 4, 1977 issued a *Statement of U.S.
Catholic Bishops on American Indians,* which puts the Church on
the side of Indian rights and development, encourages leadership,
and allows indigenous cultural adaptation. The National Council
of the Churches of Christ in the U.S.A. has been preparing a

similar statement for adoption and publication. Where recent
court decisions in land, water, and fishing claims have favored
the Native American and white fears have been creating a backlash,
state councils and regional dioceses have been manifesting their
concern. The Mennonite Central Committee and the American Friends
Service Committee engage in advocacy, but the most active of all
national Christian agencies on behalf of Native Americans is
FCNL, the Friends Committee on National Legislation.

THE NATIVE AMERICAN ACTIVIST MOVEMENT

The Red or Indian Power Movement of the end of the 1960's and
the 1970's, expressed in AIM and similar organization, has been
generally hostile to the churches, and they in turn have been
generally cool to it. It was not so much the occupation of
church property, such as the Alexian Novitiate and the dormitories
of Augustana College, which alarmed the Native American pastors
and their white colleagues as their very hostile judgements
passed upon Christianity and the churches and a rather uninformed
propaganistic effort to revive traditional religion. Some
younger pastors and missionaries are more friendly towards the
activists. Probably it is the Activist Movement that has forced
the national denominations to take Native American rights and
claims serious, to reflect on justice, and to feel a sense of
shame for the centuries of injustice. The Roman Catholic Church
has established the Campaign for Human Development, which has
funded many tribal economic projects. They may have no direct
connection with church and mission projects. From 1971 to 1977
C.H.D. has made 61 grants totaling $2,531,156. The Protestant
churches similarly set up IFCO, the Interreligious Foundation
for Community Organization, which provides technical expertise
and finds resources for the same kinds of projects.

ATTITUDE TOWARDS NATIVE CULTURE AND RELIGION

The attacks by the Activists on the churches and Christian faith
for destroying Native American culture and religion and their
attempts to revive traditional society have forced the leaders of
the churches to think more profoundly about these matters. Moreover, the concern and enlightenment about the evil of identifying
the Christian gospel with European culture and denominational
forms along with understanding of the necessity of accommodation
and acculturation accepted in overseas missions for three-quarters
of a century are now percolating into the missions to the Native
Americans. Except for Sir William Johnson, Chief Joseph Brant,
and the Rev. Charles Chauncy in the 18th century everyone engaged
in the mission had disdained Native American culture and barred
it from the churches. This was the attitude down till yesterday.
A change began to come in the mainline churches' mentality a
quarter-century ago. Anne Lively's study of 1858, *A Survey of*

The Native Christian Community in the 1970's

Mission Workers in the Indian Field [NY: NCCCUSA, 1958] revealed that 44% of Catholics and 35% of Protestants still held to the goal of complete assimilation to the white model. Yet 9% of Protestant workers and 11% of Catholics now valued Indian culture highly and advocated conservation. Furthermore, 81% of Episcopalians, 75% of Congregationalists (now U.C.C.), and 53% of the Methodists at the time regarded Indian religions as entirely or largely reconcilable with Christianity. However, little has been achieved in these 20 years. It is not the main-line churches' white personnel who oppose accommodation, but rather Indian ministers and lay leaders who are indoctrinated against their heritage by the former generation of missionaries.

The questionnaire sent out for this survey asked:

What are the attitudes and aims of your missionaries towards Indian cultural customs and values? Are they best described (check one) as: destruction of the tradition and assimilation to white society ___; or a synthesis of selected features of both ___; or conservation of Indian culture ___? Do your missionaries regard the major concepts of Indian religion as compatible ___ or incompatible ___ with Christianity? Are Indian Christians encouraged to adapt their culture to Christian faith and practice ___?

Almost without exception Roman Catholic and mainline Protestant officials and missionaries/pastors said that the prevailing desire is for conservation and adaptation of the culture, that basic Native American religious concepts are compatible, and that adaptation in theology and Christian life and practice is desireable.

Despite this new openness relatively little has yet been achieved. The Episcopalians of Navajoland have admitted medicine men into church membership and permitted them to offer prayers. Father William Stolzman has been studying with Dakota medicine men the meaning and use of the pipe in worship. There are some beginnings here and there, but little. There has been discussion of Native American perspectives on Christian theology, especially at the meetings of the National Fellowship of Indian Workers. Writing in this field, however, has been mostly by white persons, except for Vine Deloria, Jr's, *God Is Red* [NY: Grossett and Dunlap, 1973].

The large-scale opposition to cultural and religious adaptation is to be found in the very conservative Evangelical denominations, in the societies, and in the independent churches. It is taken for granted in these circles that the kind of worship and activities which they knew in their home churches is revealed and prescribed in the New Testament and may not be varied. Native American customs and religion are works of the Devil and not of God. To most of them an "indigenous church" is one where the Scripture reading, the hymn singing, and perhaps the sermon are in the vernacular language. The overseas missionaries of the churches and societies to which these people are related have been seeking indigenization for a generation, and there will be a reflex action.

Others in these quarters have been introduced to church growth principles, to the aid of anthropology, and to fundamentals of communication. They increasingly welcome adaptation which does not appear to involve syncretism and they want to forward it to speed up evangelization and church growth. The new Navajo charismatic leaders are spontaneously adapting. Dolaghan and Scates report the use of the sacred corn and bread basket in the marriage ceremony, the celebration of a baby's first laugh, and similar instances. When the link between accommodation and effective evangelism has been clearly discerned, on the one hand, and that between indigenization and church growth, on the other, Native Americans will be free both to make whatever accommodation they wish between tradition and modern white society and between their old religion and Christianity, provided they stand always under the judgement of Christ and in the illumination of the Holy Spirit.

THE BEGINNING OF THE END OF COLONIALISM

The most important fact brought forth by the survey is that the beginning of the end of the long colonial, subject status of the Native American churches appears to be in sight. Spaniard, Englishman, other Europeans, the Frenchman to a less degree, and the American before and after independence all conquered the Indian, subjugated him, and colonized him culturally, ecclesiastically as well as politically. The United States government used the missions to assimilate him. Had the Indian missions remained under the foreign mission boards, eventually the concerns for selfdetermination, devolution, autonomy and indigenity would have been applied to the Native Americans. However, under Home Mission boards the Indians and Eskimos were only one more ethnic group to be sumberged in the American melting pot. But for a decade now ethnic diversity has become prized and the melting pot is no longer an ideal and an end to be sought and glorified. All elements are taught to celebrate their ethnic origins as long as they are loyal American citizens. The Indian and Eskimo should be free now to be Native American in church and society.

The influence of the Activist Movement stimulates traditional distinctiveness. Courts have upheld the status of the tribes as nations. Legal justice and economic development both reinforce Native American ethnic aspirations rather than dissipate them.

All these forces have made for a movement towards Native American self-determination in the churches and missions. A dozen Indian ecclesiastical jurisdictions which still remain are gaining significance. Native American caucuses have been formed in denominations, including the American Baptist and United Methodist. Caucuses are unofficial but their voice is heard and they have increasing "clout." More important are the new Councils of the Native American denominational churches, which are either in control of the affairs of the Indian/Eskimo churches or relate those churches to the denominational structures. Such Councils now exist in the Episcopal Church, the United Church of Christ, the United Presbyterian Church, the Christian Reformed Church, the Reformed Church in America and the Mennonite Church General Conference. The Episcopal Church has also brought the Navajo Churches of three Dioceses together into a new Navajoland Mission, which will be under its own Bishop. The Native American Task Force of JSAC: The Joint Strategy and Action Committee, in which the Indian/Eskimo voice speaks powerfully, is a conduit to the National Council of Churches and jointly to the denominations. The power of the purse-strings still continues some colonial control. The Roman Catholic Church still appears solidly colonial, but the Federation of Catholic Indian Leaders and the National Association of Native Religious are signs of aspiration to self-determination, voice and influence. The frequently heard desire for an Apostolic Vicar for Indians, who would give the Native Americans central pastoral leadership, cohesion, and a sense of recognition indicates a growing awareness of valid aspirations. Colonial subjection may be passing after four centuries.

III
DENOMINATIONAL AGENCIES

ABBREVIATIONS

Abbreviations in order of average entry:

ord.	– ordained
lic.	– licensed
lay pas.	– lay pastor
NA	– Native American
Ind.	– Indian
w.	– white
mem.	– members, ie., communicant or regular attenders
com.	– community, ie., baptized, children, enquires, etc.
conv.	– conversions
pf.	– professions of faith
ab.	– adult baptisms
ib.	– infant baptisms
SS	– Sunday School or Church School
WS	– Women's Society, Women's Missionary Union or Ladies Aid Society
YS	– Youth Society
VBS	– Vacation or Summer Bible School

Ordained priests, pastors, ministers, deacons and sacramentalists are usually addressed as Reverend; Roman Catholic Archbishops and Bishops as The Most Reverend; and Episcopal Church Bishops as The Right Reverend.

III
DENOMINATIONAL
AGENCIES

AMERICAN BAPTIST CHURCHES IN U.S.A.

NATIONAL BAPTIST MINISTRIES
Valley Forge, Pennsylvania 19481

NATIONAL INDIAN MINISTRIES
2507 Irving, Muskogee, Oklahoma 74401   *(918)687-4185*
Ms. P. Annette Anderson, National Director (Mono)

AMERICAN BAPTIST INDIAN CAUCUS
Ms. Barbara Monoessy, President (Kiowa), Walters, Oklahoma
   73572
Mrs. Mary Horsechief, Secretary-Treasurer (Cherokee), Murrow
   Indian Children's Home, Muskogee, Oklahoma 74401

Purpose and Goals:

1. To enhance communication between local American Baptist
Indian Programs and other structures within the American
Baptists of the U.S.A.
2. To develop existing Indian programs within the American
Baptist Churches of the U.S.A. as well as to encourage the
initiation of new programming.
3. To promote the education of the Indian and non-Indian
constituencies of the American Baptist Churches, U.S.A., in
the national and international issues facing Indian people today.
4. To develop leadership within American Baptist Indian
communities.

5. To work with inter-faith agencies toward the development of cooperative and constructive programming within Indian communities.
6. To join in positive and collaborative efforts for the development of Indian communities.

ALASKA

Kodiak Baptist Mission. 1893. Aleut, Athabascan, Inuit. P. O. Box 785, Kodiak, Alaska 99615. Robert L. Childs, Superintendent, ord., w. A child care ministry begun on Woody Island in 1893 and moved to Kodiak in 1939. Purpose: "To provide care and treatment to children whose needs cannot be met in their own families, and who can benefit from the experiences offered through group living and through special- ized resources and services." A three-fold program: a receiving home for temporary care, a group home for interme- diate term aid especially to teenagers, and long term care. A staff of 12 white persons. Children served in 1977 - 51. 81% of children are Native Americans, Aleut, Athabascan, Inuit.

ARIZONA

Keams Canyon Community Church. 1909. Hopi, Navajo. Hopi Reservation. P. O. Box 67, Keams Canyon, Arizona 86034. Herbert Wilson, interim pastor, ord., w. Mem. 41, loss of 2 in 1977. Ab. in 1977 - 10. SS 100. YS 10. WS 5. Religious instruction one day per week. 250 children from BIA school. 7 Bible schools, attendance 350.

First Mesa Baptist Church. Hopi. Hopi Reservation. P. O. Box 164, Polacca, Arizona 86042.

Sunlight Baptist Mission. Hopi. Hopi Reservation. P. O. Box 727, Second Mesa, Arizona 86043.

MASSACHUSETTS

AMERICAN BAPTIST CHURCHES OF MASSACHUSETTS
88 Tremont Street, Boston, Massachusetts 02108 *(617)523-6969*
Dr. Roscoe C. Robinson, Executive Minister

Gay Head Community Baptist Church. 1670. Pawkumnawakutt. (Wampanoag) Gay Head, Martha's Vineyard, Massachusetts. (not a post office) Francis Hensley, pastor, ord., w. P. O. Box 860, 15 Spring Street, Vineyard Haven, Massachusetts 02568. (Pastor also of First Baptist Church of Vineyard Haven.) Mem. 21. Ab. in 1977 - 2. SS 8. This church, founded by Thomas Mayhew, Sr. in 1670, is the oldest Protestant Indian church in the U.S.A.

Mashpee Baptist Church. 1834, but continuing the 17th century
church. Wampanoag. Mashpee, Massachusetts 02649. Ralph J.
Davie, pastor, ord., w. 16 Shady Oak Lane, Route 2, East
Sandwich, Massachusetts 02735. *(617)888-1813*. Mem. 100.

MONTANA

AMERICAN BAPTIST CHURCHES OF THE NORTHWEST
201 South Ninth, Bozeman, Montana 59715   *(406)587-3293*
Rev. Lawrence A. Nelson, Area Minister

CROW INDIAN BAPTIST ASSOCIATION INC.   1922
P. O. Box 369, Crow Agency, Montana 59022
Mr. John Hill, Sr., Moderator/President
Rev. Laurin Kerr, Overseer

First Crow Baptist Church. 1905. Crow. Crow Reservation.
Lodge Grass, Montana 59050. Morley and Jane Langdon,
pastors, ord., w. P. O. Box 507, Lodge Grass, Montana
59050. *(406)639-2302*. Active mem. 140-150. Com. 275-300.
SS 60. YS 10. WS 15. Thursday activity group (grades K-
6) 15-25. Summer camp.

Burgess Memorial Church. 1923. Crow. Crow Reservation.
Crow Agency, Montana 59022. Laurin R. Kerr, pastor, ord.,
w. P. O. Box 369, Crow Agency, Montana 59022.
(406)638-2959. Mem. 195. SS. Wednesday prayer meeting.
Weekly sewing circle. Youth, Bible and crafts class.
Summer VBS.

Pryor Baptist Mission. (Pryor Baptist Community Church)
1914. Crow. Crow Reservation. Pryor, Montana 59066.
Harold Deuble, pastor, ord., w. Mem. 50. Com. 100. SS.
Bus ministry.

Friendship House of Christian Service. 1958. 3123 Eighth
Avenue, Billings, Montana 59101. *(406)259-5569*. Paul
Reeder, Director. Receives United Way as well as ABC support. Services low-income families, including Hispanic,
Caucasians, Blacks and Asians, as well as Indians. Group
activities: preschool, after school groups (K-6), teen
groups, recreation, adult groups for sewing, crafts,
nutrition, etc., Cadette Scouts, Civil Air Patrol and
Mental Health have teen groups here. Clothing distribution.
Referral service. Work with South Park Task Force in
community development, neighborhood improvement. 3 paid
staff, 2 part-time paid, about 35 volunteers. 1 Crow woman
aids in child care. About 160 families served, of whom

about 20-25% are Indian.

OKLAHOMA INDIAN AMERICAN BAPTIST ASSOCIATION

Area Minister: Rev. James G. Denny, P. O. Box 785, Anadarko, Oklahoma 73005

Northfield Parish. Douglas Deer, pastor, ord., w. 325 North Aurora, Geary, Oklahoma 73040.

> *Geary Indian Baptist Church.* c.1898. Arapaho. Mem. 300. SS 30. Women's quilting group.

> *Watonga Indian Baptist Church.* c.1898. Cheyenne. Watonga, Oklahoma 73772. About 300 consider themselves members, 12 adults attend. SS 10. Women's quilting group. Prayer meeting.

Rolling Plains Parish. Thomas Lucas, pastor, ord., w. R. R., Mountain View, Oklahoma 73062.

> *First American Baptist Church.* Kiowa. Hobart, Oklahoma 73651. Yale Spotted Bird, assistant pastor, layman, Ind.

> *Rainy Mountain Indian Baptist Church.* Kiowa. 4 miles southwest of Mountain View. Charles Toyebo, assistant pastor, layman, Ind. Mountain View, Oklahoma 73062.

Redstone Indian Baptist Church. 1890. Kiowa. 7 miles west of Anadarko. Victor Paddlety, pastor, lay, Ind. Route 3, Anadarko, Oklahoma 73005. *(405)247-6879.* Mem. 85, net gain of 3 in 1977. SS 24. YS 12. WS 16. Men's group 9. Wednesday night cottage prayer services. VBS. Revivals.

Wichita Mission Church. Wichita. 5 miles northeast of Anadarko. Woodrow Wills, pastor, layman. Box 785, Anadarko, Oklahoma 73005.

Apache Indian Baptist Church. Apache. 3 miles southwest of Ft. Cobb. Duke Tsoudle, Sr., pastor, layman, Ind. 101 S.W. Sixth Street, Ft. Cobb, Oklahoma 73038.

Deyo Baptist Church. Comanche. 9 miles west of Lawton. Robert Coffey, pastor, layman, Ind. 1407 Lindy, Lawton, Oklahoma 73501.

Brown Baptist Church. Comanche. 4 miles south of Walters. Ned Timbo, pastor, layman, Ind. Route 3, Box 194, Lawton, Oklahoma 73501.

Bacone College Baptist Church. All tribes. College campus church. Muskogee, Oklahoma 74401. Wayne Corzatt, pastor, ord., w.; also College Director of Religious Life. Bacone College, Muskogee, Oklahoma 74401. *(918)683-4581, ext. 207.* Average attendance 50. Ab. in 1977 - 3. SS 50. WS.

Campground. Adjacent to Wichita Mission.

Bacone College. 1880. Muskogee, Oklahoma 74401. *(918)683-4581.* Dr. Wesley N. Haines, President. An independent junior college, American Baptist Churches related, with a "personalized system of instruction" and a "core program" available where needed. Two-year course, A.A. degree. Tuition $40 per credit hour. Tuition room and board $1,200 per year. Administrative staff 6. Faculty: 4 Indians, 34 others. Students: 154 men, 383 women, including 317 Indians, 152 Caucasians, 65 Blacks, 3 Foreign, a total of 537. 99 graduated in 1976, 126 in 1977 and 571 in last 5 years. *Smoke Signals,* quarterly.

Murrow Indian Children's Home. Box 33, Bacone Station, Muskogee, Oklahoma 74401. *(918)687-4711.* Mrs. Mary Horse-chief, Executive Director. Founded by Rev. J. J. Murrow soon after Civil War. Moved to Bacone College campus in 1920's, and to site adjoining campus with cottages in 1956. Self-perpetuating Board of Trustees, 6 Trustees are local and 6 from National American Baptist Ministries. Property belongs to ABC National Ministries Division. Paid staff 11; College "fathers" are not paid, but receive board and room. Eligible children: Indians 6-14 years, but can stay through high school. Bed capacity 40, but limited to 30. More Creek than other tribes, but also Cheyenne, Kiowa, Winnebago and Pawnee. Mostly from Oklahoma and many urban.

Anadarko Christian Center. 1953. P. O. Box 785, Anadarko, Oklahoma 73005. Rev. James G. Denny, Executive Director, ord., w. Miss Barbara Johnson, Program Supervisor. Maintained by the Board of National Ministries of the American Baptist Churches:

Stated Purposes:

1. To bring a person into an intimate personal encounter with the all-encompassing love of God and to elicit a response of faith toward God through Jesus Christ and a commitment of his life to Jesus Christ as Lord and Savior.
2. To help the individual gain a healthy understanding of himself as a person. The individual must recognize his capacities and limitations and be able to live with these facts about himself with courage and creativity.

3. To develop wholesome person-to-person relationships.
4. To provide a ministry to all individuals, regardless of social, economic, racial or religious background in a planned program of participation with other agencies working in the community.
5. To inspire and assist the individual to effectively relate himself and constructively participate in the social structure of the community.

About 200 persons are served on a regular basis each year and several hundred more occasionally. These include Indians, Blacks, Mexicans and Caucasians. The Director is Area Minister to the 9 American Baptist Indian Churches in the region, and the Center is the coordinating agency for American Baptist Mission work in western Oklahoma.

ASSEMBLIES OF GOD

DIVISION OF HOME MISSIONS: 1145 Boonville Avenue, Springfield, Missouri 65802   *(417)862-2781*
National Director, Dr. T. E. Gannon

Information about the Native American Churches is not available from the Division of Home Missions. A list of persons engaged in Indian ministries was obtained from a worker and questionnaires were sent to all. Only a minority responded. It is regretable that this large commitment to Indian ministries cannot be adequately reported.

EDUCATIONAL MINISTRIES

American Indian Bible Institute, Inc. 1956. 10020 North Fifteenth Avenue, Phoenix, Arizona 85021. *(602)944-3335.* Rev. Don R. Ramsey, President. Residence: 5119 North 42nd Drive, Phoenix, Arizona 85019. *(602)937-7880.* Alma Thomas, Academic Dean. Rev. Eugene Herd, Vice President and Business Manager. Teachers: John Chisnell, Marion Herd, Eugene Hunter, David Moore. Administrative staff 4. Teachers 4. Extension staff 4 — 1 Indian on staff. A three year course leads to a diploma in "Christian Education." Admission requirements: over 18 years of age, able to handle English orally and written, have minister's recommendation, show evidence of conversion experience and have a vocation to Christian ministry. Normally expected to have completed high school. Students: 26 men, 23 women. Many tribes. Graduated between 1967 and 1977 - 72; in 1976 - 11, in 1977 - 9. Newspaper, *The AIBI Thunderer,* 4 to 6 times a year.

Eastern Indian Bible Institute. 1968. Route 1, Box 760, Shannon, North Carolina 28386. Operated by the North

Carolina District Council of the Assemblies of God. P. O.
Box 808, Dunn, North Carolina 28334. Rev. Charles Cookman,
Superintendent. Institute President, Rodger Cree. Teachers:
Rodger Cree, Charles Hadden, Hubert Boese, Esther Cree,
Jeannette Duber, Judy McKnight, Joan Morris. Two semesters.
Diploma at completion of courses. Admission requirements:
applicant should show evidence of conversion and a desire to
serve the American Indians. Pastor's recommendation
necessary.

Good Shepherd Bible School. 1967. P. O. Box 238, Mobridge,
South Dakota 57601. *(605)845-3996.* Rev. Leo Bankson,
President. VA and BIA approved. Three year course leading
to diploma. Admission requirements: 18 years of age, high
school graduation. Up to 25% non-Indians accepted. Tuition
$735 per year. Campus boarding program. Extension program
with two centers. Administrative staff 3. Campus teaching
staff 7. Extension staff 2. On campus students: 5 men, 3
women. Graduates in 1976 - 3. *The Warrior,* quarterly.

*American Indian Extension of the National Correspondence
Institute.* 2071 North Marion Avenue, Springfield, Missouri
65803. *(417)869-5117.* Ms. Pauline Mastries, Registrar.

CHURCHES, BY STATES

ARIZONA

Navajo Trail Assembly of God. 1961. Navajo. Box 64,
Cameron, Arizona 86020. Ms. Velda Brown, pastor, unordained,
w. Mem. 80, increase of 10 in 1977. Ab. 10. SS 45.
Thursday Bible study.

Indian Assembly of God. 1972. Papago. P. O. Box 1002, Casa
Grande, Arizona 85222. Ms. Betty L. Ayres, pastor, lic., w.
P. O. Box 966, Casa Grande, Arizona 85222. 8 ab. in 1977.
SS 34. WS 10. Children's Bible club 20. Kids' Crusade in
March 45.

Children's Program, Recreation Hall. Lulac Village. 1973.
Mixed tribes. Mrs. Betty F. Wheeler, lic. home missionary.
598 North McQueen, Chandler, Arizona 87224. *(602)963-2724.*
Children's hour, Tuesday at 4:00 p.m., about 40.

Dennehotso Navajo Assembly of God. 1970. Navajo. Box AA,
Dennehotso, Arizona 86535. Robert Tom, pastor, lic., Ind.
Ab. 10. Attendance about 80. SS 75. YS 15. WS. Released
time religious instruction. VBS. Summer camp meeting.

Navajo Assembly of God. P. O. Box 92, Ft. Defiance, Arizona

86504. *(602)729-5498*. Duane Johnson, pastor, ord., w. and Naomi Johnson, missionaries. SS with 11 classes - 150. Junior church service for children on Sunday. Wednesday night program for boys and girls. Women's work group on Thursday. Men's monthly fellowship.

Indian Chapel. Gila Bend, Arizona 85337. Duane E. Suit, pastor, ord., w. and Mrs. Suit. P. O. Box 380, Gila Bend, Arizona 85337.

All Tribes Assembly of God. 1947. Mixed. 902 East McKinley Street, Phoenix, Arizona 85010. *(602)253-7745*. Donald P. Keeter, pastor, ord., w. 908 East McKinley Street, Phoenix, Arizona 85010. *(602)257-1346*. Mem. 43, adherents 200. Sunday morning attendance 180. Ab. 3. SS 150. YS 13. WS 21. Men's society 11. Coffee house ministry at Phoenix Indian High School.

Hillside Chapel. 1976. Mixed tribes. Thirteenth Avenue and Cochise, Phoenix, Arizona. Eugene Herd, pastor, ord., w. 11735 North 19th Avenue, A-14, Phoenix, Arizona 85029. Mem. 50. SS 28. YS 50. Students of The American Indian Bible Institute attend this church.

Apache Assembly of God. 1937. Apache. San Carlos Reservation. P. O. Box A, San Carlos, Arizona 85550. Glenn A. Landay, pastor, ord., w. *(602)475-2389*. Mem. 40. Ab. 7, infants 10. SS 118. YS 30. WS 13. Tuesday Family Night: adult Bible study and programs for all ages. Annual Kids' Crusade. Two annual adult revivals. Summer Apache Camp meeting. Annual workers' training course.

Salt River Assembly of God. c.1960-62. Pima and Maricopa. Salt River Reservation. Route 1, Box 183, Scottsdale, Arizona 85256. Paul J. Cagle, pastor, ord., w., Anglo. Adherents about 100. SS 35. YS 12-15. WS 10. Choir. Weekly clubs.

Papago Assembly of God. Papago Reservation. P. O. Box 216, Sells, Arizona 85634. N. Hilda Garcia, pastor, ord., Ind. P. O. Box 516, Sells, Arizona 85634. *(602)383-2527*. Mem. 26. Ab. 4. SS 30-40. YS 10. Hospital visitation. Annual Kids' Crusade. Revivals.

Carrizo Apache Assembly of God. 1959. White Mountain Apaches. Ft. Apache Reservation. Route 2, Carrizo Station, Show Low, Arizona 85901. JoAnn Craver, pastor, lic., w. Mamie Beaver, co-pastor. *(602)338-4587*. Adherents 90, increase of 4. Ab. 14. SS 60-70. YS 10-15. WS. Bible training classes. Teacher training classes. Wednesday night

Bible study. Clubs for younger children, attendance 30. Crafts. Recreation.

Stanfield Assembly of God. 1950. Papago Reservation. East Arizona Drive, P. O. Box 608, Stanfield, Arizona 85272. Floyd M. Parker, pastor, ord., w. *(602)424-3794.* Mem. about 20. SS 20.

Pueblo Assembly of God. 1959. Mixed tribes. 3602 South 12th Avenue, Tucson, Arizona 85713. *(602)624-0546.* Virgil Zeigler, pastor, ord., w. P. O. Box 7292, Tucson, Arizona 85725. *(602)885-1602.* Silas Rexroat, assistant pastor, ord., w. P. O. Box 7002, Tucson, Arizona 85725. Mem. 62. Ab. 7. Infant dedications 5. SS 95-100. Royal Rangers and Missionettes (comparable to Boy and Girl Scouts with religious emphasis.) Two District Indian Youth Camps. Camp meetings. Daily VBS.

Cedar Creek Assembly of God. 1953. White Mountain Apaches. Ft. Apache Reservation. P. O. Box 327, Whiteriver, Arizona 85941. O. C. Alexander, pastor, ord., w. *(602)338-4459.* Mem. 130, increase of 24. SS 110. YS 38. WS 12. Men's society 16. Missionettes (girls' club). Royal Rangers (boys' club). Children's church, 2 groups.

Why Indian Chapel. 1977. Papago Reservation. Why, Arizona 82321. Ms. Lucille Greathouse, pastor, lic., w. P. O. Box 226, Ajo, Arizona 82321. Just now getting underway.

Indian Assembly of God. Navajo, Hopi and Apache. 617 Alfred, P. O. Box 298, Winslow, Arizona 86047. Lyle C. Wolverton, pastor, ord., w. Sunday morning and evening services. SS. WS. Wednesday evening Bible study.

Teesto Assembly of God. 1969. Navajo Reservation. Star Route, Box 315, Winslow, Arizona 86047. *(602)657-3264.* Paul C. Hodson, pastor, ord., w. SS attendance average 77. WS 16, sewing and quilting. VBS.

Cocopah Assembly of God. East Cocopah Reservation. 2815 Julie Lane, Yuma, Arizona 85364. *(602)726-7844.* Ellsworth Kennedy, pastor, ord., w. No mem. 1 ab. SS 39-40. WS 7. Children's church. Missionettes. W.M.C. Boy's hobby shop. VBS.

AMERICAN INDIAN MINISTRIES. 1962. Maricopa. Gila Bend Reservation. P. O. Box 10, Laveen, Arizona 85339. *(602)243-4893.* Harold Hanson, Director, ord., w. Mrs. June Hanson.

Laveen Indian Assembly of God. P. O. Box 2, Laveen, Arizona 85339. Adherents 75. SS 25.

Laveen Indian Children's Home. 28 children.

Nursing Home. 76 aged Indians.

Community Activities Center.

Dolaghan and Scates in *The Navajos Are Coming To Jesus* report the following additional Navajo Assemblies of God Churches: (no response to questionnaires) Average 58.6 mem.

Assembly of God Mission. Steven Brown, 311 East Erie, P. O. Box 91, Holbrook, Arizona 86025.

Broken Arrow Chapel. Elsie Watson. Indian Wells, Arizona 86031.

Cornfield Assembly of God. Rev. Mr. Musgrove. Ganado, Arizona 86505.

Gap Assembly of God. Roy Nelson. Tuba City, Arizona 86045.

Indian Assembly of God. Margaret Slane. 1729 North Main Street, Flagstaff, Arizona 86001.

Kayenta Assembly of God. A. C. Tyson. Kayenta, Arizona 86033.

Navajo Assembly of God. Roberta Goetjen. Box 165, Houck, Arizona 86506.

Shonto Assembly of God. Ken Delany. Box 885, Kayenta, Arizona 86033.

Tuba City Assembly of God. James Horne. Box 948, Tuba City, Arizona 86045.

White Cove Assembly of God. Roberta Roanhorse. Indian Wells, Arizona 86031.

Also reported to be working in Arizona, but no report:

Wilbur C. Abbott, Jr., Route 1, Box 24, Parker, Arizona 85344.

J. O. Brown, Box 868, Bapchule, Arizona 95224.

Miss Mary B. Brutenbach, P. O. Box 768, Window Rock, Arizona 86515.

Floyd L. Cruse, 3090 Lass Avenue, Kingman, Arizona 86401.

C. Jerry Frawley, P. O. Box 794, Show Low, Arizona 85901.

Leo Gilman, P. O. Box 537, Fort Apache, Arizona 85926.

Tommy Good, Box 366, Sacaton, Arizona 85247.

W. Joseph Hanna, P. O. Box J, Chandler, Arizona 85224.

T. L. Johnson, 4243 North 15th Avenue, Phoenix, Arizona 85015.

Elmer W. Kaufman, Box 1331, Cottonwood, Arizona 86326.

Thomas A. Koons, Box 788, Window Rock, Arizona 85615.

Harold McCarty, P. O. Box 5413, Mohave Valley, Arizona 86440.

James Mills, P. O. Box 8262, Bylas, Arizona 85530.

Mrs. Helen M. Rickey, 3915 W. Hubbell, Phoenix, Arizona 85009.

Mrs. Alta Washburn, 1933 East Mitchell, Phoenix Arizona 85016.

CALIFORNIA

Indian Full Gospel Church. P. O. Box 1544, Auburn, California 95603. Tim Chapdelaine, lay pas.

Table Mountain Gospel Lighthouse. 8200 Millerton Road. Mail address: P. O. Box 311, Friant, California 93626. Kenneth M. Fenwick, pastor.

Mt. Sierra Indian Assembly of God. Route 1, Box 103, Markleeville, California 96120. Archie B. Brostrum, pastor.

Assembly of God. End of Highway 169, Wanteck, California. Mail to Weitchpec Route, Hoopa, California 95546. Ruby Hoffman, pastor.

First Assembly of God. Weitchpec. Box 3C, Hoopa, California 95546. Gerald Chilson, pastor, ord., w. P. O. Box 336, Orleans, California 95556. *(916)627-3363.* Mem. 4. SS 10-15. Rest home visitation. Shut-in visitation.

Assembly of God. Community Hall, P. O. Box 218, El Portal, California 95318. Ira H. Van Houten, pastor.

COLORADO

Ignacio Assembly of God. 1975. Southern Ute Reservation.
P. O. Box 213, 145 Lakin, Ignacio, Colorado 81137.
(303)259-2069. John E. Bowersock, pastor, ord., w. Mem. 45.
Ab. 3. Ib. 6. SS 47. YS 20. Wednesday night service.
Tuesday outreach station at Boy's Reformatory in charge of
youth Indian pastor.

NEVADA

Ft. McDermitt Assemblies of God Indian Church. 1955.
Northern Paiute. Ft. McDermitt Reservation. Box 455,
McDermitt, Nevada 89421. *(702)532-8759.* Duane Hammond,
pastor, lic., w. Mem. 70, increase of 10. SS average 53.
WS 6. Camp meetings. Kids' Crusades.

Pyramid Lake Assembly of God. 1959. Paiute. Pyramid Lake
Reservation. P. O. Box 222, Nixon, Nevada 89424. Wesley E.
Erickson, pastor, ord., w. Mem. 35. Ab. 10 in 1977. SS 39.
YS 10. WS 12. VBS. Annual camp meeting.

Assembly of God Indian Church. Duck Valley Reservation. 1½
miles north of Owyhee. P. O. Box, Owyhee, Nevada 89832.
Allen Wayne Bill, pastor.

NEW MEXICO

Albuquerque Indian Assembly of God. 1950. Mixed tribes.
1119 Menaul Blvd., N.W., Albuquerque, New Mexico 87107.
William D. Lee, pastor, ord., Ind. P. O. Box 6392,
Albuquerque, New Mexico 87107. *(505)344-0568.* Mem. 94,
increase of 27 in 1977. Ab. 3. SS 90-95. YS 20. WS 15.
Men's society 15. Wednesday midweek service. VBS.

Assembly of God Revival Center. 1972. Navajo. Box 87,
Crown Point, New Mexico 87313. *(505)786-5395.* Leonard J.
Everly, pastor, ord., w. Adherents 150. SS 80-90. Summer
VBS. Camp meetings. Youth camp.

Dulce Assembly of God. 1958. Jicarilla Apache. P. O. Box
585, Dulce, New Mexico 87528. *(505)759-3279.* Boyd Wood,
pastor, ord., w. Mem. 35, increase of 10 in 1977. SS 30-35.
Wednesday night prayer and Bible study.

Pinedale Indian Assembly of God. 1965. Navajo. 25 miles
northeast of Gallup. Drawer V, Gallup, New Mexico 87301.
(505)786-5345. Lewis B. Yazzie, pastor, ord., Navajo.
Mem. 20. Ab. 11. SS 35. WS 8. Men's society 6. VBS.

Manuelito Assembly of God. Navajo. Manuelito, New Mexico (not a post office). Lee Dean Burchfield, pastor, ord., w. P. O. Box 209, Gallup, New Mexico 87301. *(505)863-3985.* Mem. 25. SS 10. VBS, about 40.

Indian Assembly of God. 1955. Jemez Pueblo. P. O. Box 32, San Ysidro, New Mexico 87053. *(505)834-7424..* Vernon Brown, pastor, ord., Ind. Mem. 42, gain of 8 in 1977. Ab. 7. SS 40. YS 12. WS 8. Summer VBS. Annual family camp.

Navajo Churches reported by Dolaghan and Scates (no response):

Carson Assembly of God. Elmer Brown. Carson, New Mexico 87517.

Core Assembly of God. Willie John Willie. Shiprock, New Mexico 87420.

Gallup Indian Assembly of God. Roy Nelson. Box 1780, Gallup, New Mexico 86301.

Independent Assembly of God. John Billy. Fruitland, New Mexico 87416.

Navajo Assembly of God. Ivan Campbell. 2121 Camino Rio, Farmington, New Mexico 87401.

Nena Nazad Navajo Assembly of God. James Yellowman. Farmington, New Mexico 87013.

Ojo Encino Assembly of God. Jack A. Bruten. P. O. Box 673, Cuba, New Mexico 87013.

Pentecostal Assembly of God. Leonard Everly. Crownpoint, New Mexico 87313.

Prewitt Assembly of God Indian Mission. Jim Reeves. Prewitt, New Mexico 87045.

Pueblo Pintado Assembly of God. Marvin Martin, Crownpoint, New Mexico 87313.

Shiprock Assembly of God. Shiprock, New Mexico 87420.

Listed as Indian workers, but no response:

Miss Ruth Droll, Box 87, Crownpoint, New Mexico 87313.

The Native American Christian Community

Miss Claudie L. Gilchrest, P. O. Box 1415, Albuquerque, New Mexico 87103.

Miss M. Imogene Hurst, Star Route 1, Box 20, Shiprock, New Mexico 87420.

Miss Marguerite Shaw, Star Route 1, Box 20, Shiprock, New Mexico 87420.

Miss Barbara Wellard, Star Route 1, Box 20, Shiprock, New Mexico 87420.

NEW YORK

First Mohawk Assembly of God. 1950. Mohawk. St. Regis Reservation. P. O. Box 339, Hogansburg, New York 13655. Marcia McCorkle, pastor, ord., w. P. O. Box 264, Hogansburg, New York 13655. *(518)358-2456.* SS 16. VBS or summer camp. An Indian is soon to become pastor.

NORTH CAROLINA

Fayetteville Assembly of God. 1959. Lumbee/Tuscarora. P. O. Box 64156, 309 Wilkes Road, Fayetteville, North Carolina 28306. *(919)425-7804.* Hubert D. Boese, pastor, ord., w. 4121 Knollwood Drive, Fayetteville, North Carolina 28304. Mem. 20. Infant dedications 6. SS 88. YS 5-10. Missionettes, Royal Rangers. Bible school classes once a week.

OKLAHOMA

Chiowaickuka Assembly of God. 1959. Choctaw. Drawer C, Wright City, Oklahoma 74766. Lula Morton, pastor, ord., w. Mem. 17. SS.

Workers listed, but no response:

Charles A. Odell, P. O. Box 131, Red Rock, Oklahoma 74651.

James Scott, Route 1, Box 96A, Longdale, Oklahoma 73755. Cheyenne-Arapaho church, reported by a former pastor.

SOUTH DAKOTA

Mission Assembly of God. 1974. Sioux/Dakota. Rosebud Reservation. P. O. Box 304, Mission, South Dakota 57555. John G. Bennett, pastor, ord., w. P. O. Box 204, Wood, South Dakota 57585. *(605)452-3244.* No mem. Infant dedications 3.

SS 15-30. Friday evening evangelistic meeting. Children's outreach. Revival meetings.

Church of the Good Shepherd. 1963. Sioux/Dakota. Standing Rock/Cheyenne River Reservation. 519 7th Avenue E., Mobridge, South Dakota 57601. *(605)845-3309.* Edward C. Maser, pastor, ord., w. 201 4th Avenue E., Mobridge, South Dakota 57601. *(605)845-3778.* No mem., about 56 adults attending. Ab. in 1977 - 1. SS 35. Kids' Crusade.

Sioux Assembly of God. Reopened 1977. Oglala Sioux. Rosebud Reservation. Drawer G, Norris, South Dakota 57560. *(605)462-6426.* James E. Black, pastor, ord., w. No mem. SS 30. YS 15-25.

Northside Indian Assembly of God. 1965. Sioux/Dakota. 831 Silver Street, Rapid City, South Dakota 57701. *(605)341-4768.* Merlin C. Neely. Ab. in 1977 - 3. SS average 40. YS 15. WS 10. Wednesday night prayer and Bible study.

TEXAS

Dallas Indian Revival Center. 1978. Mixed tribes. 2010 Ivanhoe Lane, Dallas, Texas 75208. *(214)227-2450.* L. E. Davis, pastor, ord., w. and Mrs. Davis. P. O. Box 280, Lancaster, Texas 75146. *(214)744-3923.* Ab. in 1977 - 13. Ib. 5. SS average 68. YS 24. WS 8-10. Men's society 6-8. Revivals. VBS. Camp meetings. Children's church.

Indian Village Assembly of God. 1949. Alabama and Coushatta. Alabama-Coushatta Reservation. Route 3, Box 316, Livingston, Texas 77351. *(713)563-4535.* Darrell G. Surface, D.D., pastor, ord., w. Mem. 130, increase of 15 in 1977. SS 90. YS 35. WS 25. Weekly nursery church and children's church.

Workers reported, not responding:

Tony C. Castillo, c/o Archie Talamentez, 843 E. Laramie, Dallas, Texas 75217. (Itinerating)

George D. Warren, 1209 Meadow Park Drive, Fort Worth, Texas 76108.

UTAH

Assembly of God. Ute and Navajo. P. O. Box 576, (corner Center and 4th West) Blanding, Utah 84511. *(801)678-2661.* Ms. Dorothy Blair, pastor, lic., w. Ms. Marie Johnson, co-pastor, ord., w. No mem. Increase of 12 regular attendants in 1977. Ab. 5. Child dedications 6. SS 27. Thursday night Bible study.

WASHINGTON

Elwha Assembly of God. 1944. Klallam. Elwha Reservation. P. O. Box 1712, Port Angeles, Washington 98362. *(206)457-4296.* William W. Ulin, pastor, ord., w. 237 West Third Street, Port Angeles, Washington 98362. Adherents 20. SS 25. Tuesday Bible study and prayer meeting.

All Tribes Christian Life Center of the Assemblies of God. 1976. Yakima. Yakima Reservation. P. O. Box 190, Wapato, Washington 98951. *(509)877-3084.* Ed H. Brothers, pastor, ord., w. Mem. 18. Ab. in 1977 - 5. SS 60. YS 8. Camp meeting. Children's Crusade.

Workers reported, no response:

Alfred F. Brown, 14431 S.E. 368th Place, Auburn, Washington 98002.

Miss Helen Burgess, P. O. Box 100, Harrah, Washington 98933.

Lloyd Fulton, P. O. Box 66, LaPush, Washington 98350.

Mrs. Phyllis L. Hammerbacker, P. O. Box 100, Harrah, Washington 98933.

George Kallappa, P. O. Box 113, Neah Bay, Washington 98357.

Alvin Oya, P. O. Box 102, Neah Bay, Washington 98357.

Esko Rentola, 32272 Little Boston Road, N.E., Kingston, Washington 98346.

Mrs. Mildred Schultz, 2430 N. 135th Street, Room 21, Fir Lane Con. Center, Shelton, Washington 98584.

WISCONSIN

Milwaukee All Tribes Assembly of God. 1976. Winnebago, Chippewa, Menominee, Potawatomi, Oneida. 2608 West Vliet, Milwaukee, Wisconsin 53205. *(414)445-3671.* Otho L. Cooley, ord., w. 4653 West 39th Street, Milwaukee, Wisconsin 53209. Adherents 30. Gain of 25 in 1977. Ab. 13. SS 45. Weekly midweek service and cottage prayer meetings.

Oneida Assembly of God. 1957. Oneida. P. O. Box 127, Oneida, Wisconsin 54155. *(414)869-2217.* Lonnie Johnson, pastor, ord., w. Mem. 75 with 26 adult voting members. Ab. in 1977 - 9. SS 60. WS 35. Men's society 15.

Workers reported, no response:

John E. Maracle, P. O. Box 426, Keshena, Wisconsin 54135.

WORKERS REPORTED IN OTHER STATES, BUT NO INFORMATION RECEIVED

Floyd Beckstrand, P. O. Box 396, Rolla, North Dakota 58367.

Jimmy Burnett, P. O. Box 245, Lapwai, Idaho 83540.

Carl E. Collins, 1240 Boiling Springs Road, Spartanburg, South Carolina 29303. (Itinerating)

Melvin Erickson, P. O. Box 3, Tokio, North Dakota 85379.

Rev. and Mrs. John G. Gunderson, 3231 34th Avenue, Minneapolis, Minnesota 55406.

Mrs. Grace Humphrey, P. O. Box 1076, Lander, Wyoming 82520.

Elwin Johns, P. O. Box 24, Cayuse, Oregon 97821.

Philip E. Joseph, P. O. Box 185, Harlem, Montana 59526.

Joseph Orcutt, 620 E. 11th Street, The Dalles, Oregon 97058.

Miss Barbara J. Stansberry, P. O. Box 199, Ft. Yates, North Dakota 58538.

BRETHREN IN CHRIST CHURCH

BOARD FOR MISSIONS
48½ South Market Street, P. O. Box 149
Elizabethtown, Pennsylvania 17002

NAVAJO BRETHREN IN CHRIST MISSION
Route 4, Box 6000, Bloomfield, New Mexico 87413
Rev. J. Marion Heisey, Ph. D., Director   *(505)325-2006*

Staff: total 26. 1 ord., w. minister, 2 Ind. preachers, 2 Ind. lay workers.

Navajo Chapel. Route 4, Box 6000, Bloomfield, New Mexico 87413. Cecil Wento, pastor, unordained, Ind. Mem. 20.

Chaco Chapel. Route 4, Box 6000, Bloomfield, New Mexico 87413. Peter Yazzie, pastor, unordained, Ind. Mem. 15.

Brethren in Christ School. Route 4, Box 6000, Bloomfield, New Mexico 87413. Dr. Marion Heisey, Administrator. Day and boarding. Grades K-6. Administrative staff 3. Teachers: 1 white man, 5 white women. Indian boys 34, Indian girls 3.

Other program: two extension works, small scale alcoholic rehabilitation center.

Navajo News, bi-monthly.

CHRISTIAN AND MISSIONARY ALLIANCE

Box C, Nyack, New York 10960   *(914)353-0750*
Rev. Richard Colenso, Director, Specialized Ministries
Rev. Selam Ross, Director, North American Indian Field, Cass
   Lake, Minnesota 56633   *(218)335-6734*

Navajo Mountain C. & M. A. Church. Navajo. Tonalea, Arizona 86044. 1 church, 4 chapels. 2 ord. Ind. ministers, 2 Ind. lay men workers. Mem. 60. Com. 200. Conv. 1975 - 21. SS.

Leech Lake C. & M. A. Church. Chippewa. Cass Lake, Minnesota 56633. Selam Ross, pastor, ord., w. 1 Ind. man lay worker, 3 Ind. women lay workers, 2 w. women workers. Mem. 10. 50 com. SS.

Mille Lacs C. & M. A. Church. Chippewa. Milaca, Minnesota 56353. 1 w. man lay worker. 15 mem. 40 com. SS.

Rocky Boy Church. Chippewa. Rocky Boys Reservation. Havre, Montana 59501. Pastor, ord., w. 2 w. women workers. 20 mem. 30 com. SS.

Ft. Belknap Mission. Gros Ventre. Hays, Montana 59527. Pastor, ord., Ind. 1 w. man lay worker. 10 mem. 60 com. 10 conv. in 1975.

C. & M. A. Lumbee Church. Lumberton, North Carolina 28358. Pastor, ord., Ind. 125 mem. 160 com. 5 conv. in 1975. SS.

C. & M. A. Church. Cree. Turtle Mountain Reservation. Dunseith, North Dakota 58329. Ind. lay pas. 1 w. woman lay worker. 40 mem. 75 com. 1 conv. in 1975. SS.

C. & M. A. Church. Sioux. Standing Rock Reservation. McLaughlin, South Dakota 57642. Pastor, lay Ind. 1 Ind. man lay worker. 30 mem. 50 com. 1 conv. in 1975. SS.

C. & M. A. Church. Sioux. Ft. Thompson Reservation. Ft. Thompson, South Dakota 57339. Pastor, ord., w. 1 Ind. lay worker. 20 mem. 40 com. SS.

Menominee C. & M. A. Church. Menomonie, Wisconsin 54751.

Flathead C. & M. A. Mission. Arlee, Montana 59821.

Chippewa C. & M. A. Church. White Earth Reservation. Naytahwaush, Minnesota 56566.

C. & M. A. Indian Church. Mixed tribes. Minneapolis, Minnesota. Pastor, ord., w. woman. 1 Ind. man lay worker. 30 mem. 50 com. SS.

The C. & M. A. also has the following missions and churches in Canada: *Eskimo Point Mission,* Eskimo, at Fort Churchill, Manitoba (35 mem., 50 com.); 7 Cree churches at High Prairie, Ft. McMurray; Grouvard, Kinuso and Red Earth Creek, Alberta and a mixed church in Winnipeg. 1 ord. Ind. pastor, 2 w. ord. pastors. 7 Ind. lay pastors, 2 Ind. lay workers. 365 mem. 405 com.

THE CHRISTIAN CHURCH (DISCIPLES OF CHRIST)

DIVISION OF HOMELAND MINISTRIES
P. O. Box 1986, Indianapolis, Indian 46206   *(317)353-1491*
Dr. Kenneth A. Kuntz, President

YAKIMA INDIAN CHRISTIAN MISSION. Yakima. Yakima Reservation. P. O. Box 31, Toppenish, Washington 98948. *(509)865-2979.* Dr. Barbara Graves, Interim Administrator, ord., w. Valda Hollon, Secretary. Also a licensed w. minister on staff.

Valley Christian Church. Wapapto, Washington 98951. Participating mem. 36, non-participating 17. Ab. in 1977 - 4. One addition by transfer. SS 35.

Yakima Indian Christian Church. White Swan, Washington 98952. Participating mem. 40.

Friendship House. A-7 South Toppenish Avenue, Toppenish, Washington 98948.

Friendship House. 217 South Wapato Avenue, Wapato, Washington 98951.

These two Centers offer information, referral services,
limited material aid, light recreation, counseling services.
Both staffed by Indians.

CHRISTIAN REFORMED CHURCH

BOARD OF HOME MISSIONS
2850 Kalamazoo Avenue S.E., Grand Rapids, Michigan 49508
Rev. John VanRyn, Executive Secretary   *(616)241-1691*
Rev. Peter Borgdorff, Fields Secretary
Rev. Earl Dykema, Regional Missionary for the Indian Field
  611 Vanden Bosch Parkway, Gallup, New Mexico 87301
  (505)722-5755

CHRISTIAN REFORMED COUNCIL OF INDIAN CHURCHES. A partial
classis (similar to Presbytery) is composed of three
representatives from each church. A 12 member Central
Committee. Mr. Edward T. Begay, President. 1105 Martinelli
Drive, Gallup, New Mexico 87301. Rev. Rolf Veenstra, Secretary.
Rehoboth, New Mexico 87322.

C.R.C. Box 45, Church Rock, New Mexico 87311. Navajo.
(Unorganized) Anthony Begay, pastor, ord., Navajo.
(505)722-2137. Sunday worship, English and Navajo, 10 a.m. and
7 p.m. Communicant mem. 21. Total mem. 35. Families 15.
SS 30.

C.R.C., Crownpoint. Navajo. P. O. Box 208, Crownpoint, New
Mexico 87313. *(505)786-5930.* Gordon T. Stuit, pastor, ord.,
w. Sunday worship, 10:30 a.m. and 7 p.m. Communicant mem. 83.
Total mem. 154. Families 80. SS 70. Child baptisms in 1976 -
4.

C.R.C., Farmington. Navajo. 612 West Arrington Street,
Farmington, New Mexico 87401. Sampson Yazzie, pastor, ord.,
Navajo. *(505)329-9385.* Sunday worship, 10:30 a.m. and 7 p.m.,
Navajo-English. Communicant mem. 56. Total mem. 125.
Families 30. SS Superintendent and Director of Education, Glen
Verhulst, 620 W. Arrington Street, Farmington, New Mexico 87401.

C.R.C., Fort Wingate. Navajo. (Unorganized) P. O. Box 388,
Ft. Wingate, New Mexico 87316. Gerrit Haagema, evangelist,
ord., w. *(505)488-5564.* Sunday services, 10:30 a.m. and 5 p.m.
Communicant mem. 35. Total mem. 64. Families 14. SS 310.
Children baptized 5. Pf. 2.

Bethany C.R.C., Gallup. Navajo. 1110 South Strong Drive,
Gallup, New Mexico 87301. *(505)863-9155.* Alfred E. Mulder,
pastor, ord., w. 1225 Country Club Drive, Gallup, New Mexico
87301. *(505)863-6965.* Associate ministers (3): Roger Posthuma

Zuni, New Mexico 87327; Peter D. Winkle, Chaplain, Rehoboth Hospital, Rehoboth, New Mexico 87322; Earl Dykema. Services 10 a.m. and 7 p.m. Communicant mem. 153. Total mem. 341. Families 34. SS 70. Chairman of Education: Dr. Bruce Schuurmann, 505 East Green, Gallup, New Mexico 87301. Children baptized 7. Pf. 3.

C.R.C., Naschitti. Navajo. (Unorganized) Highway 666, 43 miles north of Gallup. Naschitti, New Mexico 87325. Corwin Brummell, pastor, unordained, w. Services 10 a.m. Navajo, 7 p.m. English, 8 p.m. May to September. Families 23. Communicant mem. 35. SS 50. Children baptized 9. Pf. 5.

C.R.C., Navajo. Navajo. 1978. (Unorganized) Navajo, New Mexico 87328. Stanley Siebersma, minister, unordained, w.

C.R.C., Newcomb. Navajo. 1977. Newcomb is not a post office. Daughter congregation of Toadlena, served by same staff. Floyd Frank, pastor, unordained, Navajo. Attendance of 70.

C.R.C., Redrock. Navajo. (Unorganized) Redrock, Arizona 87420. *(505)368-4458.* Boyd Garnanez, evangelist, unordained, Navajo. P. O. Box 534, Shiprock, New Mexico 87420. *(505)368-4458.* Services 10 a.m. and 7 p.m., Navajo and English. Communicant mem. 68. Total mem. 192. Families 52. SS 65. Children baptized 1. Pf. 5.

C.R.C., Rohoboth. Navajo. Rehoboth, New Mexico 87322. Rolf Veenstra, pastor, ord., w. *(505)863-4681.* Thomas Weeda, Superintendent of Education. Box 14, Rehoboth, New Mexico 87322. Services at 10 a.m. and 6:50 p.m. Communicant mem. 92. Total mem. 153. Families 31. SS 37.

Rehoboth Christian School. 1903. Navajo. P. O. Box 41, Rehoboth, New Mexico 87322. *(505)863-6091.* Mr. Keith Kuipers, Superintendent. Cooperatively operated by the denomination and a local school board. Grades 1-12. Day school 140 students, boarding school 180. Indian boys 120, Indian girls 132. Administrative staff 2. Teachers: 2 Indian men, 7 white men, 2 Indian women, 7 white women. Support: 75% by Church, 25% tuition. Two-thirds of graduates enter collage, one-third assorted jobs. Weekly Parent Bulletin.

C.R.C., Sanostee. Navajo. (Unorganized) Sanostee, New Mexico 87461. Frank Curley, Sr., evangelist, unordained, Navajo. Box 548, Sanostee, New Mexico 87461. Services at 11 a.m. and 6 p.m. Navajo. Communicant mem. 24. Families 12. SS 25.

C.R.C., Shiprock. Navajo. (Unorganized) On Highway 66 in village of Shiprock, New Mexico 87420. *(505)368-4475.*

A.L. Koolhaas, pastor, ord., w. Box 10, Shiprock, New Mexico 87420. English services at 10 a.m. and 6 p.m., Navajo at 11:15 a.m. Communicant mem. 61. Total mem. 199. Families 34. SS 208. Children baptized 2. Pf. 2.

C.R.C., Teec Nos Pos. Navajo. (Unorganized) P. O. Box 1030, Teec Nos Pos, Arizona 86514. *(602)656-3220.* Paul H. Redhouse, pastor, ord., Navajo. Services all Navajo, 10 a.m. and 7 p.m. Communicant mem. 85. Total mem. 204. Families 32. SS 22. Children baptized 2. Pf. 1.

C.R.C., Toadlena. Navajo. (Unorganized) P. O. Box 712, Toadlena, New Mexico 87324. *(505)789-3212.* Gary Klumpenhower, evangelist, unordained, w. Floyd Frank, assistant, unordained, Navajo. Services: 10 a.m. Navajo and English, 6 p.m. Navajo. Communicant mem. 55. Total mem. 146. Families 29. SS 226. Pf 1.

C.R.C., Tohatchi. Navajo. (Unorganized) Tohatchi, New Mexico 87325. Edward Henry, pastor, ord., Navajo. Box 119, Tohatchi, New Mexico 87325. *(505)733-2238.* Services: 10:30 a.m. English translated into Navajo, 7 p.m. Navajo. Families 18. SS 35.

C.R.C., Tohlakai. Navajo. (Unorganized) 10 miles north of Gallup across highway from Tohlakai Trading Post. Mike Harberts evangelist, unordained, w. Tohatchi, New Mexico 87325. Services: 10:30 a.m. and 6:30 p.m., Navajo and English. Communicant mem. 35. Families 15. Children baptized 2.

C.R.C., Window Rock. (Unorganized) 211 Oljato; mail address P. O. Box 665, Window Rock, Arizona 85615. (602)871-4054. Charles Grey, evangelist, unordained, Navajo. 812 Laguna Circle, Gallup, New Mexico 87301. Services: 10 a.m. and 7 p.m., English and Navajo. Communicant mem. 35. Families 20. SS 60. Superintendent: Ms. Eloise De Groot, Box 665, Window Rock, Arizona 86515.

Regular Navajo Mission Services also at:
  Beclabito, Arizona (not a post office). John Talley, pastor,
    unordained, Navajo.
  Toyee, New Mexico (not a post office). Elton Woody, pastor,
    unordained, Navajo.
  Whitehorse Lake, New Mexico (not a post office). Howard
    Begay, pastor, unordained, Navajo.

Address these men in care of the Mission at Rehoboth.

C.R.C., Zuni. 1897. Zuni Reservation. (Unorganized) P. O. Box 446, Zuni, New Mexico 87327. *(505)782-4546.* Roger Posthuma,

pastor, ord., w. P. O. Box 205, Zuni, New Mexico 87327.
(505)782-4761. Services at 11 a.m. and 6 p.m. Communicant
mem. 26. Total mem. 35. Families 10. SS 53. YS 20. WS 6.
VBS. Weekly kids club. Weekly Zuni Radio broadcast. Jail and
hospital visitation.

Zuni Christian Reformed Mission School. Zuni. P. O. Box 455,
Zuni, New Mexico 87327. *(505)782-4546.* Miss Wanda Van
Klompenberg, Principal. Day school. Grades 1-8. Administrative staff 5. Teachers: 2 w men, 3 w. women. Students: Zuni
boys 49, Zuni girls 39 (1977). Graduates enter public high
school or boarding school.

American Indian Church. 1941 West Belmont, Chicago, Illinois
60657. *(312)477-5406.* Howard Bielema, pastor, w.

URBAN CENTERS:

Denver Christian Indian Center. 501 South Pearl Street, Denver,
Colorado 80209. *(303)733-3693.* Rev. Harry A. VanDam, pastor,
ord., w. A Friendship House/Church program. Mem. 8. Sunday
worship. Children's Hour and Bible Fellowship. Wednesday
evening Bible classes 35. YS. Young adult group.

Salt Lake City Christian Indian Center. 2514 South 1500 East,
Salt Lake City, Utah 84109. *(801)466-1596.* Norman Jonkman,
Director. Services and church ministries closely related to
First Christian Reformed Church of Salt Lake.

San Francisco Friendship House
  Alcoholism Rehabilitation Program. 1340 Golden Gate Avenue,
San Francisco, California 94115. *(415)922-3866.* Al Walcott,
Interim Director.

  Friendship House Christian Reformed. 89 Turquois Way, San
Francisco, California 94131. *(415)922-3866.* Donald Klompeen,
pastor, Church program.

The Christian Reformed Church also operates the Winnipeg Indian
Family Center in Winnipeg, Manitoba.

CHURCH OF CHRIST (MORMON)

P. O. Box 472, Independence, Missouri 64051   *833-3995*
Mr. William A. Sheldon, General Church Representative

This church has a mission in Yucatan, Mexico with five congregations, four or five Indian ministers and about 200 mem. It is
at present trying to find a foothold among Indians in North
Carolina and Wyoming.

CHURCH OF GOD

BOARD OF CHURCH EXTENSION AND HOME MISSIONS
P. O. Box 2069, Anderson, Indiana 46011   *(317)644-2555*
Rev. M. J. Hartman, President/Treasurer

Church of God. Dakota. Pine Ridge Reservation. Wounded
Knee, South Dakota 57770. Pastors: ord. Ind. man and w.
woman. Communicant mem. 35. Total com. 55. SS 50. WS.

Church of God. Nez Perce. Nex Perce Reservation. Lapwai,
Idaho 83540. Ord. pastors: 1 w. man, 1 w. woman. Ind.
men workers 2, woman 1. Communicant mem. 40. SS 50. WS.

Church of God. Mixed. Tulalip Reservation. Marysville,
Washington 98270. Ord. pastors: 1 Ind. man, 1 w. woman.
Ind. lay men workers 4, Ind. women 2; w. lay men workers 2,
w. women 2. Communicant mem. 55. Total com. 100. SS 100.
WS. YS. Men's society.

Navajo Church of God. Navajo. Navajo Reservation. Klagetoh,
Arizona. 1 church, 3 chapels. Ord. pastors: 2 Ind. men, 1
Ind. woman. Ind. layworkers: 5 men, 1 woman. Communicant
mem. 100. Total com. 400. SS 75.

CHURCH OF GOD IN CHRIST, MENNONITE

General Offices: Moundridge, Kansas 67107

AMERICAN INDIAN MISSIONS

Greasewood Mennonite Mission. Navajo. 3-1/2 miles south of
Greasewood Trading Post. Ganado, Arizona 86505.
(602)654-3213. Staff workers: Curt and Marge Jantz. Sewing
Circle leader: Marge Jantz. Mem. 8. Attendance 25.

Jeddito Mission. Navajo. P. O. Box 221, Keams Canyon,
Arizona 86034. *(602)736-2337.* Workers: Les and Naomi Eck.
Hopitue Trailer Park, Keams Canyon, Arizona 86034. Mem. 2.

Klagetoh Mennonite Church - Wide Ruins Mission. Navajo.
Church is ½ mile south of Klagetoh Store, 16 miles south of
Ganado, 23 miles north of Chambers. Mission is 18 miles north
of Chambers. Wide Ruins, Arizona 86502. Mission phone:
(602)652-3222. James Joe, minister. c/o Wide Ruins Store,
Wide Ruins, Arizona 86502. Workers: Mr. & Mrs. Ervin Jantz.
P. O. Box 778, Wide Ruins, Arizona 86502. Mem. 18. Average
attendance 55. SS enrollment 30.

Salina Springs Mission. Navajo. Chinle, Arizona 86503.

(602)725-3257. Workers: Albert and Malinda Schmidt. SS
enrollment 17. Average attendance 9.

Hogan Hozhoni Christian Child Care Service. Navajo. P. O.
Box 645, Window Rock, Arizona 86515. *(602)871-4021.*
Volunteer workers 10.

Christian Child Care Home. 220 West Jefferson Street, Gallup,
New Mexico 87301. *(505)863-6046.* Volunteer workers 6.

CHURCH OF JESUS CHRIST OF LATTER DAY SAINTS

50 East North Temple Street, Salt Lake City, Utah 84150

Information on the Indian churches is unavailable. The
explanation given is: "The missionary program of the Church is
currently organized on mainly geographic areas, not in terms of
racial or ethnic groups. This makes it next to impossible for
us to identify precisely all the units of the Church working on
one capacity or another with American Indians. The missionaries of each mission may work with all groups within that
area."

Dolaghan and Scates in *The Navajos Are Coming To Jesus* mention
15 to 20 Mormon Indian churches on the Navajo Reservation but
they do not list them and did not study them.

The Catawba Tribe of North Carolina in entirety belongs to the
Church of Jesus Christ of Latter Day Saints.

The Indian Student Placement Program. Begun in 1947 and became
an official pro-ram of the Church in July 1954. Up to 1976
more than 20,000 students and 10,000 foster parents had
participated. The report for the then current year in July
1976 states that more than 2,300 students from about 63 tribes
and 21 states were enrolled. Students were then placed in
foster homes in Alberta and British Columbia, Washington,
California, Idaho, Arizona and Utah. Since 1971 local priesthood leaders have assumed responsibility for student applications and orientation. The program seeks to provide Indian
children with education, spiritual, social and cultural
opportunities that would contribute to their leadership development. Foster families are carefully screened and must meet the
requirements of the local licensed agency. There is profession-
al casework supervision of every child. Foster families must
be financially able to bear costs of lodging, food, clothing,
school fees and minor medical expenses. Children visit their
own families on a regular basis. The term is for the school
year, but, as long as education continues in the same place,
the child is expected to remain in the same foster home.

CHURCH OF THE BRETHREN

GENERAL BOARD, WORLD MINISTRIES COMMISSION
1451 Dundee Avenue, Elgin, Illinois 60120   *(312)742-9100*

Lybrook Navajo Fellowship. 1950. Navajo Reservation. Star
Route 4, Cuba, New Mexico 87013. *(505)568-4378.* Russell W.
Kiester, pastor, ord., w. Communicant mem. 20. Total mem. 35-
40. SS 12-15. Adult education program preparing for GED
diploma. Crafts training program. Former clinic closed when
the Area Navajo Chapter opened one. The W.M.C. makes grants to
community projects wherein the right of self-determination is a
priority criterion for funding.

CHURCH OF THE NAZARENE

BOARD OF HOME MISSIONS
6401 The Paseo, Kansas City, Missouri 64131   *(816)313-7000*
Rev. Raymond Hurn, Executive Secretary

NORTH AMERICAN INDIAN DISTRICT   1945
Julian D. Gunn, District Superintendent, ord., Ind. *(602)227-7373*
4229 North 16th Drive, Phoenix, Arizona 85015

White ministers are not members of the District, only Indians
are members.

ZONE CHAIRMEN:

Oklahoma Zone - Owen Smith, Route 1, Box 21A, Cache, Oklahoma
73527. *(405)429-8192.*

New Mexico Zone - Will Ortega, 2315 Markham Road, S.W.,
Albuquerque, New Mexico 87105. *(505)877-0240.*

Northern Arizona Zone - Alex Riggs, Star Route, Box 76,
Winslow, Arizona 86047. *(602)669-2783.*

First Indian. All tribes. 818 Apache Avenue, N.W.,
Alququerque, New Mexico 87102. *(505)247-8241.* Floyd Fisher,
pastor, ord., w. Mem. 25. Pf. in 1977 - 1. SS 59. VBS 78.
Nazarene youth 8. Women's Missionary society 18.

Cache. Comanche. 1½ miles west of Cache, Oklahoma on Old Hwy.
62. *(405)429-8192.* Owen J. Smith, pastor, ord., Ind. Route 1,
Box 21A, Cache, Oklahoma 73527. Mem. 74. Pf. 8. SS 87.
Women's Missionary society 65. YS 9.

Canoncito. Navajo. Canoncito Navajo Reservation. New Mexico.
Leo Hudson, pastor, lic., Ind. 2315 Markham Road, S.W.,

Albuquerque, New Mexico 87105. *(505)877-0240.*

Chilchinbeto. Navajo. Navajo Reservation. 20 miles south of Kayenta, Arizona. Charlie C. Billy, pastor, lic., Ind. Chilchinbeto School, Kayenta, Arizona 86033. Johnny Grey, assistant pastor, Ind. P. O. Box 128, Kayenta, Arizona 86033. Mem. 103. SS 266. YS 72.

Dilkon. 35 miles northeast of Winslow, Arizona. Navajo. James A. Paddock, Sr., pastor, lic., Ind. P. O. Box 409, Winslow, Arizona 86047. Mem. 58. SS 92. VBS 43. Women's Missionary society 59. Nazarene youth 17.

Emerson. 6½ miles west of Walters, Oklahoma. Comanche. *(405)875-2887.* Pastor to be supplied. Nick Tahchaw-wickah, assistant pastor, ord., Ind. Mem. 46, SS 24.

Kaibeto. Navajo. Navajo Reservation. 40 miles southeast of Page, Arizona by Kaibeto Boarding School. Johnson Begay, pastor lic., Ind. P. O. Box 7043, Kaibeto, Arizona 86053. Mem. 46. Pf. 3. SS 53.

Laguna. Laguna. Paguate, New Mexico. Arthur Moendl, pastor, ord., w. 2315 Markham Road, S.W., Albuquerque, New Mexico 87105. *(505)873-1732.* SS 26.

Lehi. Pima/Maricopa. 1452 East Oak Street, Mesa, Arizona 85203. Don Blackard, pastor, lic., w. Will Ortega, assistant pastor. Mem. 41. Pf. 4. SS 98. VBS 42. Women's Missionary society 65. YS 20.

Leupp. Navajo. Leupp, Arizona 86035. Alex Riggs, Sr., pastor, ord., Ind. Star Route, Box 76, Winslow, Arizona 86047. Riley Jones, assistant pastor. Star Route, Box 77, Winslow, Arizona 86047. Mem. 88. Pf. 7. SS 137. YS 20.

Montezuma Chair. Navajo. 50 miles south of Winslow, Arizona. Joseph Curley, pastor, lic., Ind. P. O. Box 459, Winslow, Arizona 86047. Mem. 31. Pf. 3. SS 56. VBS 4. WS 16. YS 13.

Navajo Station. About 25 miles southwest of Ganado, Arizona. 1 mile east of El Paso Pumping Station. Robert and Anabelle Pino, pastors, both lic., Ind. P. O. Box 51, Ganado, Arizona 86505. Mem. 94. Pf. 6. SS 114. VBS 44. Women's Missionary society 92.

Nazarene Indian School Church. All tribes. 2315 Markham Road, S.W., Albuquerque, New Mexico 87105. *(505)877-0240.* Wayne Stark, pastor, ord., w. Mem. 38. Pf. 3. SS 64. Women's Missionary society 61. YS 21.

Needles. Mohave. 218 Market Street, Needles, California 92363. Lloyd Hughes, pastor, ord., w. 206 Market Street, Needles, California 92363. *(714)326-2419.* Mem. 39. Pf. 1. SS 182. VBS 64. WS 34.

Page Le Chee. Navajo. Le Chee community, 4 miles south of Page, Arizona. Alvin T. Tso, pastor, ord., Ind. P. O. Box 1541, Page, Arizona 86040. *(602)698-3325.* Mem. 83. Pf. 4. SS 120. WS 60. YS 10.

Parker. Mohave. 1117 Ocotillo Street, Parker, Arizona 85344. Ben and Daisy Simms, pastors, Ind.; Ben ord. P. O. Box 653, Parker, Arizona 85344. Mem. 42. SS 110. Pf. 1. VBS 61. WS 60. YS 19.

Ponca City. Ponca. 4 miles south of Ponca City, Oklahoma on Hwy. 77. Route 4, Box 271A, Ponca City, Oklahoma 74601. *(405)765-8979.* Pastor to be supplied. Mem. 39. SS 60. WS 8.

Poston. Mohave, Navajo, Hopi. 3 miles south of Poston on Mohave Road. P. O. Box NM, Poston, Arizona 85371. *(602)662-4690.* Scott Tohannie, pastor, lic., Ind. Mem. 24. Pf. 1. SS 72. YS 15.

Ramah Navajo. Ramah, New Mexico 87321. Johnny and Juanita Nells, pastors, Ind.; Johnny lic. P. O. Box 90, Ramah, New Mexico 87321. Mem. 106. Pf. 3. SS 112. VBS. WS 52. YS 16.

Ramah Pine Hill. Navajo. 23 miles south of Ramah, New Mexico. Robert Pokagon, pastor, ord., Ind. P. O. Box 6, Ramah, New Mexico 87321. Assistant pastors: Dannie Pino and Lorenza Chatto, lay, Ind. Mem. 60. Pf. 5. SS 51. VBS 42. WS 42. YS 22.

Ramah Sand Mountain. Navajo. 20 miles southeast of Ramah, New Mexico. Sheppie and Florence Martine, pastors, Ind.; Sheppie lic. P. O. Box 184, Ramah, New Mexico 87321. Mem. 81. Pf. 1. SS 161. VBS 17. WS 65.

Round Cedar. Navajo. 35 miles southeast of Flagstaff, Arizona, 5 miles south of Leupp. Rex Tsosie, pastor, lic., Ind. Star Route Box 38, Winslow, Arizona 86047. Mem. 60. SS 80. VBS 30. WS 65. YS 15.

Sells. Papago. Opposite high school at Sells, Arizona on Hwy. 86. Daniel Hasselrode, pastor, ord., w. P. O. Box 37, Sells, Arizona 85634. *(602)383-2548.* Mem. 52. SS 49. WS 49.

Smoke Signal. Navajo. 8 miles south of Hwy. 4, 40 miles south-

west of Chinle, Arizona. Ned Begay, pastor, lic., Ind. Smoke
Signal Mission, Chinle, Arizona 86503. Mem. 46. SS 167.
VBS 34. WS 55. YS 7.

Somerton. Cocopah. 3 E. George Street, Somerton, Arizona
85350. *(602)627-2040.* Ray Stillings, pastor, lic., Ind.
P. O. Box 356, Somerton, Arizona 85350. *(602)627-8438.*
Mem. 36. SS 63. WS 75. YS 10.

Tucson. Papago. 260 W. 27th Street, Tucson, Arizona 85713.
Clarence D. Liston, pastor, ord., w. P. O. Box 7185, Tucson,
Arizona 85725. *(602)622-8367.* Mem. 35. SS 63. WS 35. YS 15.

Twin Butte. Navajo. 6 miles west of Gallup, New Mexico.
Marshall Keeto, pastor, ord., Ind. P. O. Box 566, Mentmore,
New Mexico 87319. Mem. 50. Pf. 1. SS 112. VBS 87. WS 41.
YS 20.

Twin Hills and Shonto. Navajo. Twin Hills 35 miles north of
Tuba City, Arizona. Peter Riggs, Sr., pastor, lic., Ind.
P. O. Box 1148, Page, Arizona 86040. Combined mem. 63. SS 82.
WS 19.

Window Rock. Navajo. 2 miles west of stop light and ¼ mile
north of Black Rock Road, St. Michaels, Arizona. Wilfred Niedo,
pastor, lic., Ind. P. O. Box 755, Window Rock, Arizona 86515.
(602)871-4328. Mem. 23. Pf. 7. SS 53. VBS 52. WS 37.
YS 9.

Winslow First Nazarene. Navajo and mixed. 1923 West 2nd,
Winslow, Arizona 86047. J. M. Spohn, pastor, ord., w. Dennis
Johnson, assistant pastor, layman, Ind. Mem. 33. Pf. 6.
SS 83. YS 8.

Winterhaven Quechan. Quechan. 2149 "H" Street, P. O. Box 1116,
Winterhaven, California 92283. Paul R. Myers, pastor, ord.,
w. Mem. 61. SS 126. VBS 51. WS 51. YS 12.

Other ordained Indian elders:

Sarah J. Herbert, P. O. Box 634, Winterhaven, California 92283.
Raymond Kormes, 211 Market Street, Needles, California 92283.
David C. Reynolds, 9720 Stacy Ct., Box S-35, Oklahoma City,
    Oklahoma 73132.
Mike Wanqua, 6714 N.W. 43rd, Bethany, Oklahoma 73008.
Lester Whitepigeon; Lilly Sue Metzger, 2315 Markham Road S.W.,
    Albuquerque, New Mexico 87105.

Other licensed Indian ministers:

Leo Hudson, 2315 Markham Road, S.W., Albuquerque, New Mexico 87105.
Juan Martine, P. O. Box 90, Ramah, New Mexico 87321.
Morris Richards, 2315 Markham Road, S.W., Albuquerque, New Mexico 87105.
Jack Whitehorse, Dilkon Boarding School, Winslow, Arizona 86047.

All Churches have a Chairman of Christian Life, a Director of Children's Ministries, Director of Youth Ministries, a Nazarene Youth International group, a Nazarene World Mission Society, a church secretary and a treasurer.

Nazarene Indian Bible School. 2315 Markham Road, S.W., Albuquerque, New Mexico 87105. *(505)877-0240.* Rev. Merle Gray (ord., w.) Superintendent.

Totals: 31 churches and 1 branch; 14 fully ord. Ind. elders (ministers), 9 fully ord. w. elders; 18 lic. Ind. pastors, 1 w.; 1,577 mem.; 2,857 in SS; 643 in VBS; Nazarene Women's World Missionary Society mem. (WS) 1,064; Nazarene Youth International mem. (YS) 361. Raised for all purposes $189,329. Value of church buildings $545,000. Value of parsonages $225,250. Indebtedness on churches and parsonages $16,000.

CHURCHES OF GOD, GENERAL CONFERENCE

COMMISSION ON NATIONAL MISSIONS AND CHURCH EXTENSION
Rev. Donald M. Cohick, Secretary, Treasurer
P. O. Box 234, Valley View, Pennsylvania 17983

Mentmore Mission. P. O. Box 541, Mentmore, New Mexico 87319. Ronald J. Endres, missionary.

CONSERVATIVE BAPTIST HOME MISSION SOCIETY

P. O. Box 828, Wheaton, Illinois　　　　　　　*(312)665-1200*
Dr. Rufus Jones, General Director

Indian Island Baptist Church. Penobscot. Indian Island Reservation. Indian Island, Maine. Pastor, ord., w. Mem. 40. Com. about 50. SS 14. WS. YS. Children's society.

Navajo Mission. Navajo Reservation.

Tsi Bii Otseel Baptist Church. Near Indian Wells. Lamuel Yazzie, pastor, ord., Navajo. P. O. Box Y, Indian Wells, Arizona 86031.

Navajo Baptist Church of Middle Mesa. P. O. Box 254, Tuba City, Arizona 86045. John Mexicano, pastor, ord., Navajo. *(602)283-5839.* Mem. 68, increase of 12. 12 ab. SS 38. YS 14. WS 12. Young convert class. Language class. Summer VBS in June.

Preaching/Worship Points: *Shonto, Kaibeto, Red Lake.*

Working in the Mission also 1 Ind. lay minister, 1 Ind. and 1 woman worker, 1 w. layman, 2 w. laywomen.

CUMBERLAND PRESBYTERIAN CHURCH

DEPARTMENT OF INDIAN WORK OF THE DIVISION OF HOME MINISTRIES
Departmental Director: Rev. Claude Gilbert
P. O. Box 536, Idabel, Oklahoma 74745
Telephones: Office - *(405)286-3287* Home - *(405)286-5326*

CHOCTAW PRESBYTERY (Southeast Oklahoma within boundaries of the old Choctaw Nation.) 14 churches, 432 mem., 56 conv. and rededications in 1977, 3 ab., 6 ib., 6 active Choctaw ministers, several retired, 2 w. pastors. SS enrollment 206, 7 WS, 58 active mem. in Cumberland Presbyterian Women, 9 YS with 300 mem., 8 summer VBS, a men's presbyterial society, quarterly 3-day presbyterial rallies. There is a Youth Camp near Bethel. Church leaders are active in Choctaw Nation politics.

Bayou Church. 1890. Tom, Oklahoma 74762. Allen Carnes, pastor, ord., Choctaw. Box 39, Boswell, Oklahoma 74727. Mem. 8 active. SS.

Coal Creek Church. 1921. Route 3, Atoka, Oklahoma 74525. Jasper Scott, pastor, ord., Choctaw. Route 5, Atoka, Oklahoma 74525. Mem. 11 active. SS. WS.

Double Springs Church. 1925. Route 7, Lane, Oklahoma 74555. A. B. Johnson, pastor, ord., Choctaw. Mem. 12 active. SS.

Gum Creek Church. 1894. Wilburton, Oklahoma 74578. Lee Burris, pastor, ord., Choctaw. Mem. 10 active. SS. WS.

Honey Grove Church. Route 2, Broken Bow, Oklahoma 74728. Albert Jacoe, pastor, ord., w., married to Choctaw woman. Active mem. 14. SS. WS.

Lone Star Church. 1910. Wardville, Oklahoma 74576. Jasper Scott, pastor, ord., Choctaw. Route 5, Atoka, Oklahoma 74525. Mem. 28 active. SS. WS.

McGee Chapel Church. 1906. Broken Bow, Oklahoma 74728. Randolph Jacob, pastor, ord., Choctaw. Mem. 30 active. SS. WS.

Oak Hill Church. 1954. Route 2, Broken Bow, Oklahoma 74728. Claude Gilbert, pastor, ord., w. P. O. Box 536, Idabel, Oklahoma 74545. Mem. 26 active. SS.

Panki Bok Church. 1887. Eagletown, Oklahoma 74734. Allen Carnes, pastor, ord., Choctaw. Box 39, Boswell, Oklahoma 74727. Mem. 8 active. SS.

Pigeon Roost Church. 1882. Boswell, Oklahoma 74727. Jasper Scott, pastor, ord., Choctaw. Route 5, Atoka, Oklahoma 74525. Mem. 18 active.

Pine Lake Church. 1967. Broken Bow, Oklahoma 74728. Vacant. Claude Gilbert, moderator of Session. Mem. 22 active. SS. WS.

Rock Creek Church. 1914. Honobia, Oklahoma 74749. Lee Burris, pastor, ord., Choctaw. Route 1, Box 27-B, Centrahoma, Oklahoma 74534. Mem. 18 active. SS. WS.

Round Lake Church. 1929. Route 1, Box 20, Centrahoma, Oklahoma 74534. Randy Jacob, pastor, ord., Choctaw. Mem. 11 active.

Wright City Church. 1951. Wright City, Oklahoma 74766. Allen Carnes, pastor, ord., Choctaw. Box 39, Boswell, Oklahoma 74727. Mem. 13 active. SS.

THE EPISCOPAL CHURCH

Executive Council
815 Second Avenue, New York, New York 10017
Executive for Mission: Rev. Sam VanCulin
National Committee on Indian Work: Clyde Redshirt

DIOCESE OF ALASKA
P. O. Box 441, Fairbanks, Alaska 99707   *(907)452-3040*
The Rt. Rev. David R. Cochran, Bishop
The Ven. Luke Titus (Athabascan) Archdeacon for Native
  Ministry

Non-parochial Clergy:
  Anna Frank, Athabascan, ord. Health Education Coordinator
  for the Tanana Chiefs Conference. 1303 O'Connor, Box 33,
  Fairbanks, Alaska 99701. *(907)452-8251.*

Norman Nauska, Tlinget, ord. Student at Cook Christian
Training School, Tempe, Arizona.

Titus Peter, Athabascan, ord. Outreach Counselor in
Alcoholism. Diocese of Alaska. 1205 Denali Way, Fairbanks,
Alaska 99701. *(907)452-2933.*

Andrew Fairfield, ord., non-native. Coordinator of two
programs funded by the Lilly Endowment having to do with
Native Ministry and Education.

Keith Lawton, Kotzebue, Alaska 99752, ord., non-native.
Network (training Program). Associate and resource person
for the Arctic Coast.

All villages and towns except Kotzebue, Ft. Yukon, Tanana
and Barrow are virtually 100% Episcopal due to the long-
standing comity agreements. Other denominational churches
are found in those four and Fairbanks.

Sacramentalists are indicated by symbol (S). They have
been ordained to celebrate the sacraments and lead worship.
All other parochial clergy are ordained priests.
Sacramentalists as well as priests are addressed as
"Reverend."

St. John's in the Wilderness. Athabascan. Allakaket, Alaska
99720. Population 174. Village phone - *(907)968-8001.* Joe
Williams, Jr., (S), pastor. Communicants 30. Total Episcopa-
lian com. 160. Ib. in 1977 - 6, ab. 6. SS 6.

Bishop Rowe Chapel. Athabascan. Arctic Village, Alaska
99722. Population 130. Village phone - *(907)587-8001.* James
Gilbert, (S) and Trimble Gilbert, (S), pastors. Isaac Tritt,
retired pastor. Communicants 45. Total Episcopalians 130.
Ib. in 1977 - 5. SS.

Saint Timothy's. Athabascan. Chalkyitsik, Alaska 99788.
Population 130. Village phone *(907)848-8001.* David Solomon.
Communicants 55. Total Episcopalians 110. Ib. 3. SS.

Saint John's. Athabascan. Eagle, Alaska 99738. Population
80. Village phone - *(907)729-8001.* Vacant, serviced by
Diocesan staff. Communicants 30. Total Episcopalians 60..

Good Shepherd. Athabascan. Huslia, Alaska 99746.
Population 210. Village phone - *(907)829-8001.* Vacant,
serviced by Diocesan staff. Communicants 50. Total
Episcopalians 199. Ib. 11. SS.

Epiphany Church. Eskimo. Kivalina, Alaska 99750. Population 188. Village phone - *(907)289-8001.* Raymond Hawley, (S), Jerry Norton, (S), Clinton Swan, (S), Milton Swan, priest, retired. Communicants 103. Total Episcopalians 166. Ib. 1. SS 133.

St. George's-in-the-Arctic. Eskimo. Kotzebue, Alaska 99752. Population 2,000. *(907)442-3154.* James Hawley, (S), Wilfred Lane, (S). Communicants 138. Total Episcopalians 218. Ib. 7, ab. 1. SS 40.

St. Mark's Mission. Athabascan. Nenana, Alaska 99760. Population 362. The Venerable Luke Titus, pastor. Communicants 65. Total Episcopalians 284. Ib. 4, ab. 1. SS.

St. Matthew's. Mixed congregation, about 150 Indians and Eskomos regular mem. Fairbanks, Alaska 99707. Donald P. Hart, rector, ord., w. A successfully integrated congregation.

Christ Church. Athabascan. Anvik, Alaska 99558. Population 83. Village phone - *(907)462-8001.* Vacant, serviced by Shageluk priest. Communicants 12. Total Episcopalians 87. Ib. 2. SS.

\ *St. Matthew's Mission.* Athabascan. Beaver, Alaska 99724. Population 101. Village phone - *(907)628-8001.* Scott Fisher, priest, non-native. Communicants 56. Total Episcopalians 84. Ib. 3. SS.

\ *St. Stephen's Church.* Athabascan. Ft. Yukon, Alaska 99740. Population 600. *(907)662-2383.* John A. Phillips, priest, non-native. Communicants 105. Total Episcopalians 471. Ib. 13. SS 14.

St. Paul's Church. Athabascan. Graling, Alaska 99590. Population 139. Village phone - *(907)543-2682.* Vacant, served by Shageluk priest. Communicants 44. Total Episcopalians 110. Ib. 10. SS 18.

St. Barnabas. Athabascan. Minto, Alaska 99758. Population 185. Village phone - *(907)798-8001.* Kenneth Charlie, (S) and Berkman Silas, (S). Communicants 110. Total Episcopalians 185. Ib. 3. SS 35.

St. Andrew's Mission. Athabascan. Stevens Village, Alaska 99774. Population 75. Village phone - *(907)478-8001.* Vacant, serviced by the Beaver priest. Communicants 45. Total Episcopalians 70. Ib. 7. SS.

The Episcopal Congregation. Athabascan. Hughes, Alaska 99745.

Population 85. Vacant, served by Diocesan staff. Communicants 24. Total Episcopalians 75.

St. Thomas' Church. Eskimo. Point Hope, Alaska 99766. Population 386. Village phone - *(907)362-8001.* Patrick Attungana (S), Herbert Kinneeveauk (S), Nelda Kinneeveauk (S), and Donald Oktollik, retired priest. Communicants 399. Total Episcopalians 399. Ib. 10. SS.

St. Luke's Church. Athabascan. Shageluk, Alaska 99665. Population 167. Village phone - *(907)431-8001.* Jean Dementi, non-native priest. Communicants 44. Total Episcopalisna 153. SS 26.

St. James' Church. Athabascan. Tanana, Alaska 99777. Population 300. Church phone - *(907)366-7895.* Helen Peters (S), Alfred Grant (S). Communicants 44. Total Episcopalians 176. Ib. 2. SS.

Good Shepherd. Athabascan. Venetie, Alaska 99781. Population 112. Village phone - *(907)849-8001.* Paul Tritt. Communicants 63. Total Episcopalians 97. Ib. 3. SS 12.

St. Timothy's Church. Athabascan. Tanacross, Alaska 99776. Population 84. Vacant, serviced by Diocesan staff. Communicants 20. Total Episcopalians 100. SS.

Episcopal Congregation. Eskimo. Barrow, Alaska 99723. Population 2,000. Vacant.

Trinity Mission. Athabascan. Circle, Alaska 99611. Population 50. Village Phone - *(907)779-8001.* Vacant, serviced by Diocesan staff.

Totals: 18 Athabascan churches, 1 mixed, 4 Eskimo; 6 Athabascan men sacramentalists, 1 woman; 7 Eskimo men sacramentalists, 1 woman; 6 Athabascan men priests, 1 woman; 2 Eskimo and 1 Tlingit men priests, 7 non-native men priests.

DIOCESE OF ARIZONA
2311 North 55th Street, Phoenix, Arizona 85008   *(602)959-7060*
Rt. Rev. Joseph M. Harte, D.D., S.T.D., Bishop

The Navajo Good Shepherd Mission at Ft. Defiance and its associated congregations and activities have been under the Diocese of Arizona until late 1977 when the Navajo Area Mission, authorized by General Convention in the previous summer, was inaugurated as an autonomous unit. See below.

DIOCESE OF CENTRAL NEW YORK
310 Montgomery Street, Syracuse, New York 13202
Rt. Rev. Ned Cole, Bishop   *(315)474-6596*

Church of the Good Shepherd Among the Onondagas. Onondage
Reservation. Rt. 1, Nedrow, New York 13120. Albert W. Ander-
son, ord. priest, w. *All Saints' Church,* 1800 S. Salina St.,
Syracuse, New York 13205. *(315)476-6469.* Communicants 65
(1977). Total Episcopal com. 214 (1975). Total baptized 95.
Ib. in 1977 - 2. SS 10. Weekly beadwork classes.

DIOCESE OF CHICAGO
65 East Huron Street, Chicago, Illinois 60611 *(312)787-6410*
Rt. Rev. James W. Montgomery, Bishop

Saint Augustine's Center for American Indians. 4512 North
Sheridan Road, Chicago, Illinois 60640. *(312)784-1050.* With
St. Augustine's Chapel. Mrs. Amy Skenadore, Executive
Director; Fr. Peter John Powell, Spiritual Director and
Chaplain. Daily mass. Case work counseling. Family
assistance. Alcoholism program. During 1975 about 3,000
families were counseled and assisted to the benefit of about
8,000 people.

DIOCESE OF COLORADO
P. O. Box M, Capitol Hill Station, Denver, Colorado 80218
The Rt. Rev. William C. Frey, Bishop

The Diocese contributes to an emergency feeding and counseling
service for Indians and others through Episcopal Community
Services which is financed by endowments of St. John's
Cathedral.

DIOCESE OF FOND DU LAC
P. O. Box 149, Fond du Lac, Wisconsin 54935
Rt. Rev. William H. Brady, Bishop

Holy Apostles Church. c.1850. Oneida. Oneida, Wisconsin
54155. *(414)869-2565.* Charles Wallace, pastor, ord., w.
Mem. 800. There is a SS, YS, WS, and other programs.

DIOCESE OF IDAHO
P. O. Box 936, Boise, Idaho 85701   *(208)345-4440*
Rt. Rev. Hanford L. King, Jr., Ph.D., Bishop

Episcopal Church. Fort Hall Reservation (Shoshone-Bannock).
Fort Hall, Idaho 83203. Mixed congregation not for Indians
only. Mr. & Mrs. Peter Maupin, laymen in charge. P. O.
Box 534, Pocatello, Idaho 83201.

DIOCESE OF IOWA
225 37th Street, Des Moines, Iowa 50312
Rt. Rev. Walter C. Righter, Bishop

St. Paul's Indian Mission. 1883/1965. 50% Santee Sioux, 40%
other Sioux, Ponca, etc. 524 Center Street, P. O. Box 895,
Sioux City, Iowa 51103. *(712)233-2940.* James D. Marrs, Sr.,
priest, w. 211 Grove Street, Sioux City, Iowa 51103.
Communicants 76, baptized members 477. Ib. 6. SS 33. WS 18.
VBS. Cottage prayer meetings. Commission for the Community:
service to youth and elderly, housing, health, education,
recreation, alcoholism counseling, referral. Community
program now funded by Diocese of Iowa. Native American
Alcohol Treatment Program and Urban Indian Health Service use
the building. The former parish was reorganized as an
Indian Mission in 1965. St. Paul's assits the small
Episcopal Mission at Winnebago, Nebraska.

DIOCESE OF MILWAUKEE
804 East Juneau Avenue, Milwaukee, Wisconsin 53202
Rt. Rev. Charles T. Gaskell, D.D., Bishop   *(414)272-3028*

No purely Indian parishes. The following two churches have
several Indian families.

All Saints' Cathedral. 818 E. Juneau Avenue, Milwaukee
Wisconsin 53202. The Very Rev. Robert F. Stub, Dean.

St. John's Episcopal Church. 2612 W. Mineral Street,
Milwaukee, Wisconsin 53204. Malcolm P. Brunner.

DIOCESE OF MINNESOTA
309 Clifton Avenue, Minneapolis, Minnesota 55403
Rt. Rev. Philip F. McNairy, D.D., Bishop   *(612)871-5311*

Advisory and Coordinating Council for Indian Ministries
Chairman: Ms. Linda Wallace, 121 West Rustic Lodge,
Minneapolis, Minnesota 55409

St. Peter's Church. 1881. Chippewa/white. Rice Lake Reservation. P. O. Box 395, Cass Lake, Minnesota 56633. Lawrence
J. Rowe, priest. Communicants 244. Baptized mem. 453.
1977 baptisms 15. SS 20.

All Saints. 1975. Sioux/Chippewa. 3045 Park Avenue,
Minneapolis, Minnesota 55407. Marvin Red Elk, priest, Ind.
Communicants about 40. Baptized mem. about 60.

Samuel Memorial Mission. 1893. Chippewa. Rice Lake Reservation. P. O. Box 55, Naytahwaush, Minnesota 56566.

William H. Freeman, priest, w. Communicants 93. Baptized
mem. 172. Baptisms 2. SS 28. Weekly class for layreaders.

St. John's Onigun. 1880. Chippewa. Rice Lake Reservation.
Walker, Minnesota 56484. Lawrence J. Rowe, priest. w. P. O.
Box 395, Cass Lake, Minnesota 56633. Communicants 65.
Baptized mem. 69. SS 15.

Breck Memorial Mission. Chippewa. Rice Lake Reservation.
Ponsford, Minnesota 56575. Reuben Rock, priest. Communicants 103. Baptized mem. 103. 1977 baptisms 10.

Messiah. 1906. Sioux. Route 2, Prairie Island, Welch,
Minnesota 55089. Richard K. Smith, priest, resides in
Minneapolis. About 60 communicants. 100 baptized mem.

St. John's. 1876. Chippewa. Red Lake Reservation. Red
Lake, Minnesota 56671.
St. Antipas. 1878. Chippewa. Red Lake Reservation. Redby,
Minnesota 56670.
   Both: George A. Smith, priest, Ind., resides in Bemidji.
Communicants 77. Baptized mem. 270. Baptisms in 1977 - 6.
SS 12.

St. Philip's. 1876. Chippewa. Rice Lake Reservation.
Route 2, Bagley, Minnesota 56621. William Freeman, priest,
resides in Naytahwaush. Communicants 84. Baptized mem. 170.
Baptisms in 1977 - 6. SS 12.

Mazakute Memorial Mission. 1974. Chippewa/Sioux. 838
Stellar Place, St. Paul, Minnesota 55105. Leslie Bobtail
Bear, priest, Ind. Communicants 90. Baptized mem. 150.
Baptisms in 1977 - 10. SS 40.

Saint Cornelia. 1886. Sioux. Birch Coulee Reservation.
Morton, Minnesota 56270. Edward Sheppard, priest, supply
only. Communicants 59. Baptized mem. 160. Baptisms in
1977 - 5. SS 18.

Holy Light Mission. 1976. Sioux. Route 1, Shakopee,
Minnesota 55370. Marvin Red Elk, priest, resides in
Minneapolis. About 20 communicants. About 30 baptized mem.

Gilfillan Memorial Chapel. 1878. Chippewa. Rice Lake Reservation. Squaw Lake, Minnesota 56681. Lawrence Rowe,
priest, resides in Cass Lake. Communicants 34. Baptized
mem. 39.

St. Columba. 1852. Rice Lake Reservation. White Earth,
Minnesota 56591. George Parmenter, priest. Communicants 89.

Baptized residents 195. Baptisms in 1977 - 21. SS 2.

NAVAJO AREA MISSION: NAVAJOLAND EPISCOPAL CHURCH

Navajo Reservation in Utah, Arizona and New Mexico. Enacted
by General Convention in August 1977 and established on the
First Sunday in Advent, 1977, incorporating churches and
missions previously in the Dioceses of Utah, Arizona and Rio
Grande.

Rt. Rev. Frederick W. Putnam, Jr., Bishop. Ft. Defiance,
Arizona 86504.

Development Office: Fort Defiance, Arizona 86504.
Rev. Edward O. Moore, Development Officer.

Navajo Episcopal Council: Fort Defiance, Arizona 86504.
Mr. Thomas C. Jackson, Executive Secretary (Navajo).

ARIZONA CHURCHES

Good Shepherd Mission. Ft. Defiance, Arizona 86504.
Edward O. Moore, Acting Vicar, ord., w. 7 Navajo staff
members. Navajo helpers in the pre-school and after school
Enrichment Program. Communicants 193. Baptized mem. 531.
Baptisms in 1977 - 18 infants and 2 adults. SS 53. Pre-
school program 18. Each of the congregations has a sewing
group. Youth meetings on special occasions. The Mission
is comprised of the following units in addition to Good
Shepherd Church.

Preaching Points: *Jeddito* and *Many Farms*.

St. Mark's. Coal mine. Mrs. John Dick, lay field worker,
Navajo.
St. Luke's. Navajo. Mrs. John Dick.
St. Anne's. Sawmill. Mrs. Marshall Segodi, lay field
worker.
   (Mail for outstations to be addressed to GSM, Fort
   Defiance, Arizona 86504.)

NEW MEXICO CHURCHES

Lay Administrator for Navajo Congregations: Mrs. Rosella
Jim (Navajo). P. O. Box 720, Farmington, New Mexico 87401.
(505)325-2532.

Priest Trainer: Rev. Henry L. Bird (Anglo). P. O. Box 720,
Farmington, New Mexico 87401. *(505)325-2532.*

St. Luke's in the Desert. Carson's Trading Post, New Mexico 87517. Miss Inez Yazzie, lay pas., Navajo. Communicants 37. Baptized persons 72. Ib. in 1977 - 1. SS 27.

All Saints' Chapel. Farmington, New Mexico 87401. Mrs. Alice Mason, lay pas., Navajo. Eloise Martinez, assistant, Deacon, Navajo. Communicants 53. Baptized persons 101. Children baptized in 1977 - 4. SS 12.

St. Michael's. Fruitland, New Mexico 87416. Mrs. Alice Mason, lay pas., Navajo. Yazzie Mason, assistant, Deacon, Navajo. Communicants 60. Baptized persons 122. SS 23.

St. Augustine's. Shiprock, New Mexico 87420. Mrs. Uberta Arthur, lay pas., Navajo. Communicants 35. Baptized persons 71.

The Deacons are in training for the priesthood.

Totals for New Mexico: 4 churches, 185 communicants, 366 baptized persons, 11 child baptisms in 1977, SS 62.

UTAH CHURCHES

St. John the Baptizer. Montezuma Creek, Utah 84512. Steven T. Plummer, ord. priest, Navajo. Communicants 24. Baptized mem. 102. Families 50.

St. Christopher's. Bluff, Utah 84512. Communicants 778. Baptized com. 1,069. Households 359. Ib. in 1977 - 1.

St. Mary's of the Moonlight. Oljeto, Utah 84537. Communicants 44. Families 77.

DIOCESE OF NEBRASKA
200 North 62nd Street, Omaha, Nebraska 68132
Rt. Rev. James Daniel Warner, Bishop

The three Dakota churches on the Santee Reservation belong to the Niobrara Deamery of the Diocese of South Dakota: *Blessed Redeemer*, Howe Creek; *Holy Faith*, Lindy and *Our Most Merciful Savior*, Santee.

DIOCESE OF NORTH DAKOTA
809 Eighth Avenue South, Fargo, North Dakota 58102
Rt. Rev. George T. Masuda, Bishop   *(701)235-6688*

St. Luke's Church. Dakota/Sioux. Standing Rock Reservation. Box 276, Fort Yates, North Dakota 58538. Innocent Goodhouse, Vicar, ord. priest. 60 communicants. 225 baptized mem. SS.

Episcopal church women, youth organization. Alcoholics
Anonymous and other community organizations meet in the
church.

St. James' Church. Dakota/Sioux. Standing Rock Reservation.
Canon Ball, North Dakota 58528. Supervised by Innocent
Goodhouse, Vicar of St. Luke's, Ft. Yates. Communicants 65.
Baptized members 200. SS 30. Parish Hall is used for many
community activities including needs for the ageing and
handicapped.

St. Paul's Church. Arikara-Mandan-Gros Ventre. Ft. Berthold
Reservation. Emmet, North Dakota 58534. Moses Mountain,
priest, Ind. Communicants 62. Baptized mem. 135.

St. David's Episcopal Mission. New Town, North Dakota 58763.
BIA Headquarters for Ft. Berthold Reservation. Served by
Moses Mountain. Scattered families.

St. Sylvan's Episcopal Church. Chippewa. Turtle Mountain
Reservation. Dunseith, North Dakota 58329. Donald Parsons,
priest. Communicants 50. Baptized mem. 200. SS is active.
Church serves as a Community Center.

St. Thomas Episcopal Church. Dakota/Sioux. Ft. Totten
Reservation. Ft. Totten, North Dakota 58335. Vacant. About
12 communicants here and 50 scattered over the Reservation.

DIOCESE OF OKLAHOMA
P. O. Box 1098, Oklahoma City, Oklahoma 73101
Rt. Rev. Gerald N. McAllister, Bishop

Church of the Holy Family. (Originally called Whirlwind
Mission.) 1904. Cheyenne-Arapaho. Watonga, Oklahoma 73772.
Wayne Knotts, priest-in-charge, w. P. O. Box 316, Clinton,
Oklahoma 73601. Communicants 28. Baptized mem. 36. In
1976 2 baptisms.

The Diocese contributes to the support of Oklahoma Indian
Ministries, Inc. through its Community Ministries.

DIOCESE OF OLYMPIA
1551 Tenth Avenue East, Seattle, Washington 98102
Rt. Rev. Robert H. Cochrane, D.D., Bishop   *(206)325-4200*

The Diocese engages in advocacy through membership in the
Ecumenical Metropolitan Ministry of Seattle. Liaison person:
Mrs. Ruth Sterling.

DIOCESE OF THE RIO GRANDE

120 Vassar S.E., Suite 1B, P. O. Box 4130, Albuquerque, New
Mexico 87106   *(505)266-5722*
Rt. Rev. Richard M. Trelease, Jr., D.D., Bishop

The 4 Navajo churches of this Diocese are now being trans-
ferred to the new Navajo Area Mission or Navajoland Mission.
Refer to it. The parishes are: *St. Luke's in the Desert*,
Carson's Post; *All Saints' Chapel*, Farmington; *St. Michael's*,
Fruitland and *St. Augustine's*, Fruitland.

DIOCESE OF SAN DIEGO

2728 Sixth Avenue, San Diego, California 92103 *(714)291-5947*
Rt. Rev. Robert M. Wolterstorff, D.D., Bishop

The Diocese supports, contributing $4,000 annually, the San
Diego County Indian Ministry.

DIOCESE OF SOUTH DAKOTA

P. O. Box 517, Sioux Falls, South Dakota 57101 *(605)338-9751*
Rt. Rev. Walter H. Jones, Bishop

NIOBRARA DEANERY AND FIELD

CHEYENNE RIVER MISSION: Cheyenne River Reservation

> Clergy: John B. Lurvey, priest, w. P. O. Box 571, Eagle
> Butte, South Dakota 57625. *(605)964-6988.*
>
> Leslie R. Campbell, Ind. P. O. Box 82, Dupree,
> South Dakota 57623. *(605)365-3864.*

St. John the Evangelist Church. P. O. Box 80, Eagle Butte,
South Dakota 57625. John B. Lurvey, priest. Communicants
110. Baptized mem. 207. Baptisms 8. 8 confirmations in
1976.

Ascension Church. Blackfoot community (Moreau). Route 2,
Mobridge, South Dakota 57601. John B. Lurvey, priest.
Communicants 20. Baptized mem. 60. Baptisms 4. 2
confirmations in 1976.

Calvary. Marksville. R. R., Gettysburg, South Dakota
57442. John B. Lurvey, priest. Communicants 2. Baptized
mem. 28. Baptisms in 1976 - 2.

Emmanuel. White Horse, South Dakota 57661. John B. Lurvey,
priest. Communicants 45. Baptized mem. 110. Baptisms 3.
Confirmations 4 in 1976.

St. Andrew. Cherry Creek, South Dakota 57622. Leslie R. Campbell, priest. Communicants 41. Baptized mem. 72. Baptisms 3, confirmations 4 in 1976.

St. James. Bear Creek Community. Lantry, South Dakota 57636. Leslie R. Campbell, priest. Communicants 45. Baptized members 74. Baptisms in 1976 - 6.

St. Luke. Iron Lightning Community. Dupree, South Dakota 57623. Leslie R. Campbell, priest. Communicants 24. Baptized mem. 35. Baptisms 1, confirmations 4 in 1976.

St. Mary. Promise District. P. O. Box 80, Eagle Butte, South Dakota 57625. John B. Lurvey, priest. Communicants 33. Baptized mem. 65. Baptism 4, confirmations 4 in 1976.

St. Paul. La Plant. Ridgeview, South Dakota 57652. John R. Lurvey, priest. Communicants 10. Baptized mem. 16. Baptisms 2 in 1976.

St. Peter. Thunder Butte Community. Dupree, South Dakota 57623. Leslie R. Campbell, priest. Communicants 27. Baptized mem. 50. Baptisms 2 in 1976.

St. Philip. Box 82, Dupree, South Dakota 57623. Leslie R. Campbell, priest. Communicants 44. Baptized mem. 91. Baptisms 1, confirmation 4 in 1976.

St. Stephen. Red Scaffold Community. Red Scaffold Route, Faith, South Dakota 57626. Leslie R. Campbell, priest. Communicants 26. Baptized mem. 36. Baptisms 2, confirmations 1 in 1976.

St. Thomas-on-the-Tree. P. O. Box 80, Eagle Butte, South Dakota 57625. John B. Lurvey, priest. Communicants 49. Baptized mem. 67. Baptisms in 1976 - 8.

Isabel Station. Isabel, South Dakota 57633. Leslie R. Campbell, priest. Communicants 22. Baptized mem. 39. Baptisms 5 in 1976.

Cheyenne River Totals: 14 churches; 526 communicants; 905 baptized mem.; 51 baptisms, 31 confirmations in 1976.

SANTEE MISSION: Dakota. Santee Reservation. Niobrara, Nebraska 68760   *(402)857-3743*

Clergy: Ronald A. Campbell, priest, Ind. 10 Linden Avenue, Vermillion, South Dakota 57089. *(605)624-3379.*

Lay Readers: Albert Thomas, Guy Lawrence.

Blessed Redeemer Church. Howe Creek. Communicants 29. Baptized mem. 43. Baptisms in 1976 – 3.

Holy Faith. Lindy. Communicants 12. Baptized mem. 35.

Saint Paul. Communicants 18 in a previous year.

Our Most Merciful Savior. Santee. Communicants 45. Baptized mem. 98. Baptisms 7, confirmations 5 in 1976.

Advent Station. Communicants 5. Baptized 9.

St. Michael Station. Communicants 14. Baptized 27.

PINE RIDGE MISSION: Dakota. Pine Ridge Reservation.

Clergy: F. Charles Apple, priest, Ind., Superintending Presbyter. P. O. Box 56, Porcupine, South Dakota 57772.

Gary A. Hawley, priest, Ind. P. O. Box J, Pine Ridge, South Dakota 57770. *(605)867-5270.*

Francis C. Cutt, Ind. P. O. Box 929, Pine Ridge, South Dakota 57770.

Sister Margaret Hawk, C.A., Ind. P. O. Box 319, Pine Ridge, South Dakota 57770.

Vincent Two Lance, priest, Ind. P. O. Box 583, Batesland, South Dakota 57716.

Holy Cross Church. Pine Ridge. P. O. Box J, Pine Ridge, South Dakota 57770. Gary A. Lawley, priest, Ind. Lay readers: Ben Tyon, Bob Mesteth, Ursula Harsley. Communicants 284. Baptized mem. 359. Baptisms 15, confirmations 25 in 1976.

Advent. Pine Ridge, South Dakota 57770. Lay readers: Leo American Horse, Denver American Horse. Communicants 70. Baptized mem. 130. Ib. in 1974 – 5.

Christ. Red Shirt Table. Lay readers: Robert Two Bulls, Roger Campbell, James Two Bulls, Alex Wright, Todd Fox Bull. Communicants 38. Baptized mem. 83. Ib. in 1974 – 6. SS 12.

Epiphany. Wolf Creek. Lay reader: Mel Lone Hill. Communicants 11. Baptized mem. 42.

Messiah. Wounded Knee, South Dakota 57794. Lay readers: Warfield Moose, Charles Moose. Communicants 47. Baptized mem. 86.

St. Alban. Porcupine, South Dakota 57772. Lay reader: Dawson Little Soldier. Communicants 42. Baptized mem. 90.

St. Andrew. Wakpamni Lake. Lay readers: Dawson No Horse, Dennis Yellow Thunder. Communicants 58. Baptized mem. 88. SS 40.

St. James. Oglala, South Dakota 57764. Lay reader: Leo American Horse. Communicants 16. Baptized mem. 48.

St. John. Oglala, South Dakota 57764. Communicants 100. Baptized mem. 145.

St. Jude. Little White River. Lay reader: Robert Two Bulls. Communicants 9. Baptized mem. 16.

St. Julia. Porcupine, South Dakota 57772. Lay readers: Garfield Wounded Head, Fred Mesteth, Francis Apple, Jr., Cheryl Wounded Head. Communicants 78. Baptized mem. 88.

St. Luke. Porcupine, South Dakota 57772. Lay readers: Dawson Little Soldier, Guy L. Boyd, John Hugh Hawk, Pedro Quick Bear. Communicants 30. Baptized mem. 48.

St. Mark. Rocky Ford. Lay reader: Alvin Twiss. Communicants 24. Baptized mem. 40.

St. Mary. Grass Creek. Communicants 15. Baptized mem. 22.

St. Matthew. Slim Buttes. Lay reader: Wilbert Yellow Horse. Communicants 25. Baptized mem. 55.

St. Michael. Batesland, South Dakota 57716. Lay readers: Peter Red Owl, Sandra Two Lance, Peter Plenty Wound, Wilson Two Lance. Communicants 47. Baptized mem. 83.

St. Peter. Oglala, South Dakota 57764. Lay readers: Tex Broken Nose, Stephen White Maggie. Communicants 76. Baptized mem. 123.

St. Philip. Manderson, South Dakota 57756. Communicants 25. Baptized mem. 38.

St. *Thomas*. Manderson, South Dakota 57756. Lay readers: Dawson Protater, Rachel Eagle Bull. Communicants 29. Baptized mem. 63. SS 15.

CORN CREEK DISTRICT

Clergy: All churches served by Rev. Maurice Bull Bear, priest, Ind. P. O. Box 298, Wanblee, South Dakota 57577. *(605)462-6116.*

Daniel Makes Good, priest, Ind. Allen, South Dakota 57714.

Gethsemane Church. P. O. Box 298, Wanblee, South Dakota 57577. Communicants 154. Baptized mem. 164. Baptisms 8, confirmation 7 in 1976.

Inestimable Gift Church. Allen, South Dakota 57714. Communicants 42. Baptized mem. 72. Baptisms 7, confirmation 1 in 1976.

Mediator, Church of the. Kyle, South Dakota 57752. Communicants 41. Baptized mem. 134. Baptisms 3, confirmations 4 in 1976.

St. *Barnabas*. Kyle, South Dakota 57752. Communicants 129. Baptized mem. 266. Baptisms 10, confirmations 29 in 1976.

St. *Philip*. Hisle. A station. Communicants 10. Baptized mem. 10.

St. *Timothy*. Potato Creek. Communicants 35. Baptized mem. 54. Baptisms 6 in 1976.

Trinity. Allen, South Dakota 57752. Communicants 21. Baptized mem. 86.

Bad Wound Station. Communicants 10. Baptized mem. 11.

Good Shepherd. Martin, South Dakota 57551. A station. Communicants 28. Baptized mem. 39. Baptisms 7 in 1976.

St. *Mary*. Kadoka, South Dakota 57543. A station. Communicants 5. Baptized mem. 5.

ROSEBUD EPISCOPAL MISSION: Dakota. Rosebud Reservation.

Clergy: Noah Brokenleg, priest, Ind., Superintending Presbyter. P. O. Box 66, Rosebud, South Dakota 57570.

Thomas F. Newman, priest, w. P. O. Box 188,
Mission, South Dakota 57555.

LaVerne LaPointe, priest, Ind. P. O. Box 191,
White River, South Dakota 57579.

Webster A. Two Hawk, priest, Ind. P. O. Box 55,
White River, South Dakota 57579.

Lay Readers: 14

Church of Jesus. Rosebud, South Dakota 57570. Noah Brokenleg, priest. Communicants 79. Baptized mem. 98. Baptisms
4, confirmation 12 in 1976.

Trinity Church. Mission, South Dakota 57555. Communicants
100. Baptized mem. 139. Baptisms in 1976 - 1. SS 15.

Calvary. Okreek, South Dakota 57563. Communicants 99.
Baptized mem. 155. Baptisms 5, confirmation 18 in 1976.
SS 14.

Epiphany Church. Parmelee, South Dakota 57566. Communicants 24. Baptized mem. 51.

Grace Church. Soldier Creek. Communicants 45. Baptized
mem. 73. Baptisms 3 in 1976.

Holy Innocents. Parmelee, South Dakota 57566. Communicants 69. Baptized mem. 190. Baptisms 5, confirmations
1 in 1976.

Church of the Mediator. Wood, South Dakota 57585. A
station. Communicants 4. Baptized mem. 4.

Mni Wiconi. Grass Mountain. Communicants 8. Baptized
mem. 8.

St. Andrew. St. Francis, South Dakota 57572. Communicants
16. Baptized mem. 48.

St. Mark. Parmelee, South Dakota 57566. Communicants 8.
Baptized mem. 14.

St. Paul. Norris, South Dakota 57560. Communicants 55.
Baptized mem. 73. Baptisms 3 in 1976.

Saints Philip and James. White River, South Dakota 57579.
Communicants 48. Baptized mem. 105. Baptisms 1 in 1976.

St. Stephen. Norris, South Dakota 57560. Communicants 6. Baptized mem. 16.

St. Thomas. Norris, South Dakota 57560. Communicants 70. Baptized mem. 92. Baptisms 7 in 1976.

Advent. Mosher, South Dakota 57558. A station. Communicants 5. Baptized mem. 6.

St. Michael's. Belvidere, South Dakota 57521. Communicants 14. Baptized mem. 18.

LOWER BRULE MISSION: Dakota. Lower Brule Reservation.

Clergy: Clyde G. Estes, priest, Ind. Fort Thompson, South Dakota 57339.

Lay Readers: 3

Holy Comforter Church. Lower Brule, South Dakota 57548. Communicants 92. Baptized mem. 228. Baptisms 24, confirmations 9 in 1976.

Holy Name. Ft. George. Communicants 17. Baptized mem. 17.

Messiah. Iron Nation. Communicants 18. Baptized mem. 114. Baptisms 3 in 1976.

St. Alban. Fort Hole. Communicants 10. Baptized mem. 14. Baptisms 1 in 1976.

Cedar Creek Station. Communicants 6. Baptized mem. 14. Baptisms 1 in 1976.

CROW CREEK MISSION: Dakota. Crow Creek Reservation.

Clergy: Clyde G. Estes, priest, Ind. Fort Thompson, South Dakota 57339.

Lay Reader: 1

Christ Church. Ft. Thompson, South Dakota 57339. Communicants 120. Baptized mem. 202. Baptisms 43, confirmations 2 in 1976.

St. John. Pukwans, South Dakota 57370. Communicants 34. Baptized mem. 52. Baptisms 1 in 1976.

St. Peter. Shelby, South Dakota 57472. Communicants 38. Baptized mem. 52.

SISSETON MISSION: Dakota. Sisseton Reservation.

Clergy: Richard S. Miller, priest, w. Sisseton, South Dakota 57262.

Lay assistant: George Medicine Eagle.

Lay Readers: 18

St. James. Enemy Swim Lake, Wanbay, South Dakota 57273. Communicants 165. Baptized communicants 200. Baptisms 6, confirmations 9 in 1976.

St. John. Brown's Valley. Communicants 71. Baptized mem. 124. Baptisms 2, confirmations 6 in 1976.

St. Luke. Veblen, South Dakota 57270. Communicants 32. Baptized mem. 42. Baptisms 2, confirmations 2 in 1976. SS 8.

St. Mary. Old Agency, Peever, South Dakota 57257. Communicants 174. Baptized mem. 371. Baptisms 12, confirmations 4 in 1976. SS 30.

STANDING ROCK MISSION: Dakota. Standing Rock Reservation.

Clergy: Lester I. Kills Crow, priest, Ind. Wakpala, South Dakota 57658.

Fred H. Hobbs, priest, Ind. McLaughlin, South Dakota 57642.

Sidney V. Martin, priest, Ind., retired. Mobridge, South Dakota 57601.

Lay Readers: 6

Good Shepherd. Little Oak Creek. Communicants 96. Baptized mem. 375. Baptisms 1, confirmation 7 in 1976. SS 10.

St. Elizabeth. Wakpala, South Dakota 57658. Communicants 248. Baptized mem. 380. Baptisms 5, confirmations 6 in 1976. SS 12.

St. John the Baptist. Bullhead, South Dakota 57658. Communicants 102. Baptized mem. 153. Baptisms 12, confirmations 2 in 1976. SS 23.

St. Paul. Little Eagle, South Dakota 57639. Communicants 74. Baptized mem. 254. Baptisms 5, confirmations 10 in 1976.

St. Peter. McLaughlin, South Dakota 57642. Communicants 35. Baptized mem. 115. Baptisms 4, confirmations 2. SS 21.

St. Thomas. Kenel. Communicants 19. Baptized mem. 21. SS 8.

YANKTON MISSION: Dakota. Yankton Reservation.

Priest: Edmond Vock, w. Pickstown, South Dakota 57367.

Lay Readers: 4

Holy Fellowship. Greenwood. Communicants 48. Baptized mem. 179. Baptisms 7, confirmations 5 in 1976.

Holy Name. Dante, South Dakota 57320. Communicants 16. Baptized mem. 26.

St. Philip the Deacon. Lake Andes, South Dakota 57356. Communicants 34. Baptized mem. 94. Baptisms 2, confirmations 3 in 1976. SS 12.

All Saints. Herrick, South Dakota 57538. Michael Horn, priest, w. Gregory, South Dakota 57533. Communicants 18. Baptized mem. 25. SS 15.

Holy Spirit. Ideal. Richard H. McGinnis, priest, w. Winner, South Dakota 57580. 3 lay readers. Communicants 74. Baptized mem. 158. Baptisms 2, confirmations 4 in 1976.

St. Michael. Pierre, South Dakota 57501. The Ven. Vine V. Deloria, Sr., priest, Ind., retired. Communicants 27. Baptized mem. 66. Baptisms 66 in 1976.

St. Matthew's Church. 412 Adams Street, Rapid City, South Dakota 57701. *(605)342-6199.* Lyle M. Noisy Hawk, priest, Ind. *(605)343-6997.*

Total Niobara Field: Churches, chapels, stations 110; priests 24; communicants 4,366; baptized mem. 7,701; church school students (SS) 303; baptisms 416; confirmations 254. 21 ord. Ind. man, 2 Ind. deacons. 113 Ind. serving as lay w. The retired Suffragan Bishop Rt. Rev. Harold H. Jones is an Ind.

All Saints' School. Sioux Falls, South Dakota 57101. Mrs. Mary Lou Killey, Headmistress. Nursery, Kindergarden, grades 1-6.

St. Mary's School for Indian Girls. Springfield, South Dakota 57062. Mr. Kenyon Gull, Headmaster. 5th grade through High School.

Dakota Leadership Program. P. O. Box 506, Mobridge, South Dakota 57601. Rev. George Harris, Director. A joint program of the Dioceses of North and South Dakota for the development of leadership, both lay and ordained. Open also to persons of other dioceses and other denominations.

Niobara Convocation. An annually assembly of the Indian church people since 1870.

DIOCESE OF UTAH
231 East First Street, Salt Lake City, Utah 84111
Rt. Rev. E. Otis Charles, Bishop

UINTAH-OURAY EPISCOPAL CHURCH. Ute. Uintah-Ouray Reservation. P. O. Box 15A, Fort Duchesne, Utah 84026.

Church of the Holy Spirit. Randlett, Utah 84063.

St. Elizabeth's Church. White Rocks, Utah 84085. Communicants 81. Baptized mem. 300. Child baptisms in 1977 - 7, confirmations 16.

The Navajo parishes and churches of Monument Valley have been transferred to the new Navajo Area Mission. They are: *St. John the Baptizer,* Montezuma Creek; *St. Christopher's,* Bluff and *St. Mary of the Moonlight,* Monument Valley.

DIOCESE OF WESTERN NORTH CAROLINA
P. O. Box 368, Black Mountain, North Carolina 28711
Rt. Rev. William G. Weinhauer, Th.D., Bishop   *(704)669-8064*

St. Francis Church. Cherokee, North Carolina 28719. William Paul Austin, Vicar, priest, w. Communicants 15. WS 7. Occasional SS 2.

St. Bede's House of Studies. Rev. William Paul Austin, Director. Intended for the training of Indians for ministry under Canon 8, but none have as yet been enrolled and all students are white.

DIOCESE OF WYOMING
104 South Fourth Street, P. O. Box 1007, Laramie, Wyoming
82070
Rt. Rev. Bob G. Jones, Bishop

St. Michael's Mission. Northern Arapaho. Wind River Reservation. Ethete, Wyoming 82520. Kenneth Kinner, priest, w. *(307)332-2660.* Communicants 300. Baptized mem. 630. Baptisms in 1977 - 30. SS. WS. YS. Youth residence program.

Shoshone Episcopal Mission. Shoshone. Wind River Reservation. Fort Washakie, Wyoming 82514. *(307)332-4265.* Margaret H. Merrell, priest, w. P. O. Box 175, Ft. Washakie, Wyoming 82514. *(307)332-4896.* Communicants 174. Baptized mem. 957. Baptisms in 1977 - 14. SS. WS. YS.

St. Helen's. Crowheart. Mostly white, partly Indian. Wind River Reservation. Burdette Stampley, priest, w. Box 735, Dubois, Wyoming 82513.

THE EVANGELICAL CHURCH OF NORTH AMERICA

8719 Johns Drive, Indianapolis, Indiana 46234
Dr. V. A. Ballantyne, General Superintendent   *(317)297-4379*

Blue Mountain Mission. Navajo. P. O. Box 230, Prewitt, New Mexico 87045. Missionaries: Rev. and Mrs. Evan Freymiller, Rev. and Mrs. Gus Freymiller, Miss Janet Knelland, Mr. and Mrs. Robert Arndt. Mem. 18. Total com. 120. Worship services. SS. Youth work. Medical work in cooperation with the U.S. Public Health Service.

Pine Tree Mission. Navajo. Star Route 1, Box 7, Gallup, New Mexico 87301. Navajo pastor and wife: Rev. and Mrs. Joe M. Lee. Missionaries: Rev. and Mrs. Earl Whipple. Mem. 35. Total com. 150. Worship services. SS. WS. YS. Medical work in cooperation with the U.S. Public Health Service.

According to local report the Wesleyan Covenant Church merged with the Evangelical Church of North America and this action carries the following churches into the E.C.N.A.:

Black Hat Mission. Window Rock, Arizona 86515. Dennis Gardener, pastor.

Free Trinity Navajo Mission. Gamerco, Window Rock, Arizona 86515. Dennis Gardener, pastor.

Indian Holiness Mission. P. O. Box 608, Chambers, Arizona

86502. Carl Noggle, pastor.

Indian Holiness Mission. Fruitland, New Mexico 87416.

Rock Springs Mission. South Hwy. 264, Tataltey, New Mexico 86515. Rev. Mr. McCormack, pastor.

Wesleyan Holiness Mission. Gallup, New Mexico 87301. Karen Gilkinson, pastor.

EVANGELICAL COVENANT CHURCH OF AMERICA

5101 North Francisco Avenue, Chicago, Illinois 60525

THE EVANGELICAL COVENANT CHURCH OF ALASKA
Rev. Donald L. Erickson, President. Evangelical Covenant
   Church, Unalakleet, Alaska 99684

FULL MEMBER CHURCHES:

First Evangelical Covenant Church. Anchorage, Alaska 99510. Robert H. Nelson, pastor, ord. Mem. 90. SS 157.

Evangelical Covenant Church. Bethel, Alaska 99559. Walter J. Anderson, pastor, ord. Mem. 24. SS 64.

Evangelical Covenant Church. Fairbanks, Alaska 99701. Fred W. Walton, pastor, ord. Mem. 10. SS 29.

Evangelical Covenant Church. Mountain Village, Alaska 99632. Jack B. Koutchak, pastor, ord. Mem. 32. SS 45.

Evangelical Covenant Church. Nome, Alaska 99762. Albin T. Folden, pastor, ord. Mem. 38. SS 135.

Evangelical Covenant Church. Shaktoolik, Alaska 99771. Howard I. Slwooko, pastor, ord. Mem. 25. SS 35.

Evangelical Covenant Chruch. Unalakleet, Alaska 99684. Donald L. Erickson, pastor, lic. Mem. 96. SS 204.

UNORGANIZED CHURCHES NOT YET MEMBERS:

Elim, Alaska 99739. Edwin Katongon, pastor, lic.

Golovin Bay, Alaska 99762. Earl J. D. Swanson, pastor, lic.

Hooper Bay, Alaska 99604. Jonathan Johnson, pastor, lic.

Koyuk, Alaska 99753. Fred C. Weston, pastor, lic.

Mckoryuk, Alaska 99630. Peter Smith, pastor, ord.

Scammon Bay, Alaska 99662. Thomoe Tungwenuk, pastor, lic.

White Mountain, Alaska 99784. Earl D. J. Swanson, pastor, lic.

Covenant High School. 1954. Box 184, Unalakleet, Alaska 99684. *(907)624-3282.* Alfred S. White, Principal. Day and boarding. Grades 9-12. Administrative staff 2. Teachers: 3 w. men, 4 w. women, 1 Inuit woman. All staff laymen. Students: 32 Inuit (Eskimo) boys, 42 Inuit girls.

Radio Station KICY. Nome, Alaska 99762. Lay staff.

FELLOWSHIP OF BAPTISTS FOR HOME MISSIONS

P. O. Box 455, Elyria, Ohio 44035   *(216)365-7308*
Dr. Kenneth A. Muck, President

Baptist Mission. Sioux/Dakota. Rosebud Reservation. Mission, South Dakota 57555. Communicants 40. SS and YS.

Baptist Mission. Sioux/Dakota. Rosebud Reservation. Martin, South Dakota 57551. Communicants 60. SS and YS.

Baptist Mission. Mexican Water, Arizona. Communicants 30.

Other Stations: Chinle, Arizona and Cortez, Colorado

There are 2 lay Ind. ministers in the above church, 2 w. couples in South Dakota and 3 w. couples in Arizona and southwest Colorado.

FREE METHODIST CHURCH OF NORTH AMERICA

GENERAL MISSIONARY BOARD
9th and College, Winona Lake, Indiana 46590

The Farmington, New Mexico Church of the American Indian Bible Mission, Inc. is affiliated with the Free Methodist Church. Navajo. See that entry.

FRIENDS:
ASSOCIATED COMMITTEE OF FRIENDS ON INDIAN AFFAIRS

c/o Horace Smith, Executive Secretary
Route 2, Hagerstown, Indian 47346   *(317)489-4834*

Representing 15 yearly meetings. Established 1869. Supports

also Friends Committee on National Legislation in Washington.

Wyandotte Friends Church. 1871.. Wyandotte and Seneca.
Wyandotte, Oklahoma 74370. Clem and Louise Moore, pastor, w.
Box 340, Wyandotte, Oklahoma 74370. Much involved with
neighboring BIA Seneca Indian School: attendance at mid-week
school chapel 15-25; at 3 club meetings 8-10; at quarterly
chapel service 30-35; at SS 15-20.

Kickapoo Friends' Center. 1883. Kickapoo. McCloud, Oklahoma
74851. Ron and Janis Wood, pastors; Kim and Michelle Mills,
Donna Carter, associates, all w. Box 570 McCloud, Oklahoma
74851. In addition to regular Center activities there is a
ministry of visitation to Indian prisoners.

Hominy Friends Church. 1908. Osage. Hominy, Oklahoma 74035.
David E. Nagle, pastor, w. Route 1, Box 206, Hominy, Oklahoma
74035. Mem. 20.

Council House Friends. 1880. Seneca and Cayuga. Wyandotte,
Oklahoma 74370. Laurence and Lucille Pickard, pastors, w.
Route 1, Box 280, Wyandotte, Oklahoma 74370. Mem. 50.
Attendance 50-60. 1977 VBS 80 plus 20 teachers and helpers.
Ladies Aid and Ladies Missionary Societies.

All centers serve the communities as well as the tribes. All
churches or centers have monthly meetings, Sunday worship,
SS and usually adult educational programs, YS and WS. Quivering
Arrow Camp is for children of the four centers, grades 5 through
8. There is also a youth camp.

Publication: *Indian Progress.* Box 161, Frankton, Indiana
46044.

CALIFORNIA YEARLY MEETING OF FRIENDS

P. O. Box 1607, Whittier, California 90609

FRIENDS ALASKAN MISSION
P. O. Box 687, Kotzebue, Alaska 99752   *(907)442-3236; 442-3286*
Mark L. Ocker, Administrative Field Secretary; teacher
Marsha K. Ocker, Bookkeeper; teacher
P. R. Dick Martin, Administrative Assistant; teacher
Linda C. Martin, Secretary, teacher

Ambler Friends Church. Eskimo. Ambler, Alaska 99786. John
Stalker, pastor, ord., Eskimo. Mem. 30. SS 30. Wednesday
classes.

Anchorage Friends Church. Eskimo. Ermine Dr., Anchorage,

Alaska 99504. Walter Outwater, pastor, ord., Eskimo. Mem. 50.
SS 30.

Buckland Friends Church. Eskimo. Buckland, Alaska 99727.
Daniel Thomas, Jr., pastor, ord., Eskimo. Mem. 35. Wednesday
classes.

Deering Friends Church. Deering, Alaska 99736. No pastor.
Mem. 20.

Fairbanks Friends Church. 1972. Eskimo. Gillam Way, Fairbanks
Alaska 99701. Johnny Snyder, pastor, ord., Eskimo. Mem. 60.
SS 60. Wednesday service.

Kiana Friends Church. Eskimo. Kiana, Alaska 99749. Tommy
Douglas, pastor, unordained, Eskimo. Mem. 40. SS 40. Wednesday classes.

Kivalina Friends Church. Eskimo. Kivalina, Alaska 99750. Veda
Mulluk, pastor, unordained, Eskimo. Mem. 20. SS 20. Singing
and Bible study for youths.

Kotzebue Friends Church. 1897. Kotzebue, Alaska 99752.
Whittier Williams, Jr., pastor, ord., Eskimo. Mem. 200.
SS 125. United Society of Friends Women. Singing and Bible
study for youths. Wednesday classes. Singing groups.

Noatak Friends Church. Eskimo. Noatak, Alaska 99761. Raymond
Brown, pastor, ord., Eskimo. Mem. 80. SS 80. Singing and
Bible study for youths. Wednesday classes.

Noorvik Friends Church. Eskimo. Noorvik, Alaska 99763.
Mildred Sampson and Pauline Harvey, pastors, ord., Eskimo.
Mem. 100. SS 100. Youth Center. Wednesday classes.

Selawick Friends Church. Eskimo. Selawik, Alaska 99770.
Roland Booth, pastor, unordained, Eskimo. Mem. 60. SS 60.
Wednesday classes.

Shungnak Friends Church. Eskimo. Shungnak, Alaska 99773.
Lawrence Gray, pastor, unordained, Eskimo. Mem. 30. SS 30.
Wednesday classes.

Friends Bible Training School. 1930. Box 687, Kotzebue, Alaska
99752. *(907)442-3286.* Mark L. Ocker, Administrative Field
Secretary, Administrator. For Native Americans and others. Day
school. Administrative staff includes 9 Indians and 7 Eskimos.
Teachers: w. men, 2 full time, 2 part time; Eskimos, 2 men
part time, 2 women full time; 2 w. women part time. Students
mostly older men and women. Itinerant ministry has enrolled

over 200 students.

ROCKY MOUNTAIN YEARLY MEETING OF THE FRIENDS CHURCH

Mr. A. J. Ellis, Clerk, 3343 East 114th Drive, Denver, Colorado 80233

Friends Mission. Navajo. Mariano Lake, Thoreau, New Mexico 87323.

Rough Rock Friends Mission, Oakridge. Navajo. Rough Rock, Chinle, Arizona 85603. Vern Ellis, pastor, Anglo.

Rough Rock Friends Church. Rough Rock, Chinle, Arizona 86507. Vern Ellis, pastor, Anglo.

The three churches have a combined average attendance of 80. Average size is 27, largest is 40. Two Navajo pastors, two Anglos. (Dolaghan and Scates, pp 96-97.)

LUTHERAN CHURCHES

THE LUTHERAN COUNCIL IN THE U.S.A.

DIVISION OF MISSION SERVICES - Secretary for Indian Services: Eugene Crawford (Dakota), 35 East Wacker Drive, Suite 1847, Chicago, Illinois 60601   *(312)726-3791*

The members of the Lutheran Council are the American Lutheran Church, the Association of Evangelical Lutheran Churches, the Lutheran Church in America and the Lutheran Church - Missouri Synod. The Council in Indian matters works largely through the National Indian Lutheran Board and makes its Indian Services Secretary available to NILB as its executive.

LUCHIP: LUTHERAN CHURCH AND INDIAN PEOPLE

600 West Twelfth Street, Sioux Falls, South Dakota 47104

A very informal voluntary association of interested Lutherans of all Synods, not accountable to any of them, providing a focus and forum for concerned Lutherans to express and discuss Indian efforts.

It brought NILB into being and now operates as the LUCHIP SECTION in the National Indian Lutheran Board. There is an Executive Committee of four persons. Correspondence may be directed to: Mr. Solomon Mockicin, 1626 Kellog Place, Rapid City, South Dakota 57701 and Rev. Arden Dorn, Good Shepherd Lutheran Church, 2312 Harvard Avenue, Lawrence, Kansas 66044.

NATIONAL INDIAN LUTHERAN BOARD (NILB)

1970   *(312)726-3791*

35 East Wacker Drive, Suite 1847, Chicago, Illinois 60601
Executive Director: Eugene Crawford (Dakota)
Administrative Assistant: Ms. Shirley Canchola
Special Assistant: Walt Weber, 600 West 12th Street, Sioux
    Falls, South Dakota 57104

A joint organ of the American Lutheran Church, Lutheran Church
in America, Lutheran Church - Missouri Synod, and the
Lutheran Council in the U.S.A., composed of 12 representatives
from four geographical areas and the president, at least nine
of whom must be Indians. The Board is independent and is
directly related to each constituent church. It gives Indians
a voice and direct access to the Lutheran Churches and
provides a forum for discussion and decision. Its concerns are
as broad as those of the entire Native American Community, not
narrowly confessional. The Board has the dual responsibility
of serving Indian and Eskimo people on behalf of the Churches
and to give the Churches counsel on Indian affairs. In 1976
over $250,000 was distributed in small grants to 60 Indian
organizations. Lutheran resources are directed to the
specific Indian needs, and NILB educates and rallies the
Lutheran congregations and people in advocacy and support of
justice and rights.

Publication: *LUCHIP/NILB SPEARHEAD*, National Indian Board,
35 East Wacker Drive, Chicago, Illinois 60601.

Direct service to Indian people and promotion of NILB's
program are carried out through four regional offices which
are related to and sustained by the denominations in different
ways but all of which promote the work of NILB. The regions
may have their own boards. The Southwest Region Board's
chairman is Syd Beane, Executive Director of the Phoenix
Indian Center.

REGIONAL INTER—LUTHERAN COORDINATORS AND SERVICE DIRECTORS

LUTHERAN SOCIAL SERVICES OF SOUTH DAKOTA:
  Indian Concerns Consultant: Rev. Walt Weber
  600 West 12th Street, Sioux Falls, South Dakota 57104
  Special Assistant to the NILB.   *(605)336-3347*

ARIZONA INDIAN MINISTRY OF LUTHERAN SOCIAL MINISTRY
OF ARIZONA
  1500 West Maryland Avenue, P. O. Box 11541, Phoenix,
  Arizona 85061   *(602)249-3812*
  Rev. Joel T. Schlachtenhaufen, Project Director

AMERICAN INDIAN MINISTRY, CAL-NEV DISTRICT, LUTHERAN CHURCH - MISSOURI SYNOD

250 Touchstone Place, Apt. 16, West Sacramento, California 95691   *(916)441-1683*
Rev. Andy Reinap, Indian Service Coordinator
Represents also NILB and LUCHIP, ALC and LCA concerns.

INTER-LUTHERAN NATIVE AMERICAN CONCERNS

345 Randolph Avenue, Seattle, Washington 98122
Ms. Marilyn Bode, Director

AMERICAN LUTHERAN CHURCH

DIVISION FOR SERVICE AND MISSION IN AMERICA
422 South Fifth Street, Minneapolis, Minnesota 55415
Executive Director: Dr. John W. Houck

A.L.C. ESKIMO LUTHERAN MISSION. 1894. Seward Peninsula.
There is an Eskimo Committee for the Peninsula. Service and
Mission Director: Rev. Lud Siqueland, 766 John Street,
Seattle, Washington 98109. *(206)622-4552.*

Brevig Memorial Lutheran Church. Brevig Mission, Alaska
99785. An intern serves Brevig and Teller. Mrs. Joan
Jesperson, a student at Pacific Lutheran Theological
College, and her husband, George, are serving these churches
in 1978-79. Confirmed mem. 82. Baptized mem. 139.

Teller Lutheran Church. Teller, Alaska 99778. Confirmed
mem. 47. Baptized mem. 99.

Our Savior's Lutheran Church. P. O. Box 965, Nome, Alaska
99762. *(907)443-5295.* James K. Pearson, pastor, ord., w.
Confirmed mem. 122. Baptized mem. 352.

Shishmaref Lutheran Church. Shishmaref, Alaska 99772.
Duane Hanson, pastor, ord., w., (beginning September 1,
1978). Confirmed mem. 146. Baptized mem. 272.

Thornton Memorial Church. Wales, Alaska 99783. Served by
an intern, in 1977 Robert Berthold. Confirmed mem. 30.
Baptized mem. 42.

Native Outreach Ministries. 1420 Cordova, Anchorage,
Alaska 99501. John Maakestad, missionary, ord., w.
Services and ministries for Native Alaskans in Anchorage.
Not an organized congregation.

Arctic Christian Training School. 1974. P. O. Box 965,
Nome, Alaska 99762. *(907)443-5295.* Home: *(907)443-2052.*

A new director is being called. Not a formal school, but a resource to leadership persons in the congregations. The goal is to raise up and equip Eskimo leaders, working through the staff councils.

ARIZONA/NEW MEXICO - NAVAJOLAND

A.L.C. cooperates with and provides pastoral leadership for two congregations of The Navajo Evangelical Lutheran Mission. See that entry below.

White Earth Lutheran Mission. Chippewa. White Earth Reservation. Route 2, Bagley, Minnesota 56621. Stanley Goodwin, pastor, ord., Ind. Attendance 40-60. Confirmations in 1978 - 8. SS with 5 classes, 5 teachers. WS. YS 20.

St. Paul's Ojibway Lutheran Church. 1954. Ojibway. Turtle Mountain Reservation. P. O. Box 2128, Belcourt, North Dakota 58316. *(701)477-5519.* Merton E. L. Christensen, pastor, ord., w. Communicant mem. 18. Sunday worship services. SS. VBS. Summer day camp.

Tokio Lutheran Mission. 1957. Dakota and others. Tokio, North Dakota 58370. *(701)294-2298.* Arthur Ramse, pastor, layman, w. Communicant mem. 23. Baptized mem. 85. Total Lutheran com. 120. SS. Senior YS. Two junior YS. WS. Midweek Bible studies. Thursday fellowships. Instruction classes for youths and adults. Counseling.

Eben Ezer Lutheran Church. 1902. Continues the New Spring Place Mission, 1842, of the Moravian Church. Cherokee. Oaks, Oklahoma 74359. *(918)868-2196.* Elwin Bergstraesser, pastor, ord., w. Mem. 105, increase of 5 in 1977. Ib. 17. SS 60+. WS 12. VBS. Youth conventions.

Oaks Indian Mission Home. 1927. Oaks, Oklahoma 74357. *(918)868-2196.* American Lutheran Church. Rev. Elwin Bergstraesser, Director. Children admitted grades K - 12. Boys 35, girls 24. Cherokees 48, Pawnee 3, Creek 3, Choctaw 2, Otoe 1, Zuni 1, Laguna 1. Children predominately from broken homes, orphans 5%. Attend public school.

LUTHERAN CHURCH IN AMERICA

PACIFIC NORTHWEST SYNOD
5519 Phinney Avenue, N., Seattle, Washington 98103

Our Savior's Lutheran Church. 1918, organized 1958. Chippewa-Cree. *Rocky Boy's Reservation.* Rocky Boy Route,

Box Elder, Montana 59521. Robert L. Rains, pastor, ord., w. *(406)395-4307.* Communicant members 100. Confirmed members 163. Baptized members 347. SS. Two years confirmation study program. VBS. WS. YS. Camp. Crisis ministry.

LUTHERAN CHURCH—MISSOURI SYNOD

BOARD FOR MISSIONS: 500 North Broadway, St. Louis, Missouri 63102   *(314)231-6969*
Executive Secretary, Rev. Alvin Barry

There is a ten member National Indian Ministry Task Force — five Indians and five others.

NORTH WISCONSIN DISTRICT

Lutheran Church of the Wilderness. 1935. Stockbridge-Munsee. Stockbridge-Munsee Reservation. Route 1, Bowler, Wisconsin 54416. *(715)793-4975.* Jonathan Schedler, pastor, ord., w. Communicant mem. 160. Total converts in 1976 - 5. Mem. 222. Increase of 13 in 1977. Ib. 15. SS 30+. WS. Community YS. Confirmation classes. Adult instructions. VBS.

Immanuel Mohican. 1898. Stockbridge. Red Springs, Route 1, Gresham, Wisconsin 54128. Valerius Zuberbier, pastor, ord., w. 115 North Bartlett, Shawano, Wisconsin 54166. Mem. 66. SS 12. WS 8. Saturday confirmation instruction. VBS.

Our Savior's. Stockbridge. Morgan Siding, Route 1, Gresham, Wisconsin 54128. Valerius Zuberbier, pastor, ord., w. Mem. 67. SS 11. WS 7. WS. Confirmation instruction. VBS.

NORTHWEST DISTRICT

1700 N.E. Knott Street, Portland, Oregon 97212   *(503)288-8383*
District Secretary: D. C. Schroeder

Participating in Inter-Lutheran regional ministries.

Makah Evangelical Lutheran Church. 1974. Makah. Makah Reservation. Neah Bay, Washington 98357. Don Johnson, pastor, ord., Makah. P. O. Box 173, Neah Bay, Washington 98357. Communicant mem. 10. Converts in 1976 - 10. SS 20.

Lutheran Chapel. 1976. Quileute. Quileute Reservation. La Push, Washington 98350. One w. lay youth worker. No communicants or mem. as yet. SS 25. Extension of Makah ministry.

NAVAJO LUTHERAN MISSON

Navajo, New Mexico.   See Navajo Evangelical Lutheran Mission, Inc.

CALIFORNIA-NEVADA DISTRICT, AMERICAN INDIAN MINISTRY

See above under Regional Inter-Lutheran Coordinators.

CONCORDIA COLLEGE CENTER FOR INDIAN MINISTRIES AND STUDIES

800 North Columbia Avenue, Seward, Nebraska 68434
Professor James Nelesen, Director   *(402)643-3651*
Ron L. Wagoner, Field Coordinator

Supported by Concordia Teachers College and the Montana, Nebraska and Wyoming Districts.

Program objectives are thus states:
1.   To foster greater intercultural awareness, understanding and appreciation between Anglos and Native Americans.
2.   To provide needed skills for people in the church who work within and/or near Indian communities.
3.   To develop programs of teacher education and pre-professional training with Indian people.
4.   To develop new and existing resource services for Indian ministry with congregations and Districts.
5.   To provide counseling and support services to individual Anglos, Native Americans, teachers, students and administrators.

It is stated: "The essence of the organization is maintenance of the supportive contacts with people and the offering of human, spiritual and material resources to those in need."

A curriculum/program for Indian students will be worked out in the 1978-79 academic year.   The program is fluid.   There is an Inter-Disciplinary Course on Anglo culture for Indian students which is designed to facilitate their understanding of their environment.   There is an option of six hours of independent study per semester for Indian students if desired or warranted.

NAVAJO EVANGELICAL LUTHERAN MISSION

Rock Point, Chinle, Arizona 86503.   Navajo.   Navajo Reservation.   An independent, inter-Lutheran Mission, begun in 1926 by the Global Gospel Fellowship of Minneapolis, incorporated under the present name in 1960.   Rev. Wallace B. Cole, Director.   (American Lutheran Church)   Publishes: *Navajo*

Lutheran Mission Challenge.

House of Prayer Lutheran Church. 1965. A congregation of
the American Lutheran Church. Rock Point, Chinle, Arizona
86503. Wallace B. Cole, pastor, ord., w. Karl Mix, co-pastor, ord., w. 3 Navajo lay preachers. 2 other Ind. laymen
workers. 2 w. laymen workers. 1 Ind. lay woman worker.
2 w. women. Communicants 55. Total com. 130. SS 70.
Weekday religious education. An adult education school.

Rock Point Outpatient Clinic. Over 500 patients per month.
Nurse Elsie Benson and Ms. Clara Tohtsani (Navajo).

Rock Point Lutheran Elementary School. Member of American
Lutheran Education Association. Roger Rovback, Principal.
Grades 1-6. Teachers: 4 w., 1 Navajo. Boys 21, girls 22.

Navajo Lutheran Church. 1970. A congregation of the American
Lutheran Church. Box 365, Many Farms, Arizona 86538. Al
Magnuson, lay pas., w. 1 Navajo man worker, 1 Navajo woman
lay worker, 1 w. layman worker, 1 w. lay woman worker.
Communicants 10. Total com. 30. SS 10. Weekday religious
class.

Navajo Lutheran Church. 1969. A congregation of the Lutheran
Church - Missouri Synod. Box 1272, Navajo, New Mexico 87328.
Douglas May, pastor, ord., w. 1 Ind. lay worker. Communi-
cants 20. Total com. 70. Conv. in 1976 - 3. Ab. 3, ib. 3.
SS 40. Weekday religious class.

WISCONSIN EVANGELICAL LUTHERAN SYNOD

BOARD FOR WORLD MISSIONS
Rev. Edgar Hoenecke, Executive Secretary
12367 Lomica Drive, San Diego, California 92128
Rev. Frederick Nitz, Executive Chairman, Committee for Apache
   Indian Missions

EVANGELICAL LUTHERAN INDIAN MISSION. Apache.
   Superintendent: Rev. R. H. Zimmerman, 5542 West Palmaire
      Avenue, Glendale, Arizona 85301
   Visiting Elder: Rev. H. E. Hartzell, East Fork Lutheran
      Mission, East Fork, Arizona 85941
   Editor of Apache Lutheran: Rev. Alfred M. Uplegger, P. O.
      Box 27, San Carlos, Arizona 85550.

Peridot Lutheran Mission. 1895. 3 miles south of San
Carlos, Arizona. San Carlos Reservation. Dennis Meier,
pastor, ord., w. Box 118, Peridot, Arizona 85542. Communicants 201.

Peridot Lutheran School. Peridot, Arizona 85542. Grades 1-8. Teachers: Joe Beatrice, Principal; Frank Geuder, Mrs. Monica Beatrice, Mrs. Priscilla Goseyun (Apache), Mrs. Josephine Palmer (Apache). Pupils 157.

Our Saviour Lutheran Church. 1920. Coyotero Band Apaches. San Carlos Reservation. U.S. Highway 70, some 26 miles east of Peridot. General Delivery, Bylas, Arizona 85530. Lyle Sonntag, pastor, ord., w. Communicants 183.

Our Savior Lutheran School. Bylas, Arizona 85530. Willis Hadler, Principal. Teachers: Mrs. Lyla Hadler, Miss Dawn Else, Patricia Groff. Address for all: General Delivery, Bylas, Arizona 85530. Pupils 151.

Grace Lutheran Church. San Carlos Reservation. P. O. Box 27, San Carlos, Arizona 85550. Dennis Meier, interim pastor, ord., w. Alfred M. Uplegger, pastor for 60 years retired in 1977, now assistant pastor, ord., w. Communicants 190. Children attend Peridot School.

St. Peter's Lutheran Church. San Carlos Reservation. A predominately white congregation with about 20 Apache members. Orlin E. Wraalstad, pastor, ord., w. 638 North Devereaux Street, Globe, Arizona 85501. Communicants 50.

East Fork Lutheran Church. 1895. Fort Apache Reservation. 5 miles east of Fort Apache. East Fork, Arizona 85941. H. E. Hartzell, pastor, ord., w. *(602)338-4595.* Communicants 167.

> Also served by Pastor Hartzell:
> *Springerville Lutheran Church.* Springerville, Arizona 85938. Mem. 40.
> *McNary Lutheran Church.* McNary, Arizona 85930. 25 miles north of Whiteriver. Mem. 31.
> *Snowflake.*

East Fork Elementary School. Day and boarding. Five teachers. Grades K-8. Pupils 173.

East Fork High School. P. O. Box 128, East Fork, Arizona 85943. Day and boarding. Grades 9-12. James R. Opitz, Principal. Pupils 99. Teachers: Reginal Riesop, Eugene Caruss, Deborah Eaton, Nelson Zimmermann, Margo Semon, Roxanne Farrell, Peter Bauer.

Church of the Open Bible. 1920. Fort Apache Reservation. Box 516, Whiteriver, Arizona 85941. Arthur A. Guenther, pastor, ord., w. *(602)338-4496.* Communicants 178. SS 200.

Children bused to school at East Fork.

Canyon Day and Cedar Creek Churches. Fort Apache Reservation. Quincy Wiley, pastor, ord., Apache. Box 747, Whiteriver, Arizona 85941. *(602)338-4820.* Communicants: Canyon Day 48, Cedar Creek 14.

Gethsemane Lutheran Church. Fort Apache Reservation. 50 miles west of Whiteriver. P. O. Box 66, Cibecue, Arizona 85911. *(602)338-4378.* Burgess Huehn, pastor, ord., w. Communicants 130.

Gethsemane Day School. Cibecue, Arizona 85911. Grades 1-8. Wayne Cole, Principal. Miss Beth Serve, teacher. Pupils 64.

Fort Apache Lutheran Church. 4 miles south of Whitewater. Fort Apache, Arizona 85926. A. A. Guenther, pastor, ord., w. Pastor at Whitewater, at Fort Apache serves the Lutheran boys and girls including some Navajo, attending the BIA Theodore Roosevelt School. Worship and instructions. Attendance 52.

Valley Lutheran Indian Mission. 1972. 917 East Sheridan Street, Phoenix, Arizona 85006. Reuben Stock, pastor, ord., w. Communicants 56. The pastor is sick visitor to the sick and injured from the San Carlos and Fort Apache Reservation and all Indians in the hospitals and rest homes of the Phoenix area.

Many Apache members of the churches on the two reservations now living permanently or temporarily participate in the Wisconsin Synod churches in Los Angeles, San Francisco, Denver, Dallas, Chicago and St. Louis.

East Fork Lutheran Nursery. Box 55, Whiteriver, Arizona 85941. H. E. Hartzell, Superintendent, ord., w. Mrs. Virginia Burgess, Matron. Staff: 14 full time. Full care and day care. October 1977 - 31 children for varying periods of time.

Total Mission Statistics for 1975: Lutheran com. 3,095. Communicants 1,160. Baptisms: children 149, adults 12. Confirmations: children 76, adults 28. SS 330. VBS 375. Average church attendance 982. Total communed 6,413. Contributions $96,957. School enrollment: Christian Day Schools 537, East Fork High School 95. Periodical: *The Apache Lutheran.*

The Native American Christian Community

MENNONITE BRETHREN CHURCH

BOARD OF MISSIONS AND SERVICE

Crestview Mennonite Brethren Church. 3510 J. Avenue, Lawton, Oklahoma 73501. Tom Walsworth, Jr., pastor, w. *(405)357-6600.* Mem. 63.

Post Oak Mennonite Brethren Church. P. O. Box 67, Indiahoma, Oklahoma 73552. John Heidebrecht, pastor. *(405)246-3212.* Mem. 93.

Dakota Mennonite Brethren Church. P. O. Box 26, Porcupine, South Dakota 57772. Ted Standing Elk, pastor, Ind. *(605)867-5226.*

Gospel Chapel. Pine Ridge, South Dakota 57770. Earl Hedlund, pastor. *(605)867-5793.* Mem. 37.

Voluntary Service Unit. The Salt Shaker. 552 Paha Sapa, Rapid City, South Dakota 57701. *(605)348-4425.* Buffy and Marlynn Branan, Directors. 3 permanent staff plus 3-4 college age summer members. Live in Lakota Homes, a low income residential area of 198 homes. Bible clubs, Bible studies, recreation for youths. Camping. Vocational training. Open house. "Being a neighbor and friend." Those served are mostly Oglala Sioux.

MENNONITE CENTRAL COMMITTEE

21 South 12th Street, Akron, Pennsylvania 17501   *(717)859-1151*
Executive Secretary: William T. Snyder

This is the relief and service agency for 17 Mennonite and Brethren in Christ denominations. It works in Canada through the Mennonite Central Committee, Canada, 201-1483 Pembina Highway, Winnipeg, Manitoba R3T 2C8, which has a number of service units among various Native American peoples. Menno Wiebe, Director.

MCC personnel are working with Native American Concerns in the following organizations:

Institute for Development of Indian Law
925 15th Street, N.W., Suite 200, Washington, D.C. 20005
Douglas Basinger, Jackie Stahl

United Indian Planners Association
800 18th Street, N.W., Washington, D.C. 20006
Tina Mast

Friends Committee on National Legislation
245 Second Street, N.E., Washington, D.C. 20002
Jan Harmon

Houma Alliance
P. O. Box 100, Dulac, Louisana 70353
Jan Cury, Martha Byers. Day care. Research assistant.

Hoopa Tribal Council
P. O. Box 606, Hoopa, California 95546
Susan Hiebert. *(916)625-4166.* Recreation, tutoring, other
services.

Indian Member-at-large on U.S. Ministries Board:
Karen Rodner Buller, 2720 Chestnut Street, Grand Forks, North
Dakota 58201

MENNONITE CHURCH

MENNONITE BOARD OF MISSIONS
P. O. Box 370, Elkhart, Indiana 46512   *(219)294-7543*
Lupe De Leon, Jr., Secretary for Home Missions (Indian
Ministries)

Mennonite Navajo Mission. Navajo Reservation.

   Black Mountain Mission. Naswood Burbank, pastor, ord.,
   Navajo. P. O. Box 1027, Chinle, Arizona 86503.
   (602)725-3265. Mem. 44.

   Blue Gap Mission. Peter Burbank, ord., Navajo. Chinle,
   Arizona 86503. *(602)725-3265.* Mem. 14.

   Totals for the 2 churches with 2 chapels: Communicant
   mem. 65. Total Mennonite com. 75. Converts in 1976 - 10.
   Ab. 5. 2 SS with attendance of 30. WS and YS.

Pearl River Mennonite Mission. Choctaw. Mississippi Bank
Choctaw Reservation. Pearl River, Route 8, Box 14-C,
Philadelphia, Mississippi 39350. D. Glenn Myers, pastor,
ord., w. *(602)656-3514.* Mem. 16.

   Nanih Waiya Mission. Bogue Chitto Indian Community. 20
   miles north of Philadelphia. Route 1, Box 258, Preston,
   Mississippi 39354. Ethan J. Good, pastor. Route 4, Box 72,
   Macon, Mississippi 39354. *(601)326-5062.* Attendance 45.

   Crystal Ridge Mission. 35 miles north of Philadelphia.

   Choctaw Christian Church. Route 7, Louisville, Mississippi

39339. David Z. Weaver, pastor. *(601)773-7856.* Mem. 25.

Totals: 3 churches, 3 chapels: Communicant mem. 70. Total
com. 75. Converts in 1976 - 6. Ab. 4. SS 3 with
attendance of 40. WS and YS. 1 ord. Ind. minister, 3 ord.
w. ministers.

Mennonite Service Unit. Route 7, Box 273, Philadelphia,
Mississippi 39350. *(601) 656-1836.* Serving Choctaws. 5
volunteers working in adult education and consumer education.

MENNONITE CHURCH, GENERAL CONFERENCE

P. O. Box 347, Newton, Kansas 67114   *(316)283-5100*
Home Ministries: Palmer Becker, Executive Secretary

MENNONITE INDIAN LEADERS' COUNCIL. The Council is made up of
one delegate from each Mennonite Indian congregation. The
Home Ministries Commission in the summer of 1977 transferred
administrative responsibility to its Executive Committee,
which has appointed staff persons for each of the three
regions.
Chairman: Joe Walks Along, Lame Deer, Montana 59043.
Vice Chairperson: Ms. Anola Waters, Route 1, Box 6, Bessie,
Oklahoma 73622.
Secretary: Ms. Nadenia Myron, P. O. Box 39, Oraibi, Arizona
86039.
Staff: Montana - Ted Risingsun
        Oklahoma - Ric Dalke (Anglo)
        Arizona - Elmer Myron

Bacari Mennonite Church. Hopi. Hopi Reservation. P. O. Box
108, Hotevilla, Arizona 86030. Elmer Myron, pastor, layman,
Hopi. *(602)734-6638.* No official mem. Attendance 8. Total
Mennonite com. 20 adults, 2 children. SS 10-15. WS. Daily
VBS.

Moencopi Mennonite Church. Hopi. P. O. Box 232, Tuba City,
Arizona 86034. Othmar Meier, pastor, ord., w. *(602)283-5374.*
Mem. 10 adults. 2 children not mem. SS 5-10.

Oraibi Mennonite Church. Hopi Reservation. P. O. Box 181,
Oraibi, Arizona 86039. Karl Johnson, pastor, lay, Ind.
(602)734-2453. Mem. 56 adults. Children nonmembers 20+.
SS 40-50. Prayer meeting. WS. VBS.

Hopi Mission School. 1951. Hopi. Hopi Reservation. P. O.
Box 39, New Oraibi, Arizona 86039. *(602)734-2453.* Administered
by a School Board of six members selected by the four Hopi
Mennonite churches, one independent congregation and two

Baptist. Nadenia Myron (Hopi), secretary-bookkeeper. Grades
K-8. Five Hopi staff members. Other teachers are white
Mennonites. Boys 25, girls 36, total 61. There is a *Mennonite
Volunteer Service Unit* assisting the school.

Ashland Christian Fellowship. Northern Cheyenne. Ashland,
Montana 59003. John Johnson, pastor, w., (Pentecostal).
Mennonites join with the Pentecostals.

Birney Fellowship. Northern Cheyenne. Birney, Montana 59012.
Inactive.

Petter Memorial. Northern Cheyenne. On Cheyenne Reservation.
Lame Deer, Montana 59043. Joe Walks Along, pastor, ord., Ind.
(406)477-6407. Adult mem. 40. Children 10 nonmembers. SS
SS 10-20. WS. VBS.

Whiteriver Cheyenne Mennonite Church. Northern Cheyenne.
Northern Cheyenne Reservation. P. O. Box 37, Busby, Montana
59016. Willis Busenitz, pastor, ord., w. *(406)592-3643.* Mem.
56 adults. Children nonmembers 58. SS 50-60. WS. YS. VBS.

Bethel Mennonite Church. Southern Cheyenne. P. O. Box 116,
Hammon, Oklahoma 73650. *(405)473-2473.* Vacant. Chairman or
contact person: Bob Standing Water, Foss, Oklahoma 73647.
(405)664-3147. Adult mem. 50. Children 40. SS 5-10. WS.
Recreation.

Koinonia Mennonite Church. Southern Cheyenne. Route 1, Box 83,
Clinton, Oklahoma 73601. Contact person: Alice Heap of Birds,
Route 1, Box 4, Clinton, Oklahoma 73601. *(405)323-1155.* Adult
mem. 104. Children 12. SS 15-20. WS. VBS. Community
service.

Mennonite Indian Church. Southern Cheyenne. Box 411, Seiling,
Oklahoma 73663. *(405)922-4419.* Clifford Koehn, pastor, ord.,
w. Adult mem. 75. Children 20. SS 10-15. WS. YS. VBS.

Zion Church. Arapahoe. P. O. Box 427, Canton, Oklahoma 73724.
Arthur Sutton, pastor, lic., Ind. P. O. Box 381, Canton,
Oklahoma 73724. *(405)886-3225.* Adult mem. 34. Children 20.
SS 10-15. WS. YS. VBS.

MENNONITE VOLUNTARY SERVICE

MENNONITE BOARD OF MISSIONS
P. O. Box 370, Elkhart, Indiana 46512   *(219)294-7543*
Mr. John W. Eby, Secretary, Relief and Service

The several Mennonite Churches in the U.S. and Canada

participate in this program, which is administered through the
Mennonite Board of Missions of the Mennonite Church.

General Conference Mennonite Church/Home Ministries

Mennonite Service Unit. Oraibi, Arizona 86039. Hopi.
Contact persons: Judy Loganbill, Gail Wiebe, Marilyn Woelk.
(602)734-2453. Activities: Two volunteers teaching at Hopi
Mission School.

Mennonite Service Unit. General Delivery, Lame Deer,
Montana 59043. Northern Cheyenne. Contact persons: David
and Diane Klaus. Activities: Advocacy work with the
Northern Cheyennes.

Western Oklahoma Voluntary Service Unit. c/o Youth Services
Center, 1104 Circle Drive, Clinton, Oklahoma 73601. Contact
person: Diana Herlihy. *(405)323-4941.*

Mennonite Board of Missions, Home Missions Division

Mennonite Service Unit. 3629 E. 26th Street, Tucson,
Arizona 85913. Contact person: Bruce Weber, Program
Director. *(602)327-7297.* Activities: One volunteer doing
secretarial work for the House of Samuel which is an Indian
foster home and placement agency.

Mennonite Service Unit. Route #7, Box 273, Philadelphia,
Mississippi 39350. Choctaw. *(601)656-1836.* Activities:
Five volunteers working in adult education and consumer
education.

Mennonite Service Unit. Box 328, Browning, Montana 59417.
Black Feet Indians. Contact person: John Schmid, Program
Director. *(406)338-7479.* Activities: Five volunteers
working as: a nurse in a nursing home, youth recreation
program, teacher aid in special education, a woodcutting
project to sell firewood and ONHE (working at winterizing
homes).

Mennonite Central Committee, U. S. Ministries

Mennonite Service Unit. P. O. Box 100, Dulac, Louisiana
70353. Houma. Contact persons: Martha Byers, Janel
Curray. *(504)563-4501.* (Dulac Community Center).
Activities: Day care worker, research assistant.

Mennonite Service Unit. Route 3, Box 85-D, Marksville,
Louisiana 71351. Tunica. Contact persons: Steve and Anne
Egli. *(318)253-6939.* Activities: A voluntary service

couple assists the Tunica tribe in constuction and
development of a community center, working on Federal
recognition, proposal writing and adult education.

Mennonite Service Unit. Box 606, Hoopa, California 95546.
Hoopa. Contact person: Sharon Kurtz. *(916)625-4166.*
Activities: Three volunteers work with the Hoopa Indians
in recreation, tutoring and other types of assistance with
the Tribal Council

Eagle Bay, New York. Mohawk Indians. Contact person:
Richard Zehr, Route 1, Croghan, New York 13327.
(315)346-6394. Activities: In cooperation with the
Mennonite churches in Croghan, New York area MCC has
supplied canned beef and other food for a group of Mohawk
Indians. New York churches have supplied a number of pickup loads of fresh vegetables, horse-drawn agricultural
equipment and other food items.

Red Shirt Village, Pine Ridge, South Dakota. Sioux Indians.
Contact person: John B. Kliewer, Box 508, Marion, South
Dakota 57043. *(605)648-3759.* Activities: On the sugges-
tion of MCC, the South Dakota Mennonites supplied
agriculture equipment for the Red Shirt Village. MCC's
involvement in this whole project was one of support in
terms of an agreement to underwrite the cost if necessary.
Funds were supplied by other churches, so MCC funding was
not necessary.

Church of God in Christ (Mennonite)

Christian Child Care Service. 120 W. Jefferson, Gallup,
New Mexico 87301. Navajo. Contact person: Wilbur Koehn
(Cimarron, Kansas), Overseer of Program. *(505)863-6046.*
Activities: Emergency and long-term care for 13 children.

Mennonite Brethren Board of Missions/Services

Voluntary Service Unit. 552 Paha Sapa, Rapid City, South
Dakota 57701. Contact persons: Buffy and Marlynn Branam.
(605)348-4425. Activities: Volunteers work with youth in
recreation, camping, vocational training, Bible study, etc.

MORAVIAN CHURCH IN AMERICA

BOARD OF WORLD MISSION
P. O. Box 1245, Bethleham, Pennsylvania 18018
Mr. Theodore F. Hartman, Exeuctive Director

The Native American Christian Community

ALASKA MORAVIAN CHURCH
P. O. Box 545, Bethel, Alaska 99559　　　　*(907)543-2471*
Rev. Otto Dreydoppel, Superintendent

Totals: Main congregations 7, affiliated congregations 15.
Missionaries from the other 49 states: ord. 2, wives 2.
Alaska Province personnel: 5 ord., 16 unordained, wives 21.
Elders (helpers) 66. Trustees (church committee) 70.
Evangelists 1. SS enrollment 2,673.

UP-RIVER DISTRICT

Akiachuk, Alaska 99551. John P. Andrew, District pastor, ord., Eskimo.

Akiak, Alaska 99552. Andrew Jasper, lay pas., Eskimo.

Tuluksak, Alaska 99679. Joshua Phillip, lay pas., Eskimo.

Kwethluk, Alaska 99621. Frank Paul, lay pas., Eskimo.

TUNDRA DISTRICT

Atmautluak, Alaska 99641. Fred George, lay pas., Eskimo.

Napakiak, Alaska 99634. Lott George, lay pas., Eskimo.

Nunapitchuk, Alaska 99641. Melvin Egoak, lay pas., Eskimo.

Kasigluk, Alaska 99609. William Beaver, lay pas., Eskimo.

WEST COAST DISTRICT

Kongiganak, Alaska 99559. Edward Wise, District pastor, ord., Eskimo.

Kwigillingok, Alaska 99622. Teddy Brink, lay pas., Eskimo.

Kipnuk, Alaska 99614. David Paul, lay pas., Eskimo.

Tuntutuliak, Alaska 99680. Phillip Charlie, lay pas.

EAST COAST DISTRICT

Eek, Alaska 99578. Calvin Coolidge, lay pas., Eskimo.

Quinhagak, Alaska 99655. Kenneth Cleveland, lay pas., Eskimo.

Goodnews Bay, Alaska 99589. John Ekamrak, lay pas., Eskimo.

Platinum, Alaska 99651. John Ekamrak, lay pas., Eskimo. Goodnews Bay, Alaska 99589.

TOGIAK DISTRICT

Togiak, Alaska 99678. Andrew Andres, District pastor, Eskimo.

Twin Hills, Alaska 99678. Daniel Sharp, lay pas., Eskimo.

Manokotak, Alaska 99628. Alexie Mochin, lay pas., Eskimo.

DILLINGHAM DISTRICT

Dillingham, Alaska 99578. Clarence Henkelman, District pastor, ord., w.

Aleknagik, Alaska 99555. Pavila Chuckwuk, lay pas., Eskimo.

BETHEL DISTRICT

Bethel, Alaska 99559. Jacob Nelson, pastor, ord., Eskimo. William Nicholson, pastor, ord., Eskimo.

There is one Mission directly under the President of the Moravian Church. Rev. J. S. Groenfeldt, P. O. Box 1245, Bethlehem, Pennsylvania 18018. It is a congregation of the Pacific Coast District.

Morongo Moravian Church. Morongo Reservation. Banning, California 92220. Glenn F. Heintzelman, pastor, ord., w. P. O. Box 352, Banning, California 92220. Communicants 108, non-communicants 78. SS 66.

THE ORTHODOX CHURCH IN AMERICA

DIOCESE OF SITKA AND ALASKA

St. Michael the Archangel Cathedral, P. O. Box 697, Sitka, Alaska 99835
The Rt. Rev. Bishop Gregory, Bishop   (907)747-8120
The Very Rev. Archpriest Joseph P. Kreta, Chancellor, Box 65, Kodiak, Alaska 99615   (907)486-3854

Begun as Russian Mission in 1793. Priests and Deacons are addressed as the Reverand; if Very Rev. indicated.

SOUTHEASTERN DISTRICT: Mixed white, Thlinget

Angoon, *St. John the Baptist Church.* 1929. P. O. Box 132,

Angoon, Alaska 99820. *(907)788-3372.* Serviced from Sitka.
Reader: Subdeacon Ivan Jimmy George, Sr., Native American.
Teacher: Aldine Jim, Native American.

Hoonah, *St. Nicholas Church.* 1929. Hoonah, Alaska 99829.
Serviced from Juneau. Readers: Jacob Pratt, Roman Pratt,
Native Americans. Teacher: Jacob Pratt.

Juneau, *St. Nicholas Church.* 1894. 326 North Fifth Street,
Juneau, Alaska 99801. *(907)586-1023.* Theodore Fryntzko,
priest. Protodeacon John Garċia. Reader: Amos Wallace.

Sitka, *St. Michael the Archangel Cathedral.* 1848. (A
national historic landmark) Lincoln Street, Sitka, Alaska
99835. His Grace Bishop Gregory, P. O. Box 697, Sitka,
Alaska 99835. Eugene Bourdokofsky, priest, Native American.
(907)747-8120. Protodeacon Innocent Williams, Native
American. *(907)747-8350.* Reader: Ms. Anna Lazanos.
Teacher: Mrs. Evelyn Sam.

Sitka, *Annunciation of the Theotokos Chapel.* 1842. 503
Lincoln Street, Sitka, Alaska 99835.

SOUTH CENTRAL DISTRICT: Predominantly Aleut

Anchorage, *St. Innocent Church.* 1967. Mixed. 6724 East
Fourth Avenue, Anchorage, Alaska 99504. (Very Rev.)
Nicholas Harris, priest. Readers: Stavros Primis, Peter
Bourdokofsky. Teachers: Matushka Anastasia Harris, Mrs.
Eugenia Morris, Alexis Morris, Agnes Larsen, Eugenia Robins,
Athanasia Lestenkof.

Cordova, *St. Michael the Archangel Church.* 1925. Cordova,
Alaska 99574. *(907)424-7450.* Serviced from Juneau.
Readers: Fred Zachar Brizgaloff, Nicholas Kononoff.
Teachers: Matushka Mary Kompkoff, Nadezhda Totemoff.

Eklutna, *St. Nicholas Chapel.* Eklutna, Alaska 99567.
Served by Father Nicholas Harris, Anchorage.

English Bay, *SS Sergius and Herman of Valaam Chapel.* 1870.
English Bay, Alaska 99603. Serviced from St. Herman's
Seminary, Kodiak, Alaska 99615. Reader: Herman Moonin.
Teacher: Mrs. Juanita Melshiemer.

Fairbanks Orthodox Community. 1974. Serviced from Kodiak.
Contact: Ms. Angeline Purkey, 320 Farewell Avenue, Fairbanks, Alaska 99701.

Kenai, *Assumption of the Virgin Mary Church.* 1846. (A

national historic landmark) P. O. Box 3427, Kenai, Alaska 99611. (Very Rev.) Macarius Targonsky, priest. Reader: Paul Shadura.

Ninilchik, *Transfiguration of Our Lord Chapel*. P. O. Box 53, Ninilchik, Alaska 99369. Serviced from Kenai. Reader: Cecil Demidoff.

Port Graham, *Orthodox Community*. Port Graham, Alaska 99603. Serviced from St. Herman's Seminary, Kodiak, Alaska 99615. Reader: Ephim H. Moonin. Teacher: Vera Moonin.

Seldovia, *St. Nicholas Chapel*. Seldovia, Alaska 99663. Serviced from St. Herman's Seminary, Kodiak, Alaska 99615. Reader: Serguis Moonin.

Tatitlik, *St. Nicholas Church*. Tatitlik, Alaska 99677. Serviced from Juneau.

Tyonek, *St. Nicholas Church*. 1891. Tyonek, Alaska 99682. Serviced by Father Nicholas Harris, Anchorage. Choir director: Agafangel Alfred Stepetin.

Valdez, *St. Nicholas Orthodox Community*. Valdez, Alaska 99686. Serviced from Juneau.

BRISTOL BAY DISTRICT

A. Alaska Peninsula

Chignik Lake, *St. Nicholas Chapel*. Chignik Lake, Alaska 99502. Serviced from Perryville. Readers: Vasily Kucyenoff, Virginia Aleck. Teachers: Vera Aleck, Virginia Aleck.

Perryville, *St. John the Theologian Church*. 1924. Perryville, Alaska 99648. Chariton Kaiakokonok, priest, Native American. Readers: Emilian Kosbruk, Martha Kosbruk, Thomas Phillips, Elia Phillips. Teachers: Freda Kosbruk, Natalia Phillips.

Pilot Point, *St. Nicholas Church*. 1912. Pilot Point, Alaska 99649. Serviced from Perryville. Teacher: Sophia Abyo.

Port Heiden Orthodox Community. Port Heiden, Alaska 99549. Appointed starosta: John Christiansen.

B. Iliamna

Bench River, *St. Innocent of Irkutsk Chapel.* Serviced from Dillingham. Reader: Alexei Wasky. Levelock, Alaska 99625.

Egegik, *Transfiguration of Our Lord Chapel.* Egegik, Alaska 99579. Serviced from Dillingham. Reader: Andrew Krause. Teacher: Mary Alto.

Igiugig, *St. Nicholas Chapel.* Igiugig via King Salmon, Alaska 99613. *(907)775-1214.* Serviced from Dillingham. Reader: Murphy Nicholai.

Kokhonak, *SS Peter and Paul Chapel.* Kokhonak, Alaska 99625. Serviced from Dillingham. Reader: Herman Andrew. Teacher: Marie Wassilly.

Levelock, *Protection of the Virgin Mary Church.* 1937. Levelock, Alaska 99625. Serviced from Dillingham. Reader: Peter Apakitak.

Naknek, *St. John the Baptist Chapel.* Naknek, Alaska 99633. Serviced from Dillingham. Reader: Anisia McCormick.

Newhalen, *Transfiguration of Our Lord Church.* Newhalen via Iliamna, Alaska 99696. Serviced from Dillingham. Reader: Innokenty Anelon. Teachers: Myrtle Anelon, Elena Nicholi.

Nondalton, *St. Nicholas Chapel.* 1896. Nondalton, Alaska 99640. Serviced from Dillingham. Reader: Nicholas Balluta. Choir director: Nicholas Balluta. Teacher: Stephanida Evanoff.

Pedro Bay, *St. Nicholas Chapel.* 1890. Pedro Bay, Alaska 99647. Serviced from Dillingham.

South Naknak, *Elevation of the Holy Cross Church.* South Naknak, Alaska 99670. Serviced from Dillingham. Choir director: Akulina Holstrom.

C. Nushagak

Aleknagik, *Holy Resurrection Chapel.* 1938. Aleknagik, Alaska 99555. Serviced from Dillingham. Starosta: James Yako.

Dillingham, *St. Seraphim of Saro Church.* 1928. Dillingham, Alaska 99576. *(907)842-5470.* Vasily Epchook, priest, Native American. Choir director: Ms. Ingrid Andrew. Reader: Ms. Anna Johnson.

Ekuk, *St. Nicholas Chapel.* Ekuk, Alaska 99576. Serviced
from Dillingham. Reader: Nicholai Hansen.

Ekwok, *St. John Chapel.* Ekwok, Alaska 99580. Serviced from
Dillingham. Starosta: Sergei Acovak.

Kolignak, *St. Michael the Archangel Chapel.* 1870. Kolignak,
Alaska 99576. Serviced from New Stuyahok. Reader: Blunka
Ishnook.

Portage Creek, *St. Basil Church.* Serviced from New
Stuyahok. Reader: Agafangel Rockford.

New Stuyahok, *St. Sergius Chapel.* 1942. New Stuyahok,
Alaska 99363. Readers: Michael Acovak, Wassily Hansen,
Maxie Andrew. Teacher: Sophie Gust.

KODIAK DISTRICT: Predominantly Aleut

Akhiok, *Protection of the Theotokos Chapel.* Akhiok, Alaska
99615. Serviced from Kodiak. Reader: Walter Melovedoff.

Karluk, *Ascension of Our Lord Chapel.* Karluk, Alaska 99603.
Reader: Ms. Olga Panamaroff. Teachers: Ms. Olga
Panamaroff, Ms. Jessie Malutin.

Kodiak, *Holy Resurrection Church.* (1974). P. O. Box 55,
Kodiak, Alaska 99615. (Very Rev.) Joseph P. Kreta, Arch-
priest. *(907)486-3854.* John Breck, priest. Deacon Jonah
Andrew, Native American. Choir director: Ms. Janet
Maksimoff, Native American. P. O. Box 65, Kodiak, Alaska
99615.

Larsen Bay, *St. Herman Chapel.* Larsen Bay, Alaska 99624.
Serviced from Kodiak. Teacher: Mrs. Leonty Christiansen.

Monk's Lagoon, *SS Sergius and Herman of Valaam Chapel.*
1805. Grave of St. Herman of Valaam. Serviced from Kodiak.

Old Harbor, *Three Saints' Church.* 1800. Old Harbor, Alaska
99615. *(907)286-8001.* Michael Oleksa, priest. Reader:
Ms. Katerine Berntsen. Choir director: Ms. Matushka Xenia
Olesksa.

Ouzinkie, *Nativity of Our Lord Chapel.* 1849. Ouzinkie,
Alaska 99644. Yakov Parsells, priest. Reader: Ms.
Matushka Dana Parsells. Teachers: Matushka Danna Parsells,
Tanya Chichenoff, Ada Panamaroff, Angeline Anderson.

Port Lions, *Nativity of the Theotokos Chapel.* Port Lions,

Alaska 99550. Served from Ouzinkie. Reader: Sergay
Sheratine, Sr.

ALEUTIAN CHAIN DISTRICT: All Aleuts

A. Shumagin Islands

Belkofski, *Holy Resurrection Church*. Serviced from
Unalaska. Reader: Leonty Galeshoff.

False Pass, *St. Nicholas Chapel*. False Pass, Alaska 99583.
Serviced from Unalaska. Reader: Ms. Nellie Shelikot.

King Cove, *Orthodox Community*. King Cove, Alaska 99612.
Serviced from Unalaska. Reader: Sara Nezaroff. Teachers:
Dora Dushkin, Tatiana Bendixsen. Contact: Simeon Dushkin.

Sand Point, *St. Nicholas Chapel*. 1936. Sand Point, Alaska
99661. Serviced from Unalaska. Readers: Mrs. Nora
Gardner, Ms. Margaret Nelson. Teachers: Ms. Vivian
Bjornsted, Mrs. Nora Gardner.

B. Aleutian Islands

Akutan, *St. Alexander Nevsky Chapel*. 1878. Akutan, Alaska
99553. Serviced from Unalaska. Readers: Gregory Kudrin,
Artemy Stepetin. Teacher: Ms. Olga Mensoff.

Atka, *St. Nicholas Chapel*. Atka, Alaska 99502. Serviced
from Unalaska. Readers: Poda Sigaroff, Mark Sigaroff.

Nikolski, *St. Nicholas Church*. Nikolski, Alaska 99638.
(907)576-1423. Paul Merculief, priest, Native American.
Readers: Subdeacon Daniel Krukoff, Alexei Charcasen.
Teacher: M. Ermeloff.

Unalaska, *Holy Ascension of Our Lord Cathedral*. 1824.
National historical landmark. Unalaska, Alaska 99685.
Ishmael Gromoff, priest, Native American. *(907)581-1253*.
Readers: Philemon M. Tutiakoff, Mrs. Peter Dushkin, John
Tcheripanoff.

C. Pribilof Islands

St. George, *St. George Church*. 1870. St. George, Alaska
99660. Elary Gromoff, priest, retired, Native American.
Reader: Andronik Kashevarof.

St. Paul, *SS Peter and Paul Church*. (1830) St. Paul,
Alaska 99660. Michael D. Lestenkof, priest, Native American.

Readers: Parfenia Pletnikof, David Fratis, Andrew Kochutin, Audrey Mandragan. Choir directors: Stefan Lakanof, John Melovidov. Teachers: The Misses Pauline Anstigoff, Matushka Lestenkof, Augusta Buerin, Zoya Melovidov, Dorothy Shabolin.

KUSKOKWIN RIVER DISTRICT: Eskimo/Inuit

A. Kasigluk

Eek, *St. Michael the Archangel Church.* 1958. Eek, Alaska 99578. Serviced from Kasigluk and Dillingham. Starosta: Alfred Nicholai. *(907)543-2004.*

Kasigluk, *Holy Trinity Church.* 1935. Kasigluk via Nunapitchuk, Alaska 99609. Michael Tinker, priest. *(907)543-2023.* Readers: Moses Pavilla, Ms. Olga Charles, Timothy Hoover. Choir director: W. Cyril. Teachers: Maria Brink, Sophie Nicolai.

Kongiganak, *St. Gabriel Chapel.* Kongiganak, Alaska 99559. Serviced from Kasigluk and Dillingham. Readers: Frank Andrew (Kwigillingok), Noah Andrew, Roland Andrew. Teacher: Elsie Mute.

Kwigillingok, *Orthodox Community.* 1975. Kwigillingok, Alaska 99622. Contact: Frank Andrew.

Nunapitchuk, *Presentation of the Theotokos Chapel.* 1946. Nunapitchuk, Alaska 99641. Serviced from Kasigluk and Dillingham. Readers: Paul H. Brink Sr., Zach Chris.

Tuntutuliak, *St. Agaphia Chapel.* Tuntutuliak, Alaska 99680. Serviced from Kasigluk and Dillingham. Reader: Michael Wasile. Teacher: Evan Thomas.

Atmartluaq, *St. Herman of Alaska Chapel.* 1947. Atmerluaq, Alaska 99557.

B. Bethel

Bethel, *St. Sophia Church.* 1968. Bethel, Alaska 99559. Zachary Guest, priest, Native American. Readers: Constantine Efinka, Dick N. Evan.

Lower Kalskag, *St. Seraphim Chapel.* Lower Kalskag, Alaska 99607. Serviced from Kwethluk and Russian Mission. Reader: Ms. Mary M. Takumjenak.

Kwethluk, *St. Nicholas Church.* 1935. Kwethluk, Alaska

99621. Nicolai O. Michael, priest, Native American.
(907)543-2033. Readers: Daniel Olick, John Alexie, Martin
Nicholai. Choir director: Yako Fisher. Teachers: John
Alexie, Kathy Alexie, Agnes Michael.

Naspaskiak, *St. Jacob Church.* 1935. Naspaskiak, Alaska
99634. Serviced from Kwethluk. Readers: Subdeacon Stephen
Maxie, Yugo Steven, Frank Nicholai. Choir director: Wasili
Cyril.

C. Aniak

Aniak, *Protection of the Theotokos Chapel.* 1944. Aniak,
Alaska 99557. Serviced from Kwethluk and Russian Mission.

Crooked Creek, *St. Nicholas Church.* Crooked Creek, Alaska
99575. Serviced from Kwethluk and Russian Mission.

Lime Village, *SS Constantine and Helen Chapel.* Lime Village
via Sleetmute, Alaska 99668. Serviced from Kwethluk and
Russian Mission.

Little Russian Mission (Choathbaluk), *St. Sergius Chapel.*
Choathbaluk via Aniak, Alaska 99557. Philip Alexie, priest,
Native American. Reader: Mrs. Helen Simeon. Teacher:
Mrs. Sophie Saka.

Nikolai, *St. Nicholas Chapel.* 1915. Nikolai, Alaska 99691.
Serviced from Kwethluk and Russian Mission. Reader: Paul
(Bobby) Esai Sr.

Sleetmute, *SS Peter and Paul Chapel.* 1925. Sleetmute,
Alaska 99668. Serviced from Kwethluk and Russian Mission.

Talida, *St. Basil Chapel.* Talida, Alaska 99691.

YUKON RIVER DISTRICT: All Eskimo/Inuit

Ikogmute, *St. Vladimir Chapel.* Summer worship and ministry.

Kwiguk, *Orthodox Community.* Serviced from Russian Mission.
Reader: Alexie Nick, Marshall, Alaska 99657.

Marshall, *St. Michael Church.* Marshall, Alaska 99657.
Serviced from Russian Mission. Readers: Ludwig Papp,
Nicholai Andrew.

Mountain Village, *Orthodox Community.* Mountain Village,
Alaska 99632. Serviced from Russian Mission.

Pilot Station, *Transfiguration of Our Lord Chapel.* 1955. Pilot Station, Alaska 99650. Serviced from Russian Mission. Readers: Nicholai Fred Nick, Tommy Heckman. Teachers: Ms. Anna Nick, Ms. Mary Wassilie.

Pitka's Point, *SS Peter and Paul Chapel.* Pitka's Point, Alaska 99658. Serviced from Russian Mission. Reader: Vera Thompson.

Russian Mission, *Elevation of the Holy Cross Church.* 1843. Russian Mission, Alaska 99657. Gabriel Gabrieloff, priest, Native American. Readers: Alexie Nick, Subdeacon Peter Askoar, Moses Gabrieloff.

Saint Michael, *Orthodox Community.* St. Michael, Alaska 99659. Serviced from Russian Mission.

Stoney River, *Orthodox Community.* Stoney River, Alaska 99557. Serviced from Russian Mission.

St. Herman's Theological Seminary. 1973. P. O. Box 65, Kodiak, Alaska 99615. *(907)486-3524.* A 4 year program of studies leading to the B.D. degree. The Very Rev. Archpriest Joseph P. Kreta, Dean. The Rt. Rev. Gregory, Bishop of Sitka and Alaska is President.

The Seminary moved from Kenai to Kodiak in September 1974. The building was completed in March 1976. Students in year 1977-78 — 17. The purpose is to educate Native Alaskans to serve as clergy and church workers in the Diocese. One graduate was ordained priest in 1976 and one in 1977. A one-year "Reader's Program" trains Orthodox men and women to conduct services in the absence of ordained clergy. 27 students have graduated from this program. An earlier seminary at Unalaska closed in 1917.

Orthdox Church membership - 20,000.

ORTHODOX PRESBYTERIAN CHURCH

COMMITTEE ON HOME MISSIONS AND CHURCH EXTENSION
7401 Old York Road, Philadelphia, Pennsylvania 19126
Rev. George E. Haney, General Secretary   *(215)CA4-1883*

Menominee O. P. Chapel. Menominee. Zoar, Wisconsin. Missionaries, white: Neil and Lenore Tolsuma. Menominee Falls, Wisconsin 53051.

Old Stockbridge O. P. Church. Stockbridge. Gresham, Wisconsin 54128. Missionaries, white: Gordon (lic.) and Judy Peterson.

THE PENTECOSTAL CHURCH OF GOD

INTERNATIONAL HEADQUARTERS
INDIAN MISSIONS: P. O. Box 705, 211 Main Street, Joplin,
Missouri 65801   *(417)624-7050*
Director: Rev. C. Don Burke

Alphabetical entries by states. White pastors are missionaries
of the Indian Missions Department. 14 are ord. and 15 are lic.
2 additional missionaries carry on Field Bible Schools. 5 Ind.
pastors. 38 Missions. Total mem. 1,980. Most churches have a
Pentecostal Ladies Auxiliary (PLA) and a Pentecostal Young
People's Association (PYPA).

Southwest Pentecostal Indian Bible School. 2000 West Buckeye
Road, Phoenix, Arizona 85009. Will open in 1978.

Field Bible Schools: John and Eloise Prater, instructors.
Guadalupe and Kayenta, Arizona. 3 classes per month.

Chistochina Mission. Tlingit, Athabascan. Chistochina, Alaska
(not a post office). Vacant. Mem. 40.

Ketchikan Mission. Tlingit, Athabascan. Saxman Village,
Ketchikan, Alaska 99901. L. G. Streit, pastor, ord., w.
Mem. 80.

Quijotoa Community Church. Papago, Pima. Covered Wells, Sells,
Arizona 85634. Naomi Sauter and Roger Julian, pastors, ord., w.

Guadalupe Mission. Yaqui. Guadalupe, Arizona 85283. Paul
Martinez, pastor, layman, w. Mem. 100.

Holbrook Mission. Navajo. Mission Lane, Holbrook, Arizona
86025. Uva Shunk, pastor, ord., w. Mem. 40.

Kayenta Mission. Navajo. Monument Valley Road, Kayenta,
Arizona 86033. John L. Thompson, pastor, Ind. Mem. 90.

Parker Mission. Chemehuive, Mojave. Poston Road, Parker,
Arizona 85344. J. E. Hyatt, pastor, ord., w. Mem. 50.

Tolani Lake Mission. Navajo. Tolani Trading Post, Totanihake,
Arizona (not a post office). James and Helen Pio, pastors,
ord., w. Mem. 40.

Winslow Mission. Hopi, Navajo. Alder and First Streets,
Winslow, Arizona 86047. Edgar L. Hoskinson, pastor, ord., w.
Mem. 60.

Dinebito Mission. Navajo. Dinebito, Arizona (not a post office). Guy Begay, pastor, Ind. Mem. 30.

Covelo Mission. Yuroc, Kuroc. Covelo, California 95428. L. L. Ferrell, pastor, layman, w. Mem. 40.

Naturita, Colorado 81422. Navajo. No church at present time.

Mt. Pleasant, Michigan 48858. Chippewa. No church at present time.

Bena, Minnesota 55626. Chippewa. No church at present time.

Bogue Chitto Mission. Choctaw. Bogue Chitto, Mississippi 39629. Danny Figiel, pastor, layman, w. Mem. 70.

Busby Mission. Northern Cheyenne. Busby, Montana 59016. Fern Violett, pastor, laywoman, w. Mem. 40.

Lame Deer Mission. Northern Cheyenne. Lame Deer, Montana 59043. Nick Rector, pastor, layman, w. Mem. 60.

Lodge Grass Mission. Crow. Lodge Grass, Montana 59050. Howard Hunter, pastor, ord., w. Mem. 40.

Poplar Mission. Sioux, Assiniboin. Poplar, Montana 59255. Charles McGinnett, pastor, ord., w. Mem. 50.

Fallon Mission. Paiute, Shoshone. Fallon, Nevada 89406. Ralph Carpenter, pastor, ord., w. Mem. 50.

Schurz Mission. Paiute, Shoshone. Schurz, Nevada 89427. Minnie Dennis, pastor, laywoman, w. Mem. 20.

Chamisal Mission. Picuris. Chamisal, New Mexico 87521. Eva Hall, pastor, laywoman, w. Mem. 30.

Gallup Mission. Navajo, Zuni. Gallup, New Mexico 87301. Martin Kirk, pastor, layman, w. Mem. 30.

Haystack Mountain Mission. Navajo. Haystack Mountain, Prewit, New Mexico 87045. Angela Lee, pastor, Ind. Mem. 150.

Perea Pentecostal Church of God. Navajo. Old Highway 66, Fort Wingate, New Mexico 87316. Clyde V. Clark, pastor, ord., w. Mem. 125.

San Fidel Mission. Acoma, Laguna. San Fidel, New Mexico 87049. F. M. Ethridge, pastor, layman, w. Mem. 40.

Thoreau Pentecostal Church of God. Navajo. Thoreau, New Mexico 87323. Erma Tobeck, pastor, laywoman, w.

Taos Mission. Taos, Santo Domingo. Taos, New Mexico 87571. Ruth Henderson, pastor, laywoman, w. Mem. 20.

Anadarko Mission. Kiowa, Southern Cheyenne, Apache. Anadarko, Oklahoma 73005. LeRoy Carr, pastor, layman, w. Mem. 20.

Broken Bow, Oklahoma 74728. Choctaw. No church at present.

Carnegie Mission. Kiowa, Kiowa-Apache. Carnegie, Oklahoma 73015. Victor Riveria, pastor, Ind. Mem. 50.

Clinton Mission. Kiowa, Arapaho, Southern Cheyenne. Clinton, Oklahoma 73601. Johnny Bearshield, pastor, Ind. Mem. 40.

Hobart Mission. Kiowa, Otoe, Ponca, Kiowa-Apache. Hobart, Oklahoma 73651. Patsy Hobbs, pastor, laywoman, w. Mem. 30.

Lawton Mission. Kiowa-Apache, Southern Cheyenne, Comanche. Lawton, Oklahoma 73500. Vacant. Mem. 80.

Oklahoma City Mission. Choctaw, Chickasaw, Kiowa. Oklahoma City, Oklahoma. Charles Johnson, pastor, ord., w. Mem. 100.

Marietta Mission. Choctaw, Chickasaw. Marietta, Oklahoma 73448. William Strickland, pastor, ord., w. Mem. 20.

Stilwell Mission. Cherokee. Stilwell, Oklahoma 74960. Billy D. Robinson, pastor, layman, w. Mem. 35.

Omak Mission. Nespelem. Omak, Washington 98841. Burnell Hammons, pastor, ord., w. Mem. 20.

PRESBYTERIAN CHURCH IN THE UNITED STATES

SYNOD OF RED RIVER
P. O. Box 1098, Denton, Texas 76201   *(817)382-9658*
Rev. William J. Fogelman, Synod Executive

Choctaw/Chickasaw Parish. Choctaw. Simon Belvin, pastor, ord., Choctaw. P. O. Box 190, Boswell, Oklahoma 74727. 3 churches and 4 chapels. 4 lay worship leaders assist in the services. The Parish Council of 15, i.e. 2 persons from each church or chapel and the pastor, meet twice a year. The Choctaw/Chickasaw Assembly is an annual meeting of all members of the Parish.

Chishoktok. Bennington, Oklahoma 74723. Lay worship leaders. Mem. 25. Total com. 50. SS 30. YS 10. WS 6.

St. Matthews. Choctaw. RFD, Broken Bow, Oklahoma 74728. Lay worship leader. Mem. 33. Com. 66. Conv. in 1977 - 4. Ab. 1, ib. 2. SS 50. YS 15.

Sandy Creek. Chickasaw. Fillmore, Oklahoma 73434. Lay worship leaders. Mem. 39. Com. 78. SS 45. YS 12.

Indian Presbyterian Church. Alabama-Coushetta Tribe and Reservation. RFD Livingston, Texas 77351. Byron Price, pastor, ord., w. Route 3, Box 612, Livingston, Texas 77351. Mem. 163. Com. 300. Conv. in 1977 - 8. Ib. 12. SS 60. YS 20. WS 14. This church is intimately involved in the Tribal Enterprises and the pastor teaches in the Big Sandy School system attended by many children of the tribe.

Goodland Presbyterian Children's Home and Family Service Agency. Goodland Route, Hugo, Oklahoma 74743. Ralyn C. Parkhill, Executive Director. Goodland Mission School was founded in 1850 and in 1894 an Orphanage was added. The School has been replaced by a public school which operates on the campus. In 1972 the name was changed to the present form. Services include: a residential, group-living program for 40 children aged 11-18 in four coed cottages under group parents; emergency care for children in need of shelter in Choctaw County; individual care in foster homes; an adoption service; family counseling at St. Andrew's Presbyterian Church in Oklahoma City. 12 buildings on the campus. Has in the past served Choctaws, but is now open to all ethnic groups.

REFORMED CHURCH IN AMERICA

WESTERN REGIONAL CENTER - ANAHEIM
421 North Brookhurst, Suite 218, Anaheim, California 92801
Secretary for American Indian Ministries: Rev. Harold E. Brown
(714)778-2860

Apache Reformed Church. Chiricahua Apache. Apache Reservation. Apache, Oklahoma 73006. Andy Kamphuis, pastor, ord., w. and Mrs. Marjorie Kamphuis, missionaries. P. O. Box 362, Apache, Oklahoma 73006. *(405)588-3370.* Communicant mem. 77. Confessions of faith in 1975 - 21. Ab. 3, ib. 8. SS 95. WS, YS and Children's society.

Jicarilla Apache Reformed Church. Jicarilla Reservation. Dulce, New Mexico 87528. *(505)759-3349.* Russell W. Dykehouse, pastor, ord., w. and Mrs. Gen Dykehouse, missionaries; Robert and Dort Kampmara, missionaries. P. O. Box 166, Dulce, New Mexico 87528. *(505)759-3349.* 1 w. layworker. Communicant mem. 51. Ib. in 1975 - 6. SS 25. WS. Men and children societies.

The Reformed Church. Apache. Mescalero Apache Reservation. Mescalero, New Mexico 88340. Roger Bruggink, pastor, ord., w. and Mrs. Lee Bruggink, missionaries. P. O. Box 156, Mescalero, New Mexico 88340. *(505)671-4471.* Communicant mem. 81. Confessions of faith in 1975 - 1. Ib. 8. SS 62. WS. YS. Children's society.

Comanche Reformed Church. Comanche. 201 Mission Blvd., Lawton, Oklahoma 73501. *(405)355-4939.* Herman Van Galen, pastor, ord., w. and Mrs. Joyce Van Galen, missionaries. *(405)355-0213.* Communicant mem. 72. Confession of faith in 1975 - 1. Ab. 1, ib. 1. SS 25. WS. YS. Children's society.

First Reformed Church of the Omaha Indian Mission. Omaha. Macy, Nebraska 68039. Steven Farmer Sr., pastor, ord., Ind. and Mrs. Kay Farmer, missionaries. P. O. Box 57, Macy, Nebraska 68039. *(402)846-5527.* Communicant mem. 81. Confessions of faith in 1975 - 6. Ab. 4, ib. 2. SS 70. WS. YS. Children's society.

Winnebago Reformed Church. Winnebago Reservation. Winnebago, Nebraska 68071. Dirk Kramer, pastor, ord., w. and Mrs. Linda Kramer, missionaries. 1 w. lay woman worker. Communicant mem. 40. Confession of faith in 1975 - 1. SS 60. WS. YS. Children's society.

Religious Activities Center. Phoenix Indian High School, P. O. Box 7188, Phoenix, Arizona 85011. Religious Studies Coordinator: John Lucius, ord., w. Mrs. Helga Lucius. Phones: study *(602)274-7776;* home *247-1200.*

Cook Christian Training School. 708 South Lindon Lane, Tempe, Arizona 85281. Staff members: Mr. & Mrs. William J. Hocking. Phones: school *(602)968-9354;* home *966-9739.*

THE ROMAN CATHOLIC CHURCH

NATIONAL AGENCIES

BUREAU OF CATHOLIC INDIAN MISSIONS   *(202)331-8542*
2021 H. Street, N.W., Washington, D.C. 20006   1874
Board of Directors: President, His Eminence John Cardinal
  Krol; H. E. Terrence Cardinal Cooke; Most Rev. William
  Borders
Executive Director: Monsignor Paul A. Lenz

The Bureau was founded to stimulate the Church to concern for

Indian missions and to represent the missions in government relations, especially at the Federal level in Washington, D.C. It provides a center of reference for the Native American churches and ministries, collects information and makes grants to Dioceses, congregations and societies, and schools and other institutions. It presently supports the Tekakwitha Conference. *Newsletter*, monthly.

COMMISSION FOR CATHOLIC MISSIONS AMONG THE COLORED PEOPLE
  2021 H. Street, N.W., Washington, D.C. 20006 *(202)331-8542*
  Board of Directors: Chairman, H. E. John Cardinal Krol,
    H. E. Terrence Cardinal Cooke, Most Rev. William Borders
  Secretary: Msgr. Paul A. Lenz

The Commission was organized by the Third Plenary Council as trustee of the funds collected in the churches on the first Sunday in Lent for the support of Black and Indian missions in the U.S.A. Grants for Indian/Eskimo work were $826,000 in 1976.

THE AMERICAN BOARD OF CATHOLIC MISSIONS   1917
  1312 Massachusetts Avenue, N.W., Washington, D.C. 20005
  Chairman: Most Rev. John J. Sullivan

Since 1972 the ABCM has been a standing committee of the National Conference of Catholic Bishops. It is comprised of seven Archbishops and Bishops. It receives 40% of the receipts of the annual October Mission Sunday collection taken in the churches and 40% of the membership receipts of the Propagation of the Faith Society. It assists financially mission dioceses and awards special grants to mission related organizations. Native American missions, churches and organizations are aided through requests made by the Bishops.

CAMPAIGN FOR HUMAN DEVELOPMENT   1970
  1312 Massachusetts Avenue, N.W., Washington, D.C. 20005
  Acting Director: Timothy Collins

An agency of the United States Catholic Conference. The Campaign is the U.S. Catholic Church's action/education program to attack the root causes of poverty in our society. It grants funds to self-help projects for the poor and powerless, in which such people have the dominant voice in planning, implementing and policy making. Both outright and matching grants are given. No funds are allocated to Native American missions and pastoral and educational ministries. Past grants include a Sisseton Sioux cattle raising cooperative, an archery factory at Pine Ridge, an Indian Information Service at Phoenix, a marketing program

for Zuni craftsmen, Legal Aid for Ottawa Recognition and
Organization and a Native American Resource Center at
Fayetteville, North Carolina.

CATHOLIC CHURCH EXTENSION SOCIETY   1905
1307 South Wabash Avenue, Chicago, Illinois 60605
Acting President: Rev. Edward J. Slattery

The Society provides funds for church buildings and support
of clergy, religious and lay ministers in home missions. A
considerable amount each year is granted through the
dioceses or directly to the Native American churches and
ministries, but not as Indian or Eskimo purely. Grants are
made to needy home mission parishes.

MARQUETTE LEAGUE FOR CATHOLIC INDIAN MISSIONS   1904
1011 First Avenue, New York, N.Y. 10022
Director, Secretary-Treasurer: Rev. Timothy A. McDonnell

The League is now integrated into the structure of the
Archdiocese of New York but continues to collect funds and
to make grants to Indian missions on the national level.

FEDERATION OF CATHOLIC INDIAN LEADERS: FCIL   1977
Marty, South Dakota 57361
Officers for 1978:   President, Sister Inez Getty, OSBS
                     Vice President, Rev. Ed Zephier,
                     Permanent Deacon
                     Secretary, Treasurer, Rosemary Rouse
                     Priest Chaplain, Rev. Hugh Smith, OSB

The purpose of FCIL is to enable active participation by
Catholic Indian people in the implementation of leadership-
ministry programs which affect their spiritual and temporal
lives. Membership: (1) Existing Parish Councils and/or
Parish Administrative Boards in conjunction or consultation
with their local pastor will select two persons from each
reservation or urban parish to represent them at quarterly
meetings of FCIL.   (2) These two persons will be registered
as voting delegates to FCIL on an annual basis. LOCAL
CHAPTERS: (1) Local chapters of FCIL will be established
in consultation with the local pastors, and will function
in reinforcement of faith through support of Indian ministry
and leadership programs and individual service and example.
(2) Local chapters shall establish rules of order to maintain their business with emphasis on works which strengthen
the faith of the Church on the reservation or urban parish.
(3) Applications for membership in FCIL shall be made by
local chapters to any quarterly meeting for recognition and
approval.

NATIONAL ASSOCIATION OF NATIVE RELIGIOUS   1971
   Coordinator: Brother Lorenzo Martin, OFMS
   Box B, Our Lady of Blessed Sacrament, Fort Defiance,
   Arizona 86504

An association of Native Americans in religious orders,
intended to share our Lord; to help each other spiritually,
emotionally, and materially if necessary; and to help
people better understand Indian culture and life. Annual
meeting.

TEKAKWITHA CONFERENCE   1939
   Task Force: Executive Committee, Rev. Gilbert F. Hemauer,
   President.
   2021 H. Street, N.W., Washington, D.C. 20006 *(202)331-8542*

A Conference of missionaries, missiologists and persons with
interest and concern for Catholic missions and ministries to
Native Americans. The 39th annual conference is help at
St. Martin's Academy, Rapid City, South Dakota, August 7 to
10, 1978. The Conference is undergoing reorganization.

THE VENERABLE KATERI TEKAKWITHA LEAGUE
   Auriesville, New York 12016   *(518)853-3153*
   Rev. Joseph S. McBride, S.J., Vice-Postulator

A society which seeks to disseminate knowledge about the
Mohawk maiden, Kateri Tekakwitha (1656-1680) and to advance
the course of her canonization.

ARCHDIOCESES AND DIOCESES

ALASKA

ARCHDIOCESE OF ANCHORAGE
P. O. Box 2239, Anchorage, Alaska 99501   *(907)349-2535*
Archbishop: Most Rev. Francis T. Hurley

Estimated Catholics 10,000. Catholic Indians 2,000. Baptisms
in 1977 - adults 2, infants 72. All parishes have some Native
Americans attending. The following parishes minister to
Indians.

Holy Family Cathedral. Anchorage, Alaska 99501. Partial.

Holy Rosary Church. Dillingham, Alaska 99576. Indian.

Holy Family Church. Glennallen, Alaska 99588. Partial.

Mission Church. Clark's Point, Alaska 99569. Indian.

Mission Church. Seldovia, Alaska 99663. Partial. Richard Strass, CSSR, parish priest.

Chapel. Alaska Native Hospital, Anchorage, Alaska. Indian.

PERSONNEL IN INDIAN MINISTRY

Fred Bugarin, Anchorage, Alaska. Parish priest, part time.

John P. Fox, S.J., 1500 Birchwood, Anchorage, Alaska 99504. Hospital Chaplain, full time.

Eugene P. Burns, S.J., 1500 Birchwood, Anchorage, Alaska 99504. Hospital Chaplain, full time.

William Tyson, Deacon, Anchorage, Alaska. Hospital Chaplain, full time.

*500 Indian patients served by the Hospital Chaplains.

Sister Ida and Sister Margaret, based in Anchorage, religious education in the villages, including area of Dillingham, Clark's Point. Three lay persons assist. Indian participants 52.

Sister Rose, parish Sister, full time ministry to Indians.

Sister Dorothy, alcoholic counseling, 10 Indians.

Food and clothing service, Anchorage, 1000 Indians.

Summer religious education in various places by four volunteer Sisters, 20 Indians.

Retreats at Dillingham and Anchorage; Indian participants 25.

Parish liturgy at Ekok, Dillingham and Clark's Point: 6 priests, 3 lay persons, 40 Indians.

Jesuit Alaska Mission. Residence: 1500 Birchwood, Anchorage, Alaska 99504. *(907)279-4389.* Three priests in residence, two outside.

DIOCESE OF FAIRBANKS
1316 Peger Road, Fairbanks, Alaska 99701   *(907)456-6753*
Most Rev. Robert L. Wheelan, S.J., Bishop

Jesuit Alaska Mission
P. O. Box 80393, Fairbanks, Alaska 99708   *(907)479-4718*
Francis J. Fallert, S.J., Superior   *452-3523*

Personnel: 43 priests, 6 coad; total 49. There are 2
Eskimo candidates for the priesthood.

OTHER INSTITUTES AND CONGREGATIONS

Congregation of St. Paul (Paulist Fathers) - Parish and
university ministry.

Sisters of St. Joseph of Peace - Administration.

Ursuline Sisters - Education.

Sisters of Providence - Education.

Sisters of St. Anne - Social Work.

Dominican Sisters (Sinsinawa and Adrian) - Education.

School Sisters of Notre Dame - Education.

MAJOR INSTITUTIONS AND PROGRAMS

St. Mary's High School. St. Marys, Alaska 99658. James R.
Landwein, S.J., Administrator, priest, w. Sister Francis
X. Porter, OSU, Principal. Boarding, grades 9-12. Students
are Yupik (Eskimo) and Athabascan. Teaching Staff: 9
Ursuline and St. Anne Sisters, including 1 Native Alaskan;
3 Jesuit Brothers, including 1 Native Alaskan; 1 priest; 15
lay persons, including 4 Native Alaskans. 185 students in
1977-78: Eskimo 182, Indian 1, white 1. Boarding and day.

Monroe High School. 715 Monro Street, Fairbanks, Alaska
99701. Staff: Religious 10, lay 7. Students 125,
including 8 Indians or Eskimo.

Catechetical Training Program. Staff: 7 Sisters.
Participants 850, Indians and Eskimos among them 820.

Native Permanent Diaconate Training Program. Rene Astruc,
S.J., Director, priest, w. 1316 Peger Road, Fairbanks,
Alaska 99701. Charles J. Peterson, S.J., Diocesan Director
of Vocations, priest, w. (Apply to him for information.)
3248 College Road, Fairbanks, Alaska 99701. Parish councils
select candidates for the Permanent Diaconate. When
training has been completed, the Deacons are involved in
pastoral ministry in their villages. 13 have completed

training and 19 are in training in 1977–78.

Radio Station KNOM. P. O. Box 998, Nome, Alaska 99762.

All 26 parishes in the diocese, with the exception of 5 or 6, are exclusively or predominantly Eskimo or Athabascan and those 5 or 6 have some Native Alaskans. The same situation applies in the 35 missions and stations. There are approximately 8,000 Eskimo and Indian Catholics in the Diocese. There were 3 ab. and 235 ib. of Native Alaskans in 1977. 30 priests work among Native Alaskans, all but 7 full time; 6 Brothers, 2 part time; 23 Sisters, only 1 part time; 2 priests are Eskimos, 1 Brother.

Cathedral of the Sacred Heart. 1316 Peger Road, Fairbanks, Alaska 99701. *(907)456-7868.* Frs. William C. Dibb, S.J., and George E. Carroll, S.J., priests, w.

Immaculate Conception Church. 115 North Ashman Street, Fairbanks, Alaska 99701. *(907)452-3523.* Frs. Francis J. Fallert, S.J., Richard D. Case, S.J., Charles J. Fairbanks, S.J., Neill K. Murphy, S.J., Lawrence A. Nevue, S.J., Carl W. Wickart, S.J.

Home for Emotionally Disturbed Eskimo Children. Bethel, Alaska 99559. Operated by the Jesuit Volunteer Corps. Staff: 4 professionals. Patients 10–30 annually.

Little Flower of Jesus Church. Kaltag, Alaska 99748. James A. Sebastia, S.J., parish priest, w.

St. Francis Xavier Church. 1930. P. O. Box 57, Kotzebue, Alaska 99752. John E. Gurr, S.J., parish priest, w. 1 Sister, 2 lay volunteers. Catholic mem. about 250.

St. Theresa Church. Athabascan. P. O. Box 312, Nanana, Alaska 99760. *(907)832-5617.* Paul B. Miller, S.J., parish priest, w.
   Stations: Healy and Clear.

St. Joseph Church. P. O. Box 101, Nome, Alaska 99762. *(907)443-2675.* James E. Poole, S.J., parish priest, w.
   Stations at Teller, Alaska 99778 and Little Diomede Island. Harold J. Greif, S.J., missionary in charge.

Church of Our Lady of the Snows. Nulato, Alaska 99765. Charles P. Saalfild, S.J., parish priest, w. 2 Sisters. Mem. 475.
   Stations: Koyukuk and Hulsia.

Tok Junction Catholic Church. Tok Junction, Alaska 99780. Joseph P. Hebert, S.J., parish priest, w.

St. Mary's Catholic Church. P. O. Box 105, St. Marys, Alaska 99658. Radio: KLABIA and K17GOV. Jules M. Convert, S.J., parish priest, w.

St. Mary's High School. See above.

St. Ignatius Church. Eskimo. Alakanuk, Alaska 99554. Radio: KL7EPN. Francis X. Nawn, S.J., parish priest, w. 2 Sisters. Mem. 650.
  Station: Sheldon Point.

Sacred Heart Church. Eskimo. Emmonak, Alaska 99581. Henry G. Hargreaves, S.J., parish priest, w. 4 Eskimo Deacons, 30 Eskimo Catechists, 2 w. Sisters, 2 lay women. Communicants 500. Total Catholic com. 750. Teen Center. Figures include *St. Joseph's.*
  Station: *St. Joseph's Church.* Kotlik, Alaska 99620. Radio: KL7GHK. (Mem. 250.)

Holy Cross Church. Eskimo. Holy Cross, Alaska 99602. Michael J. Kaniecki, S.J., parish priest, w. 1 Sister, 2 lay helpers. 5 small stations and the following 2 churches. Mem. 260.

  St. Theresa's Church. Aniak, Alaska 99557. Mem. 120.

  Church of the Immaculate Conception. Upper Kalskag, Alaska 99607. Mem. 160.

Little Flower Church. Hooper Bay, Alaska 99604. Bernard F. McMeel, S.J., parish priest, w. Also pastor at *Scammon Bay,* Alaska 99662.

St. Lawrence Church. P. O. Box 193, Mountain Village, Alaska 99632. William P. McIntyre, S.J., parish priest, w.
  Station: Pilot Station, Alaska 99650.

Holy Family Church. Newtok, Alaska 99559. Thomas E. Provinsal, S.J., parish priest.

St. Michael Church. St. Michael, Alaska 99569. George E. Endal, S.J., parish priest. 1 Sister. Mem. 500. 1 conv. in 1977.
  Also stations at *Stebbins,* Alaska 99671, and *Unalakleet,* Alaska 99684.

St. Joseph's Church. Tununak, Nelson Island, Alaska 99681.

Daniel J. Tainter, S.J., parish priest.

DIOCESE OF JUNEAU
416 5th Street, Juneau, Alaska 99801
Archbishop Francis Hurley of Anchorage is Administrator

INSTITUTES AND CONGREGATIONS IN NATIVE ALASKAN MINISTRIES

Oblates of Mary Immaculate. Fr. Ed Cunningham, Superior.
329 5th Avenue, Juneau, Alaska 99801.

Holy Family Sisters. Sr. Marie Ann Brent, Superior. P. O.
Box 1698, Sitka, Alaska 99835. Catechetical instruction.

Holy Cross Sisters. Sr. Marguerite Gravel, Superior. 433
Jackson, Ketchikan, Alaska 99901. Catechetical instruction.

Presentation Sisters. Sr. Patrick, Superior. 525 West 9th
Street, Juneau, Alaska 99801. Day care, infant care, senior
center.

Sisters of St. Joseph. Sr. Barbara Haas, Superior. 3100
Tongun, Ketchikan, Alaska 99901. Hospital, school work.

Pastors of the 9 town parishes serve the attached village
missions regularly once a month. A team of 3 Sisters
travel regularly to logging camps and villages. All
parishes are integrated. Estimated Native Catholics 500.
In 1975 2 churches and 4 priests served Native Alaskans
exclusively or predominently and there were 4 ab. and 7 ib.

Holy Name School. 433 Jackson, Ketchikan, Alaska 99901.
(907)225-2400. Sister Andrea Nenzel, Principal/Superinten-
dent. Day school. Grades 1-6. Administrative staff: 6.
Teachers: 2 w. men, 7 Sisters. Students: 6 Ind. boys,
8 Ind. girls, 1 Aleut boy, 2 Aleut girls.

At Sitka, religious instruction is provided for children in
the BIA boarding school.

ARIZONA

DIOCESE OF PHOENIX
400 East Monroe Street, Phoenix, Arizona 85004 *(602)257-0030*
Most Rev. James Rausch, Bishop
Fr. James F. O'Brien, S.J., Indian Ministry for the Diocese
4701 N. Central Avenue, Phoenix, Arizona 85012
(602)279-9547 or *264-5291.*

INSTITUTES AND CONGREGATIONS

Order of St. Francis. St. Barbara Province. Fr. John
Vaughan, OFM, Provincial, 1500 34th Avenue, Oakland,
California 94601.

Society of Jesus. Fr. Terrence Mahon, S.J.

Franciscan Sisters of Charity. Sr. Miriam Genevieve, OSF,
20531 Carpet Drive, Walnut, California 91789. Teaching.

Mission personnel: 6 w. priests, 4 w. Brothers; 2 Ind.
Sisters, 8 w. Sisters; 4 Ind. women lay workers. 9 churches
and chapels. About 2,000 communicants. About 7,270
Catholic com. Ab. in 1977 - 7, ib. 198. Elementary
schools 2, pupils 150.

San Lucy Papago Indian Mission and *St. Michael's Church.*
Gila Bend, Arizona 85337. Partial Ind. Fr. Joseph T.
Monaghan, S.J., parish priest. P. O. Drawer F, Gila Bend,
Arizona 85337. 350 baptized.

St. John's Indian Mission. Pima. Gila River Reservation.
Laveen, Arizona 85339. Fr. Walter Holly, OFM, pastor;
Brother Bernardino Brophy, OFM, procurator; Sister Lorraine
Morin, CSJ, parish visitor and CCD director.

St. John's Elementary School. Laveen, Arizona 85339.
Sister's residence: Route 1, Box 750, Laveen, Arizona 85339.
Sister Patricia Ellen Owen, Principal and teacher. Other
teachers: Sister Malachy Donnelly, Sister St. Francis. 2
Ind. teacher's aides. Pupils 85.

St. Peter's Indian Mission. Pima. Bapchule, Arizona 85221.
Joseph Baur, OFM, parish priest. P. O. Box 886, Bapchule,
Arizona 85221. Sister Mary Schmidt, MSBT, pastoral
ministry. Sister Mary Simon Gamiel, OSF, teacher. P. O.
Box 891, Bapchule, Arizona 85221. Sister Fintan Murphy,
OSF, housekeeper. P. O. Box 891, Bapchule, Arizona 85221.

St. Peter's Elementary School. P. O. Box 891, Bapchule,
Arizona 85221. Sister Mary Casey, OSF, Principal.
Teachers: Sister Jennifer Hansen, OSF; Sister Pamela
Biehl, OSF. Ind. teacher's aide. Pupils 88.

Our Lady of Guadalupe. Yaqui. Guadalupe, Arizona 85283.
Fr. Ignatius DeGroot, OFM, parish priest. 5445 San Angelo,
Guadalupe, Arizona 85683. Brother Ivo Toneck, OFM, youth
ministry and self help construction. 5594 Encinas,
Guadalupe, Arizona 85283. Sister Georgeanna Pahl, CCD

ministry. 9004 South 54th Place, Guadalupe, Arizona 85283. Pre-school for children: Sisters (C. pp. S.) Vera Heile and Mary Ann Schiller, both at 9004 South 54th Place. About 450 families. Day care 25. Alternate school 65-70.

Salt River Indian Mission. Pima and Maricopa. Tempe, Arizona 85281. Fr. James F. O'Brien, S.J., Administrator. 2435 East McArthur Drive, Tempe, Arizona 85281. Sister Caroline Oeding, CCD ministry. Sister Stella Wener, CCD ministry. About 500 baptized.

Phoenix Indian Hospital and *Phoenix Indian School.* Fr. James F. O'Brien, S.J., ministers to Catholic patients and students. 4701 North Central Avenue, Phoenix, Arizona 85012.

OTHERS MINISTERING TO INDIANS

Sister Norma Turner, BVM, 4710 North 3rd Street, Phoenix, Arizona 85012.

DIOCESE OF TUCSON
P. O. Box 31, Tucson, Arizona 85702   *(602)792-3410*
Most Rev. Francis J. Green, Bishop
Rev. Edward Schulz, OFM, Vicar for Indians. 349 West 31st
  Street, Tucson, Arizona 85713   *(602)622-5363*

TUCSON URBAN AREA AND SAN XAVIER RESERVATION

10 church, 9 chapels. 18 w. priests, 1 Ind. Deacon. 32 w. Sisters. 8 Ind. catechists, 50 w. catechists. 40 Ind. lay men workers, 57 w. lay men workers. 49 Ind. lay women workers, 52 w. women lay workers. 1 elementary day school. Communicant mem. 2,475. Total Catholic com. 3,990. Ab. in 1977 - 16, ib. 91.

CONGREGATIONS AND INSTITUTES

American Franciscan Missions: St. Barbara Province. 1500 34th Avenue, Oakland, California 94601. *(415)536-1266.* Very Rev. John Vaughan, OFM, Provincial. Fr. Kieran McCarty, OFM, local superior. Route 11, Box 645, Tucson, Arizona 85706. Parish ministry.

Redemptorists: Fr. Ricardo Elford, CSR. P. O. Box 50172, Tucson, Arizona 85703. Cultural Awareness.

White Fathers: Fr. Eugene Moroney, WF. 602 West Ajo Way, Tucson, Arizona 85713. Parish ministry.

Carmelites: Fr. Dominic O'Callaghan. P. O. Box 2830, Tucson, Arizona 85702. Parish ministry.

Our Lady of Victory Missionary Sisters: 535 East Drachman Street, Tucson, Arizona 85705. Social work.

Dominican Sisters: 29 West 22nd Street, Tucson, Arizona 85713. Elementary education.

Franciscan Sisters of Little Falls, MN. 26 East Kelso Street, Tucson, Arizona 85705. Religious education.

Franciscan Sisters. 349 West 31st Street, Tucson, Arizona 85713. St. Nicholas Center.

Eucharistic Missionaries of St. Dominic. 822 South 7th Avenue, Tucson, Arizona 85701. Pastoral ministry.

Mother Seton Sisters of Charity. 606 West Ajo Way, Tucson, Arizona 85713. Visiting nurse.

St. Nicholas Center. Principally Papago. 314 West 31st Street, Tucson, Arizona 85713. *(602)622-5363.* Fr. Edward Schulz, OFM, Director. Sisters (OSF) Ange Mayers, Janice Weniger, Louise Bauer, 349 West 31st Street, Tucson, Arizona 85713. 5 Ind. catechists, 2 w. 2 Ind. men, 1 woman workers. 8 w. lay men workers. Learning center, emergency services, referrals, weekday religious education, adult education, social service, parish ministry. Communicant mem. 200. Total Catholic com. 300. Conv. in 1976 - 5, ab. 3, ib. 10. WS 15. YS 20. Men's society 3. General 45. Serve 3,500 yearly.

Santa Rosa Church. Yaqui, Old Pasqua. 2015 North Calle Central, Tucson, Arizona 85705. Fr. Ricardo, parish priest. 3 w. Sisters. 12 Ind. catechists, 1 w. 6 Ind. men lay workers, 5 women. 8 w. lay men workers. Communicants 200. Total Catholic com. 350. Conv. in 1976 - 5, ab. 3, ib. 50. Weekday religious instruction. Adult education. WS 40. YS 25. Men's society 15. General society 100.

Cristo Rey Iglesia. Yaqui, New Pasqua. 7509 South Camera Potam, Tucson, Arizona 85706. Fr. Maurice McCarthy, SMA, parish priest. Fr. Meno Grassman, P. O. Box 567, Tucson, Arizona 85702. 6 Sisters. 5 Ind. catechists. 20 Ind. lay men workers, 2 w. men. 10 Ind. women lay workers. Communicants 150. Total Catholic com. 600. Conv. in 1977 - 2, ab. 12, ib. 120. Weekday religious education. Adult education. WS 20. YS 20. Men's society 40. General 150. *Elementary School.*

St. Anthony Mission. Papago and Mexican. 255 West 34th Street, Tucson, Arizona 85713. Parish priest, Ind. 3 w. Sisters. 5 catechists. 4 Ind. men lay workers, 6 Ind. women. 2 w. lay men, 2 w. women workers. Conv. in 1976 - 6 ab. and 15 ib. Weekday religious education. Adult education. WS 10. Children's society 15. Men's society 20. General 40. Evangelistic ministry.

Santa Cruz Church. Partial Indian. 1200 South 6th Avenue, Tucson, Arizona 85713. *(602)623-3833.* Church and 2 chapels Parish priest, w. 3 w. Sisters. 4 Ind. catechists, 2 w. 3 Ind. lay men workers, 4 Ind. women. 5 w. men workers, 1 w. woman worker. 250 Ind. communicants. 300 total Ind. Catholic com. 6 conv. in 1976. 5 ab. 15 ib. Weekday religious education. Adult education. Societies: women 25, youth 20, children 15, men 30, general 50.

St. Augustine's Cathedral. Some Indian population. 2 chapels. 192 South Stone, Tucson, Arizona 85701. 3 w. priests. 3 w. Sisters. 5 Ind. catechists, 15 w. 3 Ind. men lay workers, 20 w. men. 7 Ind. women lay workers, 14 w. women. 200 Ind. communicants. 400 total Ind. com. Conv. in 1976 - 2. Ab. 2, ib. 18. Societies: women 50, youth 20, children 20, general 75. Senior citizens. Weekday religious education. Adult education.

Holy Family Church. Some Indian population. 338 West 3rd Street, Tucson, Arizona 85705. 2 chapels. 3 w. priests. 3 w. Sisters. 2 Ind. catechists, 15 w. 3 Ind. men lay workers, 20 w. 7 Ind. women lay workers, 14 w. 200 Ind. communicants. 400 Ind. com. Weekday religious education. Adult education. Socieities: women 20, children 15, general 40.

St. John the Evangelist Church. Some Ind. population. 602 West Ajo Way, Tucson, Arizona 85713. 3 w. priests. 5 w. Sisters. 1 Ind. catechist, 9 w. 4 Ind. lay men workers, 8 w. 3 Ind. women lay workers, 15 w. Weekday religious education. Societies: women 30, youth 20, children 20, general 60.

Our Lady of Guadalupe Chapel. Some Indian population. 401 East 31st Street, Tucson, Arizona 85713. W. priest. 3 w. Sisters. 4 Ind. catechists, 6 w. 2 Ind. men lay workers, 6 w. 3 Ind. women lay workers. 80 Ind. communicants. 240 total Ind. Catholic com. Weekday religious education. Societies: women 15, men 14, general 20.

San Martin de Porres Church. 39th Street and 10th Avenue, Tucson, Arizona 85713.

St. Christopher Church. Partial. Marana, Arizona 85238.

SAN XAVIER MISSION. Papago. Route 11, Box 645, Tucson, Arizona 85706. *Saint Francis Xavier Church,* 1 other church, 2 chapels. Fr. Kieran McCarty, OFM, superior; Fr. Edward Schulz, OFM; Fr. Lucien Pargett, OFM; Fr. Celestine Chin, OFM. 1 Ind. Sister, 3 w. Sisters. 5 Ind. catechists. 3 Ind. lay men workers, 7 Ind. lay women workers. 900 communicant mem. 900 total Catholic com. Conv. in 1976 - 18. Ab. 10, ib. 70. Weekday religious instruction. Adult education. Societies: women 100, youth 30, men 20. *San Xavier Elementary School.* 200 pupils.

SAN SOLANO MISSION. Papago. Papago Reservation. Topawa, Arizona 85639. American Franciscan Missions, St. Barbara Province, 1500 34th Avenue, Oakland, California 94601. Fr. William Sick, OFM, Superior, Topawa, Arizona 85639.

56 churches and chapels. 6 w. priests. 2 Ind. Sisters, 21 w. Sisters. 3 w. Brothers, 5 Ind. catechists 6 w. 5 Ind. men lay workers, 2 w. 4 Ind. women lay workers. 8,500 communicants. Total com. 9,040. Conv. in 1976 - 46. Ab. 46, ib. 160. Boy scouts. Girl scouts. Teenage youth clubs in about 10 villages. Social programs for elderly. Parent advisory groups for all youth programs. Weekday religious education for 5 centers. Adult Bible classes.

TOPAWA DISTRICT

St. Catherine's Mission. Topawa, Arizona 85639. Fr. Maurus Kelly, OFM, parish priest. Fr. Remy Rudin, OFM, missionary. Brother Roland Rovere, OFM, maintenance and missionary. Sister Patrica Walsh, Manitowac Sisters, missionary-catechist. Sister Viola Hubatch, Manitowac Sisters, missionary-catechist.

Our Lady of the Sacred Heart. Sells, Arizona 85634. Fr. Joseph Graff, parish priest (diocesan). Sister M. Jose Hobday, OSF, (Indian), missionary-director.

Queen of the Angels Church. San Miguel.

St. Paschal Church. Vanmori.

St. Anthony Church. Cold Fields.

Our Lady of Mt. Carmel. Sigigigskik, Sonora, Mexico.

St. Jude Church. Komalik.

Our Lady of Guadalupe. Cowlic.

St. Aloysius Church. Big Fields.

Our Lady of Lourdes. Little Tucson (Ali Chukson). Fr. Camillus Covagnaro, OFM.

St. Francis. Fresnal.

CHUICHU DISTRICT

St. Peter's Mission. St. Augustine's Church. Chuichu. Fr. Stanley Nadolny, Diocesan priest, missionary. Route 2, Box 594A, Casa Grande, Arizona 85222.

St. Ignatius. North Komalik.

St. Clare. Anegam.

St. Elizabeth. Cocklebur.

St. Francis. Kohatk.

AJO DISTRICT

St. Catherine of Sienna. Ajo, Arizona 85321.

St. Martin. Gunsight.

St. Margaret Mary. Hikivan.

St. Bonaventure. Hodaishonewos.

Immaculate Conception. Ventana.

St. Joseph's. Kaka.

St. Barbara. Vaga Chin.

PISINEMO DISTRICT

San Jose. Pisinemo, Arizona 85636. Fr. Lambert Fremdling, OFM, religious superior and missionary. Sister Ruth Speh, Notre Dame Sister, missionary-catechist. Sister Estelle VandenHeuvel, Manitowac Sister, school teacher.

Santa Cruz. Komewo's.

St. Francis. Kupk.

St. Theresa. Jevedemek.

SS Peter and Paul. Manager's Dam.

St. Joseph. GuVo's.

St. Simon. San Simon, Arizona 85032.

St. Theresa of Avila. Pioik.

St. John. Sweetwater.

COVERED WELLS DISTRICT

Sacred Heart Mission. Covered Wells, Arizona (Sells post office.) Fr. Richard Parcell, OFM, missionary priest. Sister Anne Fischer, Notre Dame Sister, missionary-catechist. Sister Dorothy Scherer, Notre Dame Sister, missionary-catechist.

St. Rose. Santa Rosa.

St. Seraphim. Akchin.

Sacred Heart. Comobabi.

St. Mary. Cobabi.

St. Agatha. Silvakya.

San Isidro. Havab Nakya.

POSTON AREA

3 churches. 1 priest. 2 Sisters. 27 lay workers.

Sacred Heart Church. Mohave, Chemehuevi and white. Colorado River Reservation. Box 814, Parker, Arizona 85344. Fr. Clemens M. Schlueter, parish priest. Catechetical School: Sister Clare Hamon, CRE; 13 lay persons. 35 Ind.

St. Margaret and St. Elizabeth Mission and Catechetical Center. Poston, Arizona 85371. 13 lay workers. 122 Ind. students.

St. John's Mission. Salome, Arizona. Box 243, Wenden, Arizona 85357. Catechetical school/trailer mission.

Sister Joyce Brown, CRE and Ms. Georgia Katrales. 16 Ind.

San Carlos Mission. Apache. San Carlos Reservation. P. O.
Box 26, San Carlos, Arizona 85550. Fr. Bartholomew Welsh,
OFM, superior.

San Carlos Mission. San Carlos, Arizona 85550. Sister
Clarita Kelly, SC, religious programs for youth. Box 338,
San Carlos, Arizona 85550. *Elementary School.* Sisters of
the Blessed Sacrament. Sr. Alice Carmel Reynolds, SBS,
Principal and kindergarden teacher; Sr. Patricia Murray,
SBS, teacher 2nd grade; Sr. Maureen Hynes, SBS, 1st grade
teacher; Sr. Regina Douglas, SBC, 3rd grade teacher.
Address for Sisters: Box 338, San Carlos, Arizona 85550.
3 lay teachers. 108 Ind. pupils. Religious education
(CCD). 75 Ind. participants.

DIOCESE OF GALLUP: ARIZONA PORTION
P. O. Box 1338, Gallup, New Mexico 87201   *(505)863-5083*
Most Rev. Jerome J. Hastrich, Bishop

St. Michael's Mission. Navajo. Navajo Reservation.
American Franciscan Missions. St. John the Baptist
Province, Vine Street, Cincinnati, Ohio. St. Michael's,
Arizona 86511. *(602)871-4171.* Frs. Martan Rademacher, OFM,
Guardian; Ivo Zirkelbach, OFM, pastor; Celestine Bauman,
OFM; John A. Cruce Lanzrath, OFM: Lawrence Schreiber, OFM:
Alexis Ripperger, OFM; Emmanuel Truckur, OFM. Lay Brothers
11.

St. Catherine. Cibecue. P. O. Box 156, Cibecue, Arizona
85901.

St. Joseph's Mission. Keams Canyon. Fr. Simon F. Conrad,
OFM. P. O. Box 128, Keams Canyon, Arizona 86034.
(602)738-2325.
  Mission: Hopi Village.
  Stations: *Cedar Springs, Teesto, Jeditto, Low Mountain,
  Castle Butte, Indian Wells, Naktee Canyon, Steamboat, Bita
  Hachee, Finger Point, Red Lake, Sand Springs, Hopi
  Reservation.*

St. Anne, Klagetoh. Fr. Gale Graishop, OFM. P. O. Box 77,
Ganado, Arizona 86505. *(602)652-3204.* 3 Dominican Sisters.
  Missions: Greasewood, *Our Lady of the Rosary.* Fr. Alex
  Ripperger, OFM.

St. Michael's Indian School. St. Michael's, Arizona 85611.
Sisters of the Blessed Sacrament. Sisters 10, lay teachers
11. Boys 173, girls 193 - Total 366.

St. Michael's High School. St. Michael's, Arizona 85611.
Sisters of the Blessed Sacrament. Sister Anne Regina,
Principal. Sisters 13, lay teachers 2. Girls 110.

Convent of Our Lady of the Angels. St. Michael's, Arizona
85611. 11 Sisters, 9 give religious instruction in
government schools.

St. Francis Apache Indian Mission. Whiteriver. Fr. Justin
Moncrief, OFM. P. O. Box 778, Whiteriver, Arizona 85941.
(602)338-4432. 2 Brothers. Mem. 250.

Summary: 18 Navajo missions, stations, churches, 1 Apache
church. 11 Franciscan priests, 13 Brothers, 42 Sisters,
13 lay teachers.

CALIFORNIA

DIOCESE OF FRESNO
P. O. Box 1668, Fresno, California 93717
Most Rev. Hugh A. Donahoe, Bishop
Msgr. Denis J. Doherty, V.C., in charge of Indian ministries

4 churches, approximately 2,500 Catholic Indians. Ab. in
1977 - 3, ib. 32.

Santa Rita Mission. Mixed. Squaw Valley, Orange Cove,
California 93646. Fr. Joseph Lipke, parish priest. Sister
Mary Clara, SBS; Sister Miriam Theresa, SBS. Mem. 125.
CCD program. Summer school of Religion, 2 Sisters.

Mater Dolorosa Church. Msgr. Maurice Lahey. Tule River
Reservation. Porterville. Weekly mass. Summer school of
Religion, 1 priest with young people.

St. Jude's Church. Kern River Valley. Rev. Mark Renner.
CCD classes and occasional mass. Aid to needy families.

Our Lady of Perpetual Help. 849 Home Street, Bishop,
California 93514. Msgr. Gilbert Meyer, parish priest. 1
lay worker. CCD program. Parish church and facilities are
used. Mem. 350. Conv. in 1977 - 10. Mission in Big Pine,
California 93513.

DIOCESE OF SACRAMENTO
P. O. Box 1706, Sacramento, California 95808   *(916)443-1996*
Most Rev. Alden J. Bell, Bishop

The Diocese reported 1 church with 1 priest and 270 Ind. mem.
in 1976.

DIOCESE OF SAN DIEGO
Alcala Park, San Diego, California 92110
Most Rev. Leo T. Maher, Bishop

INSTITUTES AND CONGREGATIONS

Sons of the Sacred Heart (Verona Fathers).   8101 Beachmont
Avenue, Cincinnati, Ohio 45230.

Sisters of the Blessed Sacrament.

San Antonio Mission. Mission Indian. Palo Reservation.
Palo Mission Road, Palo, California 92059. Fr. Bart
Battirossi, pastor. Fr. Frank DiFrancisco, assistant
pastor. Sisters' address: P. O. Box 80, Palo, California.
6 Sisters. Elementary day school, 160 pupils. CCD classes.
Mem. at Palo Wall stations 475. BIA reports population of
585. Ib. in 1976 - 15.

Rincon Reservation. Valley Center, California 92082.

Pauma Reservation. Pauma Valley, California 92061.

La Jolla Reservation. Valley Center, California 92082.

Pechanga Reservation. Fallbrook, California 92028.

Cahuilla Reservation. Anza, California 92306. Yuima
Indians.

Santa Ysabel Mission. Diguehos Mission Indians. Fr.
Dominic Pazzaglia, pastor. P. O. Box 128, Santa Ysabel,
California 92070. 7 churches at *Santa Ysabel, Mesa Grande,
Los Coyotes, Warmer Springs, Baroma, Sycuan, Inaja.* Total
Catholic com. 1,065. Ab. in 1976 - 3, ib. 26. 1 Sister
teaches catechism once a week in each mission church on
released time or after school.

St. Thomas Indian Mission. Cocopah. Ft. Yuma Reservation.
In Arizona, not California. P. O. Box 1790, Yuma, Arizona
85364. Mem. 450.

DIOCESE OF SANTA ROSA
P. O. Box 1297, Santa Rosa, California   *(707)545-7610*
Most Rev. Mark J. Hurley, Bishop

7 churches. 7 priests in full or part time service. 2,000
Indian members were reported in 1976. 5 ib. that year.

St. Mary's Church. 1690 James Road, Arcata, California 95521.

St. Anthony's Mission. Hoopa Valley Reservation. 3 priests serve the mission on a rotating basis. Mem. 160.

COLORADO

ARCHDIOCESE OF DENVER
938 Bannock Street, Denver, Colorado 80204   *(303)892-6857*
Most Rev. James V. Casey, Archbishop

Catholics 2,000. Ab. in 1977 - 1, ib. 9.

Indian Ministries in Denver:

Mass every Sunday at *Denver Native American Center*, 16th and York Street, Denver, Colorado.

Holy Spirit Neighborhood Center. 416 22nd Street, Denver, Colorado 80205. *(303)892-6909.* Our Lady of Victory Missionary Sisters. Sister Rose gives religious education every Sunday.

Marycrest Convent. 2851 West 52nd Street, Denver, Colorado. Extends emergency shelter to Indians.

Part time ministry is given to Indians by Fr. John Q. O'Connell, C.M., St. Thomas Seminary, 1300 South Steele, Denver and Fr. Timothy Sauer of *Risen Christ Church,* 4550 N. Carefree Circle, Colorado Springs, Colorado 89017.

DIOCESE OF PUEBLO
325 West 15th Street, Pueblo, Colorado 81003   *(303)544-9861*
Most Rev. Charles A. Buswell, Bishop

About 520 Catholics. Ab. 1, ib. 20 in 1977.

Towaoc Mission. Ute. Ute Mountain Reservation. Towaoc, Colorado 21334. Cared for from St. Margaret Mary Parish, 28 East Montezuma Avenue, Cortez, Colorado 81321. Fr. John J. Bulger, part time. Library at Towaoc is used. Catholic com. 50 adults and 35 children. Religious education program carried on, part time, by 3 Sisters. 40 East Montezuma, Cortez, Colorado. Sister Patricia Ann Brinker, Director; Sr. M. Margaret Flaherty; Sister Winifred Yeager. Spend 2 days on Reservation weekly. Ms. Hildy Olhtrop, commissioned lay missionary.

St. Ignatius Mission. Ute. Southern Ute Reservation.

P. O. Box 352, Ignacio, Colorado 81137. Fr. Donald Castonguay, SVD. Lay helpers in summer: Sisters Joanne Burrows and Pam Dolah, SC. About 500 Catholics. CCD program: 120 primary, 100 secondary.

IDAHO

DIOCESE OF BOISE
P. O. Box 769, Boise, Idaho 83701   *(208)342-1311*
Most Rev. Sylvester W. Treinen, Bishop

6 churches, 5 priests, 1 sister. Catholics 1,020. Ib. in 1977 - 24.

Sacred Heart Mission. Desmet, Idaho 83824. Fr. Richard R. Macy, S.J.; Fr. Thomas E. Connolly, S.J.; Cornelius Byrne, S.J. Sister Delores Ellwart, S.P.; Ms. Kathleen D'Ascendis and Elizabeth A. Snell, Jesuit Volunteers.

St. Anne's Parish. Kootenai Indian Mission, Bonners Ferry, Idaho 83805.

St. Michael's. Worley, Idaho 83876.

Our Lady of Perpetual Help. Plummer, Idaho 56748.

Sacred Heart Church. Nez Perce and white. Lapwai, Idaho. Fr. Robert J. Waldmann, pastor. Box 157, Lapwai, Idaho 83540.

Fort Hall Mission. Ft. Hall, Idaho. *St. Bernard's Parish,* 584 West Saxton Street, Blackfoot, Idaho 83221. Fr. Philip Canavan, pastor.

KANSAS

ARCHDIOCESE OF KANSAS CITY
P. O. Box 2328, Kansas City, Kansas 64141   *(913)621-4131*
Most Rev. Ignatius J. Strecker, Archbishop

Catholics 300, 1 church, 1 priest, 8 ab. in 1977.

DIOCESE OF WICHITA
424 North Broadway, Wichita, Kansas 67202   *(316)263-6262*
Most Rev. David M. Maloney, Bishop

Catholic Indians 4,673. Ab. in 1977 - 18, ib. 24.

Holy Savior Church. 1425 N. Chautanqua, Wichita, Kansas 67214.

St. Mary's Cathedral. 307 East Central, Wichita, Kansas 67202.

LOUISIANA

DIOCESE OF HOUMA-THIBODAUX
P. O. Box 9077, Houma, Louisiana 70360
Most Rev. Warren L. Boudreaux, Bishop

Catholics 6,420, priests 5, ib. in 1977 - 78.

St. Charles Borromeo. Houma. Pointe Aux Chere. Fr. Antonie Lemire, parish priest. Mem. 800.

Immaculate Conception Mission. Lower Bayou Dularge. Fr. Louis Chaisson, parish priest. Mem. 820.

Our Lady of the Isle. Houma. Grand Isle, Louisiana 70358. Fr. Thomas Hun, parish priest.

Our Lady of LaSalette Mission. Houma. Golden Meadow, Louisiana 70357. Fr. Gerald Masse, MS, parish priest.

Cure D'Ars Mission. Houma. Dulac, Louisiana 70353. Fr. Adrien Caillonet, parish priest. Catholic com. 4,000.

DIOCESE OF LAFAYETTE
P. O. Drawer 3387, Lafayette, Louisiana 70501   *(318)232-5150*
Most Rev. Gerald L. Frey, Bishop

Immaculate Conception Church. Chitimacha. P. O. Box 278, Charenton, Louisiana 70523. James W. Doiron, parish priest. Ind. mem. 55, integrated into the church. (250 Chitimachas live 1 mile east of Charenton on the banks of Bayou Teche.) Ib. in 1977 - 3.

MAINE

DIOCESE OF PORTLAND
510 Ocean Avenue, Portland, Maine 04103   *(207)773-6471*
Most Rev. Edward C. O'Leary, D.D., Bishop
Mr. Steven Cartwright, 95 Maine Street, Orono, Maine 04473,
   Director of Indian Services

Catholic Indians 4,000, priests 3, Brother 1, Sisters 11, lay teachers or aides 23. Ab. in 1977 - 1, ib. 37. 3 elementary schools, 395 pupils.

St. Ann, Indian Island. Penobscott. Fr. Donald Daigle, parish priest. Indian Island, Old Town, Maine 04468.

(207)827-2172. Mem. 250. Elementary school (maintained by the State). Sister Helen McKeough, RSM, Principal; Sister Mary Florence, RSM; Sister Theresa Rand, RSM. Address: Sisters of Mercy, Ann's Convent, Indian Island, Old Town, Maine 04468. *(207)827-4862.*

St. Ann, Peter Dana Point, Indian Township. Passamaquoddy. Fr. Raymond Picard, parish priest. Peter Dana Point, Princeton, Maine 04668. *(207)796-2237. Chapel of St. Theresa.* The Strip. Mem. 400. Elementary school (maintained by the State). Sisters of Charity: Sr. Janet Campbell, Principal; Sr. Ann Marie Kiah; Sr. Carol Letourneau, Sr. Janet Spellman. Pupils 102. Convent, Sr. Ellen Turner, Superior. Peter Dana Point, Princeton, Maine 04668. *(207)796-2359.*

St. Ann, Pleasant Point. Passamaquoddy and Micmac. Fr. Joseph Mullen, S.J., parish priest. Brother Lawrence Smith, S.J. Pleasant Point, Perry, Maine 04667. *(207)853-2934.* Elementary school (maintained by the State). Sisters of Charity: Sr. Anselma Colford, Principal; Sr. Mary Kelley; Sr. Maureen Wallace.

Parishes with part Indian memberships, off the reservations:
  St. Mary of the Visitation. 110 Military Street, Houlton, Maine 04730.
  Church of the Holy Rosary. 31 Thomas Avenue, Caribou, Maine 04736.
  St. Denis. 43 Main Street, Fort Fairfield, Maine 04742.
  St. Louis. 302 Main Street, Limestone, Maine 04750.
  St. Joseph. 262 South Main Street, Old Town, Maine 04468.

Division of Indian Services: Services, advocacy, leadership, social planning, education, interpreting.

Indian Resource Center: responsible for implementation of policies and directions established by Boards of the Diocese and Division of Indian Services.

Produces and publishes *The Wabanaki Alliance Newspaper.*

MASSACHUSSETTS

DIOCESE OF WORCHESTER
49 Elm Street, Worcester, Massachussetts 01609 *(613)791-7171*
Most Rev. Bernard J. Flanagan, Bishop

No churches, 36 Indian Catholics scattered through the Diocese. Ib. 3.

MICHIGAN

DIOCESE OF GAYLORD
P. O. Box 700, Gaylord, Michigan 74935   *(517)732-5147*
Most Rev. Edmond C. Szoka, D.D., Bishop

Catholics 1,950, 2 w. priests, 18 w. Sisters. Ab. 4, ib. 43.
1,000 non-reservation Catholic Indians in 21 counties.

Diocesan Indian Apostalate. Fr. James Gardner, Director.
P. O. Box 59, Suttons Bay, Michigan 49682. Fr. John B.
Tupper, Associate Director. 202 E. Sherman, Whittemore,
Michigan 48770. 5 other priests, 3 pastors and 2
associates, minister to the Indian people of this extended
parish.

Immaculate Conception Church. Ottawa. Peshabestown. c/o
P. O. Box 59, Sutton's Bay, Michigan 49682. Ind. congrega-
tion. Fr. James Gardiner, parish priest. 200 mem.
Peshabestown Center.

Holy Childhood Church. Partially Indian. 150 West Main
Street, Harbor Springs, Michigan 49740. *Holy Childhood
Indian Boarding School.* School Sisters of Notre Dame:
Sr. Helen Setterston, Principal. 11 other Sisters.

Holy Cross Church. Lake Shore Drive, Cross Village,
Michigan 49723. Ind. congregation. Fr. George Phillips.
Mem. 10.

St. Mary Church. P. O. Pellstown, Burt Lake, Michigan
49717. Partial.

St. Ignatius. Middle Village, c/o Cross Village, Michigan
49723. Partial.

Nishnabe Danawing Summer Camp. c/o Immaculate Conception
Church, 720 West 2nd Street, Traverse City, Michigan 49684.

Diocesan Indian Youth Apostalate. c/o Peshabestown Center.
Sister Marjorie Redmond, RSM, Director. Route 1, Box 125,
Sutton's Bay, Michigan 49682.

DIOCESE OF MARQUETTE
P. O. Box 550, Marquette, Michigan 49855   *(906)225-1141*
Most Rev. Charles A. Salatka, Bishop

Catholic Indians 4,620, churches 10, priests 5, Sisters 11.
Ab. in 1977 - 6, ib. 70.

St. Isaac Joques, Sault Ste Marie. Fr. Joseph Lawless, S.J.
pastor and missionary. Fr. Michael Steltenkamp, Associate
pastor. Mem. 400. Summer religious education. 7 Sisters
part time, 6 lay workers. 195 participants, 155 Ind.
Religious education during school year: 6 Sisters, 10 lay
persons, 150 Ind.

St. Catherine, Bay Mills, Brinley, Michigan 49715.

Sacred Heart, Sugar Island, Sault Ste Marie.

St. Catherine. Zeba, L'Anse, Michigan 49946. Fr. Elmer
Staffel, OFM Cap., pastor. Clothes House, 2 lay persons.
25 Ind.

Holy Name of Jesus. Assinins, Baraga, Michigan 49908. Fr.
John Haskall, OFM Cap. Pastor of Assinins Mission and
Western Upper Peninsula Missions. 1 Sister. Religious
education program. Ind. language and culture programs.
450 Ind.

St. Kateri. Hannahville Reservation. Hannahville,
Michigan. Fr. Francis Dobrzenski, pastor, part time. St.
Patrick's, Escanaba, Michigan 49829. About 40 attendance.
106 baptized Catholics. Sister Martha Napier, O.P.,
catechist and pastoral assistance. Sister Doris Prybilla,
C.S.P.S., catechist and pastoral assistant. Box 131,
Harris, Michigan 49845. 120 Ind. in catechetical and Ind.
Cultural Programs.

Immaculate Conception. Watersmeet Indian Mission. Watersmeet, Michigan 49969. Religious education program:
Sisters Joyce Rybarczyk and Gretchan Greening, O.P.

Partially Indian parishes:
  St. George. Bark River, Michigan 49807.
  Sacred Heart. L'Anse, Michigan 49946.
  St. Ann. Baraga, Michigan 49908.

DIOCESE OF SAGINAW
2555 Wienecke Road, Saginaw, Michigan 48603   *(517)799-7910*
Most Rev. Francis F. Reh, Bishop

Catholics 200-300 out of 2,316 Ind. No Ind. churches or
schools. 20 Ind. children attend 8 Catholic parochial
schools in 1975-76. A grant of $4,875 from the Committee on
Human Development was given to the Mt. Pleasant Chippewa
Reservation for a self-help program.

MINNESOTA

DIOCESE OF CROOKSTON
P. O. Box 610, Crookston, Minnesota 56716   *(218)281-4533*
Most Rev. Victor H. Balke, Ph.D., D.D., Bishop

Catholic com. 3,087, priests 5, Sisters 17, Brothers 3. Ab. 1, ib. 66.

INSTITUTES AND CONGREGATIONS

Benedictines of Collegeville, Minnesota 56321. Abbot John Eidenslunk, OSB. Pastoral ministry.

Benedictines of St. Joseph, Minnesota 56374. Mother Evin Rademacher, OSB. Education.

St. Mary's Mission. Chippewa. Red Lake Reservation. Red Lake, Minnesota 56671. Fr. Patrick Okasa, OSB, pastor. Brothers Julius Boechermann and Gabriel. Sr. Jane Weber, parish ministry. Sr. Delphine Heier. Sr. Lucy Revering, Sr. Dorothea Lez. Baptized com. 3,700. Ib. in 1977 - 1.

St. Mary's Mission School. Red Lake, Minnesota 56671. Sr. Elizabeth Theis, Principal. Teachers: Srs. Marlene Schwinghammer, Marcella Weber, Dominica Freund. Sr. Constette, Secretary. Sr. Caroline Eckroth, Librarian and Special Education. Sr. Kayleen Nehner, Religious Education. Sr. Loretta Rothskin, store. Sr. Barbara Zinner, Title I teacher. 2 w. men teachers, 4 Ind. women aides. Students: 142 Ind. children (66 boys, 76 girls), 2 others. The School is cooperatively maintained by the Diocese, St. John's Abbey and St. Benedict's Convent.

St. Benedict's Mission. Chippewa. White Earth Reservation. White Earth, Minnesota 50591. Fr. Robert Wieber, OSB, pastor. Fr. Ignatius Candrian, OSB, assistant pastor. Sisters 4, catechists 15. Members: Ind. 345, w. 196. 2 chapels. 1 ab., 20 ib. CCD. Teachers: Srs. Ruth Ann Schneider, Delise Bialke, Mary Dengel, Ansger Willenbring, OSB, Brother Gabriel, OSB.

St. Francis Cabrini Church. Big Elbow Lake, 20 Ind., 23 w. *Most Holy Redeemer Church.* Ogena. 24 Ind., 428 w. *St. Theodore's.* Ponsford. Fr. Alto Butkowski, pastor. 319 Ind., 119 w. CCD program. 2 Sisters.

Tri-parish Religious Education Center. St. Benedict's, White Earth. 4 Sisters, 15 lay workers including 3 Ind.

St. Anne's Church. Naytahwaush, Minnesota 56566. Fr. Jordan Stovik, OSB, pastor. St. Joseph's Church, Route 2, Mohnomen, Minnesota 50557. Mem. 200. CCD program: 1 Sister, 1 w. lay person, 1 Ind. lay person.

DIOCESE OF DULUTH
215 West 4th Street, Duluth, Minnesota 55806   *(218)727-6861*
Most Rev. Paul F. Anderson, Bishop

Churches 16, Catholics 4,239, priests 5, Sisters 8, 49 ib.

Holy Cross Church. Partial. P. O. Box 218, Orr, Minnesota 55771. Fr. Thomas Hitpas, OMI, pastor. Sr. Yvonne Campbell, OSB. Sr. Theresa OPR.

St. Joseph's. Buyck, Minnesota 55771.
Our Lady of Fatima. Kinmount, Minnesota.

Immaculate Conception. Nett Lake, Minnesota 55772. Fr. Thomas Hitpas, OMI, pastor.

Vermillion Reservation. Tower, Minnesota 55790. 2 OMI novices for 2 months each year. Weekly Eucharist, 25 Ind.; released time catechetics 45. Enrichment program for children in Advent and Lent 40. Summer recreation program 40.

St. Joseph Church. Box 61, Ball Club, Minnesota 56622. 2 Missions.

St. Anne's. Bena, Minnesota 56626.
Sacred Heart. Federal Dam, Minnesota 56641.

St. John's. P. O. Box 548, Grand Marais, Minnesota 55604. Fr. Henry Anderl, OSB. Summer School: 2 Sisters.

Holy Rosary. Grand Portage, Minnesota 55605.

St. Charles Church. Partial. 308 Central Avenue, Cass Lake, Minnesota 56633. Fr. R. H. Growbowski, pastor. Religious education program: 6 lay women teachers, once a week, 35 Ind. Fr. Jude Koll, OSB, St. John's Abbey, Collegeville, summer ministry.

Holy Family Church. 280 Reservation Road, Cloquet, Minnesota 55720. Fr. Alban Furth, OSB, pastor. 108 families, 462 souls. Catechetical summer school: Sr. Agnines Coleman, OSB; Sr. Marceline Neeser, OSB; Sr. Mary Jo LaDuk.

SS Mary and Joseph. Sawyer, Minnesota 55780. 85 families, 318 souls.

St. Patrick's. Brookston, Minnesota 55711. 35 families, 120 souls.

St. Catherine's. Partial. Squaw Lake, Minnesota. Fr. Vincent Fitzgerald, OMI, pastor. Sr. Ethel Radthke, OSB, volunteer. St. Cathern's Motor Cahpel. *Kateri Alcohol Center.* Alcoholics counseling, weekly A.A.

St. Charles Church. Pennington, Minnesota 56603.

Office of Social Concern. 215 West 4th Street, Duluth, Minnesota 55806. Contributes to Duluth Indian Action Council towards matching grant.

DIOCESE OF ST. CLOUD
214 Third Avenue, S., St. Cloud, Minnesota 56301
Most Rev. George H. Speltz, D.D., Bishop   *(612)251-2340*

Church 1, priest 1, Sisters 3, catechists: 1 Ind. 2 w. 1 conv. in 1976. Ib. 9.

Congregation of Women: Order of St. Benedict. Mother Evin Rademacher, Convent of St. Benedict, St. Joseph, Minnesota 56374.

Little Flower Mission. Chippewa. Mille Lacs Reservation. Star Route, Onamia, Minnesota 56359. Fr. William Straka, OSC, pastor. OSB Sisters: George, M. Phyllis, M. Alphonse, teachers and pastoral workers. Released time and other religious education. Emergency assistance, good neighbor ministry.

Church of St. Therese of Vineland. Chippewa. 50 communicants. 80 Ind. Catholics. 3 ib.

Holy Cross Church. Onamia. Partial.

ARCHDIOCESE OF SAINT PAUL AND MINNEAPOLIS
226 Summit Avenue, St. Paul, Minnesota 55102   *(916)222-1745*
Most Rev. John R. Roach, Archbishop
Rev. Theodore F. Zuern, S.J., Office of Ministry to Native Americans, 2424 18th Avenue, S., Minneapolis, Minnesota 55404.

The office of Ministry to Native Americans was inaugurated in January 1975. It is developing a staff and program of ministries to the 4,000-5,000 Catholic Indians and others of the approximately 15,000 urban Indians in the Twin Cities.

Churches ministering to Indians 3, estimated Catholic Ind.
4,500, priests 6, Deacon 1, Sisters 12, Brothers 3. Ab. in
1977 - 7, ib. 31.

Ascension Church. Partial. 1723 Bryant Avenue, N.,
Minneapolis, Minnesota 55403. Msgr. William Coates, pastor.
Teachers: Srs. Darlene Daley, Sylvia Krawfeyk, Mary Helen,
Caroline Ciatti, Eleta.

St. Stephen's Church. Partial. 2211 Clinton Avenue, S.,
Minneapolis, Minnesota 55404. Fr. Edward Flahavan, pastor.
Fr. Greg Welsh, assistant pastor. Fr. Steve Levi,
assistant pastor.
St. Stephen's School: Sr. Jean Funk, Principal. Teachers:
Srs. Jackie Lawson, Carol Ann Richter, Margaret Brown. 8
lay teachers. 2123 Clinton Avenue, S., Minneapolis,
Minnesota 55404. 38% of pupils or 64 are Ind.
St. Stephen's Guild Hall: 1 Sister, 5 lay workers.
Chemical Dependency and Senior Citizens, participants 2,000,
Ind. 1,500.
St. Stephen's Parish Senior Citizens: 1 Sister, 2 lay
persons. Participants 500, Ind. 100.

Holy Rosary Church. 2424 18th Avenue, S., Minneapolis,
Minnesota 55404. Fr. David Staszak, O.P., pastor. Fr. John
Schwind, O.P., assistant pastor. Sr. Theresa Zorn, Liaison
person, the parish and South High community. John Spears,
Deacon.
Holy Rosary School: 2430 18th Avenue, S., Minneapolis,
Minnesota 55404. Sr. Kathleen Hayes, Principal. Sisters 6,
lay teachers 5. Pupils 160, Ind. 95.
Holy Rosary Social Program: 1 Sister. 100 Ind. and
families.
Day Education Workshop: 3 Sisters, 6 lay persons. 25 Ind.

Kateri Prayer Group. 2424 18th Avenue, S., Minneapolis,
Minnesota 55404. 1 Sister. 30 Ind.

Ascension Church. 1726 Dupont Avenue, N., Minneapolis,
Minnesota 55411. 6 Sisters, 12 lay persons. 30 Ind.

Catholic Charities, Branch I. Neighborhood Social Service
Center, 1308 East Franklin, Minneapolis, Minnesota 55404.
Staff: Sr. Joan Connors, 6 lay persons. 7,000 Ind.
participate.

Catholic Charities, Branch II. Neighborhood Social Services
Center, 901 Hennepin Avenue, Minneapolis, Minnesota 55414.

Staff: 15 lay persons. 1,500 Ind. participate.

De La Salle High School. 25 West Island Avenue,
Minneapolis, Minnesota 55401. Teachers: 6 religious, 24
lay persons. Ind. 18.

Assignment of 3 Brothers and 3 Sisters is not clear.

MISSISSIPPI

DIOCESE OF NATCHEZ-JACKSON
P. O. Box 2248, Jackson, Mississippi 39205   *(601)948-6553*
Most Rev. Joseph B. Brunini, Bishop

Catholics in 1976 - 1,020. 3 churches, 2 priests, 3 ab., 15
ib.

MISSOURI

ARCHDIOCESE OF SAINT LOUIS
4445 Lindell Blvd., St. Louis, Missouri 63108   *(314)533-1887*
His Eminence John Cardinal Carberry, Archbishop

Catholic Indians are estimated at 4,000 to 5,000. There are
no Ind. churches.

Msgr. John A. Shocklee is the responsible officer for Indian
matters, at Chancery office. He is the Liaison person with
the 8 member Indian Pow-Wow Committee. This Committee and
the Mid-American Indian Cultural Center refer needy cases to
him.

MONTANA

DIOCESE OF GREAT FALLS
P. O. Box 1399, Great Falls, Montana 59403   *(406)453-9389*
Most Rev. Eldon B. Schuster, Bishop

Churches 19. Catholics 7,500, priests 15, Sisters 30+,
Brothers 2+. Conv. in 1977 - 17. Ab. in 1977 - 25, ib. 225.
Reservations of Ft. Peck, Ft. Belknap, Rocky Boy.

St. Paul's Mission. Hays, Montana 59527. 1 church, 1
chapel, 2 stations. Fr. Joseph Ritzel, pastor. Fr. E. F.
Simonean, co-pastor. 5 Franciscan Sisters, 2 Dominicans, 1
Jesuit Brother. Lay workers 5. Parish mem. 1,000. Conv.
in 1977 - 2. *Primary School:* 63 pupils.

St. Thomas Church. Lodge Pole.

St. Joseph's. Zortman, Montana 59546.

Sacred Hearth Church. (east of) Harlem, Montana 59526. Fr. Howard Moran, S.J., pastor.

Saint Labre Indian Mission. Cheyenne. Ashland, Montana 59003. Fr. Ronald Smith, OFM Cap., Superior and Director of the Mission. Fr. Paul Reichling, OFM Cap., co-pastor. Fr. Reynold Rynda, co-pastor. Parish mem. 850. Conv. 2.

Saint Labre Indian School. Ashland, Montana 59003. Ray Streater, Superintendent; Fred Mestel, Principal. School Sisters of St. Francis (Rochester) 14. Lay staff 85. Primary pupils 350. High School students 296.

Saint Labre Indian School Association, Inc. Ashland, Montana 59004. Fr. Ronald Smith, OFM Cap., Director. North Cheyenne and Crow Reservations. Staff: 30 priests, Brothers, Sisters. 1 Catholic primary school 60. Religious work with 2 community primary schools, 370 pupils. 1 community High School, 200 students.

Sacred Heart Church. Cheyenne. Birney, Montana 59012.

St. Charles Mission Church. Crow. Pryor, Montana 59066. Fr. Randolph Graczyk, pastor. 4 religious, 3 lay workers. Parish mem. 350. Conv. 4.

Primary School: 58 pupils.

St. Xavier Mission Church. Crow. Pryor, Montana 59066. Fr. Larry Abler, OFM Cap., pastor.

Our Lady of Loretto Church. Crow. Lodge Grass, Montana 59050. Team of Sisters.

Kathryn Tequawitha Church. Crow. Wyola, Montana 59089. Mission of Lodge Grass.

St. Dennis Church. Crow. Crow Agency, Montana 59022. Fr. Raymond Kopka, OFM Cap., pastor.

Our Lady of Lourdes Church. Assiniboine and Sioux. Fort Peck Reservation. Poplar, Montana 59255. Fr. Dick Schlosser, pastor.

St. Thomas. Assiniboine and Sioux. Fort Peck Reservation. Brokton, Montana 59213. Fr. Dick Schlosser, pastor.

St. Anne Church. Assiniboine/Sioux. Fort Peck Reservation. Chelsea, Montana.

Immaculate Conception Church. White/Assiniboine/Sioux. Not a reservation. P. O. Box 789, Wolf Point, Montana 59201. Fr. James Reynolds, pastor. 2 Sisters, 47 lay helpers.

St. Joseph Church. Frazer, Montana 59225. (west side of Ft. Peck Reservation) Confirmed parish mem. 1,268 including 300 Indians at Wolf Point and 20 at Frazer. Conv. 5.

Schools: Confraternity of Christian Doctrine. Pre-school through 8th grade - 225; grades 9 through 12 - 80.

St. Anthony and St. Mary. Rocky Boy Reservation. Box Elder, Montana 59521.

St. Margaret Mary. Big Sandy, Montana 59520. Fr. Peter E. Guthneck.

Blessed Sacrament Church. Cheyenne. Lame Deer, Montana 59043. Fr. Pascal Silver, OFM Cap. Brother Tomkro. 2 Sisters. Mem. 150 active, 400 inactive. Conv. 4.

Christ the King Church. Cheyenne. Busby, Montana 59016.

Religious Research Center, Inc. Ashland, Montana 59003. Fr. Gilbert Hemauer, OFM Cap., President and Director.

DIOCESE OF HELENA
P. O. Box 1729, Helena, Montana 59601   *(406)442-5820*
Most Rev. Elden F. Curtiss, Bishop

Churches 8. Catholic Indains about 7,200, priests 7, Sisters 5. Ab. in 1977 - 3, ib. 200.

St. Ignatius. 1854. Flathead Reservation. St. Ignatius, Montana 59865. *(406)745-2768.* Co-pastors: Frs. Job Obersinner, S.J.; Edmund Robinson, S.J.; Joseph E. Shiney, S.J. Fr. Ignatius Dumbeck, S.J., hospital ministry. Ursuline Sisters Pat Funderheide, Mary Dostol and K. C. Young do religious education and parish visitation on the Flathead Reservation.

St. Anne's Church. Heart Butte, Montana 59448. *(406)338-3412.* Fr. Egon E. Mollman, pastor.

Little Flower Mission. Blackfoot. Browning, Montana 59417. Frs. Steven Tallman and John Murray, co-pastors.

Sister Kevin Marie Flynn, SCL and Sister Teresa Klepoc, SCL, parish visitation and religious education.

Queen of the Universe Church. Partial. Babb, Montana 59411.

St. John Birchmans. Jocko, Montana.

Sacred Heart Church. Starr School, Montana.

Sacred Heart Church. Arlee, Montana 59821.

Holy Family Mission. Holy Family, Montana.

NEBRASKA

ARCHDIOCESE OF OMAHA
100 North 62nd Street, Omaha, Nebraska 68132   *(402)558-3100*
Most Rev. Daniel E. Sheehan, Archbishop

Churches 2. Catholics 407, priests 2, Sisters 3, ib. 101.

St. Augustine's Indian Mission. Winnebago and Omaha. Winnebago, Nebraska 68071. Churches 1, chapels 1, stations 1. Msgr. Francis J. Hulsman, Director. Fr. Michael Malone, OSB, associate Director. 3 Missionary Benedictine Sisters. Lay helpers 7. Total com. 280. Conv. in 1977 - 2. Ib. 31. *Primary School:* 101 pupils.

NEVADA

DIOCESE OF RENO-LAS VEGAS
515 Court Street, Reno, Nevada 89501   *(702)392-9274*
Most Rev. Norman F. McFarland, Bishop

Churches 1. Catholic Indians about 400, ib. in 1977 - 2.

Corpus Christi Church. Predominantly Indian. P. O. Box 12, Stewart, Nevada 89437. About 100 Ind. mem. Bernard Sheerin, S.J., pastor. Sisters: 1 full time, 2 part time.

Catholic Student Chaplaincy. Stewart Indian School, Stewart, Nevada 89437. Fr. Bernard Sheerin, S.J., chaplain. Sister Ellen Jordan, SDSH. CCD classes. Sister Marlene Brochu, SDSH. CCD classes.

Franciscan Center. P. O. Box 7339, Las Vegas, Nevada 89101. Fr. Louis Vitale, OFM, Director. 1420 West Bartlett Avenue, Las Vegas, Nevada 89106. Sr. Evelyn Montez, OP, community action.

St. John's Church. P. O. Box 493, Overton, Nevada 89040.
Fr. Edward Fronske, OFM, part time. Indian ministry.

Indian mem. in w. churches: St. Theresa, Reno 6; Holy
Cross, Sparks 20; St. Joseph, Elko 12; St. Patrick, Tonopah
21; St. Paul, Winnemucca 6; St. James, Las Vegas 11, St.
John, Overton 5.

NEW HAMPSHIRE

DIOCESE OF MANCHESTER
135 Ash Street, Manchester, New Hampshire 03104 *(603)669-3100*
Most Rev. Odore J. Gendron, Bishop

Catholic Indians about 100.

NEW MEXICO

DIOCESE OF GALLUP
P. O. Box 1338, Gallup, New Mexico 87301   *(505)863-5083*
Most Rev. Jerome J. Hastrich, D.D., Bishop

Churches in N.M. 46. Indian Catholics 12,060, priests 31,
Sisters 21, Brothers, Permanant Deacons. Ab. in 1977 - 256,
ib. 481. See ARIZONA for 54 churches.

DIOCESAN INSTITUTIONS AND SERVICES

Vocations Office. Primary purpose is to promote Native
vocations.

Apostolic Formation Program. Purpose is to promote Native
vocations as well as to serve those who come from outside,
providing the distinctive training for which the unique
nature of the Diocese calls.

Cristo Rey Seminary. High School and College Divisions.
205 East Wilson Avenue, Gallup, New Mexico 87301. For male
students. For girls: *Casa Reina.* 217 East Wilson Avenue,
Gallup, New Mexico 87301.

Brothers of Our Lady of Guadalupe. 500 South Woodrow Drive,
Gallup, New Mexico 87301. A diocesan brotherhood for team
ministry with Diocesan missionary priests.

Permanent Diaconate Program. Cristo Rey Seminary, Diaconate
Division, 415 East Green Avenue, Gallup, New Mexico 87301.
4 year course, one weekend a month for nine months of the
year.

Southwest Volunteer Apostolate. P. O. Box 626, Gallup, New Mexico 87301. Out of 300 applicants 60 persons are approved for summer service and 25 for year round service.

CURSILLOS/SEARCH. CURSILLO Office - 415 East Green Avenue, Gallup, New Mexico 87301. SEARCH Office - P. O. Box 309, St. John's Arizona 85936.

Stephanites. A Semi-contemplative community, with the status of a Pious Union, for working among Navajo Indians. Priests and Brothers. Mother House at Crownpoint, New Mexico 87313.

INSTITUTES AND CONGREGATIONS with missionaries in the Diocese

Franciscans. St. John the Baptist Province. Very Rev. Andrew Fox, OFM, Provincial. 1615 Vine Street, Cincinnati, Ohio 45210. Pastoral work and evangelization.

Franciscans. St. Barbara Province. Oakland, California. Pastoral work and evangelization.

Dominicans.

Holy Ghost Fathers.

Society of Jesus.

Women's Congregations minister in teaching, nursing, social work and parish visiting.

Maryknoll Sisters. Maryknoll, New York 10545.

Sisters of St. Francis. Colorado Springs, Colorado.

Sisters of St. Francis. Amarillo, Texas

Sisters of the Blessed Sacrament. Cornwells Heights, Pennsylvania 19020.

Dominican Sisters. Brighton, Massachusetts.

Franciscan Missionaries of Mary. New York City, New York.

Franciscan Sisters of the Poor. Brooklyn, New York.

Ursuline Sisters. Maple Mount, Kentucky.

Acoma Indian Missions. Acoma (Pueblo). *San Esteban.* P. O. Box 116, San Fidel, New Mexico 87049. Fr. Sean Murnan, OFM, pastor. *(505)522-6236.* Ursuline Sisters 2. Most of 3,000 parishioners baptized.
Missions: *St. Anne Acomita, Santa Maria de Acoma, McCartys.*

Laguna. Laguna Pueblo. *St. Joseph.* P. O. Box 21, New Laguna, New Mexico 87038. Frs. Maurus Pax, OFM; Kilian Huber, OFM; Mathias Crehan, OFM. *(505)552-9429.* Sisters of the Blessed Sacrament 4. Sr. Beatrice Maria, Directress.
Missions: *Encinal, Mescita, Paquote, Parase, Seama.*

Zuni. Zuni Pueblo. *St. Anthony.* 1922. P. O. Box 486, Zuni, New Mexico 87327. Fr. Meldon Hickey, OFM; Donald Miller, OFM. *(505)782-4477.* 1 Brother. *St. Anthony Mission School.* K - 8th grade. Sisters of St. Francis of Perpetual Adoration 4. Lay teachers 9. 1 Ind. man, 10 Zuni aides. Pupils 252. Old church, *Our Lady of Guadalupe.* 1629.

Christ the King Church. Navajo. P. O. Box 610, Shiprock, New Mexico 87420. Fr. Adam Wethington, OFM. Fr. Bart Pax, OFM. *(505)368-4532.*
Stations: In New Mexico - *Sanastee, Todalena, Nava.* In Arizona - *Red Rock, Cove, Teec Nos Pos.*

Sacred Heart. Navajo. Star Route, Box 10, Waterflow, New Mexico 87421. *(505)598-5454.* Fr. Clemintin Wottle, OFM.
Station: *Fruitland,* New Mexico 87416.

St. Bernard. Navajo. P. O. Box 123, Navajo, New Mexico 87328. Fr. Niles Kraft, OFM. 2 Sisters. 2 lay helpers. Parish mem. 100.

St. Eleanor. Navajo. Fort Wingate, New Mexico 87316.

St. Francis. Partial. P. O. Box 940, Gallup, New Mexico 87301.

St. Francis of Assisi. Partial. P. O. Box 68, Lumberton, New Mexico 87547. *(505)759-3300.* Fr. Donan Herbe, OFM. School: Poor Sisters of St. Francis Seraph of the Perpetual Adoration 2. Lay teachers 5. Pupils 95.

St. Hubert. P. O. Box 156, Gallup, New Mexico 87301.

St. Jerome. P. O. Box 1760, Gallup, New Mexico 87301.

St. Joseph. Partial. Box 7, San Fidel, New Mexico 87049.

(505)552-6236. Fr. Cecil J. Kleber, OFM. *School:* Ursuline Sisters 3. Lay teacher 1. Pupils 92.
Mission: *Our Lady of Light.* Cubero, New Mexico 87014.

St. Mary. Navajo. Box 39, Tohatchi, New Mexico 87321. *(505)733-2243.* Fr. Cormac Antram, OFM; Daniel Wefer, OFM. Mission: *Naschitti.*
Stations: *Coyote Canyon, Mexican Springs, Twin Lakes, Sheep Springs, Chuska.*

St. Paul. Navajo and w. P. O. Box 268, Crownpoint, New Mexico 87313. Fr. Albert Pinheiro, OFM. 3 Maryknoll Sisters.

St. Philip. Navajo. Church Rock, New Mexico 87311. *(505)863-4073.*

St. Valerian. 506 West 66th Street, Gallup, New Mexico 87301.

St. William. Box 64, Gallup, New Mexico 87301.

Sacred Heart. Navajo. Farmington, New Mexico 87401. OFM Frs. Kenneth Robertson, Theophil Meyer, Conran Runnebaum. 414 North Allen Avenue, Farmington, New Mexico 87401. *(505)325-9743. School:* Ursuline Sisters. Sister Charles Marie, Supr. 6 Sisters. 6 lay teachers. Pupils 265.

Santo Nino. Aragon, Catron County. Fr. Ismael Manero, OFM. P. O. Box 493, Reserve, New Mexico 87830. *(505)533-6240.*
Missions: *Reserve, Lower San Francisco, Horse Spring.*
Stations: *Apache Creek, Cruzville.*

Saint Joseph. 500 North Mesa Verde Street, Aztec, San Juan County, New Mexico 87410. *(505)334-6535.* Fr. Gregg Petri, OFM.

St. Rose. Navajo. P. O. Box 417, Blanco, San Juan County, New Mexico 87412. *(505)632-2064.* Fr. Myron Uhl, OFM.
Mission: *Navajo Dam.*

St. Mary. Navajo. P. O. Box 669, Bloomfield, New Mexico 87413. *(505)632-2014.* Fr. Gerard H. Geiger, OFM.

St. Hubert Indian Mission. Chickitah, McKinley County. Msgr. Arthur McDonald, Administrator. P. O. Box 156, Gallup, New Mexico 87301. 2 Maryknoll Sisters.

St. Bonaventure Mission. Navajo. P. O. Box 610, Thoreau, New Mexico 87323. Fr. Douglas A. McNeill. 1 Sister.

4 lay helpers. Conv. 5. Churches 2, stations 1.

ARIZONA PORTION OF GALLUP DIOCESE: See under Arizona

Churches at Chinle, Kayenta, Ft. Defiance, Pinon, Ganado, Cibecue, Lukachukai, Keams Canyon, Tuba City, Houck and St. Michael's - all Navajo and an Apache Mission at Whiteriver. Major schools at St. Michael's.

ARCHDIOCESE OF SANTA FE
202 Morningside Drive, S.E., Albuquerque, New Mexico 87108
Most Rev. Robert F. Sanchez, Archbishop   *(505)268-4572*

Churches 25. Catholic Indians 17,700, priests 12, Sisters 37. Ab. in 1977 - 11, ib. 370.

Sandia Pueblo. Fr. Manuel Alvarez, pastor.

Nambe Pueblo. Fr. John Rodriquez, pastor. Pojoaque, New Mexico 87501.

San Juan Pueblo. Fr. Albert Povin, pastor. San Juan Pueblo, New Mexico 87566.

Picuris Pueblo. Fr. George Weisenborn, Penasco, New Mexico 85753.

Isleta Pueblo. Fr. James Banke, pastor. Isleta Pueblo, New Mexico 87022. Religious education program: 4 Sisters, 6 lay teachers, 200 participants, 2,000 baptized and not joined Protestant churches.

San Diego Mission, Jemez Pueblo. Fr. Emeric Nordmeyer, pastor. Fr. Victorian Bachus, OFM, assistant pastor. Brother Kenneth Beetz, catechist. Jemez Pueblo, New Mexico 87024. *(505)834-7300.* 2 priests, 2 Brothers, 7 Sisters (catechists), 2 lay teachaers, 12 teacher aides. Parish mem. 3,000 Ind., 1,500 Spanish. Churches 7, chapel 1.

> *San Diego Mission School.* Sr. Alberta Wieser, Principal. Day School, grades K - 8. Administrative staff 2. Teachers: 2 w. men, 1 Ind. woman, 9 Ind. aides. Students: 83 Ind. boys, 82 Ind. girls.

Santo Domingo Pueblo. Santo Domingo Pueblo, New Mexico 87052.

Zia Pueblo.

Santa Felipe Pueblo.

Santa Anna Pueblo.

Taos Pueblo. Fr. Luis Jaramillo, pastor. Fr. Michael Thull, assistant pastor. Sr. Margaritta McGrath, catechist. P. O. Box 8888, Taos, New Mexico 87571. Mem. about 1,000.

San Juan Pueblo. San Juan Pueblo, New Mexico 87566.

Cochiti Pueblo. Pena Blanca, New Mexico 87041.

Santa Clara Pueblo.

San Ildenfonso Pueblo.

Tesuque Pueblo. Tesuque, New Mexico 87574.

Pena Blanca Missions. P. O. Box 1248, Pena Blanca, New Mexico 87041. Frs. Chrysostom Partee, OFM and Killian Huber, OFM, co-pastors. SBS Sisters Mary Frances, Benita, Conradine and Marguerite, catechists. 3 lay helpers. 300 participants.

Queen of Angels Chapel. Albuquerque Indian School, P. O. Box 12137, Indian School Road, Albuquerque, New Mexico 87105. Fr. John Uhl, OFM, Director. 1 Permanent Deacon. Religious education program: 175 participants.

Cathedral Missions. Fr. Larry Dunham, OFM, pastor. Srs. Florence Marie Young, SBS and Mary Delorenz, SBS, catechists. Brother Dennis Huff, OMS, catechist. P. O. Box 1883, Santa Fe, New Mexico 87501.

St. Catherine Indian School. P. O. Box 1883, Santa Fe, New Mexico 87501. *(505)982-1889.* Sr. Katherine, Director. Grades 7-12. Sisters 17. Day school 32; boarding school 206. Boys 108, girls 98, all Indian.

The general belief has been that Gallup Diocese has the largest number of Catholic Indians, but the Archdiocese of Santa Fe has reported more. All Pueblo Indians are baptized in infancy, but few become active Catholics.

NEW YORK

DIOCESE OF OGDENSBURG
624 Washington Street, Ogdensburg, New York 13369
Most Rev. Stanislans J. Brzana, S.T.D., Bishop *(315)393-2920*

Church 1, chapel 1. Catholics 5,100 (850 families). Report was 2,000 in 1976. 1 Ind. priest, 1 w. priest. 2 w. Brothers.

Sisters: 3 full time, 3 part time. Ib. in 1977 - 113.

St. Regis Indian Mission. P. O. Box 327, Hogansburg, New York 13655.

Kateri Tekawitha Center. Fr. Michael Jacobs, S.J. and Fr. Gordon B. Bazinet, S.J., (Ind.), co-pastors. Brother Eustache Savard, S.J., Brother Bertrand Girard, S.J., Atonement Sisters Benidicta McWeeney and Margaret M. O'Rourke, catechetics.

Cornwall Island School. Sr. Kateri Mitchell, SSA. 3 SSJ Srs. of Ogdensburg, New York engage part time in adult education and social work, also a priest from Pottsdam, New York.

NORTH DAKOTA

DIOCESE OF BISMARCK
P. O. Box 1575, Bismarck, North Dakota 58501   *(701)223-1237*
Most Rev. Hilary B. Hacker, Bishop

Churches 8, Catholics 3,491, priests 3, Sisters 7. Ab. in 1977 - 3, ib. 129.

Benedictine Fathers of Conception Abbey, Conception, Missouri 64433.

St. Peter. Sioux. Standing Rock Reservation. Ft. Yates, North Dakota 58538. Fr. David Clements, OSB, pastor. Fr. Adrian Mundt, OSB. 4 chapels. 2,000 Catholics under care. 72 ib. Brother Mark Kosiba, OSB.

St. Bernard Mission School. P. O. Box 394, Ft. Yates, North Dakota 38538. *(701)854-7430.* Sr. Marilyn Heck, OSB, Principal. Teachers: 4 Benedictine Sisters, 1 Sister of Providence. 4 Ind. teacher's aides. Enrollment total 106, Ind. 85. CCD program.

St. James. Porcupine.

St. Elizabeth. Cannonball, North Dakota 58528. Vacation religious school 28.

Assumption. Kenel. Vacation religious school 42.

St. Anthony. Mixed. Mandoree, North Dakota 58757. Fr. Stephen Kranz, OSB, pastor. Brother Bernard Vogel, OSB, teacher. Parish mem. 449, under care 1,070, also w. 52. Ib. 32. Summer camp: 100 Ind., 9 w.

Sacred Heart, Whiteshield. Fr. Terrence Carroll, OSB, pastor. CCD program. Sr. Mary John Majusiak, OSB, Sr. Jean Warner, OSB, CCD teaching.

St. Joseph. Twin Buttes. CCD program.

St. John. Trenton, North Dakota 58853. CCD program.

DIOCESE OF FARGO
1310 Broadway, Fargo, North Dakota 58102   *(701)235-6429*
Most Rev. Justin A. Driscoll, Bishop

Churches 14. Catholic Indians 16,131, priests 11, Sisters 32. Ab. in 1977 - 18, ib. 403.

Institute of Men: Order of St. Benedict. Blue Cloud Abbey, Marvin, South Dakota 57251.

Immaculate Heart of Mary Mission and St. Louis Church. Dunseith, North Dakota 58329. Fr. Joseph Zimmer, SAC. 6 religious, 3 lay helpers. Parish mem. 1,590.

St. Anne's Indian Mission. Belcourt, North Dakota 58316. Fr. George Lyon, OSB. Fr. Benno Fellinger, OSB. Fr. John McMullen, OSB. 9 religious, 7 lay workers. Parish mem. 12,000.
    Missions: *St. Anthony, St. Benedict.*

Seven Dolors Indian Mission. Ft. Totten, North Dakota 58335. Fr. Dennis Quinkart, OSB. 4 religious, 2 lay workers. Parish mem. 1,000.

St. Jerome's Indian Mission of Crow Hill. Ft. Totten, North Dakota 58335. 1 religious, 2 lay helpers. Parish mem. 137.

St. Michael's Mission. St. Michael, North Dakota 58370. Fr. Wilfred Lambertz, OSB. 2 religious, 2 lay workers. Parish mem. 1,000.

Christ the King Mission. Tokio, North Dakota 58379. 1 religious, 1 lay worker. Parish mem. 108.

St. James Indian Mission. Warwick, North Dakota 58381. 1 religious, 2 lay workers. Parish mem. 247.

St. Boniface. Walhalla, North Dakota 58282. Partial. Msgr. Raoul Longpre, part time. 4 religious, 3 lay workers. Parish mem. 200.

St. John's. St. John, North Dakota 58369. Partial. Fr.
Theophane Gonnelly, OSB. 1 religious, 2 lay workers.
Parish mem. 220.

Sacred Heart of Olga. Langdon, North Dakota 58249. Partial.
Fr. Dennis Schue. 1 religious, 2 lay workers. Parish mem.
40.

St. Joachim's. Rolla, North Dakota 58367. Partial. Fr.
Louis G. Veit. 1 religious, 2 lay workers. Parish mem. 180.

Newman Student Parish, at BIA Indian School. Wahpeton,
North Dakota 58057. Fr. Martin T. Cullen. 1 religious, 3
lay workers. 460 participants.

OKLAHOMA

ARCHDIOCESE OF OKLAHOMA CITY
P. O. Box 18838, Oklahoma City, Oklahoma 73118
Most Rev. Charles A. Solatka, Archbishop

Churches 3. Catholic Indians 2,750, priests - 2 w., 4 Ind.,
Sisters 13.

There have been 2 large campaigns for Human Development, and
there is a legal aid program for the Cheyenne and Arapaho
Tribes. The Archdiocese supports Oklahoma Indian Ministries,
Inc. Participates in Public Inebriate Alternative.

St. Patrick's Church. Mixed tribes and w. P. O. Box 628,
Anadarko, Oklahoma 73005. Fr. Michael Chapman. Sr.
Cecilia Schmidt, IHM; Sr. Francine Malzone, IHM.

St. Anthony's Church. Cheyenne, Arapaho and w. P. O. Box
268, Okeene, Oklahoma 73736. Fr. Joseph Burger.

St. Benedict's Church. Potawatomi, Kickapoo and w. 632
North Kickapoo, Shawnee, Oklahoma 74801. Fr. M. J. Brown,
pastor. 5 religious, 15 lay workers. About 1,000 Ind.

Legal Aid Program. Fr. Joe Burger, P. O. Box 268, Okeene,
Oklahoma 73763.

3 Sisters and 7 lay workers at each of 2 BIA Schools conduct
religious education classes. Concho Indian School at El
Reno and Chilocco Indian School at Newkirk. 75 participants
at each school.

DIOCESE OF TULSA
P. O. Box 2009, Tulsa, Oklahoma 74104   *(918)587-3115*
Most Rev. Bernard J. Gantner, Bishop

Churches 9. Catholics 900, priests 5, Sisters 8. 1 high
school. Ab. 24, ib. 35.

Immaculate Conception Church. Osage. 1314 Lynn Avenue,
Pawhuska, Oklahoma 74056. Fr. Daniel Keohane, pastor.
Sister Catherine Coles, pastoral assistant. 2 lay workers.
Mem. 750, Ind. 700.

St. Joseph's Church. 421 South Petit, Hominy, Oklahoma
74035. Fr. Timothy Daley, MM. Mission in Cleveland. Mem.
150, Ind. 110.

Sacred Heart Church. Partial. 333 South 8th Street,
Fairfax, Oklahoma 74637. Fr. James Greenwell, pastor. 4
religious, 2 lay workers. Parish mem. 336, Ind. 60.
  Missions: *St. John's Church.* Pawnee, Oklahoma 74058.
  Ind.
  St. Ann's Church. Shidler, Oklahoma 74652. Partial.

St. Brigid's Church. Partial, Cherokee Capital. Tahlequah,
Oklahoma 74464. Fr. Stephen Fogerty, OSA. P. O. Box 747,
Tahlequah, Oklahoma 74464.

St. John's Church. P. O. Box 220, McAlester, Oklahoma
74501. Partial. Fr. Herman J. Foken, pastor.

Kiamichi Area Catholic Ministry. Covers 9 counties,
including 3 parishes and 4 missions. P. O. Box 220,
McAlester, Oklahoma 74501. Team of 3 priests and 3 Sisters.
Fr. Herman J. Foken. Sisters Mary Maloney, Dorothy Rasche,
Gilchrist Conway. P. O. Box 1225, McAlester, Oklahoma
74501.

Bishop Kelley High School. 3905 South Hudson, Tulsa,
Oklahoma 74135. *(918)627-3390.* Sister Ida Marian Deville,
Principal. Grades 9 - 12. Staff 37, including 1 Ind.
teacher. Ind. boys 51, girls 56. *Perspective,* every four
weeks.

OREGON

DIOCESE OF BAKER
P. O. Box 826, Baker, Oregon 97814   *(503)523-2373*
Most Rev. Thomas J. Connolly, Bishop

Churches 3. Catholic Indians about 800, priests 2, Sisters 2.

Adult baptisms 2, infant baptisms 35.

St. Andrew's Mission. Umatilla, Cayuse and Walla Walla. Umatilla Reservation. Route 1, Box 515, Pendleton, Oregon 97801. *(503)276-6155.* Fr. James P. Hurley, S.J., pastor. Catholic com. about 350. Ib. 31, ab. 2. Sr. Dolores, religion teacher. CCD classes at *St. Mary's,* Pendleton, Oregon 97801. Religious vacation school, 34 Ind.

St. William. Warm Springs Reservation. Warm Springs, Oregon 97801. Partial. Msgr. Matthew Crotty, part time. P. O. Box 786, Madras, Oregon 97741. Ind. mem. 40. CCD program.

Our Lady of Mt. Carmel. P. O. Box 296, Chiloquin, Oregon 97624. Partial. Fr. Thomas R. Scanlan, pastor. 6 catechists. Members: Ind. 129, w. 168. Conv. 6. 4 ib. Religious vacation school, 19 Ind.

ARCHDIOCESE OF PORTLAND
P. O. Box 351, Portland, Oregon 97207   *(503)234-5334*
Most Rev. Cornelius M. Power, Archbishop

Chapel 1. Catholic students 140, priest 1, lay workers 3.

Chemawa High School Chaplaincy. Chemawa Indian High School, Salem, Oregon 97308. Chapel. Fr. John F. de Paemelaere, OFM, chaplain to Catholic students. 3 lay workers. About 140 Catholic students.

SOUTH DAKOTA

DIOCESE OF RAPID CITY
P. O. Box 678, Rapid City, South Dakota 57701   *(605)343-3541*
Most Rev. Harold J. Dimmerling, Bishop

Churches. Catholic Ind. 15,000, priests 36. Sisters: 2 Ind. and 24 w. 4 Permanent Deacons, Ind. Brothers 11. Ab. 11, ib. 289 in 1977. 2 elementary schools, 1 high school.

Society of Jesus, Wisconsin Province

EDUCATIONAL INSTITUTIONS

Red Cloud Indian Grade School. Pine Ridge, South Dakota 57770. Staff: religious 4, lay persons 37. Ind. pupils 274.

Red Cloud Indian High School. Holy Rosary Mission. Pine Ridge, South Dakota 57770. Fr. William Kiley Stolz, S.J.,

Principal. Staff: religious 9, lay persons 31. Ind. students 231.

Our Lady of Lourdes Elementary School. Box 2, Porcupine, South Dakota 57772. Staff: religious 4, lay persons 16. Ind. pupils 174.

Permanent Diaconate Program. Fr. John Hatcher, S.J., Patrick McCorkell, S.J., Damien O'Connell, S.J., James Stehr, S.J. Plainview, South Dakota 57771.

PINE RIDGE RESERVATION. Oglala Sioux. *Holy Rosary Mission.* Pine Ridge, South Dakota 57770. Fr. Earl J. Kurth, S.J., Director of Missions; Fr. Joseph D. Sheehan, Superior of the Jesuits and pastor of the churches; Fr. John Hennessy, S.J.; Fr. William Fitzgerald, S.J.; Fr. Paul Steinmetz, S.J.; Fr. Donald Rouscher, S.J.; Fr. Martin Schlitz, S.J.; Fr. Glendon R. Welshons, S.J.; Fr. David M. Shields, S.J.; Fr. Jim Dixon, S.J.; Fr. James R. Strvzok, S.J., Superintendent of Schools; Fr. William Kiley Stolz, S.J., Principal of Red Cloud High School; Fr. Ronald S. Seminara, S.J.; Fr. Leonard J. Fencl, retired; Fr. Anthony Dagelen, S.J.; Fr. Charles Leute, O.P.

Religious 60. Sisters 12, Brothers 5, Permanent Deacons 2, lay helpers 25. 10 Ind. catechists. 100 Ind. lay men workers, 30 w. 100 Ind. lay women workers, 20 w. Churches 5, chapels 9, station 1. Communicants 5,500. Total Catholic com. 8,100. Conv. in 1975 – 18. Ab. in 1975 – 18, ib. 530.

PARISHES PREDOMINANTLY INDIAN

Holy Rosary. Pine Ridge, South Dakota 57770.

Sacred Heart. Pine Ridge, South Dakota 57770.

Our Lady of Sorrows. Box 229, Kyle, South Dakota 57772. Fr. Glendon R. Welshons, S.J.

St. Stephen's. North of Kyle.

St. Agnes. Manderson, South Dakota 57756.

St. Henry's. Potato Creek, near Allen. Fr. Glendon R. Welshons, S.J.

St. John of the Cross. Allen, South Dakota 57714. Fr. Glendon R. Welshons, S.J.

Sacred Heart, Wounded Knee. P. O. Box 359, Wounded Knee, South Dakota 57794. Fr. James C. Milota. 2 Sisters.

Our Lady of the Sioux. Oglala, South Dakota 57764.

Our Lady of Good Counsel. No water.

St. Bernard. Red Shirt Table, Oglala, South Dakota 57764.

Christ the King. Porcupine, South Dakota 57772.

St. Paul's on the Creek. Porcupine, South Dakota 57772.

ROSEBUD RESERVATION. Brule Sioux. *St. Francis Mission*. St. Francis, South Dakota 57572. Very Rev. Bernard D. Fagan, S.J., Director of Mission. Fr. J. Robert Hilbert, S.J., Superior of Jesuits. Fr. Raymond Berger, S.J.; Fr. Robert Demeyer, S.J.; Fr. Harry S. Eglsoer, S.J.; Fr. Joseph C. Gill, S.J.; Fr. George Haas, S.J.; Fr. Albert A. Janka, S.J.; Fr. Richard T. Jones, S.J.; Fr. William F. Stolzman, S.J.; Fr. Kenneth T. Walleman, S.J.; Fr. Harry Zerner, S.J.; Fr. Hal Dessell, S.J.

2 Ind. Sisters, 10 w. Sisters. 2 Permanent Deacons, 4 w. Brothers. 10 Ind. catechists. 100 Ind. lay men workers, 30 w. 100 Ind. lay women workers, 30 w. 5 churches, 7 chapels. 3 Diocesan parish churches. Communicants 4,000. Total Catholic com. in 1976 - 7,250. Conv. in 1975 - 20. Ab. 20 in 1975, ib. 500. CCD program on released time through the Reservation.

PARISHES PREDOMINANTLY INDIAN

St. Charles Church. St. Francis, South Dakota 57572. Fr. Richard T. Jones.

St. Patrick. Spring Creek, near St. Francis. Fr. Richard T. Jones.

St. Rose of Lima. Soldier Creek, near Norris, South Dakota 57560. Fr. Harry Zerner.

Sacred Heart. Ring Thunder, near Norris.

St. Peter's. Okreek, South Dakota 57566. Fr. Raymond Burger.

St. Agnes. Parmalee, South Dakota 57566. Fr. Robert Demeyer.

Sacred Heart. Upper Cut Meat District, near Parmalee. Fr. Robert Demeyer.

St. Brigit's. Rosebud, South Dakota 57570. Fr. George Haas.

Immaculate Conception. Two Strike, near St. Francis. Fr. Kenneth T. Walleman.

St. Charles Barromeo. Batesland, South Dakota 57716.

Sacred Heart. Little Eagle, South Dakota 57639.

St. Thomas the Apostle. Mission, South Dakota 57555. Fr. Lawrence Helmueller.

Holy Family. North Antelope. Fr. Lawrence Helmueller.

St. Catherine Church. Promise, near White Horse, South Dakota 57661.

St. Francis Xavier. Ponca, near Bonsteel, South Dakota 57317.

St. Luke. Thunder Butte, near Dupree, South Dakota 57623.

St. Theresa. White Horse, South Dakota 57661.

St. Ignatius. White River, South Dakota 57579. Fr. William Stolzman. 1 Sister, 1 lay worker. Mem. 350. 2 chapels. Also, *Sacred Heart,* White River, white.

CHEYENNE RIVER RESERVATION

St. Joseph. Cherry Creek, South Dakota 57662. Fr. Lawrence Rucker, SCJ, Brother Paul Rosonke, CSC.

All Saint's Church. Eagle Butte, South Dakota 57625. Fr. Paul Casper, SCJ, Fr. Joseph Poirer, SCJ.

St. Mary's Church. Lower Brule, South Dakota 57548. Fr. Patrick Lloyd, SCJ, pastor. Parish mem. 200.

St. Aloysius. Bullhead, South Dakota 57621. Fr. Joachim Schieber, OSB. Mem. 100.

St. Bede. Wakpala, South Dakota 57658. Fr. Joachim Schieber of St. Bernard Church. Mem. 30.

Total Catholic com. at Bullhead and Wakpala 285. 2
Sisters. 2 w. catechists. 6 Ind. men workers, 6 women.

Mother Butler Center. St. Isaac Joques. Rapid City,
South Dakota 57701. Fr. Richard G. Pates, S.J., Director.
Brother Paul Rosonke, CSC. Church and Urban Center.

Sioux Spiritual Center.

DIOCESE OF SIOUX FALLS
423 North Duluth Avenue, Sioux Falls, South Dakota 57104
Most Rev. Lambert Hoch, Bishop, resigned   *(605)334-9861*

Churches 19. Catholic Indians 1,720, priests 14, native
Permanent Deacon 1, Sisters 11, Brothers 11, lay workers 57.
Baptisms in 1977 - adults 19, infants 97.

INSTITUTES AND CONGREGATIONS

Order of St. Benedict, SDB: Blue Cloud Abbey, Marvin, South
Dakota 57251. Reservation ministry in North and South
Dakota.

Oblates of Mary Immaculate, OMI: 104 North Mississippi
Blvd., St. Paul, Minnesota 55104. School and reservation
ministry.

Sacred Heart Fathers, SCJ: North American Province, Hales
Corners, Wisconsin 53130. School ministry.

Benedictine Sisters, OSB: Mother of God Priory, Watertown,
South Dakota 57201. Teaching.

Oblate Sisters of the Blessed Sacrament, OSBS: St.
Sylvester's Convent, Marty, South Dakota 57361. Teaching
and child care.

Sisters of the Blssed Sacrament, SBS: Cornwells Heights,
Pennsylvania 19020. Teaching.

INDIAN MISSIONS AND CHURCHES

St. Paul Indian Mission. Yankton Dakota Reservation.
Marty, South Dakota 57201. *(605)384-3234.* Frs. Michael
O'Reilly, OSB, Hugh Smith, OSB, and Augustine Edele, OSB.
Permanent Deacon Ed Zephier. 1 OSB Brother. 10 SBS and
OSBS Sisters. 5 lay helpers.
    St. Francis Solano. Lake Andes, South Dakota 57356.
    St. John the Evangelist. Greenwood, South Dakota.

Immaculate Conception. Dakota. Crow Creek Reservation. Stephan, South Dakota 57346. *(605)856-2215.* Fr. Julius Armbruster, OSB, Cletus Miller, OSB, and Daniel Modlon, OSB. 2 OSB Sisters. 5 cburches, 2 stations, religious education in 5 areas.
> *St. Catherine Church.* Big Bend.
> *St. John.* Piere, South Dakota 57501. Mission to city Indians.

St. Joseph. Dakota. Crow Creek Reservation. Ft. Thompson, South Dakota 57339. *(605)245-5500.* Fr. Thomas Roznowski, OSB, pastor.

St. Catherine Indian Church. Dakota. Sisseton Reservation. Sisseton, South Dakota 57262. Fr. Jonas Grey, OMI. 2 other priests, 1 OMI Brother, 1 OSB Sister. 2 missions, 2 chapels. 300 mem.
> *St. Matthew.* Veblen, South Dakota 57270.
> *St. Joseph.* Pickerel Lake, Wanbay, South Dakota 57273.

Tekakwitha Indian Mission, Inc. Sisseton, South Dakota 57262. *(605)698-7518.* Fr. Leonard Baldus, OMI, secretary-treasurer.

Our Lady of the Sioux. Dakota. Brule Reservation. Chamberlain, South Dakota 57325.
> *St. Joseph's Indian School.* Frs. Thomas Cassidy, SCJ, Superintendent; William Pickcavage, SCJ; Thomas Lind, SCJ; Patrick Lloyd, SCJ. Deacon Joseph DiVenuto, Principal. 6 Brothers, 17 lay teachers. Pupils 210.

Flandreau Indian School. Flandreau, South Dakota 57028. Ministry to Catholic children in this BIA boarding school. Fr. Odo Gogel, OSB. 2 lay workers. 300 children.

Pierre Government Indian School. Pierre, South Dakota 57501. Fr. Cletus Miller, OSB. 138 children.

American Indian Cultural Research Center. Blue Cloud Abbey, Marvin, South Dakota 57251. Fr. Stanislaus Maudlin, OSB, Director.

Dakota Catholic Leadership Program. St. Paul's Mission, Marty, South Dakota 57361. Fr. Hugh Smith, OSB, Director. Diaconate and other leadership training.

Tekakwitha Indian Children's Home. Sisseton, South Dakota 75262. *(605)697-7557.* Fr. Robert Reitmeier, OMI. 2 Brothers. 64 children.

TEXAS

DIOCESE OF EL PASO
1200 North Mesa Street, El Paso, Texas 79902   *(915)533-5549*
Most Rev. Sidney Matthew Metzger, Bishop

Churches 2. Indian Catholics 300, priest 1. Ab. in 1977 - 1,
ib. 41.

> *St. Joseph's Mission.* Mescalero Apache. Mescalero Reservation. P. O. Box 177, Mescalero, New Mexico 88340. Fr. George Carr, OFM, missionary. 5 week summer school of religion by 4 Sisters from St. Louis. 65 participants.

> *Guadelupe Chapel,* Bent. Partial.

UTAH

DIOCESE OF SALT LAKE CITY
333 East Temple Street, Salt Lake City, Utah 84111
Most Rev. Joseph Lennox Federal, Bishop   *(801)328-8641*

Churches 2. Catholic Indians approximately 800, priests 2, Sisters 3. Ib. 7.

> *St. Henry's.* Partial. Brigham City, Utah 84302. Priest 1, Sister 1. CCD program.

> *St. Helen's.* Partial. P. O. Box 415. Roosevelt, Utah 84066.

> *Religious Education Program.* Brigham City, in connection with Intermountain Indian School. Fr. John Wright, S.J., and Sister Marce, OLVM. 200 Catholic students.

> *Ute Reservation.* Ute. Duchesne, Utah 84021. Reservation Indians attend church in Roosevelt. Sister Mary Michael, SA. Roosevelt and Duchesne.

WASHINGTON

ARCHDIOCESE OF SEATTLE
907 Terry Avenue, Seattle, Washington 98104   *(206)622-8880*
Most Rev. Raymond G. Hunthausen, Archbishop

1976 Statistics: Churches 3. Indian Catholics 4,000. 3 Priests.

The Native American Christian Community

DIOCESE OF SPOKANE
1023 West Riverside Avenue, Spokane, Washington 99201
Most Rev. Bernard J. Topel, Bishop   *(509)456-7100*

Churches 8. Indian Catholics 2,793, priests 5, Sisters 1.
Ab. 13, ib. 98.

> *St. Mary Mission.* Omak, Washington 98841. A mission of the
> Oregon Province of the Society of Jesus. Fr. Eugene E.
> Pierre, S.J. Sister Margaret Ball, SNJM. Ministry to sick
> and aged.

> *St. Joseph's Church.* East Omak.

> *Pastoral Center.* Omak, Washington 98841. Fr. Jake Morton,
> S.J.

> *Sacred Heart Mission.* P. O. Box 214, Wellpinit, Washington
> 99040. Fr. John G. Birk.

> *Our Lady of Lourdes Church.* Partial. Westend, Washington.

> *St. Philip's.* Ford, Washington 99013.

> *Our Lady of Sorrows.* Kalispel Reservation. Cusick,
> Washington 99119.

> *Sacred Heart Mission.* P. O. Box 70, Nespelem, Washington
> 99155. (Jesuit Mission annexed to Omak.) Fr. Patrick J.
> Twohy, pastor.

> *St. Michael Mission.* Inchelium, Washington 99115.

Fr. Dominic Doyle, S.J. 12224 Euclid Avenue, Spokane,
Washington 99207. Part time.

DIOCESE OF YAKIMA
P. O. Box 901, Yakima, Washington 98907   *(509)248-6857*
Most Rev. Nicholas E. Walsh, Bishop

Catholic Indians 1,000.

A few Catholic Yakimas live in St. Joseph parish in downtown
Yakima. More live on the Reservation in the parishes of St.
Mary, White Swan, St. Aloysius, Toppenish and St. Peter
Claver, Wapato.

A few Coville Indians are in St. Anne Parish, Bridgeport, in
St. Francis Church, Chelan, and the parishes at St. Joseph,
Wenatchee and Holy Apostles, East Wenatchee.

WISCONSIN

DIOCESE OF GREEN BAY
P. O. Box 66, Green Bay, Wisconsin 54305   *(414)435-4406*
Most Rev. Aloysius J. Wycislo, Bishop

Churches 2. Catholic Indians 1,800, priests 3, Sisters 12,
Brothers 1. 1 day school. Ib. in 1976 - 22. The Diocese
has an Indian Ministry Task Force.

INSTITUTES AND CONGREGATIONS

Franciscan Fathers. St. Louis, Missouri. Parish ministry.

Sisters of St. Joseph of Corondolet. St. Louis, Missouri.
School and Outreach ministry.

St. Michael's. Menominee. Menominee Reservation. Keshena,
Wisconsin 54135. Church and a chapel. 2 w. priests, 6 w.
Sisters, 1 w. Brother. Cathechists: 2 Ind., 2 w. Communi-
cant mem. 250. Total Catholic com. 800. Ib. in 1976 - 10.

St. Joseph's School. 1873. Menominee. P. O. Box 488,
Keshena, Wisconsin 54135. Sisters of St. Joseph of
Corondelet: Sister Mary Cornelius, CSJ, Prinipal. Grades
1 - 8. Originally entirely Native American, now also serves
St. Joseph's Parish. Administrative staff of 8 includes 6
Indians. Teachers: 5 Sisters. Indian students: 42 boys,
42 girls.

St. Anthony's. Menominee. Neopit, Wisconsin 54150. 1 w.
priest, 6 w. Sisters, 1 w. Brother. 2 Ind. catechists, 6
w. catechists. 1 w. lay woman worker. Communicants 300.
Total Catholic com. 1,000. Ib. in 1976 - 12.

ARCHDIOCESE OF MILWAUKEE
345 North 95th Street, Milwaukee, Wisconsin 53226
Most Rev. William E. Cousins, Archbishop   *(414)476-2101*

Churches 10 (partial Indian). Catholic Indians nearly 2,000.
The Diocese has a Permanent Diaconate Program for Indians,
Blacks and Latins. Minsitry for migrant workers mostly
Mexican half-Indians.

St. Anne. 2474 North 37th Street, Milwaukee, Wisconsin
53210.

St. Charles Borromeo. 5571 South Marilyn Avenue, Milwaukee,
Wisconsin 55221.

St. Florian. 1233 South 45th Street, Milwaukee, Wisconsin 53214.

Gesu. 1210 West Michigan Avenue, Milwaukee, Wisconsin 53233.

Holy Trinity-Guadalupe. 613 South 4th Street, Milwaukee, Wisconsin 53204.

St. Leo. 2470 West Locust Street, Milwaukee, Wisconsin 53206.

St. Michael. 1445 North 24th Street, Milwaukee, Wisconsin 53205.

St. Patrick's. 723 West Washington, Milwaukee, Wisconsin 53204.

St. Thomas Aquinas. 1968 North 36th Street, Milwaukee, Wisconsin 53208.

St. Rose. 540 North 31st Street, Milwaukee, Wisconsin 53208.

DIOCESE OF SUPERIOR
1201 Hughitt Avenue, Superior, Wisconsin 54880
Most Rev. George A. Hammes, Bishop   *(715)392-2937*

Churches 10. Catholic Indians 3,455, priests 9, Brothers 1, Sisters 12. 2 elementary schools. Ab. in 1977 - 2, ib. 86.

INSTITUTES AND CONGREGATIONS

Franciscan Fathers. Sacred Heart Province. Fr. Vitus Duschinsky, 3140 Meramac, St. Louis, Missouri 63118. Parish ministry.

Franciscan Sisters of Perpetual Adoration. Sister Patricia Alden, Marywood, Woodruff, Wisconsin 54568. Teaching and parish ministry.

Congregation of the Third Order of St. Francis and Mary Immaculate. Sr. Ann James Murray. 520 Plainfield Avenue, Joliet, Illinois 60435. Teaching and parish ministry.

School Sisters of St. Francis. Sr. Lauretta Mather. 1501 South Layton Blvd., Milwaukee, Wisconsin 53215. Indian school ministry.

St. Francis of Solanus. Chippewa. Reserve. Route 2, Stone
Lake, Wisconsin 54876. Fr. Kurt Buranich, pastor. 3 w.
Sisters, 3 w. catechists. Communicants 680. Total com.
680. 26 ib. in 1976.

St. Francis of Solanus Elementary Day School. Sr. M.
Felissa Zander, OSF, Principal. Sr. Mary Rose Theobold,
OSF, Sr. Polykarp Haseidle, OSF. Pupils 98.

Holy Family Church. Chippewa. Box 469, Bayfield, Wisconsin
54814. Fr. David Oberts, pastor. Sr. Cyrinus Flaska,
pastoral ministry. Communicants 210. Total com. 525. 1
conv. 14 ib. 2 w. catechists.

Holy Family Elementary School. Mr. John Dill, Principal.
Sr. Catherine Lukamich and Sr. Anne Arnold, teachers. 3
lay teachers. 75 pupils.

St. Ignatius Mission. Chippewa. New Post, Route 2, Stone
Lake, Wisconsin 54876. Fr. Laurus Rhode, pastor. Communicants and com. 218. Ib. in 1976 - 2.

St. Ignatius School. 1 Sister, 4 lay teachers. Pupils
75. Charity program: 120 Indians.

St. Mary. Chippewa. Odanah, Wisconsin 54861.

St. Agnes. Ashland, Wisconsin 54806. Fr. Medard Buvolo,
pastor. 106 Second Avenue, E., Ashland, Wisconsin 54806.
Fr. Michael Fowler, OFM, parish and catechetical ministry.
Fr. Isadore Langhein, OFM, parish and catechetical ministry.
Brother John Hettel, OFM, parish and catechetical ministry.
Sr. Catherine Kaiser, FSPA, Principal and catechetical
worker. Sr. Joyce Miller, FSPA, parish and catechetical
ministry. 4 other Sisters, teachers. Communicants 415.
Total com. 465. Ib. in 1976 - 6. Weekday religious
education.

St. Agnes Consolidated School. Ashland. 6 Sisters. 45
Indian children. St. Mary's Visitation Program. 478
Indians.

St. Anthony. Chippewa. Lac Du Flambeau, Wisconsin 54538.
Fr. Alexis Pruemer, pastor. 465 Communicants. Total com.
465. Ib. in 1976 - 13. Weekday religious education.

Our Lady of Perpetual Help. Chippewa, Partial. Danbury,
Wisconsin 54830. Fr. Edward Senn, pastor. P. O. Box 7,
Webster, Wisconsin 54893. Communicants 81. Com. 239. Ib.
in 1976 - 1. Weekday religious education.

St. Francis. Red Cliff. Fr. Myron Landolt, pastor. Brother Joseph Weithman, OFM.

St. Louis. Superior, Wisconsin 54880. Fr. James Dluge, pastor. 512 Grand Avenue, Superior, Wisconsin 54880.

St. Mary Magdalene. Couderay, Wisconsin 54828. Fr. Fabian Pakosta, pastor. P. O. Box 216, Winter, Wisconsin 54896.

WYOMING

DIOCESE OF CHEYENNE
P. O. Box 426, Cheyenne, Wyoming 82001   *(307)638-9394*
Most Rev. Hubert M. Newell, Bishop

Churches 3. Catholic Indians approximately 1,050, priests 4, Brothers 2, Sisters 17. Ab. in 1977 - 6, ib. 68.

St. Stephen's Indian Mission. Arapaho. Wind River Reservation. P. O. Box 294, St. Stephens, Wyoming 82524. Fr. Carl F. Starkloff, S.J., pastor. Active mem. about 600. Total Mission staff: Priests 4, Sisters 17, Brothers 2, Ind. catechists 1, w. catechists 5, Ind. lay men workers 7, w. lay men workers 5, Ind. lay women workers 6, w. women 2. Conv. in 1975 - 1. Ab. 9, ib. 27 (1977 - 6 and 68). 2 weekday religious education programs. 1 adult education program. 2 WS. 1 YS. 1 men's society. 2 general societies. Family counseling, Cultural Program.

St. Joseph's. Arapaho. Ethete, Wyoming 82502. Active mem. 300.

Blessed Sacrament. Shoshone. Ft. Washakie, Wyoming 82502. Active mem. 150.

St. Stephen's School. Pupils 210. Government pays mission staff.

Tekawitha Alcohol Center.

RELIGIOUS ORDERS

PRIESTS AND BROTHERS

BENEDICTINES. Order of St. Benedict (OSB). *St. John's Abbey,* Collegeville, Minnesota 56321. Rt. Rev. John Eidenschink, OSB, Abbot. 7 Indian missions in the Diocese of Crookston, Minnesota. *Assumption Abbey,* Richardton, North Dakota 58652. Rt. Rev. Robert West, OSB, Abbot. 2 Indian missions.

Conception Abbey, Conception, Missouri 66433. Rt. Rev. Jerome Hanus, OSB, Abbot. Mission in Diocese of Bismarck. *Blue Cloud Abbey*, Marvin, South Dakota 57251. Rt. Rev. Alan Berndt, Abbot. Missions in the Dioceses of Fargo and Sioux Falls. *Mount Angel Abbey*, St. Benedict, Oregon 97373. Very Rev. Anselm Galvin, OSB, Abbot. *Mission in Diocese of Boise.*

CAPUCHIN FRIARS (OFM CAP) *Province of St. Joseph,* 1740 Mt. Elliott Avenue, Detroit, Michigan 48207. Very Rev. Lloyd Thiel, OFM Cap, Provincial. Cheyenne Indians, Diocese of Great Falls.

FRANCISCAN MISSIONS. (OFM) *St. John the Baptist Province,* 1615 Vine Street, Cincinnati, Ohio 45210. Very Rev. Andrew Fox, Provincial. Rev. Aloys Held, Mission Promoter. Missions: Navajo, Pueblo, and Hopi in the Diocese of Gallup. *The Padres' Trail,* monthly, St. Michael's, Arizona. *Sacred Heart Province,* 1434 West 51st Street, Chicago, Illinois 60609. Very Rev. Vitus Duschinsky, OFM, Provincial. Missions at Keshena and Lac du Flambeau, Wisconsin. *St. Barbara Province,* 1500 34th Avenue, Oakland, California 94601. Missions in the Dioceses of Tucson and Phoenix: Papago, Pima, Apache, and others.

MARIST FATHERS (SM) *San Francisco Western Province,* 625 Pine Street, San Francisco, California 94108. Very Rev. Leonard Ferringo, SM, Provincial. Diocese of Boise

JESUIT MISSIONS. SOCIETY OF JESUS. (SJ) *Jesuit Missions, Inc,* 1717 Massachusetts Avenue, N. W., Washington, D. C. 20036. Rev. Simon E. Smith, SJ, Executive Secretary. *Oregon Province,* 2222 N. W. Hoyt, Portland, Orgegon 97210. Very Rev. William J. Loyens S. J., Provincial. Dioceses of Fairbanks, Anchorage, and Juneau, and stations in Idaho, Washington, and Oregon including Desmet, Lapwai, Harlem, Heart Butte, St. Ignatius, and Pendleton. *Wisconsin Province.* 2120 West Clybourn Street, Suite 200, Milwaukee, Wisconsin 53233. Very Rev. Bruce F. Bevier, SJ, Provincial. Missions in Diocese of Rapid City

MISSIONARY OBLATES OF MARY IMMACULATE. (OMI) *Central Province.* 104 North Mississippi Boulevard, Saint Paul, Minnesota 55104. Very Rev. William H. Woestman, OMI, Provincial. Missions: Sisseton, South Dakota; Squaw Lake, Minnesota; Orr, Minnesota.

REDEMPTORIST FATHERS. (CSSR) *Oakland Province*. 3696 Clay
Street, San Francisco, California 94118. Very Rev. William
Lockman, Provincial. Diocese of Boise.

Priests and Brothers of other religious communites are scattered
throughout the Indian parishes.

RELIGIOUS COMMUNITIES OF WOMEN

BENEDICTINE SISTERS. (OSB) *St. Benedict's Convent*. St.
Joseph, Minnesota 56374. Mother Evin Rademacher, OSB, Prioress.
Three Indian missions, Crookston and St. Cloud Dioceses. *St.
Scholastica Priory*. Kenwood Avenue, Duluth, Minnesota 55811.
Mother Grace Marie Braun, OSB, Prioress. Indian ministries 3 in
the Dioceses of Duluth, Phoenix and St. Paul-Minneapolis.
Mother of God Priory. Watertown, South Dakota 57201. Sister
Josita Pitz, Prioress. Diocese of Sioux Falls, South Dakota.
Priory of St. Gertrude. Cottonwood, Idaho. Mother Mary Marge
Goechener, OSB, Prioress. Diocese of Boise.

SISTERS OF THE BLESSED SACRAMENT FOR INDIANS AND
COLORED PEOPLE. (SBS) 1891. Mother house: *St. Elizabeth
Convent*. Cornwells Heights, Pennsylvania 19020. Sister Mary
Elizabeth Fitzpatrick, President. The Sisters, including four
Indians, staff schools at Marty, South Dakota; Santa Fe, New
Mexico; St. Michaels, Arizona; San Carlos, Arizona; and Pala,
California with a total of 46 Sisters and 1,111 pupils. They
operate St. Valerian Catholic Indian Center at Gallup, New
Mexico and give religious instruction and make visitations at
two missions in Old Laguna and Pena Blanca, New Mexico.

OBLATE SISTERS OF THE BLESSED SACRAMENT. (OSBS) 1935.
Mother house: *St. Sylvester's Convent*. Marty, South Dakota
57361. *(605)384-3305*. Sister Inez T. Jetty (Indian), Superior
General. 11 professed Sisters. Founded as a Native American
community, but later opened to others. Indian missions in
Dioceses of Rapid City and Sioux Falls.

SISTERS OF PROVIDENCE. (SP) *Province of the Sacred Heart*.
1511 Third Avenue, Seattle, Washington 98101. Sister Louise
Gleason, SP, Provincial. Dioceses of Anchorage and Fairbanks,
Alaska.

DOMINICAN SISTERS. ORDER OF ST. DOMINIC. (OP)
Congregation of the Holy Cross. Rosary Heights P. O. Box 280,
Edmonds, Washington 98020. Reports an Indian Apostolate.
Diocese of Crookston. Dominican Sisters serve in a number of
parishes and missions but the summaries of the Congregations in
the *Official Catholic Directory* do not differentiate them from
ordinary parishes.

FRANCISCAN MISSIONARIES OF MARY. (FMM) *US Province*. 225 East 45th Street, New York, N.Y. 10017. Sister Elizabeth Ann Conyers, FMM, Provincial. Navajo missions in Arizona, Gallup Diocese.

FRANCISCAN SISTERS OF THE ATONEMENT. (SA) Graymoor. St. Francis Convent. Garrison, New York 10524. Sister Julia Coyle, SA, Supr. General. Indian minitry in Ogdensburg Diocese.

FRANCISCAN SISTERS OF LITTLE FALLS, MINNESOTA. (OSF) St. Francis Convent, Little Falls, Minnesota 56345. Indian ministry in Tucson. There are numerous Franciscan Sisters in the Indian missions and parishes, but their specific communities are not specified in the reports, and Indian ministry is not differentiated from diocesan and parish ministries in the *Official Catholic Directory*.

SCHOOL SISTERS OF NOTRE DAME. (SSND) *Mequon Province*. 700 West Highland Road, Mequon, Wisconsin 53092. Sister Mary Jacqueline Buckley, SSND, Provincial Leader. One Indian school.

SCHOOL SISTERS OF ST. FRANCIS. (OSF) St. Joseph Convent, 1501 South Layton Blvd., Milwaukee, Wisconsin 53215. Sr. Louretta Mather. School ministry in Diocese of Superior.

SISTERS OF THE HOLY CROSS. (CSC) *Western Region*. 5401 E. 17th Avenue, Parkway, Denver, Colorado 80220. Sr. Patricia Mulvaney, CSC, Regional Superior. Diocese of Boise.

SISTERS OF ST. JOSEPH OF CARONDOLET. *Province of St. Luke*. 6400 Minnesota Avenue, St. Louis, Missouri 63111. Sister Mary Catherine O'Harman, Provincial Superior. Diocese of Green Bay.

URSULINE SISTERS. *Western Province*. 639 Angela Drive, Santa Rosa, California 95401. Sister Dolores Helbling, OSU, Provincial Prioress. St. Mary's School, Fairbanks, Alaska and St. Ignatius, Montana. *Mt. St. Joseph Ursuline Motherhouse* (Owensboro), Maple Mount, Kentucky 42356. Sister Annalita Lancaster, Major Superior. Diocese of Gallup.

Numerous other communities of women participate in the missions and parishes but have not been identifed as to Order and Mother house.

THE SALVATION ARMY

NATIONAL HEADQUARTERS
120-130 West 14th Street, New York, N.Y. 10011

The Salvation Army has Indian members in the Corps across the country and in many places ministers to Indians through social services, but only in a few areas, notably Alaska, are there Indian or Eskimo units.

ALASKA DIVISIONAL HEADQUARTERS
P. O. Box 1459, Anchorage, Alaska 99510   *(907)276-2515*
Major Arthur Smith, Divisional Commander

> *Anchorage.* Thlingit and some Eskimos. P. O. Box 40606, Anchorage, Alaska 99509. Lt. Gerald Akin. Willow Park area in Anchorage - Youth Program (Sunbeams) for girls. Boy's club.

> *Fairbanks.* Eskimo. (Social Services), Indian - youth meetings. Box 405, Fairbanks, Alaska 99701. A/Capt. Colin MacDonald.

> *Haines.* Thlingit. Box 157, Haines, Alaska 99827. Lt. Dan Hughes. Indian youth group. Ladies group.

> *Hoonah.* Thlingit. Box 238, Hoonah, Alaska 99829. Lt. Josephus Govaars. Indian youth groups. Ladies groups. Works with Alcoholism Council in the village and there is a feeding program.

> *Juneau.* Thlingit. Box 110, Juneau, Alaska 99802. Lt. Floyd Bacon. Several youth programs for Native and white young people.

> *Kake.* Thlingit. Box 300, Kake, Alaska 99830. Capt. Herbert Miller. Senior, youth and ladies groups. Senior Citizen feeding program.

> *Ketchikan.* Thlingit, Haida and Tsimshian. Box 5157, Ketchikan, Alaska 99901. Major George Driver. Ladies group. Youth programs.

> *Metlakatla.* Tsimshian. Box 5157, Ketchikan, Alaska 99901. Major George Driver. Ladies groups. Youth program.

> *Klawock.* Thlingit. Box 29, Klawock, Alaska 99925. Ray Skan, Thlingit Indian. Youth programs for village children.

> *Petersburg.* Thlingit. Box 514, Petersburg, Alaska 99833.

Capt. Ken Daneker. Ladies and men's group weekly. Youth program. Senior Citizen's feeding program.

Saxman Corps. Thlingit. Box 5184, Ketchikan, Alaska 99901. A/Capt. Mnester McKay. Ladies, men's, and youth programs.

Wrangell. Indian and caucasian. Lt. Joe Murray, part Sioux, his wife is Thlingit. Music. Youth groups. Ladies group.

Social Services Center, Anchorage. Capt. David Clitheroe. 735 East 8th Avenue, Anchorage, Alaska 99501.

Alcoholism Services, Anchorage. Capt. David Boyd. Box 4-992, Anchorage, Alaska 99509.

SOUTHERN TERRITORIAL HEADQUARTERS reports:

Within this area the Salvation Army does not have a "church", as such, ministering predominantly to Indians. However, our spiritual ministry is projected toward all persons of any national origin, including Indians. In the State of Oklahoma we have our largest concentration of Indians who are "Salvation Army Soldiers", meaning they are members of the organization just as a person may be a member of a church. No distinction is made to the fact that they are Indians. All of the Indian tribes who live in Oklahoma are included among our constituents. These include Cherokee, Osage, Choctaw, Comanche and others.

In addition to our spiritual ministries, a considerable amount of our social service, group work activities, character building programs and camping activities include the various Indian tribes in the State of Oklahoma.

In other areas of the Southern Territory, our social services, particularly, touch the lives of many Indians. These social services would be direct financial relief, counseling, visitation and individual services in medical hospitals and other programs. Areas of the South where we are rendering these services would include South Florida, the Seminoles; the Cherokees of Western North Carolina and Georgia; the Powhatans and other tribes in Eastern North Carolina.

NORTHWEST DIVISIONAL HEADQUARTERS reports:

"We do have Indians who attend our corps in Havre, Montana and Great Falls, Montana but they are a small part of the constituency."

"We also treat some Indians in our Harbor Light Center in

Seattle but again, this is not a major part of our
constituency."

CASCADE DIVISION states:

At the Dales, Oregon, 23 Indians are attending services,
Sunday School and a variety of clubs and activities.

THE WISCONSIN AND UPPER MICHIGAN DIVISION reports that several
Indian families attend the Green Bay Corps and a large family
attend the Milwaukee South Corps.

THE SIOUX CITY, IOWA, CORPS states that persons belonging to the
Winnebago, Macy and Sioux Tribes come for various services:
welfare, religious worship, game rooms, recreational
activities and meals for the elderly.

ABERDEEN, SOUTH DAKOTA CORPS reports that a large percentage of
recipients of services are American Indians. Work is
basically meals and lodgings for transients and for residents
of the county. Some assistance in job placement and some
cooperation with BIA offices. There is involvement in
alcoholic referral and hospitalization services.

CORPS COMMUNITY CENTER, RAPID CITY, SOUTH DAKOTA reports:

1. We work with the Lakota and Sioux Indian people in South
   Dakota.
2. We have in our Sunday School and in our Sunbeam Troop
   approximately 12 Indian girls.
3. We have our Black Hills Salvation Army Camp located 12
   miles south of Rapid City and have for the two years of
   1975 and 1976 had 340 Indian persons, children and adults
   numbering 340 for those two camping experiences.
4. Our work in Welfare Assistance is approximately 85%
   Indian persons - supplying them with lodgings, meals,
   grocery orders, gasoline and bus transportation to one of
   the five reservations that surround Pennington County,
   Rapid City, South Dakota.
5. We also visit with regularity the Veterans Hospitals at
   Sturgis, South Dakota and Hot Springs, South Dakota and
   serve the Indian veteran there in our game nights and our
   Seasonal distributions.
6. We have a Divisional Camp located at Omaha, Nebraska and
   have in the last four years, 1974-1977, taken youth from
   6 to 14 for a week of camping. In these four years we
   have taken with us 4 to 6 Indian boys and girls.
7. We have with regularity supplied clothing and appliances
   from our Salvage Store to many Indian families.

SIOUX FALLS, SOUTH DAKOTA CORPS ministers to Indians mostly in welfare: food, clothing, furniture, lodging, meals, gasoline, toys for children, counseling. A number of children are connected with the Community Center Program.

OMAHA, NORTHEAST DIVISIONAL HEADQUARTERS reports slight involvement through services to the Aging Department.

CHICAGO INNER CITY SERVICES

The Tom Seay Service Center. 1025 West Sunnyside at Broadway, Chicago, Illinois 60640. *(312)271-6182.* Directors: Captain and Mrs. David Dalberg. Located in Chicago's Uptown District where there is a large Indian population. The Center provides for Indians and other ethnic groups these services: alcoholic treatment residence, crisis counseling center, daily free nutrition program, food pantry, daily religious services, therapy programs, New Life House for runaway teenage girls, summer day camp.

TERRITORIAL HEADQUARTERS, NEW YORK

There is social service assistance to Indians in Western New York, especially in the Salamanca area, where food and clothing are the principal emergency needs. There is similar service in Northern New England, particularly in the Bangor, Maine area.

SEVENTH-DAY ADVENTISTS, GENERAL CONFERENCE OF NORTH AMERICAN DIVISION

6840 Eastern Avenue, N.W., Washington, D.C. 20012 *(202)723-0800*
Mr. R. A. Wilcox, General Field Secretary

Holbrook S.D.A. Church. 1945. Navajo. Holbrook, Arizona 86025. Burton Wright, pastor, ord., w. Mem. 165 (mixed). Sabbath school, etc.

Indian Mission School. 1945. Navajo. P. O. Box 880, Holbrook, Arizona 86025. Earl Spaulding, Principal. Mem. 44.

Monument Valley S.D.A. Church. 1961. Navajo. Monument Valley, Utah 84536. Robert Nickell, pastor, ord., w. Mem. 228 (mixed). Sabbath school, etc.

Monument Valley S.D.A. Hospital. 1961. Navajo. P. O. Box 6, Monument Valley, Utah 84536. Tom Cummings, Medical Director. 33 employees. 27 beds.

La Vida Mission. 1962. Navajo. P. O. Box 1289, Farmington, New Mexico 87401. A. L. Moore, Director. Mem. 35. Sabbath school, etc. *School:* pre-school to 9th grade. Administrative staff 2. Teachers: 4 Ind. women. Students 27 boys, 31 girls.

Maricopa Indian Mission. About 1930. Maricopa. Laveen, Arizona 85339. E. A. Ricketts, pastor, ord., w. Mem. 25. Sabbath school, etc.

Pine Ridge S.D.A. Mission. Dakota. P. O. Box 380, Pine Ridge, South Dakota 57770. Elder Max Slinghurst, Director, ord., w. Mem. 45. Sabbath school, etc.

Pine Ridge S.D.A. Mission School. Pine Ridge, South Dakota 57770. Guy L. Gatewood, Principal. Mem. 42.

Waccainauw and *Pembroke Groups.* About 1928. North Carolina. Obed Klein, pastor, ord., w. Mem. 50. Sabbath school, etc.

SOUTHERN BAPTIST CONVENTION

HOME MISSION BOARD. DEPARTMENT OF LANGUAGE MISSIONS
1350 Spring Street, N.W., Atlanta, Georgia 30309 *(404)873-4041*
Dr. Oscar I. Romo, Director
Dr. James N. Lewis, Jr., Assistant Director

ALABAMA BAPTIST STATE CONVENTION
2001 East South Blvd., P. O. Box 11870, Montgomery, Alabama
36111 *(205)288-2460*
Department of Special Missions: Rev. Jere Allen, Director

SOUTHWEST ALABAMA MISSION FIELD
P. O. Box 352, Citronelle, Alabama 36522 *(205)886-5369*
Rev. E. R. Isbell, General Missionary

Locally these people are called *Cajuns,* but have no relationship to the Louisiana Cajuns. Three ordained ministers.

Bethel Church. E. R. Isbell, pastor. P. O. Box 352, Citronelle, Alabama 36552. Mem. 34. Conv. in 1977 - 0. SS 12.

Cedar Creek. Claude Cox, pastor. Rural Route, Citronelle, Alabama 36552. Mem. 160. Ab. 2. SS 60.

Level. Malcolm, Alabama 36556. E. R. Isbell. Mem. 60. SS 20.

Memorial. McIntosh, Alabama 36553. David Curtis, pastor. Cov. in 1977 - 4. SS 62. Training Union 27. WS 10. YS 3.

Mt. Moriah. Route 1, Box 165, McIntosh, Alabama 86553.

L. D. Neese, pastor. Mem. 210. Conv. in 1977 - 1. Ab. 1.
SS 69. Training Union 31.

Mt. Pleasant. Route 1, Box 174, McIntosh, Alabama 86553.
Bennet Weaver, pastor. Mem. 95. Conv. 4. Ab. 1. SS 58.

Oak Hill. Malcolm, Alabama 36556. Greg George, pastor.
Mem. 124. Conv. 4. SS 37.

Reeds Chapel. McIntosh, Alabama 36553. J. E. Parker,
pastor. Mem. 382. Conv. 3. Ab. 3. SS 138. Training
Union 73. WS 27. YS 12.

Rivers. General Delivery, Sims Chapel, Alabama 36577.
Galsneed Weaver, pastor. Mem. 76. Conv. 5. Ab. 3. SS 23.

Lambert Grove. c/o First Baptist Church, Chickasaw,
Alabama 36611. James Warren, pastor. Mem. 73. Conv. 5.
Ab. 4. SS 50. Training Union 50.

ESCAMBIA BAPTIST ASSOCIATION
Route 4, Box 205, Atmore, Alabama 36502
Rev. Fred E. Brown

Poarch Indian Mission. c.1953. Creek. Sponsored by First
Baptist Church, Atmore. *(205)368-2181.* Mission pastor:
Camerone Byrant, Route 4, Box 421, Atmore, Alabama 36502.
(205)368-5186. Mem. 60. SS 20+. Wednesday Prayer meeting.

The Association began a week ministry in 1977. Four units
that can draw from weekday ministries: Poarch Mission,
Judson Church, McCullough Church and Lottie Church. Weekday
ministry at Creek Indian School. Director of Weekday
Ministries: Ms. Joyce Presley, Star Route A, Box 159, Atmore,
Alabama 35602

ALASKA BAPTIST CONVENTION
SRA Box 1791, Anchorage, Alaska 99507   *(907)344-9627*
Rev. John H. Allen, Director of State Missions

East Third Avenue Mission. Eskimo. 802 East 3rd Street,
Anchorage, Alaska 99501. *(907)279-3631.* Willie Johnson,
pastor, ord., Eskimo. Mem. 65. Conv. in 1977 - 5. Ab. in
1977 - 5.

Fairview Baptist Center. Eskimo/Indian/Athabascan. 1120
East 13th Street, Anchorage, Alaska 99501. *(907)272-6913.*
Jim Hearn, pastor, lay, w.

King Salmon Chapel. Eskimo/white. P. O. Box 95, King Salmon,

Alaska 99613. *(907)246-3365.* Don Rollins, pastor, ord., w.

Ekwok Mission. Yupik Eskimo. General Delivery, Ekwok, Alaska 99580. Rick Hale, pastor, lay, w. Conv. in 1977 - 3. Baptisms in 1977 - 5.

Friendship Mission. Eskimo/Indian/Athabascan. 1501 Lacey, Friendship, Alaska 99701. *(907)456-4542.* J. D. Back, pastor, ord., w. Valeria Sherard, white lay.

Fort Yukon Mission. Indian/Athabascan. General Delivery, Clear, Alaska 99704. *(907)832-5533.* Rendell Day, pastor, lay, w. Reopened June 15, 1978.

Chalkyitsik. Indian/Athabascan. General Delivery, Clear, Alaska 99704. Darrell White, pastor, lay, w. Begun August 1977.

Venetie. Indian/Athabascan. Venetie, Alaska 99781. Closed.

Emmonak. Eskimo. Emmonak, Alaska 99581. Closed.

Kotzebue. Inupiaq Eskimo/white. Box 26, Kotzebue, Alaska 99752. *(907)442-3294.* Elmer Hatfield, pastor, ord., w. Eskimo mem. 42. Conv. in 1977 - 2. Ab. 1.

Selawik. Eskimo. Box 102, Selawik, Alaska 99770. *(907)442-3375.* Harley Shield, pastor, ord., w. Mem. 5.
  Kiana. Mem. 5.
  Shungnak. Mem. 7.
  Ambler. Mem. 4.
  Kobuk. Mem. 5.

ARIZONA SOUTHERN BAPTIST CONVENTION
400 West Camelback Road, Phoenix, Arizona 85013
Language Missions: Dr. Delbert G. Fann, Director

First Navajo Baptist Church. P. O. Box 1198, Tuba City, Arizona 86045. *(602)283-6402.* Navajo. Jerry Sloan, pastor, ord., Navajo. *(602)283-5849.* Mem. 100. Ab. in 1977 - 10. SS 60. YS 15. WS 16. Men's group 10. Wednesday Bible study and prayer. VBS. BIA released time classes.

Navajo Trail Southern Baptist Church. P. O. Box 215, Tuba City, Arizona 86045. *(602)283-5364.* Vacant. Navajo. 1 Navajo layworker. Mem. 87. Com. 100. Ab. in 1976 - 6. SS 99. WS.

Cameron. Cameron, Arizona 86020. Navajo. Jasper Jones, pastor, ord., Navajo. 3221 Elder Drive, Flagstaff, Arizona

86001. Mem. 15. Com. 30. SS 18.

Dry Lake. Navajo. Lemuel Littleman, pastor, ord., Navajo.
43 Brannon Homes Circle, Flagstaff, Arizona 86001. Mem. 60.
Total com. 100. SS 30.

Leupp. Navajo. Leupp, Arizona 86035. Wallace (Bill) Parham,
pastor, ord., w. P. O. Box 848, Winslow, Arizona 86047.
Mem. 29. Com. 75. SS 34. WS. Weekday religious classes.

Many Farms. Navajo. Box 8, Many Farms, Arizona 86503.
Vacant. Mem. 29. Com. 60. Ab. in 1976 - 15. SS 76. WS.
Weekday religious classes.

Dilkon. Navajo. Wallace Parham, pastor. Mem. 13. Com. 35.
SS 30.

West White Cove. Navajo. Jack Begay, pastor, lic., Navajo.
Dilkon Bdg. School, Winslow, Arizona 86047. Founded 1977.
Mem. 13. Com. 20. Ab. 3. SS 25. VBS.

Indian Wells. Navajo. Allison Holman, pastor. 905 West
Aspinwall, Winslow, Arizona 86047. Mem. 10. Com. 30. SS 10.

Whiteriver. Apache. John Mouser, pastor, ord., w. P. O.
Box 278, Whiteriver, Arizona 85941. *(602)338-4468.* Mem. 131.
Com. 200. Ab. in 1976 - 7. SS 123. WS.

San Carlos. Apache. Tom Muskrat, pastor, ord., Apache. P.
O. Box 481, San Carlos, Arizona 85550. *(602)475-2686.* Mem.
47. Com. 60. SS 60. WS.

Ferguson Memorial. Pima. Arnold Enos, pastor, ord., Ind.
1275 East Thomas, Mesa, Arizona 85201. Mem. 95. Com. 200.
Ab. in 1976 - 17. SS 67. WS.

Sacaton. Pima. George Caruso, pastor, ord., w. Box E,
Sacaton, Arizona 85247. *(602)779-0088.* SS 26. WS.

San Tan. Pima. J. J. Johnston, pastor, ord., w. P. O. Box
68, Chandler Heights, Chandler, Arizona 85227. *(602)988-2012.*
Mem. 29. Com. 50. SS 14.

Blackwater. Pima. 694 West Coolidge Place, Coolidge, Arizona
85228. Gerald Brown, pastor. Mem. 61. Com. 75. Ab. in
1976 - 1. SS 27. WS.

Casa Blanca. Pima. 115 West Main Avenue, Casa Grande,
Arizona 85222. Truett Johns, pastor, ord., Ind. Mem. 34.
Total com. 54. SS 15.

Siloam. Pima. Route 1, Box 723C, Leveen, Arizona 85339. Alexander Lewis, Jr., pastor, ord., Ind. Mem. 71. Com. 40. SS 40. WS.

First Papago Baptist Church. Sells, Arizona 85634. Virgil Stoneburner, pastor, ord., w. P. O. Box 276, Sells, Arizona 85634. Mem. 129. Com. 75. SS 93. WS.

Chui-chui. Papago. L. E. Johns, pastor. 115 West Main Ave., Casa Grande, Arizona 85222. *(602)836-8473.* Mem. 10. Com. 25. SS 14.

McNary. Apache. Bob Price, pastor, ord., w. Box C-P, Payson, Arizona 85541. *(602)334-2336.* Mem. 136. Com. 40. SS 17.

Casa Grande. Mixed mem. L. E. Johns, pastor, ord., Ind. 115 West Main Ave., Casa Grande, Arizona 85222. *(602)836-8473.* Mem. 63. Com. 75. SS 46. WS. Men's society.

Phoenix First Indian Baptist Church. Mixed. Victor Kaneubbe, pastor, ord., Ind. 2014 West Rancho Drive, Phoenix, Arizona 85015. *(602)246-7524.* Mem. 50. Com. 125. Ab. in 1976 - 5. Ord. Ind. assistant pastor. SS 54. WS.

Flagstaff. Navajo and Hopi. A. A. Moore, pastor, ord., w. P. O. Box 1794, Flagstaff, Arizona 86001. *(602)774-6231.* Mem. 104. Com. 204. Ab. in 1976 - 6. SS 55.

Winslow First Indian Baptist Church. Navajo and Hopi. Allison Holman, pastor, ord., w. 905 West Aspinwall, Winslow, Arizona 86047. *(602)289-3022.* Mem. 44. Com. 75. Ab. in 1977 - 2. SS 41. WS. VBS.

SOUTHERN BAPTIST GENERAL BAPTIST CONVENTION OF CALIFORNIA

P. O. Box 5168, 678 East Shaw, Fresno, California 93755
Language Missions: Rev. E. J. Combs, Director   *(209)229-9533*

Most churches have SS and a Women's Missionary Union (WS).

NEVADA CHURCHES

General Missionary, Northern Nevada: LaVern Inzer, full time. P. O. Box 605, Carlin, Nevada 89822. *(702)754-6837.*

Schurz Indian Mission. Walker-River Reservation. Paiute. Star Route 1, Hawthorne, Nevada 89415. John A. Ashcraft, pastor, w., associate missionary, unordained. Church founded June 1973. Mission in December 1976. No formal membership as yet. Tuesday evening Bible study. VBS 30-40.

McDermitt Baptist Church. 1966. Paiute. P. O. Box 42, McDermitt, Nevada 89421. Frank Shuler, pastor, ord., w. *(702)532-8769.* Mem. 32, increase of 6. Ab. 3. SS 39. YS 10. WS 4. Senior Citizen's Bible Club. Backyard Bible Club. Sewing class.

CALIFORNIA CHURCHES

San Jose American Indian Baptist Church. 143 Fleming Ave., San Jose, California 95127. Leroy McDermott, pastor, self-employed. 464 Cestaric, Milpitas, California 95035.

American Indian Baptist Church. Creek. 422 Leland, San Francisco, California 94134. George H. Smith, pastor, ord., Ind., self-employed. 858 Florida Street, San Francisco, California 94110. *(415)648-0693.* Mem. 68. SS 30. WS 12. Wednesday prayer service and Children's Bible study.

American Indian Baptist Church. 660 South Third Street, El Cajon, California 92021. Lawrence Snow, pastor, self-employed. 5398 Waring Road, San Diego, California 92120. *(714)582-9233.*

First Baptist Church. P. O. Box 546, Hoopa, California 95546. Hoopa and Witchepek. Vacant.

First Southern Baptist Church. 5621 East Clara, Bell Gardens, California 90201. Vacant.

American Indian Baptist Church. 1315 102nd Ave., Oakland, California 94601. Vacant.

Mrs. Irene Dalby, retired. 8209 Specht Street, Bell Gardens, California 90201. *(213)927-6433.*

COLORADO BAPTIST GENERAL CONVENTION
5400 South Syracuse Street, P. O. Box 22005, Denver, Colorado 80222   *(303)771-2480* State Missions Department: Rev. Don Murray, Director

Ignacio Baptist Indian Mission. Southern Ute Reservation. Allen Seward, pastor, ord., w. Ignacio, Colorado 81137. Mem. 66. SS 40. Church training class 26. Off-station points served by Allen Seward: Towaoc on the Reservation and Rico in Uncompahgre National Forest, both Bible Fellowships. Summer student missionaries assist at Rico in the summer.

Four Corners Christian Mission. Box 376, Cortez, Colorado

81321. Ministry: a fellowship.

Rico Baptist Mission. Box 376, Cortez, Colorado 81321.

Towac Indian Bible Study. Ute. Ute Reservation. Box 376, Cortez, Colorado 81321. *(303)508-7402.* Allen Seward. *(303)565-7928.*

FLORIDA BAPTIST STATE CONVENTION
1230 Hendricks Avenue, Jacksonville, Florida 32208
Rev. Harold C. Bennett, Executive Director

Department of Language Missions: Home Mission Board S.B.C. and State Convention.
  Missionary to the Seminole Indians:
  Rev. Genus E. Crenshaw, 4701 Sterling Road, Ft. Lauderdale,
    Florida 33314

First Seminole Baptist Church. 4701 Sterling Road, Ft. Lauderdale, Florida 33314. Vacant, currently supplied. Mem. 137. Conv. in 1977 - 7 youths. SS 52. WS 16. Youth group weekly attendance 46. Self-supporting.

Big Cyprus First Baptist Church. Star Route, General Delivery, Big Cyprus, Florida. Junior Billie, pastor, Ind., lic. Mem. 176. Conv. in 1977 - 6 (3 adults). SS 63. WS 22. YS 32. Self-supporting.

First Indian Baptist Church. Brighton, Route 6, Box 616, Okeechobee, Florida. Howard Micco, lic. and ord. pastor. Mem. 156. Conv. in 1977 - 6 youth. SS 65. WS 19. WS 40. Partial subsidy.

Indian Trail Baptist Chapel. Tamiami Trail at 40 Mile Bend, Ochopee, Florida 33943. Jay Mawhorter, ord. pastor. Mem. 46. Conv. in 1977 - 3 (2 adults). SS 33. WS 8. YS 10. Minister paid by sponsoring church, Miami Springs Baptist Church.

Turners River Chapel, a preaching point operated by First Seminole.

Immokalee Chapel, a preaching point operated by Big Cyprus Church.

Four small independent Baptist churches are in this area. There are approximately 700 professing Christians among the Seminoles and Miccosukees in Florida. These churches are members of the local Baptist Association. An Indian Fellowship meets 3 times a year for a weekend. An Annual Assembly meets during Thanksgiving week. These churches contribute

together an annual sum of $10,000 to world missions. Total
Seminole population is about 1,900.

KANSAS-NEBRASKA STATE CONVENTION OF SOUTHERN BAPTISTS
5410 West Seventh Street, Topeka, Kansas 66606

Haskell Indian Mission. 140 Indian Lane, Lawrence, Kansas
66044. *(913)842-0040.* Vacant. Mem. ? Ab. in 1977 - 10.
SS 16. WS 20. Men's group 16. VBS 51.

BAPTIST STATE CONVENTION OF MICHIGAN
15635 West Twelve Mile Road, Southfield, Michigan 48076
Rev. Eugene Bragg, Director, Language Missions   *(313)557-4200*

An American Indian Baptist Church, not affiliated with the
Southern Baptist Convention, meets in the Baptist Center in
Detroit. Rev. Washington Doxtator, 15865 Plainview, Detroit,
Michigan 48233. *(313)533-3010.*

Page Avenue Baptist Church. 5023 Page Avenue, Jackson,
Michigan 49202. *(517)764-1255.* R. R. Jack Neyome, associate
minister, ord., Ottawa (Grand River) of Isabell (Mt. Pleasant)
Reservation. 225 North Forbes, Jackson, Michigan 49202. Mr.
Neyome conducts a church membership training class before
Sunday night service, Wednesday night Bible study. Half-hour
radio program Sunday noon. VBS. Annual revivals. He
preaches at a Rest Home every Saturday night. Evangelistic
ministry is to Native Americans in Michigan's Upper Peninsula
and New York State, mostly to Ojibways and Senecas.

MISSISSIPPI BAPTIST STATE CONVENTION

BAPTIST INDIAN CENTER
P. O. Box 265, Philadelphia, Mississippi 39350   *(601)656-2161*

A cooperative ministry of the Home Mission Board of the
Southern Baptist Convention and the State Mission Board of
the Mississippi Baptist Convention to the Choctaw Indians.
Rev. and Mrs. Dolton Haggan, General Missionaries to the
Choctaws.

All pastors are ordained Choctaw Indians. 46 baptisms in
1977. Other statistics are 1976.

Bethany Church. Emmett Denson, pastor. Route 7, Box C-45,
Philadelphia, Mississippi 39350. *(601)646-6286.* Mem. 69.
SS 21. WS 5. YS 3.

Bogue Chitto Church. Calvin Gibson, pastor. Route 1,
Conehatta, Mississippi 39057. Mem. 123. SS 54. YS 25.

Bogue Homa Church. Route 1, Hedelberg, Mississippi 39439. Calvin Gibson, pastor. Mem. 42. SS 20. WS 4. YS 8.

Calvary Church. Newton St. Union. Jack Polk. Route 7, Box 323-A, Carthage, Mississippi 39051. Mem. 45. SS 12. WS 7. YS 5.

Canaan Church. Route 7, Box 34, Philadelphia, Mississippi 39350. Emmett Denson, pastor. Mem. 90. SS 40. YS 10.

Choctaw Central Church. Clay Gibson, pastor. Route 7, Box 253, Philadelphia, Mississippi 39350. Mem. 37. SS 30. YS 11.

Corinth Church. Dolphus Henry, pastor. Route 2, Box R-68, Philadelphia, Mississippi 39350. Mem. 107. SS 45. WS 12. YS 13.

Hope Church. Ellis Thompson, pastor. Route 2, Box 105, Philadelphia, Mississippi 39350. Mem. 54. SS 25. WS 5. YS 3.

Hopewell Church. A. J. Anderson, pastor. P. O. Box 13, Walnut Grove, Mississippi 39189. Mem. 123. SS 41. WS 13. YS 20.

Macedonia Church. Homer Gibson, pastor. Route 1, Conehatta, Mississippi 39057. Mem. 130. SS 50. WS 14. YS 25.

Mt. Zion Church. Thomas Nickey, pastor. Route 1, Box 315, Conehatta, Mississippi 39057. Mem. 170. SS 51. WS 20. YS 11.

Old Canaan Church. Ike Anderson, pastor. Route 4, Box 233, Union, Mississippi 39365. Mem. 76. SS 13. WS 10. YS 1.

Pine Bluff Church. Arthur Ben, pastor. Route 7, Box M-1, Philadelphia, Mississippi 39350. Mem. 30. SS 23. WS 8. YS 4.

Three Missions. SS 60.

Total Membership 1,096. Baptisms 45. SS 485. WS 98. YS 139.

BAPTIST CONVENTION OF NEW MEXICO
P. O. Box 485, Albuquerque, New Mexico 87103   *(505)247-0586*
Rev. Chester C. O'Brien, Executive Director
Rev. Don Brent, Director, Missions
Rev. A. Kenneth Chadwick, Language Missions Program Leader

Albuquerque Indian Mission and Southwest Indian Polytechnic Ministry. Mixed. Claudio Iglesias, pastor, ord., San Blas Ind. 11013 Morris Court, N.E., Albuquerque, New Mexico 87112. Church mem. 84 (average 60 in morning). SS 31. Ab. 12.

Santa Fe Mission to Students. Mixed. Russell Begay, ord., Navajo. Santa Fe Center, 1420 Cerrilos Road, Santa Fe, New Mexico 87501.

NAVAJO CHURCHES AND MINISTRIES

Farmington Indian Center. Mrs. Irene Diswood, Director, Navajo. Mel Peterson, pastor, ord., w. Box 1892, Farmington, New Mexico 87401. A mission to 2,000 city Indians. Children's Bible Club.

First Baptist Church, Shiprock. Gerald Lawton, pastor, ord., w. P. O. Box 907, Shiprock, New Mexico 87420. Associate pastor, George Nez. Mem. 162. SS 92. Services in Navajo and English. Ministry to boarding school pupils, social work. WS. Seminary extension program.

Teec Nos Pos Indian Baptist Church. Tom Nelson, pastor, ord., w. P. O. Box 916, Teec Nos Pos, Arizona 86514. Mem. 31. SS 35. Services in Navajo and English. Weekday program. Center for a number of small missions.

Fort Wingate Mission (of First Indian Baptist Church of Gallup). Ft. Wingate, New Mexico. 12 miles east of Gallup. Ministers to about 300 children in BIA school. SS 35. Weekday Bible study 56. Also ministers to adult Navajo and other Indians.

Tinian. Cecil Willeto, pastor, ord., w. Box 75, Cuba, New Mexico 87013. Mem. 65. SS 18. WS. YS. Sunbeams. Tuesday evening prayer meeting.

Fruitland Indian Church. Kenneth Norton, pastor, ord., w. P. O. Box 233, Fuitland, New Mexico 87416. Mem. 29. SS 45.

Alamo. Dennis Apechito, Navajo lay minister. Box 722, Magdalena, New Mexico 87825. On small reservation separated from main reservation, 35 miles north of Magdalena. Mem. 121. SS 35.

The Native American Christian Community

Magdalena. Magdalena, New Mexico 87825. Associated with Alamo. Abel Becara, ordained regional catalytic missionary. Phil Dooley, assistant. Student center across street from dormitories which house Alamo children at BIA school. About 285 children involved.

Crownpoint. Crownpoint, New Mexico 87313. Vacant. Mem. 22. SS 22. Ministry to people of several tribes and to Anglos. Leadership training, literary education, music teaching.

Gallup First Indian Baptist Church. W. C. Buie, pastor, ord., w. 501 South Third, Gallup, New Mexico 87301. Mem. 130. SS 46. Ministers to mixed tribes, especially to persons who work for the BIA in Gallup; also to Navajos in Gallup. Sponsors a mission at Ft. Wingate.

Tohatchi Mission. Paul Klopfer, pastor, ord., w. P. O. Box 267, Tohatchi, New Mexico 87325. A mission of First Baptist Church, Gallup. Mem. 51. SS 49.

Pine Hill. Box 44, Counsellor, New Mexico 87918. Wallace Castello, ord., Ind. Bible schools and hogan visitation in area. Mem. 60. SS 25. Church type ministry with outreach programs. Ministry to BIA school children.

White Horse Lake Mission. Austin Toledo, pastor, layman, Navajo. Box 176, Crownpoint, New Mexico 87313. Mem. 56. SS 58.

Canoncito. James Calvert, pastor, w. 2133 Alvardo N.E., Albuquerque, New Mexico 87110. Mem. 66. SS 15.

Standing Rock. Austin Toledo, layman, Navajo. Box 176, Crownpoint, New Mexico 87313. Mem. 10. SS 16.

Dalton Pass. Between Standing Rock and Crownpoint. A mission of the First Baptist Church of Crownpoint, begun in 1970. Austin Toledo, layman, Navajo. Mem. 21. SS 17.

Mexican Springs. Supplied by Paul Klopfer, Tohatchi. 20 miles north of Gallup. Mem. 3. SS 48.

Nagiizi. On reservation north of Tohatchi. Mrs. Irene Diswood. Christians meet in homes. Fellowship. A WS. Supervision of Paul Klopfer, Tohatchi.

San Juan Association. Andrew Begay, laymen, Navajo. Associational Apprentice (San Juan Association). P. O. Box 266, Shiprock, New Mexico 87420.

Beclabito Indian. Vernon Barton, pastor, Navajo. P. O.
Box 907, Shiprock, New Mexico 87420. Mem. 26. SS 24.

Church Rock Indian. Keith Begay, Navajo. P. O. Box 15,
Church Rock, New Mexico 87311.

Ramah Indian. (Bird Springs) Ollie Blevins, Navajo. P. O.
Box 2905, Grants, New Mexico 87020. Mem. 25. SS 18.

Northwest Catalytic Missionary. Dalton Edwards, ord., w.
P. O. Box 87301, Gallup, New Mexico 87301.

Cuba Catalytic Missionary. David McKenzie, Navajo, ord.
P. O. Box 26, Cuba, New Mexico 87013.

APACHE CHURCHES

Mescalero Baptist Church. Mescalero Apache. James Huse,
pastor, ord., w. P. O. Box 258, Mescalero, New Mexico
88340. Mem. 43. SS 84.

Jicarilla Baptist Church. Jicarilla Apache Reservation.
Eugene Branch, pastor, ord., w. P. O. Box 126, Dulce, New
Mexico 87528. Mem. 32. SS 50.

PUEBLO CHURCHES AND MISSIONS

Isleta Indian Mission. Vacant. P. O. Box 244, Isletta,
New Mexico 87022. Mem. 12. SS 7.

Jemez Valley Indian Chapel. Michael Toledo, pastor, layman,
Ind. 959 Buena Vista S.E., Albuquerque, New Mexico 87106.
Mem. 35. SS 17.

Taos Indian Church. Bennie Romero, pastor, Taos Ind. layman. P. O. Box 246, El Prado, New Mexico 87529. Mem. 29.
SS 54.

Zuni Indian Church. John Bailey. P. O. Box 427, Zuni, New
Mexico 87327. Mem. 31.

Laguna-Acoma Mission. At Cubero, New Mexico. Audley
Hamrick. Route 1, Cubero, New Mexico 87014. Mem. 105.
Com. 250. SS 71. Religious class in school, once a day in
summer.

Santa Clara Indian. Ben Yelrington. Route 2, Box 56,
Espanola, New Mexico 87532. Mem. 32. SS 86. A mission is
carried on from here to Tewa speaking Pueblos near
Espanola, serving the Pueblos of San Juan (Weekday Bible

study 17), Nambe (weekday Bible study 39), Tesuque (weekday Bible study 13), Pojoaque (weekday Bible study 39), San Ildefonso (weekday Bible study 18). Weekday Bible study also at Pecuris 60.

Southern Pueblo Catalytic Missionary. James Bowen. 12444 Towner N.E., Albuquerque, New Mexico 87112.

Reports by Missionaries for 1976: Additions - baptisms 43, by letter 58, by profession of faith 266.

BAPTIST STATE CONVENTION OF NORTH CAROLINA

CHEROKEE BAPTIST ASSOCIATION
Mr. James M. Parris, Moderator; Cherokee, North Carolina 28719.
Rev. Haven C. Lowe, Clerk; P. O. Box 395, Cherokee, North Carolina 28719.
Rev. Luther Osment, Area Missionary; 22 Cowan Street, Sylvia, North Carolina 28770. *(704)586-6630.*

Cherokee Baptist Church. P. O. Box 395, Cherokee, North CArolina 28719. *(704)497-2761.* Haven C. Lowe, pastor, ord., w. Resident mem. 324. Total mem. 462. Ab. in 1976 - 12. Other additions 11. SS 142. VBS 86. Training Union enrollment 70. WS 15.

Children's Home Chapel. Cherokee, North Carolina 28719. J. D. Griffin, pastor. w. P. O. Box 507, Cherokee, North Carolina 28719. Resident mem. 95. Total mem. 115. Baptisms in 1976 - 10. Other accessions 8. SS 95. VBS 87. Training Union 55.

Echota. Cherokee, North Carolina 28719. Thomas Lambert, pastor, Ind. Mem. 48. Ab. in 1976 - 9. Other additions 5. SS 40.

Little Snowbird. Roy French, pastor, Ind. Cherokee, North Carolina 28719. Resident mem. 60. Total mem. 165. Ab. in 1976 - 12. Other additions 11. SS 30. VBS 23.

Piney Grove. No address. Able Lossiah, pastor, Ind. Cherokee, North Carolina 28719.

Rock Springs. Cherokee, North Carolina 28719. Dock A. Smith, pastor, w. Mem. 150. Ab. in 1976 - 4. Other additions 1. SS 95. VBS 57. Training Union 57.

Waterfalls. Cherokee, North Carolina 28719. Johnny Walkingstick, pastor, Ind. Star Route, Cherokee, North

Carolina 28719. Resident mem. 25. Total mem. 39. Ab. in 1976 - 2. Other additions 2. SS 19.

Wright's Creek. Cherokee, North Carolina 28719. Dalton Stanton, pastor, w. Route 1, Sevierville, Tennessee 37862. No information.

Yellow Hill. Star Route, Box 3, Cherokee, South Carolina 28719. Roland E. Whitaker, pastor, w. Route 5, Box 324, Ashville, North Carolina 28803. Resident mem. 152. Total mem. 188. Ab. in 1976 - 2. Other additions 10. VBS 50.

BURNT SWAMP BAPTIST ASSOCIATION Lumbee Indians
Clerk: John L. Carter, Route 1, Box 266, Pembroke, North Carolina 28372.
Director of Associational Missions: Rev. Tom E. Brewington, P. O. Box 997, Pembroke, North Carolina 28372 *(919)521-9850.*

Earlier known as Croatan Indians. Churches are mostly in Robeson County. The Association has 56 ordained ministers and 52 licentiates. All pastors are Indian.

Antioch. Route 1, St. Paul's, North Carolina 28384. 1919. Steve Brewer, pastor, ord. Route 8, Lumberton, North Carolina 28358. Resident mem. 98. Total mem. 100. Baptisms in 1976 - 18. SS 158. VBS 129.

Bear Swamp. 1882. Pembroke, North Carolina 28372. T. M. Swett, pastor, ord. Route 1, Box 343, Rowland, North CArolina 28383. Resident mem. 200. Total mem. 262. Baptisms in 1976 - 16. SS 312. VBS 153. Training Union 24. WS 16. Brotherhood 25.

Benson Chapel. 1970. Rowland, North Carolina 28383. Vacant. Resident mem. 86. Total mem. 89. Baptisms in 1976 - 11. Other additions 12. SS 209. VBS 183. Training Union 47. Brotherhood 25.

Berea. 1926. P. O. Box 835, Pembroke, North Carolina 28372. Sydney Oxendine, pastor, ord. Box 1296, Pembroke, North Carolina 28372. Resident mem. 285. Total mem. 335. Baptisms in 1976 - 8. Other additions 2. SS 254. VBS 138. Training Union 27. WS 10.

Bethel Mill. 1918. Route 3, Box 309, Lumberton, North Carolina 28358. Glassie Locklear, pastor, ord. Route 4, Box 246C, Red Springs, North Carolina 28377. Resident mem. 87. Total mem. 98. Baptisms in 1976 - 10. Other additions 2. SS 126. VBS 92.

The Native American Christian Community

Beulah. 1939. Route 1, Rowland, North Carolina 28383. Manford Locklear, pastor, ord. Mem. 60. Baptisms in 1976 - 10. Other additions 2. SS 102. VBS 45. WS 40. Brotherhood 77.

Burnt Swamp. 1879. Route 4, Box 707, Lumberton, North Carolina 28358. A. A. Lockee, pastor, ord. P. O. Box 595, Pembroke, North Carolina 28372. Mem. 85. SS 140. VBS 51. WS 50.

Cape Fear. 1922. 2618 Dinsmore Drive. Fayetteville, North Carolina 28801. Grady Cummings, pastor, ord. Route 1, Box 11, Pembroke, North Carolina 28371. Mem. 139. Baptisms 9. Other additions 1. SS 249. VBS 125. WS 64. Brotherhood 39.

Cedar Grove. 1930. 608 Morro Street, Fairmont, North Carolina 28340. Vacant. Resident mem. 33. Total mem. 39. SS 75.

Cherokee Chapel. 1949. Route 1, Box 7, Chadbourn, North Carolina 28431. O. J. Burns, pastor, lic. 28 Canal Street, Lumberton, North Carolina 28358. Mem. 62. Baptisms in 1976 - 6. SS 84. VBS 40.

Deep Branch. 1882. Route 2, Box 213B, Pembroke, North Carolina 28372. Chesley McNeill, pastor, ord. Route 8, Box 826, Lumberton, North Carolina 28358. Resident mem. 176. Total mem. 181. SS 227. VBS 101. Training Union 41. WS 34. Brotherhood 9.

Dogwood. 1951. Route 2, Rowland, North Carolina 28383. James D. Dial, pastor, ord. Route 2, Box 345, Pembroke, North Carolina 28372. Resident mem. 48. Total mem. 54. SS 94. VBS 53. WS 17. Brotherhood 7.

Dundarrach. 1972. Route 1, Box 12E, Parkton, North Carolina 28371. Vacant. Mem. 9.

Elizabeth Heights. 1951. P. O. Box 608, Lumberton, North Carolina 28358. King Maynor, pastor, ord. Route 3, Box 860, Lumberton, North Carolina 28358. Resident mem. 59. Total mem. 64. Baptisms in 1976 - 6. SS 90. VBS 96. WS 9.

Elrod. 1972. Route 1, Rowland, North Carolina 28383. Tommy W. Hagans, pastor, ord. Route 4, Box 343A, Lumberton, North Carolina 28358. Mem. 110. Baptisms in 1976 - 20. SS 114. VBS 220.

Gallilee. 1952. Route 4, Red Springs, North Carolina 28377. Isaiah Locklear, Wakulla. Resident mem. 55. Total mem. 69. Baptisms in 1976 - 5. SS 112. VBS 80.

Gospel Tabernacle. 1954. Route 1, Box 206, Maxton, North Carolina 28364. Vacant. Resident mem. 88. Total mem. 103.

Gray Pond. 1911. Route 1, Box 311, Laurinburg, North Carolina 28352. Glassie Locklear, pastor, ord. Route 4, Box 246C, Red Springs, North Carolina 28377. Resident mem. 60. Total mem. 63. SS 86.

Harpers Ferry. 1888. Pembroke, North Carolina 28372. Steve Jones, pastor, ord. P. O. Box 11, Pembroke, North Carolina 28372. Resident mem. 199. Total mem. 201. Baptisms in 1976 - 5. SS 405. VBS 105. WS 43.

Island Grove. 1954. Route 2, Box 173B, Pembroke, North Carolina 28372. C. M. Cummings, pastor, ord. Route 3, Box 105A, Maxton, North Carolina 28364. Mem. 132. Baptisms in 1976 - 2. SS 336. VBS 159. Training Union 54. WS 46.

Leith Creek. 1949. James D. Dial, pastor, ord. Route 2, Box 345, Pembroke, North Carolina 28372. Resident mem. 20. Total mem. 27. SS 64. VBS 20.

Lowry's Chapel. 1954. Route 1, Raeford, North Carolina 28376. Chalmers Kerns, pastor, lic. Route 1, Box 542, Lumberton, North Carolina 28358. SS 40. VBS 50.

Mount Airy. 1915. Route 1, Pembroke, North Carolina 28372. Kelly K. Sanderson, pastor. P. O. Box 288, Pembroke, North Carolina 28372. Mem. 396. Baptisms in 1977 - 22. SS 380. VBS 154. Training Union 65. WS 82. Brotherhood 64.

Mount Bethel. 1958. P. O. Box 4, Hollister, North Carolina 27844. C. H. Richardson, pastor, ord. P. O. Box 100, Hollister, North Carolina 27844. Resident mem. 345. Total mem. 477. Baptisms in 1976 - 22. Other additions 5. SS 269. VBS 120. WS 88.

Mount Elim. 1924. Route 4, Box 283½, Red Springs, North Carolina 28377. David Hunt, pastor, layman. Resident mem. 123. Total mem. 125. Baptisms in 1976 - 17. Other additions 3. SS 242. VBS 125. WS 36.

Mount Moriah. 1887. Route 3, Lumberton, North Carolina 28358. Harvey E. Brewington. P. O. Box 596, Pembroke, North Carolina 28372. Mem. 97. Baptisms in 1976 - 2. SS 166. WS 27. Brotherhood 18.

Mount Olive. 1886. Route 3, Lumberton, North Carolina 28358. Grady Cummings, pastor, ord. Resident mem. 58. Total mem. 68. Baptisms in 1976 - 3. SS 160. VBS 65.

New Bethel. 1910. Route 1, Clinton, North Carolina 28328. Michael Cummings, pastor, ord. Route 1, Box 78D, Clinton, North Carolina 28328. Resident mem. 190. Total mem. 212. Baptisms in 1976 - 4. Other additions 3. SS 180. VBS 112. WS 13. Brotherhood 31.

New Hope. 1945. Route 1, Bolton, North Carolina 28423. C. E. Locklear, pastor, ord. P. O. Box 5, Pembroke, North Carolina 28372. Resident mem. 220. Total mem. 241. SS 325. VBS 231.

New Point. 1945. Route 6, Box 168, Lumberton, North Carolina 28358. Sanford Locklear, pastor, ord. Route 1, Box 178, Pembroke, North Carolina 28372. Resident mem. 144. Total mem. 172. Baptism in 1976 - 1. SS 162. VBS 71. Training Union 50. WS 13. Brotherhood 20.

Oak Grove. 1896. Route 3, Box 281, Laurinburg, North Carolina 28352. R. W. Maynor, pastor, ord. P. O. Box 442, Pembroke, North Carolina 28372. Resident mem. 68. Total mem. 78. Baptisms in 1976 - 4. SS 112. VBS 53.

Pee Dee Chapel. 1891. Route 1, Box 264, Clio, North Carolina 29525. Elbert Chavis, pastor, lic. Route 3, Maxton, North Carolina 28364. Resident mem. 38. Total mem. 54. Baptisms in 1976 - 11. SS 85. VBS 77.

Pembroke First. 1895. P. O. Box 956, Pembroke, North Carolina 28372. Chesley Hammonds, pastor, ord. Resident mem. 93. Total mem. 106. Baptisms in 1976 - 2. SS 106. VBS 45. Training Union 21. WS 13.

Piney Grove. 1880. Route 1, Fairmont, North Carolina 28340. R. W. Maynor, pastor, ord. Mem. 197. Baptisms in 1976 - 6. SS 208. VBS 70. WS 35.

Pleasant View. 1904. Route 1, Box 42, Fairmont, North Carolina 28340. Vester Oxendine, pastor, ord. Route 3, Fairmont, North Carolina 28340. Mem. 178. Baptisms in 1976 - 8. SS 183. VBS 105. Training Union 57. WS 55. Brotherhood 46.

Reedy Branch. 1881. Route 3, Fairmont, North Carolina 28340. C. W. Maynor, pastor, ord. Route 1, Pembroke, North Carolina 28372. Resident mem. 352. Total mem. 355. Baptisms in 1976 - 5. Other Additions 5. SS 350. VBS 71.

St. James. 1902. Route 1, Box 412, Hallsboro, North Carolina 28442. Winford Locklear, pastor, ord. Route 1, Pembroke, North Carolina 28372. Mem. 141. Baptisms in 1976 - 3. SS 162.

Shady Grove. 1974. Route 3, Box 272, Laurinburg, North Carolina 28352. Donald Bullard, pastor, ord. Route 2, Box 165A, Maxton, North Carolina 28364. Mem. 56. Baptisms in 1976 - 17. SS 74. VBS 72.

Smyrna. 1888. Route 5, Lumberton, North Carolina 28358. Douglas Mitchell, pastor, ord. Route 1, Box 315, Rowland, North Carolina 28383. Resident mem. 120. Total mem. 126. SS 205. VBS 212. WS 66.

South Hoke. 1967. Route 1, Box 626, Red Springs, North Carolina 28377. Governor Ray Hunt, pastor, ord. 113 Indian Drive, Fayetteville, North Carolina 28301. Resident mem. 55. Total mem. 60. Baptisms 9. SS 131. VBS 60.

South Walnut. 1976. 301 South Walnut Street, Lumberton, North Carolina 28358. Grady Carter, pastor, ord. Mem. 18. SS 53.

Tabernacle. 1954. P. O. Box 65, Pembroke, North Carolina 28372. Noah Locklear, pastor, ord. Mem. 104. Baptisms in 1976 - 8. SS 178. VBS 85. WS 12.

Ten Mile Center. 1924. Lumberton, North Carolina 28358. James Strickland, pastor, ord. Route 1, Box 137½, Pembroke, North Carolina 28372. Resident mem. 91. Total mem. 93. SS 145. VBS 72. WS 28. Brotherhood 9.

Thompson. 1965. Route 6, Box 277, Lumberton, North Carolina 28358. Gary Sampson, pastor, layman. Route 4, Box 47, Lumberton, North Carolina 28358. Resident mem. 80. Total mem. 83. SS 73.

Union. 1927. Lumberton, North Carolina 28358. Wade Locklear, pastor, ord. Route 4, Red Springs, North Carolina 28377. Resident mem. 138. Total mem. 177. SS 194. VBS 153. Trianing Union 81. WS 19. Brotherhood 12.

Union Light. 1928. Route 1, Maxton, North Carolina 28364. Grady Hunt, pastor, ord. Route 5, Box 579, Lumberton, North Carolina 28358. Resident mem. 101. Total mem. 102. Baptisms 5. SS 79.

West End. 1974. Fairmont, North Carolina 28340. Welton

Lowry, pastor, ord. Route 2, Box 368, Pembroke, North
Carolina 28372. Resident mem. 45. Total mem. 50.
Baptisms in 1976 - 5. Other additions 5. SS 118. VBS 105.

Zion Hill. 1919. Route 1, Shannon, North Carolina 28386.
Steve Brewer, pastor, ord. Resident mem. 97. Total mem.
99. Baptisms in 1976 - 7. Other additions 2. SS 245.
VBS 212.

NORTHERN PLAINS BAPTIST CONVENTION
P. O. Box 1278, Rapid City, South Dakota 57709   *(605)343-5572*
Rev. C. Clyde Billingsley, Director of Missions

Wolf Point Indian Mission. Sioux/Dakota and Assiniboine.
Fort Peck Reservation. Wolf Point, Montana 59201. Oliver W.
Marson, pastor, ord., w. *First Baptist Church*, P. O. Box
1135, Poplar, Montana 59255. *(605)768-3774. Mission* also at
Brockton 59213. Mem. 104. Ab. in 1977 - 1. SS 90. WS 12.
Men's group. Children's choir weekly. VBS at Frazer, Poplar,
Brockton and Wolf Point.

Morning Star Baptist Chapel. P. O. Box 114, Lame Deer,
Montana 59043. Vacant.

First Baptist Church-Mission. Sisseton and Wapheton Dakota/
Sioux. Lake Traverse Reservation. P. O. Box 141, Sisseton,
South Dakota 57262. Wilbert D. Robertson, pastor, ord.,
Sioux. *(605)698-7914.* Mem. 2. SS 20. YS 3. Children meet
after school every Thursday. VBS every summer. Youth camp
in summer. Mission was started 5-10 years ago, but present
pastor is the first resident and 1977-78 is his first year.
He is the first Sioux in the Southern Baptist ministry in
North and South Dakota and Montana.

First Baptist Church. Dakota. Cheyenne River Reservation.
P. O. Box 170, Eagle Butte, South Dakota 57625. Ballard
White, pastor. P. O. Box 170, Eagle Butte, South Dakota
57625.

La Plant Baptist Chapel. Dakota? Cheyenne River Reservation.
Served by Ballard White, pastor at Eagle Butte.

Lakota Baptist Church. 1970. Dakota/Sioux. Pine Ridge
Reservation. P. O. Box 352, Pine Ridge, South Dakota 57770.
(605)867-5395. Harold Heiney, pastor, ord., w. Mem. 21.
SS 18. YS 4. Weekly Bible study in a Rest Home. VBS.

Oglala Baptist Church. Oglala Dakota/Sioux. Pine Ridge
Reservation. Harold Heiney, pastor, ord., w., also pastor
at Lakota Baptist Church. P. O. Box 352, Pine Ridge, South

Dakota 57770. *(605)867-5395.* Mem. 27. SS 20. VBS.

Wookiye Baptist Church. 1975. Sioux/Dakota. Standing Rock
Reservation. Cannon Ball, North Dakota 58528. Ted R.
Samples, pastor, ord., w. P. O. Box 447, Ft. Yates, North
Dakota 58538. *(701)854-7540.* Mem. 20. Ab. in 1977 - 5.
SS 35. YS 10. WS 6. VBS in about 12 small towns on the
Reservation. Sponsored Wowicada Church in Ft. Yates,
organized formally in 1977. Sponsors a mission in Little
Eagle, South Dakota and a large church-type mission in
Mobridge, South Dakota.

First Baptist Church, formerly *Wowicada Baptist Chapel,*
organized officially August 21, 1977. Dakota. Standing Rock
Reservation. Bill Tiger, pastor, ord., Seminole/Creek.
P. O. Box 455, Ft. Yates, North Dakota 58538. *(701)854-7581.*
Mem. 29. Baptisms in 1977: adults 4, children 8-16 years 9.
SS 28. YS 10. WS 10. VBS. Backyard Bible study. Spring
and fall revivals. January - three day Bible study. Bible
Study at DETOX Center and Youth Ranch on Tuesday and Thursday.

Sioux Baptist Chapel and *Waka Waste Baptist Owacekiye* (Red
Shirt Mission). Chapel - Sioux, Black and Mexican. Mission -
all Sioux. Pine Ridge Reservation. P. O. Box 897, Rapid
City, South Dakota 57701. *(605)342-7574.* Calvin Sandlin,
pastor, ord., w. *(605)341-5517.* Mem., including Mission, 98.
Baptisms in 1977: adults 5, children over 8 years 2. SS 35.
YS 12. WS 5. Men's group 3. Bible clubs and VBS every
summer in various places.

Glacier View Baptist Chapel. 1976. Blackfeet. Blackfeet
Reservation. P. O. Box 186, Browning, Montana 59417.
(406)338-7122. Preston North, pastor, ord., w. Mem. 8,
increase of 8 in 1977. Ab. in 1977 - 3. SS 25. YS 10.
Weekly Thursday night adult Bible class. Weekly Wednesday
afternoon children's Bible club. VBS.

First Baptist Church. Dakota/Sioux. Ft. Peck Reservation.
P. O. Box 716, Wolf Point, Montana 59201. Ray Self, pastor,
ord., w.

NORTHWEST BAPTIST CONVENTION
1033 N.E. 6th Street, Portland, Oregon 97232
Executive Director: Rev. Dan C. Stringer

Warm Springs Baptist Church. Allen Elston, ord., w. P. O.
Box 237, Warm Springs, Oregon 97761. Warm Springs Federated
Tribes. Mem. approximately 100.

Indian Baptist Church. 5641 N.E. 60th Avenue, Portland,

Oregon 97218. Dale Pirtle, ord., w. 4815 Buffalo Drive, Salem, Oregon 97301.

Queets Bible Fellowship. Quinalt Tribe. Queets, Washington. c/o Rev. A. J. Whitfield, First Baptist Church, P. O. Box 505, Forks, Washington 98331. This church has also conducted a VBS at Queets.

Hoh Tribe, Forks, Washington 98331. The First Baptist Church of Forks conducts a VBS.

BAPTIST GENERAL CONVENTION OF OKLAHOMA
1141 North Robinson, Oklahoma City, Oklahoma 73103 *(918)756-5567*
Cooperative Missions: Robert Haskins, Director
Indian Consultant to the S.B.C. Board of Home Missions: Dr. B. Frank Belvin, 1724 East 9th Street, Okmulgee, Oklahoma 74447

CHEROKEE INDIAN BAPTIST ASSOCIATION   1869
Secretary: Rev. John Stand, Route 3, Box 172, Stilwell,
             Oklahoma 74960   *(918)774-7171*
General Missionaries to the Cherokees: Rev. and Mrs. J. R.
             Stogsdill, 1305 Cedar Street, Tahlequah, Oklahoma
             74464   *(918)456-9620*

Antioch Baptist Church. 1845. North of Stilwell, Peavine Community. John Stand, pastor, ord., Ind. Route 3, Box 172, Stilwell, Oklahoma 74931. Mem. 84. SS 18. WS 3.

Ballou. 1926. 8 miles south of Locust Grove. Robert Ballou, pastor, ord., Ind. Route 2, Box 153, Locust Grove, Oklahoma 74352. Mem. 185. Ab. in 1977 - 16. SS 108. WS 43.

Bellefonte. 1968. 11 miles northwest of Muldrow. Martin Cochran, pastor, ord., Ind. Route 1, Stilwell, Oklahoma 74960. Mem. 130. Ab. 1. SS 120. WS 10.

Brush Creek. 1958. Joshua Davis, pastor, ord., Ind. Route 1, Box 506, Grove, Oklahoma 74344. Mem. 81. Ab. 7. SS 92. WS 34.

Cedar Tree. 1907. 6 miles east of Tahlequah. Kenneth Littledove, pastor, ord., Ind. Route 1, Salina, Oklahoma 74365. Mem. 134. Ab. 8. SS 54. WS 24.

Cherry Tree. 1914. 8 miles south of Stilwell. Rex Vann, pastor, ord., Ind. Route 2, Proctor, Oklahoma 74457. Mem. 224. Ab. 3. SS 80. WS 5.

Chuculate. 1926. 12 miles southwest of Stilwell. Vacant.

(Secretary, Liza Salazar, Route 1, Stilwell, Oklahoma 74960) Mem. 20. Ab. 12. SS 100. WS 6.

Cloud Creek. 1952. Arch Foreman, pastor, ord., Ind. Route 2, Colcord, Oklahoma 74338. Mem. 71. SS 69. WS 10.

Echota. 1913. 12 miles west of Stilwell. Woodrow Allen, pastor, ord., w. Route 3, Tahlequah, Oklahoma 74464. Mem. 126. Ab. 5. SS 98. WS 23.

Elm Tree. 1953. Tahlequah. Sam Chaudoin, pastor, ord., Ind. Star Route, South, Locust Grove, Oklahoma 74352. Mem. 102. Ab. 5. SS 94. WS 8.

Euwasha. 1915. Kenwood. Bert Spade, pastor, ord., Ind. Route 1, Rose, Oklahoma 74364. Mem. 187. Ab. 1. SS 78. WS 48.

Fairfield. 1909. 3 miles northeast of Stilwell. Andy Gonzales, pastor, ord., Ind. Route 1, Stilwell, Oklahoma 74960. Mem. 228. Ab. 14. SS 110. WS 49.

Fellowship. 1977. Edward Baker, pastor, ord., w. Route 3, Muldrow, Oklahoma 74948. Mem. 32. Ab. 4. SS.

Fourkiller. 1975. Key Ketcher, pastor, ord., Ind. P. O. Box 599, Stilwell, Oklahoma 74960. Mem. 29. SS 43. WS 16.

Hillside. 1926. Jay Bluff, 4 miles southeast of Jay. John Pickup, pastor, ord., Ind. Route 1, Eucha, Oklahoma 74342. Mem. 80. Ab. 3. SS 53. WS 16.

Illinois River. 1950. Joe Pershica, pastor, ord., Chickasaw. Route 1, Watts, Oklahoma 74964. Mem. 144. Ab. 11. SS 80. WS 48.

Johnson Prairie. 1958. Arch Foreman, pastor, ord., Ind. Route 2, Colcord, Oklahoma 74338. Mem. 84. SS 84. WS 16.

Keener. 1953. John Gonzales, Jr., pastor, ord., Ind. Route 1, Bunch, Oklahoma 74931. Mem. 125. Baptisms 8. SS 126. WS 14.

Little Rock. 1912. Robert Nofire, pastor, ord., Ind. General Delivery, Kansas, Oklahoma 74347. Mem. 91. Ab. 2. SS 37. WS 12.

Long Prairie. 1850. Albert Robbins, pastor, ord., Ind. Route 1, Hulbert, Oklahoma 74441. Mem. 127. Ab. 20. SS 136. WS 25.

Mulberry Tree. 1924. Sanders McLemore, pastor, ord., Ind. Route 3, Stilwell, Oklahoma 74960. Mem. 136. Ab. 16. SS 105. WS 37.

New Baptist. Johnson Vann, pastor, ord., Ind. Route 1, Stilwell, Oklahoma 74960. Mem. 100. Ab. 7. SS 100. WS 20.

New Green. 1944. Bill Youngbird, pastor, ord., Ind. Loop Route, Tahlequah, Oklahoma 74464. Mem. 84. Ab. 1. SS 124. WS 8.

New Greenleaf. No report. WS 4.

New Jordan. 1944. Richard Pickup, pastor, ord., Ind. P. O. Box 352, Sadina, Oklahoma 74365. Mem. 205. Ab. 20. SS 174. WS 63.

New Mission. 1905. Vacant. Mem. 80. SS 82. WS 16.

Oak Grove. 1915. Stanley Shell, pastor, lic., Ind. Route 1, Bunch, Oklahoma 74931. Mem. 48. Ab. 4. SS 47.

Oak Ridge. 1974. Frank Acorn, pastor, ord., Ind. Route 1, Stilwill, Oklahoma 74960. Mem. 13. Ab. 3. SS 19.

Old Green. 1947. Martin Cochran, pastor, ord., Ind. Route 1, Stilwell, Oklahoma 74960. Mem. 63. SS 71.

Olive. Bill Youngbird, pastor, ord., Ind. Loop Route, Tahlequah, Oklahoma 74464. Mem. 36. SS 42. WS 8.

Pine Ridge. 1969. Rufus King, pastor, ord., Ind. P. O. Box 44, Jay, Oklahoma 74346. Mem. 44. Ab. 1. SS 38. WS 15.

Piney. 1897. Sam Hider, pastor, ord., Ind. Route 4, Jay, Oklahoma 74346. Mem. 131. Ab. 6. SS 124. WS 10.

Ribbon. 1960. 3 miles southeast of Spavinaw. Lewis Ross, pastor, ord., Ind. Route 2, Spavinau, Oklahoma 74366. Mem. 92. Ab. 18. SS 92. WS 51.

Rock Fence. 1907. 12 miles southeast of Stilwell. Frank Mink, pastor, lic., Ind. Route 1, Stilwell, Oklahoma 74960. Mem. 68. Ab. 4. SS 107. WS 5.

Round Springs. 1860. Eucha. Mike Kingfisher, pastor, ord., Ind. P. O. Box 172, Salina, Oklahoma 74365. Mem. 168. Ab. 7. SS 161. WS 33.

Salem. 1896. 7 miles southeast of Stilwell. Lawrence Eagle, pastor, ord., Ind. Mem. 317. Ab. 10. SS 144. WS 24.

Sequoyah. 1914. 8 miles southwest of Stilwell. John Stand, pastor, ord., Ind. Route 3, Box 172, Stilwell, Oklahoma 74960. Mem. 76. SS 47. WS 7.

Snake Creek. 1956. Southeast of Locust Grove. Ezekiel Vann, pastor, ord., Ind. General Delivery, Salina, Oklahoma 74365. Mem. 73. Ab. 1. SS 70. WS 12.

Standing Rock. 1905. 4 miles southeast of Salina. Joe Chuculate, pastor, ord., Ind. P. O. Box 133, Hulbert, Oklahoma 74441. Mem. 83. Ab. 6. SS 76. WS 56.

Steeley. 1946. 10 miles east of Salina. Alex Sawney, pastor, ord., Ind. Route 1, Salina, Oklahoma 74365. Mem. 136. Baptisms 2. SS 162. WS 30.

Swimmer. 1885. Ned Bridge, pastor, ord., Ind. General Delivery, Salina, Oklahoma 74365. Mem. 56. Ab. 10. SS 75. WS 10.

Sycamore Springs. 1975. Calvin Turner, pastor, ord., Ind. Route 4, Jay, Oklahoma 74346. Mem. 46. Ab. 3.

Tahlequah. Sunday Stopp, pastor, lic., Ind. Route 2, Tahlequah, Oklahoma 74464. Mem. 70. Baptism 1. SS 25. WS 8.

Twin Oaks. 1964. Dick Pickup, pastor, ord., Ind. Route 1, Box 359, Salina, Oklahoma 74365. Mem. 153. Ab. 17. SS 74. WS 45.

Totals: 44 churches; 4,591 members; 257 baptisms; 3,558 Sunday School enrollment; 881 Women's Missionary Union enrollment. All but 3 pastors are Cherokee - 1 is Chickasaw and 2 are "Anglo".

OTHER CHURCHES:

Elm Prairie. About 1860. Neal Leach. Ross M. Bolin, Sr., pastor. Star Route, South, Locust Grove, Oklahoma 74352.

Tyor. SS 10.

OTHER ORDAINED INDIAN MINISTERS:

Tim Wilson. Route 3, Tahlequah, Oklahoma 74464.

John Goodrich. Route 1, Stilwell, Oklahoma 74960.
Stanley Sojourn. P. O. Box 580, Stilwell, Oklahoma 74960.
Leroy Backwater. Route 1, Salina, Oklahoma 74365.
Abraham Proctor. P. O. Box 244, Twin Oakes, Oklahoma 74368.
Stanton Dew. Loop Route, Tahlequah, Oklahoma 74464.
Albert Six. P. O. Box 84, Disney, Oklahoma 74340.
Samson Mouse. 819 Guinn, Tahlequah, Oklahoma 74464.
Charlie Swimmer. Route 3, Stilwell, Oklahoma 74960.
Leonard Ballou. Route 2, Locust Grove, Oklahoma 74352.
Windy Staller. Tahlequah, Oklahoma 74464.
William Rooster. 803 Harrison, Tahlequah, Oklahoma 74464.
Guy Pickup. 2841 East 41st Place, N., Tulsa, Oklahoma 74105.
Charlie Sands. 505 West South Street, Tahlequah, Oklahoma 74464.
J. L. Craeger. P. O. Box 606, Salina, Oklahoma 74365.

OTHER LICENSED INDIAN MINISTERS:

Martin Ballou. Route 1, Box 6-E-1, Locust Grove, Oklahoma 74352.
Jim Sevenstar. Route 3, Muldrow, Oklahoma 74949.
Larry Kingfisher. Box 58, Jay, Oklahoma 74346.
Clifford Loftis. Route 4, Jay, Oklahoma 74346.
Leo Littledeer. Route 1, Stilwell, Oklahoma 74960.
George Chair. Stilwell, Oklahoma 74960.
Ellis Foster. Route 4, Stilwell, Oklahoma 74960.
Tom Sands. Route 4, Box 21, Tahlequah, Oklahoma 74464.
Robert Belt. Box 782, Tahlequah, Oklahoma 74464.
Raymond Jones. Route 2, Tahlequah, Oklahoma 74464.
Daylight Batt. Route 3, Stilwell, Oklahoma 74960.
Steven Gourd. Route 1, Hulbert, Oklahoma 74441.
Mack McLemore. Star Route E, Locust Grove, Oklahoma 74352.
Jim Cochran. Star Route, Kansas, Oklahoma 74347.
Joe O'Field. Star Route, Kansas, Oklahoma 74347.
Jess Fields. Kansas, Oklahoma 74347.
Raymond Cochran. Box 99, Kansas, Oklahoma 74347.
Tom Peters. Route 1, Box 125, Rose, Oklahoma 74364.
Fox Blackfox. Box 233, Twin Oaks, Oklahoma 74368.
Willie Cochran. Route 1, Colcord, Oklahoma 74338.
Fred Cypert. Route 2, Box 81-A, Locust Grove, Oklahoma 74352.
Isaac Hummingbird, Jr. Stilwell, Oklahoma 74960.
Ralph Ketcher. Route 2, Box 27, Stilwell, Oklahoma 74960.
Woodrow Fourkiller. Route 3, Stilwell, Oklahoma 74960.
Bob Keener. 601 D SE, Miami, Oklahoma 74354.
Eli L. Fields. Box 143, Kansas, Oklahoma 74347.
Nelson Kingfisher. Route 1, Colcord, Oklahoma 74338.
Johnson Jones. Route 4, Jay, Oklahoma 74346.
Tommy Sands. Kansas, Oklahoma 74347.
Charley Sultzer. Eucha, Oklahoma 74342.

Homer Sapp. Route 1, Salina, Oklahoma 74364.
Terry Standingwater. Route 1, Salina, Oklahoma 74365.
Sam Blossom. Box 63, Salina, Oklahoma 74365.
Sam Hair. Route 1, Hulbert, Oklahoma 74441.
Steven Crittenden. Route 1, Salina, Oklahoma 74365.
George Cochran. Star Route, Kansas, Oklahoma 74347.
Thomas Gourd. Box 48, Kansas, Oklahoma 74347.
Claude Kingfisher. Route 1, Box 56, Salina, Oklahoma 74365.
Sanford Cummings. Loop Route, Tahlequah, Oklahoma 74464.
Joe McCarter. Loop Route, Tahlequah, Oklahoma 74464.
Curley Turtle. Box 3, Oaks, Oklahoma 74359.
Ned Watt. Route 2, Box 232, Westville, Oklahoma 74965.
Chester Jones. Route 2, Colcord, Oklahoma 74338.
Dick Davis. 12630 E. 10th, Tulsa, Oklahoma 74128.
Mose Hair. Star Route, Spavinaw, Oklahoma 74366.
Chester Jones. General Delivery, Stilwell, Oklahoma 74960.
Daniel Proctor. Route 1, Colcord, Oklahoma 74338.
Jess Robbins. 610 Russell, Tahlequah, Oklahoma 74464.
Hoover Crittenden. Route 1, Hulbert, Oklahoma 74441.
W. G. Whitekiller. Route 1, Hulbert, Oklahoma 74441.
Sanders Dew. Box 634, Tahlequah, Oklahoma 74464.
Sammy Hogshooter. Route 1, Colcord, Oklahoma 74338.

CHOCTAW-CHICKASAW BAPTIST ASSOCIATION   1871
Secretary: Mrs. Delois Vaughn, Hoxbar Route, Box 190,
            Ardmore, Oklahoma 73401
Regional Missionary: Rev. Jack Comer, Box 461, Atoka,
            Oklahoma 74525

Antioch. East of Antlers. A. P. Jefferson, pastor. P. O.
Box 242, Achille, Oklahoma 74720.

Bacon Springs. Achille. A. P. Jefferson, pastor. P. O.
Box 242, Achille, Oklahoma 74720. Mem. 68. Baptism 1. WS.

Bethel. 6 miles south of Stigler. Milton Lewis, pastor.
P. O. Box 341, Keota, Oklahoma 74941. Mem. 20. WS.

Boiling Springs. 1 mile northwest of Wilburton. Silas
McFarland, General Delivery, Hugo, Oklahoma 74743. Mem. 51.
Baptisms 7. WS.

Brushy. 3 miles southeast of Blanco. Isaiah Wesley,
pastor. 4204 S. 24th W., Tulsa, Oklahoma 74104. Mem. 18.
WS.

Capernaum. 8 miles northeast of Antlers. Silas McFarland,
pastor. General Delivery, Hugo, Oklahoma 74743.

Cedar. 7 miles north of Red Oak. Erie Taylor, pastor.

34A Bourland, Ardmore, Oklahoma 73401. Mem. 31. WS.

Concord. Ardmore. Abner White, pastor. 704 E. Florida, Durant, Oklahoma 74701. Mem. 21. Baptisms 1. WS.

Corinth. 1951. Ft. Towson. Ruble C. Green, pastor. Route 2, Antlers, Oklahoma 74523. *(405)587-2251.* Communicants 35. Total com. about 100. Baptisms 2.

Double Springs. 16 miles southwest of McAlester. H. M. Pierce, pastor. P. O. Box 207, Wilburton, Oklahoma 74578. SS 25. YS 15.

Durwood. 10 miles northeast of Ardmore. Shon Bradley, pastor. 611 South 13th, Duncan, Oklahoma 73533. Mem. 25. Ab. 3. WS.

Friendship, Hugo. Kellus Walker, pastor. 1022 W. 7th, Apt. 25, Shawnee, Oklahoma 74801. Mem. 47. Baptisms 2.

First Indian Baptist, McAlester. Gilbert Frazier, pastor. 235 W. Chickasaw, McAlester, Oklahoma 74501. Mem. 148. Baptisms 5. WS.

Green Hill. 3 miles east of Talihina. Vacant. Baptisms 7. Mem. 36. WS.

High Hill, Krebs. Vacant.

Macedonia. 6 miles east and 11 miles south of Atoka. Erie Taylor, pastor. 34A Bourland, Ardmore, Oklahoma 73401. Mem. 66. Baptisms 2. WS.

Mission, Broken Bow. Not meeting.

New Hope. 2 miles south of Keota. A. P. Jefferson, pastor. P. O. Box 242, Achille, Oklahoma 74720. Mem. 53. Ab. 2.

New Jerusalem. Southwest of Hugo. Philip Wade, pastor. Soper, Oklahoma 74759.

Pine Gorve, Talihina. Leslie Clark, pastor. 1002 W. 7th Street, Apt. 25, Shawnee, Oklahoma 74801. Mem. 41. WS.

Rock Creek. 7 miles south of Red Oak. Kuben Kemp, pastor. 701 W. Harrison, McAlester, Oklahoma 74501. Mem. 46. Baptism 1.

Sardis. 18 miles south of Hartshorne. Wayne Scott, pastor. 608 E. Ash, Wilburton, Oklahoma 74578. Mem. 48. Baptisms 7.

Sobol Mission. Lee Carshall, pastor. Route 1, Red Oak, Oklahoma 74653.

Thessalonia, Red Oak. Otis Taylor, pastor. 110 E. Main, Ardmore, Oklahoma 73401. Mem. 33. Baptisms 5. WS.

Zion. Vacant. Mem. 12.

Total: Mem. 862. Ab. in 1976 – 45.

CHI-KA-SHA ASSOCIATION
Regional Missionary: Jack Comer, Box 461, Atoka, Oklahoma
          74525
Associational Missionary: Peter Wall, Box 865, Davis,
          Oklahoma 73030
Moderator: Henry Marris, Route 1, Box 91-A, Madill, Oklahoma
          73446

Ada, First Indian. Howard Baker, pastor. 701 W. 13th, Ada, Oklahoma 74820.

Blue. Northwest Connerville. Joshua Wesley, pastor. Box 461, Stratford, Oklahoma 74856.

Chi-Ka-Sha. 1973. 971 F Street, S.E., Ardmore, Oklahoma 73401. Roy Sockey, pastor. 602 Park S.E., #16, Ardmore, Oklahoma 73401. *(405)226-4707.* Mem. 61. Ab. 30. SS average 40. Midweek prayer service.

Hickory Hill. Northwest of Fittstown near Ada. Willie Brown, pastor. Box 142, Sulphur, Oklahoma 73086.

High Hill, Ada. Southeast. Jack Vines, pastor. Route 1, Allen, Oklahoma 74828.

Indian Baptist, Ardmore. Coolidge Coley, pastor. 1116 Douglas S.E., Ardmore, Oklahoma 73401.

McAlester, Indian. Overbrook. Dale Reynolds, pastor. 112 Mimosa, Weatherford, Texas 76086.

Midway. North of Stratford. Willie Brown, pastor. Box 142, Sulphur, Oklahoma 73086.

Oak Grove. Northwest of Roff. Henderson Cravatt, pastor. General Delivery, Millcreek, Oklahoma 74856.

Only Way. Keota. Marvin Lewis, pastor. Box 188, Millcreek, Oklahoma 74856.

Pickens. McMillan. Henry Marris, pastor. Route 1, Box 91-A, Madill, Oklahoma 73446.

Sandy. Northwest of Sulphur. Elias Brown, pastor. Route 1, Box 209, Davis, Oklahoma 73030.

Sandy Hill. Southwest of Stratford. Emerson Sealy, pastor. Route 1, Box 25, Roff, Oklahoma 74865.

St. York. Southeast of Marlow. Albert Farve, pastor. 3216 S.W. 49th, Oklahoma City, Oklahoma 73119.

Members approximately 900.

MUSKOGEE-SEMINOLE-WICHITA ASSOCIATION
Regional Missionary: Jimmy Anderson, 403 North Washington,
         Shawnee, Oklahoma 74801
Associational Missionary: Dan Phillips, Jr., Route 2,
         Stidham, Oklahoma 74461
Moderator: George Jesse, Box 237, Sasakwa, Oklahoma 74867

65 pastors are ordained, 2 are licensed. 2 are "Anglo", 1 married to a Creek wife. Membership is approximately 4,000.

Alabama. 2 miles northwest of Weleetka. James Harjo, pastor. Box 632, Weleetka, Oklahoma 74880. WS.

Arbeka. 3 miles southwest of Bryant. Louis Birdcreek, pastor. Route 1, Weleetka, Oklahoma 74880.

Artusse. 3 miles southwest of Eufaula. Edmond Barnett, pastor. Route 3, Eufaula, Oklahoma 74432.

Baptist Sunday School Mission. Inactive.

Beaver. Daylight Owl, pastor. Route 1, Bunch, Oklahoma 74931.

Bemo. 2 miles northwest. Victor Wesley, pastor. 703 Rutherford, Muskogee, Oklahoma 74401.

Big Arbor. Fame. Boney McIntosh, pastor. General Delivery, Stidham, Oklahoma 74461. WS.

Birdcreek. 1888. 4 miles southwest of Sasakwa. Seminole. John Factor, pastor, ord. P. O. Box 177, Sasakwa, Oklahoma 74867. Mem. 50.

Butler Creek. 5 miles northeast of Oktaha. Thompson Billy, pastor. 609 North G. Street, Muskogee, Oklahoma 74401.

Cedar Creek. Near Coweta. Barney Porter, pastor. Box 211, Coweta, Oklahoma 74429.

Cedar Creek Eufaula. 2 miles east of Maud. Herman Bender, pastor. P. O. Box 1138, Seminole, Oklahoma 74868.

Cedar River. 3 miles southwest of Holdenville. Washie Foster, pastor.

Cedar Spring. 4 miles southeast of Gore. Tom Phillips, pastor. General Delivery, Braggs, Oklahoma 74423.

Cold Spring, Seminole. 15 miles south Wold Com. Homer Lee Emarthle, pastor. Route 1, Maud, Oklahoma 74854.

Deep Fork Hilliabee. 4 miles southwest of Checotah. Bill Welch, pastor. Box 116, Checotah, Oklahoma 74426. WS.

First Indian, Okmulgee. John Dyson, pastor. 310 N. Mission Road, Okmulgee, Oklahoma 74447. WS.

Forrest Creek. Terry Walker, pastor. 205 W. College, Seminole, Oklahoma 74868.

Grave Creek. 1 mile west of Hitchita. Victor Wesley, pastor. 703 Rutherford, Muskogee, Oklahoma 74401. WS.

Greenleaf. 3 miles southwest of Okemah. C. D. Harjo, pastor. Route 2, Box 26, Okemah, Oklahoma 74859.

Hickory Ground #1. 6 miles southeast of Henryetta. Artussee Fields, pastor. 1339 N. 78 E. Avenue, Tulsa, Oklahoma 74115.

Hickory Ground #2. 7 miles southeast of Henryetta. Solomon Lee, pastor. Box 692, Henryetta, Oklahoma 74437.

High Spring (Creek). 3 miles south of Okemah. William Wind, pastor. 744½ N. Cheyenne, Tulsa, Oklahoma 74106.

High Spring (Seminole). William Wind, pastor. 744½ N. Cheyenne, Tulsa, Oklahoma 74106.

Hillabee. 4 miles northwest of Hanna. Sam Brown, pastor. Route 3, Eufaula, Oklahoma 74432.

Hutchechuppa. Oscar Harjo, pastor. Route 2, Henryetta, Oklahoma 74437.

Little Coweta (Lenna). 20 miles southeast of Henryetta.

Earnest Best, pastor. 800 Forrest Avenue, Eufaula, Oklahoma 74432. WS.

Little Cussetah. 1 mile north and 1½ miles east of Sapulpa. Solomon Bullett, pastor. WS.

Little Quarsarity. 3 miles southeast of Cromwell. Eddie Lindsey, pastor. Route 2, Box 102, Wewoka, Oklahoma 74884. WS.

Many Springs (Holdenville). 5 miles south and 1½ miles east of Winding Road. Tom Bear, pastor. Box 95, Eufaula, Oklahoma 74432.

Mekusukey. 2 miles south of Seminole. Willie Herrod, pastor. Route 2, Wetumka, Oklahoma 74883.

Middle Creek #1 (Carson). 20 miles south of Henryetta. Johnston Roberts, pastor. Route 1, Dustin, Oklahoma 74839. WS.

Middle Creek #2. 3 miles west of Holdenville. Major Hawkins, pastor. Route 1, Box 349, Wewoka, Oklahoma 74884.

Montezuma. 3 miles northwest of Okfuskee. Edward Leader, pastor. P. O. Box 1022, Sapulpa, Oklahoma 74066. WS.

New Arbor. 2 miles west of Eufaula. Luke McIntosh, pastor. Route 1, Checotah, Oklahoma 74426.

New Life. 1365 East 46th N., Tulsa, Oklahoma 74126. *(918)425-2771.* Jim B. Foreman, pastor, ord., Cherokee. Mem. 25. SS 50. YS 12. WS 15. Men's group 12. VBS.

Nuyaka. 2½ miles east of Morse, 10 miles east of Okmulgee. Wesley Roberts, pastor. Route 4, Okmulgee, Oklahoma 74447. WS.

Okfuskee. Creek. 1½ miles southeast of Eufaula. Willie Kelley, pastor, ord., Creek. P. O. Box 554, Eufaula, Oklahoma 74432. Communicant mem. 35. Total com. 90. WS 20. Men's society 15.

Okmulgee. 1 mile west. James McCosar, pastor. 212 N. Frisco, Tulsa, Oklahoma 74103.

Pigeon. 3 miles northwest of Cromwell.

Ponca Indian (Ponca City). Eddie Lee Lindsey, pastor. 1809 Richway, Ponca City, Oklahoma 74601.

Prairie Spring (Castle). Joe Smith, pastor. Castle, Oklahoma 74833. WS.

Randell. 7 miles northwest of Henryetta. Taylor Johnson, pastor. Route 1, Box 234, Henryetta, Oklahoma 74437.

Rock Spring (Anadarko). 3 miles north and just east of highway. Mark Standing, pastor. 112 W. Virginia, Anadarko, Oklahoma 73005. WS.

Ross Mission. Inola Wildcat, pastor. Route 1, Gore, Oklahoma 74435.

Salt Creek. 3½ miles north of Wetumka. Mose Scott, pastor. Route 3, Box 115, Okemah, Oklahoma 74859.

Sand Creek. 5 miles northeast of Wetumka. Gene Harjo, pastor. 501 N. Martin, Okmulgee, Oklahoma 74447. WS.

Sand Creek Eufaula. 4 miles southwest of Wewoka. Joe Tiger, pastor. Route 1, Wewoka, Oklahoma 74884.

Sand Spring. 1½ miles southwest of Braggs. Ward Coachman, pastor. Route 1, Braggs, Oklahoma 74423. WS.

Seminole Arbeka. 4 miles east of Konawa. William Burgess, pastor. 119 N. Okfuskee, Wewoka, Oklahoma 74884.

Seminole Baptist. 4 miles east of Konawa. Alex Burgess, pastor. Route 1, Box 203, Konawa, Oklahoma 74849.

Silver Spring. 9 miles east of Henryetta. Felix Tiger, pastor. P. O. Box 537, Henryetta, Oklahoma 74437. WS.

Snake Creek #1 (Creek). 1 mile southeast of Bixby. George Doyle, pastor. 3 E. Rosedale, Tulsa, Oklahoma 74127. WS.

Snake Creek #2 (Seminole). Little, 10 miles northeast of Seminole. Bryant Jesse, pastor. WS.

Spring. 2 miles west of Sasakwa. George Jesse, pastor. Box 237, Sasakwa, Oklahoma 74856. WS.

Thewahle. 1½ miles northeast of Dustin, William West, pastor. Bowlegs, Oklahoma 74830.

Texanna Mission. Inola Wildcat, pastor. Route 1, Gore, Oklahoma 74435.

Tookparfka. 11 miles northeast of Calvin. Robert Herrod,

pastor. Star Route, Calvin, Oklahoma 74531.

Trenton. 5 miles west of Hanna. Roley Haynes, pastor. Box 604, Weleetka, Oklahoma 74880.

Tulmochussee. 3 miles south of Hanna. Raymond McGirt, pastor. 608 E. Popular, Holdenville, Oklahoma 74848.

Tuskegee. 6 miles west, 3/4 mile south of Eufaula. James McComb, pastor. Box 402, Eufaula, Oklahoma 74432. WS.

Vian Creek. 7 miles north of Vian. Harley Barnoski, pastor. 814 N. Utica, Tulsa, Oklahoma 74110.

Wekiwa. 4 miles west of Sand Springs. Marvin Kelly, pastor. 2530 S. 65th West Avenue, Tulsa, Oklahoma 74107. WS.

Weogufkee. 1870. Creek. 2 miles west of Hanna. Dave McCombs, pastor, ord., Creek. Route 1, Dustin, Oklahoma 74839. *(918)656-3463.* Worship in Creek language. SS and Church Training in Creek and English. SS 15. YS 8. WS 4. Men's society 5. Mission study. Week of prayer. Revivals. Bible studies.

West Eufaula. 2½ miles west and 1 mile south of Eufaula. Washie Lewis, pastor. Box 304, Eufaula, Oklahoma 74432.

Wetumka. 1¼ mile southeast. Charlie Tiger, pastor. Wetumka, Oklahoma 74883.

Wewoka. John Leitka, pastor. Box 837, Wewoka, Oklahoma 74884. WS.

Yardika. 7 miles southeast of Henryetta.

INDIAN CHURCHES IN OTHER ASSOCIATIONS

Membership approximately 3,087.

American Indian Baptist, Oklahoma City. Roy Weavel, interim pastor. 1205 N.W. 1, Harrah, Oklahoma 73045.

Bowen Place Indian Chapel, Tulsa. 1950. Osage. Tulsa Association. Tulsa, Oklahoma 74127. *(918)584-6015.* Paul Whitaker, pastor, ord. 632 East 57th Street, N., Tulsa, Oklahoma 74126. Ab. in 1977 - 21. SS 121. YS 29. WS 33. Men's society 29. MWF Food service. VBS.

Broadway Indian Church, Kingfisher. Ron Moses, pastor.

Mem. 187. Baptisms in 1975 - 9. SS 92. WS 25.

Calument Indian Mission. Preaching Point of Broadway.

Canton Indian Church, Canton. Jerry Jones, pastor. Box 576 Canton, Oklahoma 73724. Mem. 148. Baptisms in 1975 - 5. SS 77.

Carnegie Indian Mission, Carnegie. Reuben Boland, pastor. P. O. Box 559, Carnegie, Oklahoma 73015. Mem. 45. SS 16.

Central Indian Church, Oklahoma City. 828 N.W. 8th, Oklahoma City, Oklahoma 74106. Mem. 247. Baptisms in 1975 - 21. SS 162.

Chilocco Indian Mission, Newkirk. Lloyd Jones, pastor. Box 473, Newkirk, Oklahoma 74647.

Claremore Immanuel Church. Mem. 89. Baptisms in 1975 - 13. SS 83.

Cooper Memorial Church, McLoud. Lester Patterson, pastor. Box 537, McLoud, Oklahoma 74851. Mem. 86. Baptisms in 1975 - 13. SS 121.

Concho School, El Reno. Pat Bowers, pastor. Route 2, Box 48, El Reno, Oklahoma 73036.

Elk City Indian Mission. Preaching Point of Hammon.

First Caddo Indian Church, Ft. Cobb. Amon Harjo, pastor. 313½ W. Kentucky, Anadarko, Oklahoma 73005.

First Indian Baptist Mission. 1953. Cheyenne-Arapaho. 320 North 4th Street, Clinton, Oklahoma 73601. Concord-Kiowa Association. Max Malone, pastor, ord., Ind. P. O. Box 157, Hammon, Oklahoma 73650. Mem. 156. SS 75. WS 10. Midweek prayer service. VBS. Two revivals yearly.

First Indian Church, Enid. John Hubbard, pastor. Box 166, Enid, Oklahoma 73701. Mem. 99. Baptisms in 1975 - 3. SS 47.

First Indian Church, Shawnee. Tom Anderson, pastor. P. O. Box 1561, Shawnee, Oklahoma 74801.

Gethsemane Mission, Oklahoma City. Willis Knight, pastor. 7205 Melrose Lane, Apt. 18, Oklahoma City, Oklahoma 73109. 2515 S.W. Grand, Oklahoma City, Oklahoma 73108.

Glorieta Indian Baptist Church. 1961. Cherokee. 200 S.E. 70th Street, Oklahoma City, Oklahoma 73149. *(405)632-0108.* Capital Association. John E. Hummingbird, pastor, ord. 717 Plaza Drive, Moore, Oklahoma 73160. *(405)799-6688.* Communicant mem. 75. Total com. 125. Ab. in 1977 - 20. SS 65. WS 10. Wednesday night prayer service and Bible study. VBS. Revivals.

Harmon Indian Church. 1950. Cheyenne. P. O. Box 157, Hammon, Oklahoma 73650. Beckham-Mills Association. Max Malone, pastor, ord., Ind. P. O. Box 157, Hammon, Oklahoma 73650. Communicant mem. 132. Ab. in 1977 - 5. SS 64. WS 8. Men's society 5. Midweek prayer service. VBS. Daily hot meal provided for elderly in cooperation with Tribe. Sponsors Mission Fellowship in Elk City, Oklahoma Sponsors A.A. meetings.

Independent Indian Church, Walters. Videll Yacheschi, pastor. Walters, Oklahoma 73572. Comanche-Cotton Association.

Indian Capitol Church, Anadarko. Bridge Chuckluck, pastor. Route 1, Anadarko, Oklahoma 73005. Caddo Association.

Community Baptist Church, Tulsa. Lloyd Kingfisher, pastor. 1301 S. Quincy, Tulsa, Oklahoma 74120. Tulsa Association.

Indian Fellowship Church, Tulsa. Jim Alexander, pastor. 6130 S. 58th, Oakhurst, Oklahoma 74050. Mem. 52. Baptisms in 1975 - 6. SS 34. WS 11. Tulsa Association.

Indian Nations Church, Seminole. Bill Barnett, pastor. P. O. Box 2533, Shawnee, Oklahoma 74801. Pottawatomie-Lincoln Association.

Lawton Indian Church, Lawton.

Little Springs Church, Oklahoma City. Billy S. Jones, pastor. 4000 S.E. 51, Oklahoma City, Oklahoma 73135. Capital Association. Mem. 219. SS 123. WS 45.

Muskogee First Indian, Muskogee. Frank Sweger, pastor. 1176 Walnut, Muskogee, Oklahoma 74401. Mem. 163. SS 51. WS 14. Muskogee Association.

New Trinity Baptist Mission, Oklahoma City. Marcey Gibson, pastor. 4305 South Nebraska, Oklahoma City, Oklahoma 73129. Capital Association.

Only Way Indian Church, Stroud. Allen K. Morris, pastor.

Route 3, Box 227A, Stroud, Oklahoma 74079. Mem. 45. SS 26.
WS 11. Cimarron Association.

Osage Indian Church, Pawhuska. Fred Wright, pastor. Abbott
Avenue and ·Okesa Road, 619 Kiagkah, Pawhuska, Oklahoma
74056. Washita-Osaga Association.

Otoe Indian Church, Red Rock. A. B. Jones, pastor. 310
Taz, Morrison, Oklahoma 73061. Mem. 184. SS 32. WS 8.
Perry Association.

Ottawa Indian Church, Wyandotte. Mem. 109. Baptisms in
1975 - 5. SS 85.

Pawnee Indian Baptist Church. 1908. Pawnee. Route 2,
Box 2-A, Pawnee, Oklahoma 74058. *(918)762-2356.* Cimarron
Association. Floyd Freeman, pastor, ord., w. Resident
mem. 90. Ab. in 1977 - 3. SS 40. WS 5. VBS. Services in
a local Rest Home.

Salateeska Indian Mission, Shawnee. Victor Cope, pastor.
Route 5, Box 224A, Shawnee, Oklahoma 74801. Pottawatomie-
Lincoln Association.

Seneca Indian School, Wyandotte.

Spring River Indian Church, Quapaw. Fred Von Moss, pastor.
Box 130, Cardin, Oklahoma 74335. Northeastern Association.
Mem. 260. Baptisms in 1975 - 23. SS 131. WS 11.

El Reno Indian Mission, El Reno. John Goat, pastor. 4028
S.W. 25, Oklahoma City, Oklahoma 73108. Central
Association. Mem. 10. Baptisms in 1975 - 4.

Swappingback Indian Church, El Reno. J. M. James, pastor.
'Box 921, El·Reno, Oklahoma 73036. Central Association.

Westwood Indian Church, Oklahoma City. Mem. 38. SS 46.
Capital Association.

TENNESSEE BAPTIST CONVENTION

P. O. Box 347, Brentwood, Tennessee 37027   *(615)373-2255*
Rev. Leslie R. Baumgartner, Director of Missions

First Indian Baptist Church. Choctaw. Star Route, Ripley,
Tennessee 38063. Michael Powers, pastor. ord., w. 94 .
Russell Road, Jackson, Tennessee 98301. Mem. 40. SS 39.
Church training class 39.

Wright's Creek Baptist Church. Cherokee. Dalton Stanton.

Route 1, Sevierville, Tennessee 37862.

THE BAPTIST GENERAL CONVENTION OF TEXAS
Language Missions Section, 305 Baptist Building, Dallas, Texas 75201   *(214)741-1991*
Rev. Leobardo C. Estrada, Coordinator

First Indian Baptist Church. K. P. Hohannan, pastor. 603 South Beacon, Dallas, Texas 75223. 1976 report: mem. 241, ab. 16, SS 105, WS 39, total income $20,164.

James Avenue Baptist Church. Frankie Rainey, pastor. 5745 James Avenue, Fort Worth, Texas 76134. This church has a small Indian Department.

Cliff Temple Baptist Church. A. Douglas Watterson, pastor. P. O. Box 3770, Dallas, Texas 75208. Some Indian families are members or attend this church.

Friendship Baptist Church. Route 2, Box 1141, Midland, Texas 79701.

UTAH-IDAHO SOUTHERN BAPTIST CONVENTION
P. O. Box 2545, Salt Lake City, Utah 84110   *(801)322-3565*
Rev. Darwin E. Welsh, Executive Director

Intermountain Baptist Indian Chapel. 634 South Fourth Street, Brigham City, Utah 84302. Bruce Conrad, pastor, ord., Anglo. Participants 50. Adjacent to Intermountain Indian School. Various tribes. All programs are youth-oriented.

Ute Baptist Indian Church. Ute tribe. Unitah an Ouray Reservation. Route 1, Box 154, Roosevelt, Utah 84066. John Blake, ord., Anglo. Mem. 125. SS. WS. Youth programs.

Fort Hall Indian Mission. Shoshone-Bannock. P. O. Box 488, Blackfoot, Idaho 83221. Mike McKay, pastor, ord., Anglo. Mem. 44. SS. WS. Youth programs.

VIRGINIA BAPTIST CONVENTION
Virginia Baptist Building, Monument Avenue at Willow Lawn, Richmond, Virginia 23226
Language Missions: Rev. George Joslin, Director

All pastors are ordained and white.

Indian View Baptist Church. Pamunkey. King William, Virginia 23086. Dr. Charles A. Morgan. 3328 West Franklin Street, Richmond, Virginia 23111. *(804)353-9937.* Mem. 123. Ab. in 1977 - 1. SS 40. Other programs.

Mattaponi Baptist Church. Mattaponi. Route 1, West Point, Virginia 23181. Charles Colonna, supply. 563 Logan Place, Apt. 11, Newport News, Virginia 23601. *(804)595-6538*. Mem. 30. SS 15. Midweek prayer meeting. VBS.

Pamunkey Baptist Church. Pamunkey. King William, Virginia 23086. Curtis P. Cleveland. 4309 Chamberlayne, Apt. 2, Richmond, Virginia 23227. *(804)262-7124*.

Rappahannock Baptist Church. Route 1, Tappahannock, Virginia 22560. William Durrett. P. O. Box 5028, Fredericksburg, Virginia 22401. *(703)373-8037*.

Samaria Baptist Church. Route 1, Box 330, Providence Forge, Virginia 23104. Charles Evans, interim pastor. Route 1, Box 245-H, Sandston, Virginia 23150.

Tsena Commoko Baptist Church. 1922. Eastern Chickahominy. Providence Forge, Virginia 23140. Thomas L. Parlett. 2108 Avondale Drive, Mechanicsville, Virginia 23111. Mem. 41. SS 41. WS 5. B.T.U. annual training course.

UNITED CHURCH OF CHRIST

CAIM: COUNCIL FOR AMERICAN INDIAN MINISTRIES
122 West Franklin Avenue, Room 321, Minneapolis, Minnesota 55404
Edward Decorah, Chairman   *(612)870-3679*
Ms. Juanita Helphrey, Secretary-Treasurer
Rev. Mitchell Whiterabbit (Winnebago), Executive Director
Ms. Jackie Owen, Executive Secretary

The National agency of the UCC responsible for ministry to American Indians and the resource agency for the Indian churches. Allocations from the UCC to the churches are routed through CAIM. Concerned with social, legal and treaty rights, with the urban Indian situation, with ecumenical cooperation, and with religious issues relating to the American Indians and their cultures.

DAKOTA ASSOCIATION: The Indian churches
Rev. Percy Tibbets, Acting-Director (retired minister, Dakota)
P. O. Box 213, Rapid City, South Dakota 57701

Arickara U.C.C. 1885. Arickara. Ft. Berthold Reservation. Emmet, North Dakota 58534, near Garrison. Robert Fox, pastor, ord., Arickara. Roseglen, North Dakota 58775. Mem. 84.

Memorial. 1899. Arickara. Ft. Berthold Reservation. Emmet, North Dakota 58534, near Parshall. Robert Fox, ord., Arickara. Roseglen, North Dakota 58775. Mem. 60.

Twin Buttes. 1922. Arickara. Ft. Berthold Reservation. Halliday, North Dakota 58636. Gerald Geske, ord., w. Mem. 60. SS 42.

Independence. 1916. Arickara. Ft. Berthold Reservation. Mandaree, North Dakota 58757. Vacant. Mem. 57. SS 8.

Mandaree. 1955. Arickara. Ft. Berthold Reservation. Mandaree, North Dakota 58757. Vacant. Mem. 28. SS 17.

Snow Bird Chapel. 1955. Arickara. Ft. Berthold Reservation. New Town, North Dakota 58763. George Gillette, pastor, ord., Arickara. Mem. 33. SS 20.

Shell Creek. 1922. Arickara. Ft. Berthold Reservation. George Gillette, pastor, ord., Arickara. New Town, North Dakota 58763. Mem. 33. SS 20.

Congregational Church. Arikara. Ft. Berthold Reservation. New Town, North Dakota 58763. David Holsinger, pastor, ord., w. Mem. 41. SS 35.

Bazille Creek Church, Niobrara. 1888. Santee Reservation. Bazille Creek, Nebraska. Paul N. Robertson, pastor, lic., Santee Sioux. Niobrara, Nebraska 68760. Mem. 17.

Memorial. 1912. Dakota. Standing Rock Reservation. Cannon Ball, North Dakota 58528. Vacant. Mem. 69. WS.

Cherry Creek Church. 1890. Cherry Creek, South Dakota 57622. Owen Hale, pastor, lic., Cheyenne River Dakota. Mem. 80.

Frazier Memorial. 1924. Dakota. Howes, South Dakota 57748. Douglas Widow, pastor, ord., Cheyenne River Dakota. Faith, South Dakota 57626. Mem. 44. WS.

Upper Cheyenne. 1910. Dakota. Howes, South Dakota 57748. Douglas Widow, pastor, ord., Cheyenne River Dakota. Mem. 52. WS.

Red Scaffold Church. 1941. Dakota. Eagle Butte, South Dakota 57625. Vacant. Mem. 50.

Virgin Creek. 1894. Dakota. LaPlant, South Dakota 57637. Francis Lee, pastor, lic., Cheyenne River Dakota. Ridge View, South Dakota 57652. Mem. 43.

Elkhorn Hill. 1894. Dakota. Little Eagle, South Dakota 57639. Moses Zephier, pastor, lic., Lower Brule Dakota. Mem. 100. WS.

Messiah. 1891. Dakota. Little Eagle, South Dakota 57639.
Angus Long Elk, pastor, ord., Lower Brule Dakota. Mem. 100.
WS.

Ponca Creek Church. 1891. Dakota. St. Charles, South Dakota
57571. Hampton Andrews, pastor, lic., Rosebud Dakota. Mem.
73. SS 25. YS.

Parmalee. 1908. Dakota. Parmalee, South Dakota 57566.
Taylor Bald Eagle, part time pastor, Cheyenne River Dakota.

Bear Creek. 1925. Dakota. Lantry, South Dakota 57636.
Dennis Dog Eagle, pastor, part time, Standing Rock Dakota.
Mem. 32.

Buffalo Church. 1976. Dakota. Eagle Butte, South Dakota
57625. Henry Good Bear, pastor, part time, lic., Cheyenne
River Dakota. Mem. 11.

Green Grass. 1895. Dakota. Eagle Butte, South Dakota 57625.
Moses Bad Male, pastor, lic.

Pine Church. 1973. Dakota. Little Eagle, South Dakota
57625. Charles Shell Track, Sr., pastor.

Retired ministers: Rev. Jonah Little Wounded
                     Dupree, South Dakota 57625

                     Rev. Percy Tibbets
                     P. O. Box 213, Rapid City, South Dakota
                                                        57701
SOUTH DAKOTA CONFERENCE supports in finance and leadership
Milk's Camp Industries, Bonesteel, South Dakota 57317.

WISCONSIN CONFERENCE, WISCONSIN NORTHWEST ASSOCIATION

Winnebago U.C.C. 1878/1922. Winnebago Indian Mission.
Black River Falls, Wisconsin 54615. James Selmser, pastor,
ord., w. R.D. 5, Box 393, Black River Falls, South Dakota
54615. Mem. 90. Confessions of faith in 1976 - 2.
Confirmations 4. SS 47.

Total for U.C.C.:   24 churches (there are a number of
additional inactive ones). Mem. 1,083.

THE UNITED METHODIST CHURCH

The Indians missions of the Methodist Churches were always the
joint responsibility of the regional Conferences and the
national Missionary Society or Board, and today the churches

continue in that dual relationship. The National agency most concerned is:

THE NATIONAL DIVISION OF THE BOARD OF GLOBAL MINISTRIES
475 Riverside Drive, New York, N.Y. 10027   *(212)678-6161*
Dr. Randolph Nugent, Associate General Secretary
Miss Billie Nowabbi (Indian), Director of Field Work, Native
    American Churches

Other agencies related to the Indian ministries are:

WOMEN'S DIVISION
475 Riverside Drive, New York, N.Y. 10027
Ms. Theressa Hoover, Associate General Secretary

BOARD OF HIGHER EDUCATION AND MINISTRY
P. O. Box 871, Nashville, Tennessee 37202
Division of the Ordained Ministry: Douglas Fitch, Indian
    Concerns
Office of Personnel: Ruben Salcido, Indian Concerns

COMMISSION ON RELIGION AND RACE
100 Maryland Avenue, N.E., Washington, D.C. 20002
Woodie W. White, Executive Secretary

The voice of the Indian churches and members is the:

NATIVE AMERICAN INTERNATIONAL CAUCUS
Ms. Diane Moats, President

Five regional organizations elect six members each to the
national Caucus.

A self-study is underway.

STUDY COMMITTEE ON NATIVE AMERICAN MINISTRIES
P. O. Box 4808, Mesa, Arizona 85201   *(602)834-8179*
Raymond G. Baines, Exeutive Director

NEW YORK WEST AREA
3049 East Genesee, Syracuse, New York 13224   *(315)446-6731*
Bishop Joseph H. Yeakel

CENTRAL NEW YORK CONFERENCE

Onondaga Indian Mission. Onondaga. Richard Dickinson,
pastor, ord., w. 226 Davis Street, Syracuse, New York
13204. Mem. 45. Ib. 4. SS 14. WS 12.

Four Corners. Group meeting. No pastor.

Directory - Denominational Mission Agencies

NORTHERN NEW YORK CONFERENCE

Hogansburg. Akwasasne (Mohawk). St. Regis Reservation. Box 116m, Hogansburg, New York 13655. Bruce C. Clark, ord., w. R.D. 2, Masena, New York 13662. *(315)769-5618.* Mem. 143. WS 15. Summer School.

Two ordained Indian pastors serve white churches: Kenneth Snyder, 212 East Main St., Arcade, N.Y. 14009. Marvin Abrams, P. O. Box 8522, Rochester, N.Y. 14619.

Another is on the staff of the Board of Church and Society: Thomas Fassett, 100 Maryland Ave., N.E., Washington, D.C. 20002.

The Central New York Conference provides transportation to Indians for medical care and Senior Citizens activities and has cooperated with the State Council of Churches in mediation of disputes.

NORTH CAROLINA CONFERENCE
Council on Ministries   *(919)828-0568*
P. O. Box 10955, Raleigh, North Carolina 27605
Rev. Simeon F. Cummings, Coordinator of Outreach Ministries

LUMBEE CHURCHES

First United Methodist Church. 1906. Breece Street, Pembroke, North Carolina 28372. *(919)521-4943.* Jerry J. Juren, pastor, ord., w. *(919)521-4018.* Mem. 183. Ab. in 1977 - 4, ib. 2. SS 149. YS 15. WS 20. VBS. Children's choir.

Prospect United Methodist Church. Route 3, Maxton, North Carolina 28364. 1874. Harvey Lowry, pastor, ord. Mem. 670. Accessions in 1977 - 34. SS average 399. WS 25. Men's society 25. YS 74. Total budget $61,000.

Collins Chapel. 1960. Route 1, Lumber Springs, North Carolina. Wilton Cummings, part time pastor, deacon. Route 2, Box 347, Pembroke, North Carolina 28372. *(919)521-2291.* Mem. 56. SS 77. VBS.

Sandy Plains Charge. Milford Oxendine, Jr., pastor, ord., Ind. Route 1, Box 67A, Pembroke, North Carolina 28372. *(919)521-3775.*

Branch Street. 1962. West 5th Street, Lumberton, North Carolina 28358. Mem. 110. SS 152. WS 15. VBS.

Sandy Plains U. M. C. 1908. Route 1, Box 67A, Pembroke, North Carolina 28372. Mem. 195. Ab. in 1977 - 4. SS 191. YS 15. WS 13. VBS.

Fairview. 1912. Route 2, Hamer, South Carolina 29547. Theodore R. Brady, Jr., pastor, unordained, w. 2414 Roberts Avenue, Lumberton, North Carolina 28358. *(919)738-9011.* Mem. 132. Ab. in 1977 - 4. SS 40. VBS.

Hickory Grove. 1910. Route 1, Clio, South Carolina 29525. Theodore R. Brady, Jr., pastor, unordained, w. 2414 Roberts Avenue, Lumberton, North Carolina 28358. *(919)738-9011.* Mem. 82. Ab. in 1977 - 9. SS 35. VBS.

Philadelphus. 1958. Highway 71, Red Springs, North Carolina 28377. Wilton Cummings, part time pastor, Ind. deacon. Route 2, Box 347, Pembroke, North Carolina 28372. *(919)521-2291.* Mem. 140. Ab. in 1977 - 4. SS 67. VBS.

Pleasant Grove. 1912. Route 1, Rowland, North Carolina 28383. Simeon Dufrene Cummings, Ind. student pastor. P. O. Box 348. Pembroke, North Carolina 28372. Mem. 95. Ab. in 1977 - 11, ib. 4. SS 152. WS 11. VBS

Ashpole Center. 1906. Route 1, Rowland, North Carolina 28383. Simeon Dufrene Cummings, Ind. student pastor. P. O. Box 348, Pembroke, North Carolina 28372. *(919)521-9602.* Mem. 60. SS 154. WS 20. VBS.

Coharrie. 1963. Highway 421, Clinton, North Carolina 28328. James Lee Jacobs, part time pastor, Ind. deacon. 104 Westwood Drive, Goldsboro, North Carolina 27530. *(919)734-8645.* Mem. 62. Ab. in 1977 - 5. SS 48. VBS.

WESTERN NORTH CAROLINA CONFERENCE

Cherokee United Methodist Church Mission. P. O. Box 367, Cherokee, North Carolina 28919. *(919)497-2948.* Tim Boles, pastor, ord., w. Mem. 214. Methodist com. 315. Conv. in 1977 - 6, ab. 4, ib. 2. Indian men layworkers 3, Ind. women workers 4, Black men layworkers 3, w. men 3, w. women 4. SS 60. Day nursery 16. WS 12. YS 15. Men's society 17.

Big Cove. Meet as one congregation at Cherokee. Big Cove Church is used for summer recreational programs, Wednesday night prayer meetings and emergency housing.

FLORIDA CONFERENCE
Council on Ministries
P. O. Box 3767, Lakeland, Florida 33802   *(813)688-5563*
Victor L. Rankin, Associate Council Director for Missions

Brighton Mission. Church not yet organized. Seminole.
Brighton Reservation. Begun 11/09/73. Naomi F. Orpurt,
pastor, ord., Seminole. P. O. Box 280, Moore Haven, Florida
33471. *(813)946-6615.* Mem. approximately 60. WS 15.
Personal work. Community development projects. The Methodist
churches have presented a library building to the Seminole
Tribal Council and Florida United Methodist women have
provided a mobile home unit for the 4-H organization and
extension worker.

NORTH CENTRAL REGION
2111 Woodward Avenue, Detroit, Michigan 48201
Bishop Edsel A. Ammons

Michigan Area Indian Mission Worker's Conference: Lewis W. E.
Church, chairman. Route 5, Allegan, Michigan 49101. Meets
spring and fall. Maintains a training program for new
ministers with the aid of Garrett Theological Seminary.

DETROIT CONFERENCE

MARQUETTE DISTRICT

Zeba Mission. 1832. Chippewa. Chippewa Reservation
(near L'Anse). Howard Shaffer, pastor, ord., w. 227
Front Street, L'Anse, Michigan 49946. *(906)524-7939.*
Mem. 45. SS 30. VBS. Camp meeting. Indian student
works with youth in summer.

SAGINAW BAY DISTRICT

Oscoda Methodist Indian Mission. Chippewa. 1970.
Oscoda, Michigan 48750. Lawrence A. Nahgahwon, lay pas.,
Chippewa. Route 1, Mikado, Michigan 48745. *739-9837.*
James Smith. 120 West Doyht Street, Oscoda, Michigan
48750. Conducts English service on Thursday night and
sacraments, weddings and funerals. *739-5147.* Mem. 35.
Total village attached to church. SS - adult and 1
primary class. Women unorganized but meet socially and
work. Fall revival meetings. Bazaar in Spring and Fall.

Saginaw Mission. 1974. Supplied by pastor at Standish.
Clem Bollingar.

WEST MICHIGAN CONFERENCE

GRAND TRAVERSE DISTRICT

Greensky Hill. 1833 or 1844. Ottawa. Charlevoix, Michigan 49720. *(616)547-2654.* Austin Regier, pastor, ord., w. 106 State Street, Charlevoix, Michigan 49720. *(616)547-5168.* Mem. 14. Loss in 1977 - 3 by death. WS 8. One week "Indian Heritage" youth conference. Annual camp meeting.

Kewadin Mission. Ottawa. Box 78, Kewadin, Michigan 49648. Harry Johns, Sr., pastor, Indian in training will be commissioned and licensed by Bishop. Route 4, Box 371, Peninsular Trails, Traverse City, Michigan 49684. Mem. 17. Bible study on Monday evenings.

Northport Mission. Ottawa. Tom John, pastor, Ind. Crain Hill Road, Box 575, Traverse City, Michigan 49684. Mr. John and wife, Phyllis, are in training and will be commissioned and licensed by the Bishop. *(616)946-6181.* Mem. 40. Ib. 4. Summer camp meeting.

CENTRAL DISTRICT

Chippewa Hill Mission.

Mt. Pleasant. Chippewa. Saginaw Chippewa Reservation. 1954. Joseph Sprague, Ind., local lay pas. about to be lic. 7320 East Broadway, Mt. Pleasant, Michigan 48858. Mem. 72. Serves about 600 population of the Saginaw Chippewa Reservation. SS. WS. YS. Summer camp meeting.

North Branch Mission. Chippewa. Mt. Pleasant, Michigan 48858. Kenneth Mankota, Ind. lay pas.

GRAND RAPIDS DISTRICT

Bradley Mission. Ottawa/Pottawatomie. Bradley, Michigan 49311. Lewis Church, pastor, ord., Ind. Route 5, 128 Avenue, Allegan, Michigan 49101.

Salem Mission. Ottawa/Pottawatomie. Salem, Michigan 48175. Lewis W. E. Church, pastor, ord., Ind. Route 5, 128 Avenue, Allegan, Michigan 49101. *(616)793-4111.* Mem. 29. Ab. in 1977 - 2, ib. 2. SS 20. WS 12. Midweek prayer meeting.

Saganing Mission. Paul I. Greer, pastor, ord., w. P. O. Box 186, Standish, Michigan 48658. (Also pastor of the

U.M.C. in Standish.) Mem. 9. Ib. in 1977 - 3. SS 17. Summer camp. Unite with Standish Methodist Church for VBS.

WISCONSIN CONFERENCE
Council on Ministries
325 Emerald Terrace, Sun Prairie, Wisconsin 53590 *(608)837-7328*
Donald A. Ott, Program Associate

Oneida Indian Mission. Route 4, De Pere, Wisconsin 54115. *(414)869-2927.* Eldon Riggs, pastor, ord., w. Church organized in 1832 when a large company of Methodist Oneidas moved from New York. Communicant mem. 235. Total Methodist com. 348. Conv. in 1976 - 9. Infant and adult baptisms 21. Layworkers 12. SS 106. WS 5-20. WS 20.

Menominee Ministry. 1968. Menominee Reservation. 626 S. Franklin, Shawano, Wisconsin 54166. *(715)526-6297.* James Feay, pastor, ord., w. A chaplaincy-type ministry: spiritual adviser at large, jail ministry, senior citizens and counseling, juvenile detention work, work service projects.

Odanah Mission Church. 1897. Ojibway and Chippewa. Bad River Reservation. Odanah, Wisconsin 54861. Chomingwen Pond, pastor, ord., w. P. O. Box 27, Washburn, Wisconsin 54891. *(715)373-2528.* Mem. 29 (19 are non-resident).

The Conference participates in the ecumenical Wisconsin Indian Resource Program and the Indian Ministry Special Program of the Wisconsin Council of Churches.

MINNESOTA CONFERENCE
122 West Franklin Avenue, Minneapolis, Minnesota 55404
Bishop Wayne C. Clymer

Pine Bend United Methodist Mission. Ojibway. White Earth Reservation. R. R. Lengby, Minnesota 56651. (Rev. Delton Krueger, District Superintendent, 1114 Broadway, Alexandria, Minnesota 56308.) Carl E. Clausen, pastor, ord., w., (also serves 20 other churches). A Lutheran Indian minister partly Methodist funded also gives some service. Communicant mem. 20. Total Methodist com. 50-70.

Nett Lake United Methodist Church. Orr, Minnesota 55771.

Native American Community Ministry. Based in Emmanuel United Methodist Church, 1900 Eleventh Avenue, South, Minneapolis, Minnesota 55404, carried out by Associate Pastor Larry W. Mens. *(612)870-9931.* Funded by National Division and Conference. Some 10,000 Indian people in neighborhood.

The Minnesota Conference also participates in the Division of Indian Work of the Minneapolis Council of Churches.

LOUISIANA CONFERENCE

Duloc Community Center. Houma. P. O. Box 100, Duloc, Louisiana 70353. Spiller Milton, Executive Director, ord., w. *(504)563-4501.* Purpose: "To assist the Indians of the Houma Tribe to preserve their heritage with pride and dignity; to secure ready acceptance in the social, business and political life of the communities; to secure an education that will equip them to cope with life and free them to develop their natural interest and follow their life ambitions; and to develop a deep sense of the spiritual presence of God in their lives through the experience of Jesus Christ." Day care for 3 and 4 year olds - 23. Adult education school. Homebound program. Scouting. Recreation. WS. YS. Personal and family counseling.

Clanton Chapel. Now operating independently of Center. Communicant mem. 174. Total Methodist com. 200. **Conv.** in 1977 - 15, ab. 2, ib. 17.

MISSISSIPPI CONFERENCE
P. O. Box 931, Jackson, Mississippi 39205
Bishop Mack B. Stokes

Methodist Indian Mission. Choctaw. 1799. Pearl River and Red Water Reservation. (103 Methodists remained behind and did not move to Oklahoma.) Route 7, Box 27-A, Philadelphia, Mississippi 39350. *(601)656-4045.* Dr. L. Shaw Gaddy, Director, ord., Choctaw.

Green Hill Church. 1822. Mem. 182. Methodist com. 500. Conv. in 1976 - 14. Ab. 4, ib. 10. Indian men layworkers 4, w. 1; Indian women workers 2, w. 1. 2 SS 108. YS 16.

OKLAHOMA CONFERENCE
P. O. Box 60565, Oklahoma City, Oklahoma 73106
Bishop Paul W. Milhouse

Four Indian Ministers with full status on special assignments:
  David Adair, Director of Council of Ministries of the
    Oklahoma Indian Missionary Conference
  Lee L. Chupco, Director of Finance and Program, Indian
    Mission, Oklahoma City
  Forbis P. Durant, Indian Mission, Talihina
  Robert Pinezaddleby, Director of Oklahoma Indian Ministries,
    Inc., Oklahoma City

OKLAHOMA INDIAN MISSIONARY CONFERENCE
Bishop Paul W. Milhouse
2420 North Blackwelder, P. O. Box 60565   *(405)521-1471*
Oklahoma City, Oklahoma 73106

Rev. David Adair, Director of Ministries   *(405)525-2252*
1707 North Broadway, P. O. Box 60427, Oklahoma City, Oklahoma
73106

All ministers are Indian.

NORTHEAST DISTRICT
Superintendent: Rev. Sampson Parish
P. O. Box 142, Jenks, Oklahoma 74037

22 charges, 36 churches.

Bristow: Muttleloke Memorial. Eucha. J. B. Dunn. P. O.
Box 661, Okemah, Oklahoma 74859. *(918)623-2649.* Mem. 87.
1 addition by transfer in 1976. SS 23, teachers 7.

Bristow: Choska Circuit. William Smith. Okemah, Oklahoma
74859. *(918)623-2067.*
   Arbeka Church. Creek. Mem. 31. SS 42, teachers 8.
   Choska Church. Eucha/Creek. Mem. 48. SS 35, teachers 8.
   Grant Chapel. Creek. Mem. 16. SS 9, teachers 6.

Broken Arrow: Broken Arrow Indian U.M.C. Creek. George
Miller. 102 West Urbana, Broken Arrow, Oklahoma 74012.
Mem. 73. Gain of 8 in 1976, including 3 confessions of
faith. SS 46, teachers 4. WS 11.

Bixby: Bixby Circuit. Creek. Willie Gooden. P. O. Box
415, Preston, Oklahoma 74756. *(918)756-1505.*
   Choncharty Church. Mem. 124. Confessions of faith 2.
   SS 37, teachers 4. WS 24.
   Davis Chapel. Mem. 28
   Baikey Chapel. Mem. 54.
   Springtown.

Jay: Jay Tsalagi Church. Cherokee. Joe Lowe, Jr. P. O.
Box 552, Jay, Oklahoma 74346. *(918)253-8833.* Mem. 40.
SS 25, teachers 3. WS 8.

Tahlequah: Etchieson Circuit. Cherokee. Scott Bread.
412 W. Seneca, Tahlequah, Oklahoma 74464. *(918)456-8667.*
   Etchieson Chapel. Mem. 74. Confessions of faith in
   1976 - 12. SS 11, teachers 6. WS 9.
   Stroh's Chapel. Mem. 20.

Muskogee: Fife Memorial. Creek/Cherokee. Lee L. Chupco. 1011 South Utah, Muskogee, Oklahoma 74401. *(918)687-1438.* Mem. 89. SS 27, teachers 4. WS 8.

Okmulgee: New Town. Creek. Thomas Long. 1000 Airview, Okmulgee, Oklahoma 74447. *(918)756-8697.* Mem. 128. Confessions of faith in 1976 - 2. SS 47, teachers 7. WS 30.

Okemah: Honey Creek Circuit. Creek. Ben Burgess. P. O. Box 186, Henryetta, Oklahoma 74436. *(918)652-8320.*
  Big Cusseta. Mem. 135. Confessions of faith in 1976 - 2. SS 41, teachers 6. WS 24.
  Honey Creek. Mem. 45. SS 36, teachers 5. WS 24.
  Little Cusseta. Mem. 37. Confessions of faith in 1976 - 2. SS 28, teachers 6.
  Springfield. Mem. 42. SS 41, teachers 8.

Oklahoma City: Billy Hooten Memorial. Mixed. 2445 W. Sheridan Drive, Oklahoma City, Oklahoma 73137. *(405)235-9029.* Dave Long, Jr. 508 Tompkins Drive, Oklahoma City, Oklahoma 73127. *(405)787-2695.* Mem. 57. Confessions of faith in 1976 - 3. SS 42, teachers 5. WS 12.

Salina: Salina Circuit. Cherokee. Roy Big Pond. Route 1, Box 73, Mounds, Oklahoma 74047. *(918)366-3920.*
  Claremore Christ Church. Mem. 34.
  Salina Mission. Mem. 23. SS 16, teachers 3.

Sapulpa: Pickett Chapel. Creek/Eucha. Jess Sullivan. Route 2, Box 199, Sapulpa, Oklahoma 74066. *(918)321-3109.* Mem. 167. Confessions of faith in 1976 - 3. SS 75, teachers 9. WS 33.

Seminole: Seminole Hitchitee. Seminole. Sam Chupco. P. O. Box 537, Seminole, Oklahoma 74868. *(405)382-2502.* Mem. 280. Confessions of faith in 1976 - 1. SS 50, teachers 6.

Stilwell: Stilwell Indian U. M. Church. Cherokee. Richard Blackburn. Route 2, Stilwell, Oklahoma 74960. *(918)744-2092.* Mem. 104. SS 66, teachers 6. WS 20.

Tulsa: Indian United Methodist. Mixed. *(918)936-9741.* Vacant. Parsonage, 1645 North College Street, Tulsa, Oklahoma 74110. *(918)936-4505.* Mem. 146. Confessions of faith in 1976 - 7. SS 65, teachers 8. WS 15.

Tulsa: Witt Memorial U. M. Church. *(918)425-5968.* Jake Wildcat. 1114 E. 59th Place, North, Tulsa, Oklahoma 74110.

Mem. 83. Confessions of faith 4. SS 67, teachers 7.

Vian: Vian Circuit. Cherokee. Levi Flute. General
Delivery, Vian, Oklahoma 74962. *(918)773-5771.*
Canterbury Chapel. Mem. 34. SS 22, teachers 2.
Sycamore Indian U. M. Church. Mem. 42. SS 24, teachers
3.

Marble City: Pettit Circuit. Cherokee. Adam Canoe.
General Delivery, Marble City, Oklahoma 74945.
Covers Chapel. Mem. 20.
Pettit Chapel. Mem. 29.

Wetumka: Wetumka Circuit. Creek. Charles O'Niell. P. O.
Box 185, Wetumka, Oklahoma 74883. *(405)452-5136.*
Thlopthlooco. Mem. 91. Confessions of faith in 1976 - 1.
SS 44, teachers 3. WS 9.
Salt Creek. Mem. 87. Confessions of faith in 1976 - 1.
WS 10.

Yeager: Yeager Circuit. Creek. Vernon Haney. Route 3,
Box 209-N, North Seminole, Oklahoma 74868. *(405)382-1447.*
Kaney Chapel. Mem. 20. SS 26, teachers 4.
Thlewahley. Mem. 33. SS 23, teachers 4.
Wewoka. Mem. 39. SS 38, teachers 6.
Yeager Mission. Mem. 28. Confessions of faith in 1976 -
1. SS 37, teachers 5.

Shawnee: Nagawu. Pottawatomie. John Lowe. 1429 S.W.
26th, Oklahoma City, Oklahoma 74367. *(405)634-8867.* Mem.
47. SS 23, teachers 3.

SOUTHEAST DISTRICT
Superintendent: Rev. James Sockey
P. O. Box 278, Atoka, Oklahoma 74525   *(405)889-3557*

15 charges, 44 churches.

Ada: Mitchell Memorial. Choctaw. Callen Burris. 1000 S.
Mississippi, Ada, Oklahoma 74820. *(405)436-2246.* Mem. 50.
Confessions of faith in 1976 - 7. SS 26, teachers 6.
WS 6.

Allen: Jesse Circuit. Jefferson Frazier. Route 1, Allen,
Oklahoma 74825. *(405)845-2264.*
Boiling Spring. Choctaw. Mem. 78. Confessions of faith
in 1976 - 2. SS 27, teachers 5.
Johnson Chapel. Chickasaw. Mem. 66. Confessions of
faith in 1976 - 2. SS 55, teachers 7. WS 7.
Red Spring. Choctaw. Mem. 61. SS 34, teachers 7.

Kallihoma. Choctaw. Mem. 32.

Antlers. Choctaw. Justin Graham. P. O. Box 147, Finley, Oklahoma 74543. *(405)298-5349.*
  Big Lick. Mem. 48. SS 17, teachers 3.
  Nelson. Mem. 19. SS 16, teachers 3.
  Old Cedar. Mem. 68. SS 33, teachers 4.
  Sugar Loaf. Mem. 33. Confessions of faith in 1976 - 1. SS 10, teachers 4.

Antlers Charge. Hugo. Choctaw. Lester Tims. General Delivery, Hugo, Oklahoma 74743. *(405)326-5431.*
  Bobb Myers. Mem. 51. Confessions of faith in 1976 - 1. SS 29, teachers 4. WS 8.
  Jacob Memorial. Mem. 26. SS 23, teachers 4.
  William Anderson Memorial. Mem. 40. SS 21, teachers 5. WS 12.

Atoka Circuit. Choctaw. Pipin Gibson. Route 2, Box 150, Atoka, Oklahoma 74525.
  Buffalo Creek. Mem. 21. SS 15, teachers 2. WS 5.
  Cane Hill. Mem. 30. SS 23, teachers 3.
  Pine Grove. Mem. 21. SS 8, teachers 2.

Broken Bow: Boktuklo Circuit. Choctaw. Route 2, Box C13-A, Broken Bow, Oklahoma 74728.
  Bethel Hill. Mem. 85. Confessions of faith in 1976 - 1. SS 47, teachers 4. WS 14.
  Goodland. Mem. 54. SS 33, teachers 3.
  Kullichito. Mem. 107. Confessions of faith in 1976 - 2. SS 165, teachers 5. WS 14.
  Nanichito. Mem. 44. SS 22, teachers 5. WS 9.
  Towali. Mem. 90. Confessions of faith in 1976 - 5. SS 83, teachers 5. WS 20.
  Yasho. Mem. 62. Confessions of faith in 1976 - 1. SS 46, teachers 4. WS 14.

Connersville: Chickasaw Circuit. Choctaw. Edgar E. Tims. P. O. Box 516, Connersville, Oklahoma 74836. *(405)836-7143.*
  Pennington. Mem. 49. SS 11, teachers 3.
  Seeley Chapel. Mem. 80. Confessions of faith in 1976 - 2. SS 44, teachers 6. WS 12.
  Yellow Spring. Mem. 16. SS 10, teachers 3.

Dallas: Dallas Indian Mission. Mixed. P. O. Box 4506, Dallas, Texas 75208. *(214)331-8261.* Lindy Waters. 1205 S. Hollywood Street, Dallas, Texas 75208. *(214)337-4946.*

Pennington: Hugo Circuit. Choctaw. William Louis. Route 2, Box 14, Pennington, Oklahoma 74723. *(405)847-2653.*

Sulphur Springs. Mem. 41. Confessions of faith in 1976 -
2. SS 29, teachers 6.
White Sand. Mem. 49. Confessions of faith in 1976 - 1.
SS 18, teachers 5. WS 5.

Idabel Circuit. Choctaw. Arthur Crosby. Route 1, Box 57,
Idabel, Oklahoma 74745.
   Bukchito. Mem. 81. Confessions of faith in 1976 - 8.
   SS 67, teachers 6. WS 29.
   Kullitukla. Mem. 128. Confessions of faith in 1976 - 4.
   SS 52, teachers 8. WS 16.
   Living Land. Mem. 29. SS 26, teachers 6.
   Water Hole. Mem. 14. SS 10, teachers 1.
   White Sand. Mem. 34. Confessions of faith in 1976 - 3.
   SS 17, teachers 3.

Oklahoma City: Mary Clark Lee Church. Mixed. 504 S.
Dewey, Oklahoma City, Oklahoma 73125. *(405)236-4243.* Dave
Long, Sr. 2309 S. Kate, Oklahoma City, Oklahoma 73129.
(405)677-0995. Mem. 181. Confessions of faith in 1976 - 4.
SS 73, teachers 14. WS 31.

Quinton: McCurtain Circuit. Choctaw. James Sockey.
R.F.D. 1, Box 203, Quinton, Oklahoma 74561. *(918)469-2976.*
   Middle San Bois. Mem. 22. SS 20, teachers 3.
   Siloam Springs. Mem. 47. SS 21, teachers 3. WS 6.

Rufe: Rufe Charge. Choctaw. Stephen Billy. P. O. Box 192
Rufe, Oklahoma 74755. *(405)933-4358.*
   Black Jack. Mem. 38. SS 18, teachers 3.
   Choctaw Academy. Mem. 46. SS 22, teachers 5.
   Goodwater. Mem. 75. Confessions of faith in 1976 - 2.
   SS 53, teachers 5.
   Hampton Chapel. Mem. 57. Confessions of faith in 1976 -
   5. SS 30, teachers 5. WS 12.
   High Hill. Mem. 34. Confessions of faith in 1976 - 1.
   SS 19, teachers 4.

Talihina: St. Paul U. M. Church. Choctaw. Forbis Durant.
P. O. Box 649, Talihina, Oklahoma 74571. *(918)567-2091.*
Mem. 101. Confessions of faith in 1976 - 1. SS 58,
teachers 6. WS 18.

Whitesboro: LeFlore Charge. Choctaw. Joseph Wilkin.
P. O. Box 115, Whitesboro, Oklahoma 74571.
   James Folsom Memorial. Mem. 17. SS 7, teachers 2. WS 7.
   Good Spring. Mem. 63. SS 14, teachers 3. WS 8.

WESTERN DISTRICT
Superintendent: Rev. Reuben Ahhaitty
P. O. Box 642, Anadarko, Oklahoma 73005   *(405)247-2900*

14 charges, 24 churches.

Angie Smith Memorial Church. Mixed. *(405)632-5610.* Dan
Sexton. 426 S.W. 32nd Street, Oklahoma City, Oklahoma
73109. *(405)632-6756.* Mem. 333. Confessions of faith in
1976 - 5. SS 294, teachers 24. WS 14.

Horse Circuit. Kiowa. Melvin Boyiddle. P. O. Box 835,
Carnegie, Oklahoma 73015.
  Albert Horse Memorial. Kiowa. Mem. 50. Confessions of
  faith in 1976 - 3. SS 45, teachers 6. WS 14.
  Wetselline. Mem. 47. Confessions of faith in 1976 - 2.
  SS 41, teachers 5. WS 5.

Cedar Creek. Kiowa. Charles Quetone. P. O. Box 930,
Carnegie, Oklahoma 73015. Mem. 370. Confessions of faith
in 1976 - 3. SS 78, teachers 5. WS 15.

Clinton Church/Thomas Church. Cheyenne. Malcom Fire. 521
West Franklin Street, Weatherford, Oklahoma 73906. Mem. 69.

El Reno Circuit. Joe Wesley. 1938 N.W. 12th Street,
Oklahoma City, Oklahoma 73108. *(405)528-8697.*
  El Reno. Mixed. Mem. 48. SS 33, teachers 3. WS 8.
  Kingfisher. Cheyenne. Mem. 61.

Anadarko: J. J. Methvin. Kiowa. 613 East Broadway,
Anadarko, Oklahoma 73005. Spencer Alpeatone. P. O. Box
997, Anadarko, Oklahoma 73005. Mem. 217. Confessions of
faith in 1976 - 5. SS 29, teachers 4. WS 6.

Lawton Circuit. Emerson. George Saumty. P. O. Box 1611,
Lawton, Oklahoma 73501. *(405)353-1670.*
  Lawton. Comanche. Mem. 125. SS 15, teachers 7. WS 6.
  Emerson. Kiowa. Mem. 84. SS 13, teachers 3. WS 6.

Little Washita. Comanche. John Padacony. General Delivery,
Anadarko, Oklahoma 73005. *(405)247-6716.* Confessions of
faith in 1976 - 2. SS 63, teachers 4. WS 8.

Mt. Scott Circuit. Comanche. Virgil Yeahquo. Route 1,
Elgin, Oklahoma 73538.
  Mt. Scott. Comanche. Mem. 210, SS 70, teachers 10. WS 12.
  Petarsky. Mem. 64. SS 29, teachers 4.

Mt. Scott Kiowa Circuit. Kiowa. Sherwood Tsotigh. Star

Route, Box 146-E, Lawton, Oklahoma 73501.
Cache. Mem. 167. Confessions of faith in 1976 - 3. SS 83, teachers 7. WS 19.
Mt. Scott Kiowa. Mem. 82. SS 76, teachers 6. WS 15.

Mulkahay Circuit. Comanche. Joe Pedro. Route 1, Apache, Oklahoma 73005. *(405)588-3612.*
Masetky. Mem. 137. Confessions of faith in 1976 - 10. SS 60, teachers 5. WS 25.
Mulkahay. Mem. 75. Confessions of faith in 1976 - 2. SS 31, teachers 4.

St. Luke's Circuit. Lincoln Tartsah, Sr. P. O. Box 88, Hobart, Oklahoma 73651.
Lone Wolf Chapel. Caddo. Mem. 49. Confessions of faith in 1976 - 5. SS 17, teachers 5. WS 5.
St. Luke. Comanche. Mem. 63. Confessions of faith in 1976 - 3. SS 10, teachers 8. WS 3.

Stecker Mission, Ware's Chapel. Cheyenne. John Chaino. 601 West Oklahoma, Anadarko, Oklahoma 73005. Mem. 414. Confessions of faith in 1976 - 4. SS 77, teachers 4.

Watonga Circuit. Floyd Blackbear. P. O. Box 364, Watonga, Oklahoma 73772. *(405)623-4520.*
Watonga. Cheyenne. Mem. 71. SS 55, teachers 13.
Colony. Cheyenne/Arapaho. Mem. 78.

NORTH DISTRICT
Superintendent: Rev. Steve Chibitty
505 N. Stephens, Ponca City, Oklahoma 75601   *(405)762-7991*

9 charges, 10 churches.

Arkansas City, Arkansas City Mission. Mixed. (Serves Indian School) Minnie Bowen. 718½ S. "B" Street, Ponca City, Kansas 67005. Mem. 10. SS 29, teachers 5.

Horton Mission. Kickapoo. Grover James. P. O. Box 202, Horton, Kansas 66439. Mem. 65.

Lawrence Mission. Mixed. (Serves Haskell Jr. College) Harry D. Folsom. 48 Wiowna Street, Lawrence, Kansas 66044. *(913)842-6423.* Mem. 50 (average attendance 55). SS 36, teachers 8. WS 8.

Dewey: New Hope. Delaware. William Littlesun. 1238 North Choctaw, Dewey, Oklahoma 74029. Mem. 55.

Pawnee U. M. Church. Pawnee. Earl Dunson. 302 E. Kansas,

Pawnee, Oklahoma 74058. Mem. 31.
Tryon. Box 277, Tryon, Oklahoma 74375. *(918)762-3567.*

Phil Deschner Church. Ponca. Rony Cere. Route 6, Box 215A, Ponca City, Oklahoma 74601. Mem. 35.

Topeka: Sullivan Chapel. Pottawatomie. George Evans. 1937 N. Madison, Topeka, Kansas 66608. Mem. 93. SS 26, teachers 3.

Wichita Mission. Wichita. Luther Blackbear. 1445 West Haskell, Wichita, Kansas 67213. Mem. 66. SS 32, teachers 3.

White Eagle, Ponca Mission. Thomas Roughface, Sr. P. O. Box 2573, Ponca City, Oklahoma 74601. *(918)762-2112.* Mem. 274. SS 67, teachers 9. WS 26.

Tyrone, Omaha/Ponca. Mem. 10. (new)

Totals for Conference: 60 charges, 113 churches; 8,029 members; 151 confessions of faith; 2,566 average Sunday service attendance; 506 Sunday School leaders; 3,874 Sunday School membership; 2,105 average Sunday School attendance; 694 United Methodist Women membership.
Ministers: full connectional membership 39, associate members 28, probationary members 5.
On special appointment - 3:
  Harry Long, Yuma (Arizona) Indian Mission.
  Oliver Neal, American Indian Ministry, Los Angeles.
  Kenneth Deere, Associate Executive Secretary, Commission on Religion and Race, 100 Maryland Avenue, N.E., Washington, D.C. 20002.

NEW MEXICO CONFERENCE

First United Methodist Church. Shiprock. Navajo. Paul N. West, pastor, ord., w. P. O. Box 657, Shiprock, New Mexico 87420. Communicant mem. 150. Methodist com. 250. Conv. in 1976 - 5, ab. 5. Ord. Ind. minister. Ind. men layworker 1. SS 45. WS. Men's society.

Navajo Methodist Mission School. 1200 West Apache Street, Farmington, New Mexico 87420. Boarding 7 - 12 grades. 100 students.

First United Methodist Church. 1971. Navajo. P. O. Box 668, Window Rock, Arizona 96515. Chee D. Benallie, pastor, unordained, Ind. Mem. 4. SS 15. YS 10. WS 2-4. Men's group 2.

YELLOWSTONE CONFERENCE
2200 South University Blvd. Denver, Colorado 80210
Bishop Melvin E. Wheatley, Jr. (Denver Area)   *(303)733-3736*

Blackfeet United Methodist Mission. Blackfeet Reservation.
Mostly Blackfeet, some Cree. P. O. Box 578, Browning, Montana
59417. *(406)338-7313.* Communicant mem. 82 in Browning, 30
in Babb. Mailing list of 140. Total Methodist com. about
200. Ab. in 1977 - 3, ib. 6. SS 30. WS 8. YS 8. Men's
weekly breakfast 8-10.

OREGON CONFERENCE
1505 S.W. 18th Avenue, Portland, Oregon 97201
Bishop Jack M. Tuell

Beatty United Methodist Church. 1898. Modoc, Klamath,
Paiute. Beatty, Oregon 97621. Gerald T. McCray, Sr., pastor
ord., w. Chiloquin, Oregon 97624. Mem. 26. SS 6. YS 12.
Prayer and Bible study. VBS.

Williamson River United Methodist Church. 1876. Klamath,
Modoc. Gerald T. McCray, Sr., pastor, ord., w. Star Route 1,
Box 82A, Chiloquin, Oregon 97624. *(503)783-2875.* Mem. 34.
Ab. in 1977 - 3, ib. 7. SS 12. YS 35. WS 12. Prayer
meeting. VBS 70.

PACIFIC NORTHWEST CONFERENCE
920 Second Avenue, Suite 800, Seattle, Washington 98104
Bishop Wilbur W. Y. Choy

Indigenous Community Developer: Mrs. Edith George (Nez Perce)
13309 54th Street, S.E., Everett, Washington 98204.

Native American Caucus, Chairman: Mr. Hollis Woodward
(Yakima) P. O. Box 2, White Swan, Washington 98952.

Noosack Indian Mission. Noosack Reservation. 6605 Mission
Road, Everson, Washington 98247. Mrs. John W. Martin, pastor,
ord., w. 821 Hoag Road, Mt. Vernon, Washington 98273.
Communicant mem. 38. Total Methodist com. 72. Ib. in 1976 -
1. SS 16.

Nespelem United Methodist Church. Colville Tribe. Colville
Reservation. P. O. Box 220, Nespelem, Washington 99155.
Kenneth Edwards, pastor, ord., w. *(509)634-4224.* Communi-
cant mem. 36. Methodist com. 53. Ib. 10.

Wilbur Memorial United Methodist Church. Yakima. Yakima
Reservation. P. O. Box 50, White Swan, Washington 98952.
Milton C. DeArmand, pastor, ord., w. *(509)874-2736.* Church

now mostly white. Ind. mem. 13%. Communicant mem. 111.
Methodist com. 222. SS 20. YS 5. WS 34. VBS. 2 Bible
study groups.

Nez Perce Indian Mission. Nez Perce Reservation. Lapwai,
Idaho 83540. J. Richard Cook, pastor, ord., w., serves also
Orchards United Methodist Church, Lewiston. 1213 Burrell,
Lewiston, Idaho 83501. *(208)743-9201, 743-7991.* Communicant
mem. 14. Methodist com. 85. Ib. 7.

The Pacific Northwest Conference provides workers at the above
churches and is erecting a new building at Lapwai. A summer
youth program is maintained at Lapwai. Contributions have
been made to the Blackfeet Indian Center Social Service
Programs in Seattle, to a multi-purpose cabin at fisheries on
Squaxin Island and to an Indian People-to-People employment
and referral program in Silverdale, Washington. The Seattle
District supports a Native American Community Outreach person
who handles crisis situations in the urban area, relating to
housing, food and clothing and referral services.

PACIFIC SOUTHWEST CONFERENCE
5250 Santa Monica Blvd., Los Angeles, California 90029
Bishop Charles F. Golden

Native American Ministries. 1575 West 14th Street, Los
Angeles, California 90015. *(213)385-2441.* Oliver B. Neal,
minister, ord., Ind.

United Methodist Indian Church. 1976. 1575 West 14th Street,
Los Angeles, California 90015. Oliver B. Neal, pastor, ord.,
Chickasaw. Mem. 100. Ab. in 1977 - 60, ib. 30. SS 40.
YS 18. WS 14. Men's society 7.

Yuma Indian United Methodist Church. 1900. Quechan and
Cocopah. Ft. Yuma Reservation. Box 844, Yuma, Arizona 85364.
(602)572-6564. Harry Long, pastor, ord., Muskogee Creek.
565 South 10th Avenue, Yuma, Arizona 85364. *(602)782-2094.*
Mem. 96. Ab. in 1977 - 1, ib. 9. SS 25-30. Day care. VBS.
A.A. meetings.

CALIFORNIA-NEVADA CONFERENCE
Bishop C. F. Golden

Round Valley Indian Mission. Mixed. Round Valley Reservation
Mark M. Stahnke, pastor, ord., w. 286 School Street, Willits,
California 95490. *(707)459-2855.* Mem. 16. Weekday Bible
School 5-15 children. Tribes represented: Yuki, Pit River,
Nomlacki, Concaw, Pomo, Walacki, Little Lake.

Schurz Mission. 1875. Paiute. Walker River Reservation.
221 North Main Street, Yerington, Nevada 89447. John L.
Dodson, part time pastor, ord., w. Mem. 24. WS 8. Other
programs. Plans for an Indian pastor in 1978 are under way.

UNITED PRESBYTERIAN CHURCH IN THE U.S.A.

The local churches have standing in the Presbyteries and receive
some oversight and ministries from Synods. The denominational
concern and ministry to the Native American churches and peoples
are lodged in
THE PROGRAM AGENCY
475 Riverside Drive, New York, N.Y. 10027
Dr. J. Oscar McLoud, General Director

Native American Consultative Committee   *(212)870-2244*
Gene Begay, Associate, Native American Ministries

NORTHEAST SYNOD

LONG ISLAND PRESBYTERY

Shinnecook U. P. C. Southampton, New York 11968.
Shinnecook. Matthew H. Thies, pastor, ord., w. Mem. 189.

WESTERN NEW YORK PRESBYTERY

Tonawanda Indian Presbyterian Church. 1968. Seneca Reservation. Box 681, Basom, New York 14013. *(716)937-7528.*
Seneca. Roger Dean Kemp, ord., w. Mem. 43. Ab. 1.
Wednesday school, average attendance 8. WS 14. Summer
vacation program in cooperation with Cook Christian Training
School. Thursday morning Bible study. Seneca Chorus,
vernacular language, travels.

Iroquois Wright Memorial Presbyterian Church. 1827.
Cattaraugus Reservation. RFD, Irving, New York 14081.
(716)549-3686. Seneca. Dr. Lauchlin D. MacDonald, ord.,
w. 187 Chestnut Street, Fredonia, New York 14073.
(716)679-1857. Mem. 47, increase of 2. Ib. 6. SS 16-20.
YS 23. WS 14. VBS - 3 separated weeks during summer.

Jimmerstown Presbyterian Church. Allegheny Indian Reservation. Salamanca, New York 14779. George Mighells, pastor,
ord., w. Route 3, Lyndon Road, Cuba, New York 14727. Mem.
139.

The Native American Christian Community

SYNOD OF THE LAKES AND PRAIRIES
Associate for Indian Ministries: Rev. Simon Looking Elk
3729 West Chicago, Rapid City, South Dakota 47701 *(605)348-4223*

All ministers are ordained.

CHIPPEWA PRESBYTERY

Lac DuFlambeau. Lac DuFlambeau, Wisconsin 54538. David
Knapp, w. Mem. 84.

White Fish. Stone Lake, Wisconsin 54876. Vacant. Mem. 26.

Red Eagle Memorial. Box 288, Brockton, Montana 59213. Paul
Firecloud, Ind. Mem. 149.

DAKOTA PRESBYTERY
Rev. Simon Looking Elk, Executive Presbyter
3729 West Chicago, Rapid City, South Dakota 47701

Makaicu. Box 288, Brockton, Montana 59213. Paul Firecloud,
Ind. Mem. 30.

Lindsey Memorial. Box 155, Poplar, Montana 59255. Eugene
Ammon, w. Mem. 67.

Bdecan. Tokio, North Dakota 58379. Phillip Todd, w.

Goodwill. RD 2, Sisseton, South Dakota 57262. Floyd
Heminger, Ind. Mem. 47.

Longhollow. Sisseton, South Dakota 57262. Floyd Heminger,
Ind. Mem. 72.

Mayasan. Veblen, South Dakota 57270. Harvey Allison, Ind.
Mem. 29.

Ascension. Route 1, Peever, South Dakota 57257. Vacant.
Mem. 133.

Buffalo Lakes. Eden, South Dakota 57232. Vacant. Mem. 69.

Lake Traverse. Browns Valley, Minnesota 56219. Vacant.
Mem. 25.

Pejutazizi. Granite Falls, Minnesota 56241. Irving Tang,
Chinese. Mem. 32.

Cottonwood. Cottonwood, Minnesota 56229. Irving Tang,
Chinese. Mem. 47.

First. Box 86, Flandreau, South Dakota 57028. Peter Vanderveen, w. Mem. 45.

Hill. Route 3, Wagner, South Dakota 57380. Steven Spider, Ind. Mem. 28.

Greenwood. Greenwood, South Dakota 57343. Joseph Dudley, Ind. Mem. 76.

Cedar. Ravinia, South Dakota 57356. Joseph Dudley, Ind. Mem. 29.

Conkicakse. Fort Thompson, South Dakota 57339. C. Arlin Talley, w. Mem. 34.

Mniska. Dixon, South Dakota 57530. C. Arlin Talley, w. Mem. 45.

Porcupine. Porcupine, South Dakota 57772. Samuel Rouillard, Ind. Mem. 64

Johnson Memorial. Wounded Knee, South Dakota 57772. Samuel Rouillard, Ind. Mem. 28.

Makasan. Box 61, Oglala, South Dakota 57764. Harry Lee Weston, Ind. Mem. 145.

NORTH CENTRAL IOWA PRESBYTERY

Mesquakie. RD 2, Box 16, Tama, Iowa 52339. Vacant. Mem. 25.

SYNOD OF THE SUN

EASTERN OKLAHOMA PRESBYTERY
505 West Olmulgee Avenue, Suite 5, Muskogee, Oklahoma 74401
Dr. Coy C. Lee, Executive Presbyter   *(918)683-5232*

Choctaw Parish - 16 churches, 2 in Washita Presbytery. Continues the fellowship of the former Choctaw Presbytery. Miss Rena Sampson, Administrative Assistant and Treasurer, Star Route, Box 17, Broken Bow, Oklahoma 75728. *(405)494-6576.* Also in charge of children's work program and youth work. Served by two ord. Choctaw ministers, Rev. Eli Samuels and Rev. Gene Wilson and five certified Choctaw worship leaders. Total mem. 541.

Mt. Zion. Battiest, Oklahoma 47422. Mem. 43.

Kulli Chito. Bethel, Oklahoma 74724. Mem. 66.

Homers Chapel. Boxwell, Oklahoma 74727. Mem. 5.

Oka Achukma. Star Route 17, Broken Bow, Oklahoma 74728. Mem. 41.

Mt. Fork. Eagletown, Oklahoma 74734. Mem. 10.

Spring Hill. Honobia, Oklahoma 74549. Mem. 52.

Philadelphia. Box 536, Idabel, Oklahoma 74745. Mem. 10.

St. John's. Rufe, Oklahoma 74755. Mem. 9.

Big Lick. Smithville, Oklahoma 74957. Mem. 20.

Nanih Chito. Smithville, Oklahoma 74957. Mem. 14.

Wadeoille. Talihina, Oklahoma 74576. Mem. 5.

Buffalo. Watson, Oklahoma 74963. Mem. 30.

Kulli Tuklo. Watson, Oklahoma 74963. Mem. 6.

Luksokla. Wright City, Oklahoma 74766. Mem. 30.

Cherokee Hills. RFD 1, Stilwell, Oklahoma 74960. Cherokee. Charles E. Sanders, ord., Cherokee. Mem. 18.

WASHITA PRESBYTERY

Dixon Chapel. Byars, Oklahoma 74831. Choctaw Parish, ministers see above. Mem. 44.

Salem, Sulpher, Oklahoma. General Delivery, Roff, Oklahoma 74865. Choctaw Parish, ministers see above. Mem. 60.

Achena. Route 2, Maud, Oklahoma 74854. Seminole. Vacant. Mem. 60.

Cheyarha. Route 2, Seminole, Oklahoma 74868. Seminole. Vacant. Mem. 21.

Tallahasse. Route 2, Seminole, Oklahoma 74868. Seminole. Vacant. Mem. 47.

First Indian. Box 134, Wewoka, Oklahoma 74884. Seminole. Vacant. Mem. 47.

Dental and Medical Clinic. Wright City, Oklahoma 74766. One weekend per month. Volunteer physicians and dentists.

Mrs. Theda Monahans, LPN, coordinator. Choctaw.

Annual conference of the Seminole churches - 50th held in 1977.

SYNOD OF THE ROCKY MOUNTAINS

YELLOWSTONE PRESBYTERY
Mission Consultant for Montana: Rev. Howard R. VanDyke
412 Fifty-First Street, South, Great Falls, Montana 59405
(406)727-4949

United Dakota Presbyterian Church. Fort Peck Reservation.
Wolf Point, Montana 59201. Dakota/Sioux. Robert Lodwick,
ord., w. Chapels at Frazer and Wolf Point. Combined mem.
87. Two other congregations on the Fort Peck Reservation
have a few Indian members - First Presbyterian Church, Wolf
Point and First Presbyterian Church, Poplar.

WESTERN COLORADO PRESBYTERY

Ute Mountain U. P. C. Ute Mountain Reservation. Towaoc,
Colorado 81334. Carl Dickson, ord., Ind. Mem. 44.

SYNOD OF ALASKA-NORTHWEST
720 Seneca Street, Seattle, Washington 98101 *(206)623-4973*
Dr. W. W. Rosco, Synod Executive
Rev. Harold E. Penhalurick, Associate Synod Executive,
Presbytery of North Puget Sound and Synod Administration and
Mission Resource

ALASKA PRESBYTERY
1209 West 29th Avenue, Anchorage, Alaska 99503
Rev. Gordon Corbett, Associate Executive

Sunday School and adult education programs are usual in the
churches. Pastors are white unless otherwise indicated.

U. P. C. Angoon, Alaska 99820. Tlingit. Lou Rookers,
pastor, ord. Mem. 28.

First Presbyterian. Craig, Alaska 99921. Tlingit/Haida.
Vacant. Mem. 38.

Northern Light. Juneau, Alaska 99801. Tlingit. John
Tindell, pastor, ord. Mem. 343.

Hoonah Presbyterian. Box 86, Hoonah, Alaska 99829.
Tlingit. Vacant. Mem. 125.

Hydaburg U. P. C. Hydaburg, Alaska 99922. Haida. Arden Fritz, pastor, ord. Mem. 73.

Kake Memorial. Box 249, Kake, Alaska 99830. Tlingit. Timothy Doty, pastor, ord. Mem. 45.

Ketchikan U. P. C. Box 1409, Ketchikan, Alaska 99901. Haida/Tlingit. Robert Frye, pastor, ord. Mem. 85.

Klukwan U. P. C. Klukwan, Alaska 99831. Tlingit. Robert Cameron. Mem. 30.

Metlakatla. Box 37, Metlakatla, Alaska 99926. Tsimshian. Norma Crader, pastor, Mem. 98.

Yakutat U. P. C. Box 225, Yakutat, Alaska 99689. Tlingit. Donald Smith, pastor, ord. Mem. 22.

Sheldon Jackson College. 1878. Sitka, Alaska 99835. Accredited 2-year Junior College. Hugh H. Holloway, President. 170 full time students. See: Schools and Colleges.

MV Anna Jackman, Juneau home port. Rev. Ward Murray.

YUKON PRESBYTERY
1209 West 29th Avenue, Anchorage, Alaska 99503
Rev. Gordon Corbett, Associate Executive

Chapel in the Mountains. Anaktuvuk Pass, Alaska 99721. Inuit. James Nageak, Inuit. Mem. 58.

Utkeagvik U. P. C. Box 236, Barrow, Alaska 99723. Inuit/white. Richard Wayne. Mem. 628.

Kaktovik U. P. C. Kaktovik, Alaska 99747. Inuit. James Negeak, Inuit. Mem. 54.

Savoonga U. P. C. Savoonga, Alaska 99769. Inuit. Alice Green. Mem. 254.

Oleonik U. P. C. Wainright, Alaska 99782. Inuit. Samuel Simmons, Inuit. Mem. 144.

Gambell U. P. C. St. Lawrence Island, Alaska 99742. Inuit. Dean Hickox. Mem. 144.

Nome U. P. C. Nome, Alaska 99762. Inuit. John Staffer. Mem. 44.

Nuiqsut P. C. Nuiqsut, Alaska 99716. Inuit. James Nageak, Inuit.

INLAND EMPIRE PRESBYTERY
S. 324 Cedar Street, Spokane, Washington 99204
Dr. William Kelley, Associate Executive

North Fork. Orofino. Ahsahka, Idaho 83544. Indian.
Vacant. Mem. 10.

Meadowcreek. U. P. C. c/o 1309 Birch, Lewiston, Idaho 83501.
Indian. Vacant. Mem. 6.

First U. P. C. Kamiah, Idaho 83536. Indian. Vacant.
Mem. 67.

Second U. P. C. Kamiah, Idaho 83536. Indian. Vacant.
Mem. 15.

First U. P. C. Spalding, Idaho 83551. Indian. Vacant.
Mem. 48.

First U. P. C. Wellpinit, Washington 99040. Indian. John
W. Hubbard. Mem. 22.

NORTH PUGET SOUND PRESBYTERY

Neah Bay U. P. C. Box 308, Neah Bay, Washington 98357.
Indian. Vacant. Mem. 49.

OLYMPIA PRESBYTERY

Indian Fellowship. 2232 E. 28th Street, Tacoma, Washington
98404. Indian. Vacant. Mem. 28.

SYNOD OF THE PACIFIC
1 Hallidie Plaza, Suite 405, San Francisco, California 94102
Rev. Richard E. Moore, Executive

For Indian Churches refer to:

Rev. John C. Matthew - Associate Synod Executive
Snake River Area, 2308 North Cole Road, Suite H, Boise, Idaho
83703   *(208)345-4069*

Rev. Bryce Little, Jr., Sierra Mission Area
2431 H. Street, Sacramento, California 95816

EASTERN OREGON PRESBYTERY

Tutuilla U. P. C. Umatilla Reservation. Box 781, Pendleton, Oregon 97801. Umatilla and Cayuse. David N. Stewart, ord., w., mobile minister, wife a Delaware. 251 S.W. 2nd Street, Pendleton, Oregon 97801. Mem. 42. SS. Sponsors Tutuilla Farms Inc., a cooperative farming project under Self-Development of People.

NEVADA PRESBYTERY

Valley U. P. C. Paiute. Robert E. Dodson, ord., w. 2112 West Line, Bishop, California 93514. Mem. 42. SS. YS.

Owyhee U. P. C. Paiute and Shoshone. Charles Proudfoot, ord., w. Owyhee, Nevada 89832. Mem. 103. SS. YS.

CASCADES PRESBYTERY
0245 S.W. Bancroft Street, Portland, Oregon 97201
Rev. Tom M. Castlen, Associate Synod Executive *(503)227-5486*

Warm Springs U. P. C. 1875. Warm Springs Reservation. Warm Springs Tribe? P. O. Box 458, Warm Springs, Oregon 97761. Calvin Y. Chinn. 3/4 Indian - mem. 60. SS. Adult education program. VBS. Programs for children and youth. Family retreat. Community support services. Developing house churches at Simnasito and Kahneata.

REDWOODS PRESBYTERY

Church of the Mountains. G. Woody Garvin, ord., w. P. O. Box 398, Hoopa, California 95546. Mem. 75.

SOUTHWEST SYNOD
10 Roanoke Avenue, Phoenix, Arizona 85004 *(602)264-2528*
Dr. Roe B. Lewis, Director of Indian Ministries

GRAND CANYON PRESBYTERY

Yah-Ki. Pima. Box 870, Bapchule, Arizona 85221. Howard Smith, pastor, non-Indian. SS.

Stotonic Chapel. Pima. Box 870, Bapchule, Arizona 85221. Howard Smith, pastor, non-Indian. SS.

Good Year Chapel. Pima. Box 870, Bapchule, Arizona 85221. Howard Smith, pastor, non-Indian. SS.

NOTE: Combined mem. of the three above is 80.

Blackwater. Pima. Box 95B, Blackwater, Arizona 85228. Ralph Dixon, pastor, Ind. SS.

Sacaton Flats Chapel. Pima. Box 95B, Blackwater, Arizona 85228. Ralph Dixon, pastor, Ind. SS.

NOTE: Combined mem. of the two above is 75.

Trinity. Navajo. Box 367, Chinle, Arizona 86503. Richard Lupke, pastor, non-Indian. Mem. 136.

Emmanuel. Yavapai. Box 271, Clarkdale, Arizona 86324. James Douthitt, pastor, non-Indian. Mem. 15. SS.

Fort Defiance. Navajo. Box 317, Fort Defiance, Arizona 85604. Kenneth Schellback, pastor, non-Indian. Mem. 72. SS.

Ganado. Navajo. Box 389, Ganado, Arizona 86505. James VanDyke, pastor, non-Indian. Mem. 151. SS. WS.

Indian Wells. Navajo. Indian Wells Trading Post, Arizona 86025. Mem. 34.

Kayenta. Navajo. Box 277, Kayenta, Arizona 86033. James Morelli, pastor, non-Indian. SS. WS.

Oljato Chapel. Box 277, Kayenta, Arizona 86033. James Morelli, pastor, non-Indian. SS. WS.

NOTE: Combined mem. of the two above is 47.

Gila Crossing. Pima. Box 785, Laveen, Arizona 85339. Delbert Lewis, pastor, Ind. SS. WS.

Co-op Chapel. Pima. Box 785, Laveen, Arizona 85339. Delbert Lewis, pastor, Ind. SS. WS.

Maricopa First. Pima/Maricopa. Box 785, Laveen, Arizona 85339. Delbert Lewis, pastor, Ind. SS. WS.

NOTE: Combined mem. of the three above is 145.

First. Navajo. Leupp, Arizona 86035. John Cook, Ind. Mem. 66. SS. WS.

Parker Valley. Mohave/Chemehuevi. Box 704, Parker, Arizona 85344. Robert Hoffman, pastor, non-Indian. Mem. 35.

Central. 37 East Indian, Phoenix, Arizona 85012. Joedd

Milled, pastor, non-Indian. Mem. 89.

First. Pima. Sacaton, Arizona 85247. Kenneth Sneed, pastor, Ind. SS. WS.

Upper San Tan Chapel. Pima. Sacaton, Arizona 85247. Kenneth Sneed, pastor, Ind. SS. WS.

Lower San Tan Chapel. Pima. Sacaton, Arizona 85247. Kenneth Sneed, pastor, Ind. SS. WS.

NOTE: Combined mem. of the three above is 183.

Ft. McDowell. Pima. Box 1344, Mesa, Arizona 85201. Russell Durler, pastor, non-Indian. Mem. 26. SS. WS.

Lehi. Pima. Box 1344, Mesa, Arizona 85201. Russell Durler, pastor, non-Ind. Mem. 34. SS. WS.

Salt River. Pima. Box 1344, Mesa, Arizona 85201. Russell Durler, pastor, non-Indian. Mem. 63. SS. WS.

First. Navajo. Tuba City, Arizona 86045. Harold Borhauer, pastor, non-Indian. Mem. 63. SS. WS.

DE CRISTO PRESBYTERY

Sells. Papago. Box 158, Sells, Arizona 85634. Roger Smith, pastor, Ind. SS. WS.

Topawa & San Miguel. Papago. Box 158, Sells, Arizona 85634. Roger Smith, pastor, Ind. SS. WS.

Vamori & Santa Rosa. Papago. Box 158, Sells, Arizona 85634. Roger Smith, pastor, Ind. SS. WS.

NOTE: Combined mem. of the three above is 199.

SANTA FE PRESBYTERY

Jemez Springs. Pueblo. Jemez Springs, New Mexico 87025. Paul Stevens, pastor, non-Indian. Mem. 24. SS.

United. Laguna Pueblo. Laguna, New Mexico 87026. Mem. 65. WS.

THE WESLEYAN CHURCH

General Department of Extension and Evangelism
Box 2000, Marion, Indiana 46952   *(317)674-3301*
Joe C. Sawyer, General Secretary

Wesleyan Indian Missions
Drawer 891, Hot Springs, South Dakota 57747   *(605)745-4077*
Neal Phipps, Director
Leston N. Phipps, Assistant Director

30 churches or chapels; 1 elementary day school; 2 boarding
schools; 35 ord. Ind. ministers; 5 Ind. lay pas.; 15 Ind.
teachers; 15 Ind. in other ministries; 6 w. male teachers, 12
women; boarding pupils 70.

Pine Ridge Wesleyan Chapel. Dakota. Pine Ridge, South
Dakota 57770.

Rapid City Sioux Chapel. Dakota. Rapid City, South Dakota
57701.

Pine Ridge Christian Academy. Dakota. Pine Ridge, South
Dakota 57770. Boarding school.

Brainard Indian School. 1946. Star Route, Box 167, Hot
Springs, South Dakota 57747. *(605)745-3733.* Rev. J.
Franklin Heer, President and Principal. Boarding school
grades 7-12 and a 4 year Bible School. Indians plus children
of mission staff. Administrative staff 2. Teachers: 6 w.
men, 5 w. women. Other staff: 6 w. men, 13 w. women.
Students: 9 Ind. boys, 21 Ind. girls. Mostly Sioux.
Supported by Church and private gifts. *Broken Tomahawk,*
quarterly.

Radio Ministry.

LATE ADDITIONS AND CORRECTIONS

ASSEMBLIES OF GOD

Casa Blanca Assembly of God. Pima. Gila River Reservation.
P. O. Box 868, Bapchule, Arizona 85221. *(602)562-3410.*
J. Brown, w. Ab. in 1977 - 3. 6 infant dedications. SS 80.
YS 35. WS 20. Kid's Crusade and VBS.

CHURCH OF GOD. Anderson, Indiana

The Yearbook for 1978 reports the following personnel in Indian
ministry:
  Mark Blackcalf, Jr., Box 41, Gordon, Nebraska 69361.
  Mr. & Mrs. Keith Plank, P. O. Box 203, Scottsbluff, Nebraska
    69361.
  Mr. & Mrs. B. Adam Williams, Star Route, Box 745, Marysville,
    Washington 98270.
  Mr. & Mrs. Fred Mamaloff, P. O. Box 437, Crow Agency, Montana
    89022.
  Mr. & Mrs. Donald Mink, Hickory Route, Box 1-A, Alliance,
    Nebraska 69361.
  Mr. & Mrs. Bahe Woodman, Box 152, Sanders, Arizona 86512.

CHURCH OF JESUS CHRIST OF LATTER DAY SAINTS

The Navajo Times, vol. 19, no. 30, July 27, 1978, carries a
major article entitled: SPECIAL REPORT. MORMONS ON THE
RESERVATION. Report 20,000 Mormons on the Reservation.

EPISCOPAL CHURCH

DIOCESE OF IDAHO

Good Shepherd Parish. P. O. Box 608, Ft. Hall, Idaho 83203.
Name and Statistics added: communicants 50, baptized members
250. SS. WS.

DIOCESE OF SOUTH DAKOTA

YANKTON MISSION: Full address of Priest-in-charge - Rev.
Edward G. Vock, P. O. Box 686, Pickstown, South Dakota 57367.
(605)487-7775.

St. Michael, Pierre. Closed.

Retired Diocesan Indian Clergy:
Rt. Rev. Harold S. Jones, retired Suffragan Bishop. 2408
Central Blvd., Rapid City, South Dakota 57701.

The Venerable Vine Deloria, Sr., retired Archdeacon. 401
North Harrison St., Pierre, South Dakota 57501.
(605)224-4834.

EVANGELICAL COVENANT CHURCH OF AMERICA

Ethnic identy of pastors:
Peter Smith, Eskimo, ordained.
Jack B. Koutchak, Eskimo, ordained.
Howard I. Slwooko, Sr., Eskimo, ordained.
Robert Nelson, Athabascan, ordained.
Walter Anderson, Athabascan, ordained.
Albin Folden, Athabascan, ordained.
Fred Walton, Native Canadian, licensed.
Earl Swanson, Athabascan, licensed.
Edwin Kotongan, Sr., Eskimo, licensed.
Thomas Tungwenuk, Sr., Eskimo, licensed.
Fred Weston, Eskimo, licensed.

ROMAN CATHOLIC CHURCH

CAMPAIGN FOR HUMAN DEVELOPMENT. Total grants to Native
American projects (61) from 1971 to 1977 were $2,531,156.

TEKAKWITHA CONFERENCE

Officers elected August 1978:
Executive Committee: Fr. Gilbert F. Hemauer, Capuchin,
Chairman, St. Patrick's Parish, P. O. Box 166, Medicine
Lake, Montana 59247. *(406)789-2371*; Sister Genevieve
Cuny; Francis Hairychin.

Advisory Council: (Ministry) Ben Black Bear, Jr.;
(Catechism) Sister Patricia Mylot, OSBS; (Evangelical
Liberation) Fr. Stanislaus Maudlin, OSB; (Liturgy) Fr. Carl
Starkloff, S.J.; (Education) Sister Christine Hudson;
(Family) Dallas Chief Eagle.

ALASKA: DIOCESE OF FAIRBANKS.

St. Catherine Church. Yupik, Eskimo. Chefornak, Alaska
99561. Norman E. Donohus, S.J., parish priest, w. 3 deacon
candidates. About 12 CCD workers. Communicants 200. Total
community 250.

The Native American Christian Community

Sacred Heart Church. Eskimo. Chevak, Alaska 99563. Richard D. Case, S.J., parish priest, w. 3 deacons, 20 layworkers. Mem. 450. A theology and catechetical program for students in BIA school and grade school.

IV
NONDENOMINA—
TIONAL SOCIETIES
AND INDEPENDENT
CHURCHES

A.
NONDENOMINATIONAL
SOCIETIES

These are voluntary, independent societies, "faith missions," nondenominational in character, but often called interdenominational because they draw personnel and support from congregations and members of many denominations. See also Schools and Childcare Agencies, many of which are organized as independent societies.

AMERICAN INDIAN BIBLE MISSIONS, INC.

P. O. Box 230, Farmington, New Mexico 87401
Mr. Clifford Cheeseman, President
Mrs. Sheila Cheeseman, Superintendent

Cheehaalgeed Church. Burnham. 1966. 20 communicants, 10 conv. in 1976. 6 ib. 3 ord. Ind. men, 1 ord. Ind. woman. SS attendance 12. Head Start program.

Sanostee Church. Sanostee. 1957. 30 communicants, 18 conv. in 1976. 10 ab, 8 ib. 1 ord. Ind. man, 2 ord. Ind. women. SS 16.

Nahoo Chapel. Outstation. 10 communicants, 6 conv. in 1976. 1 Ind. woman layworker, 1 w. woman layworker.

Farmington Church. Farmington, New Mexico. 1957. (Free Methodist affiliation.) 30 communicants, 15 conv. in 1976. 16 ab. 1 Ind. man layworker, 1 w. man layworker, 3 w. women layworkers. SS 20. Indian/Anglo congregation.

Camp meetings with attendance over 100. VBS, adult classes. *Nan N Jia* Prayer bulletin since 1954.

The Native American Christian Community

AMERICAN MINISTRIES INTERNATIONAL
(Formerly American Indian Missions)
P. O. Box 3718, West Sedona, Arizona 86340   *(602)282-7381*
R. L. Gowan, President

A ministry of Christian literature for Indians. Formerly published *Indian Life*, which has now been turned over to *CHIEF*, but funding continues. All present ministering also to other minorities. Staff of 3.

ARCTIC MISSIONS, INC.
Box 512, Gresham, Oregon 97030
Mr. John Gillespie, General Director

Primary purpose is evangelism of Native Alaskans and Canadians and the goal is to plant churches in communities where a group of growing believers is not present.

5 churches, 6 chapels: (ALL ATHABASCAN and/or WHITE)

Grayling, Alaska 99590. *Chapel*. Regular attendance approximately 6.
Ruby, Alaska 99768. *Chapel*. Attendance 2.
Tanana, Alaska 99777. *Chapel*. Attendance 10.
Nenana, Alaska 99760. *Chapel*. Attendance 10.
Cantwell, Alaska 99729. *Chapel*. Attendance 10.
Talkeetna, Alaska 99676. *Church*. Attendance 50.
Trapper Creek. *Church*. Attendance 30.
Palmer, Alaska 99645. *Church*. Attendance 60.
Mile 95, Glenn Highway. *Chapel*. Attendance 40.
Nondalton, Alaska 99640. *Church*. Attendance 2.
McGrath, Alaska 99647. *Church*. Attendance 12.

In each case the community is at least twice the number given for regular attendance. Conv. 60-100 in 1976. Ord. ministers: 1 Ind., 14 whites. Total ord. force 20. Lay ministers 8. SS at each place with attendance of 25-100. Occasional boys and girls clubs. "New Life Fellowship" in Anchorage with attendance of 80-150. Correspondence course, 150-200 enrolled. 15 minute radio program "Crosswinds."

Boarding Schools: *Victory High School*, Palmer; *Arctic Bible Institute*, Palmer, 4 year post high school; *Native Institute of Canada*, Quesnell, B.C. Ind. teachers - 2 men, 1 woman. Other teachers - 20 men, 15 women. Boarding students 80-90.

Arctic Voice.

BEREAN MISSION, INC.

3536 Russell Blvd., St. Louis, Missouri 63104   *(314)773-0110*
Rev. Donald A. Urey, General Director

Berean Navajo Church. P. O. Box 700, Thoreau, New Mexico
87323. 1963. Jones Dehiga, Navajo, unordained, pastor.
Box 520, Gallup, New Mexico 87301. Glenn E. Marshall,
missionary, w. Average attendance 30. "Members" of unorganized group 8-10. Family night 6-8. Weekly classes at 2 BIA
schools. VBS usually 2 one-week sessions. Midweek service.
Ministry to alcoholics. Navajo language classes.

Huerfano and Little Tree. 1977. Navajo. Navajo lay
pastors. Churches unorganized but approximately 20 baptized.
Average attendance at Huerfano 30. Children's church. SS.
Midweek prayer meetings. Class at BIA school. Youth center.
VBS. Cassette library.

Preaching Points: *Mariano Lake Station and Blanco Canyon.*
Near Huerfano. Average attendance 17 at former, 12 at latter.
SS at Blanco Canyon. Midweek prayer meeting. Youth center.
Mariano - class at BIA school.

Elementary School. Huerfano. Boarding. Missionary teachers
5. Students 55.

CENTRAL ALASKAN MISSIONS, INC.

A division of Far Eastern Gospel Crusade
Box 5, Glennallen, Alaska 99588   *(907)882-3291, 3321*
Leander Rempel, Alaskan Director

Unorganized churches. Athabascan.

Copper Center Community Chapel. Copper Center, Alaska
99573. Jim McKinley and Harry Johns, pastors, ord., w.
Average attendance 56.

Gulkana Community Chapel. Gakona, Alaska 99586. Ven
Neeley and Fred Ewan, pastors, ord., w. Average attendance 38.

Tanaross Community Chapel. Delta Junction, Alaska 99737.
Mike Matthews, lay pastor, w. M.P. 1324.5 Alaska Highway,
Delta Junction, Alaska 99737. Average attendance 24.

Alaska Bible College. Box 289, Glennallen, Alaska 99588.
(907)882-3201. Bob Lee, President. 1966. Boarding.
Entrance requirements: high school graduation, born-again
believer, open admission for academics. 4 years course leads
to B.A., 3 years to A.A., 2 years to Bible certificate.

Teaching staff: 7 full time, 6 part time. Tuition $25.00
per credit hour. Students: 20 men, 20 women, including
Indians, Eskimos, Aleut, white, others. Graduated in 1976 -
7, in 1977 - 7, from 1967-1977 - 33. 95% are in pastorate or
church related ministries.

Faith Hospital and Clinic. 1 physician, 4 nurses, 4 other
staff. Patients treated in year 10,000.

CHIEF INC.: CHRISTIAN HOPE INDIAN ESKIMO FELLOWSHIP INC.

1432 North 7th Street, Suite C. Phoenix, Arizona 85006
Rev. Tom Claus, Executive Director (Mohawk)

CHIEF promotes acquaintance, understanding and consultation
among Native Americans through travel, conferences, short
courses and literature, conducts revivals and evangelistic
campaigns; sponsors pastors' and leadership conferences; engages
in relief to needy; runs family camps; assists ministerial
candidates with scholarships; promotes training for ministry;
stimulates spiritual life; publishes a variety of literature
especially the newspaper *Indian Life,* bimonthly. P. O. Box
2600, Orange, California 92669.

CHRISTIAN INDIAN MINISTRIES, INC.

(1965-1973 Open Door Indian Bible Mission, founded by Rev.
Bertram Bobb)
P. O. Box 4221, Dallas, Texas 75208   *(214)941-9210*
Rev. Wesley Woodard, Jr., Administrative Director
Miss Rose Marie Charlie, Athabascan

Christian Indian Chapel. 521 South Cumberland Avenue, Oak
Cliff, Dallas, Texas 75203. *(214)941-9210.* Richard Sootenay,
pastor, ord., Kiowa-Apache. *(214)942-7678.* Services Sundays
and Thursday evenings.

Christian Indian Broadcast. Radio Station KIHN, Hugo,
Oklahoma 74743. 1340 on dial, Monday - Friday at 12:50 p.m.
Rev. Bertram Bobb, Director. P. O. Box 9, Antlers, Oklahoma
74523. *(405)298-5195.*

Christian Indian News. Quarterly. Circulation of 6,000.

Christian Indian Campground. Pine Creek Lake in southwestern
Oklahoma. Camping for Indian children, teens and adults.

Oklahoma Indian Evangelism. P. O. Box 9, Antlers, Oklahoma
74523. *(405)298-5195.* Bertram Bobb, Choctaw, Director.
Ministry primarily to Choctaws: personal evangelism, home
Bible studies, Bible correspondence courses, course work, etc.

EVANGELICAL NAVAJO FELLOWSHIP

Not a missionary society, but a fellowship of missionaries and Navajo church workers. Persons in neighboring tribal areas and interested individuals in the Navajo region may be associate members. Applicants for constituent and associate membership must affirm seven articles of faith set forth in a moderate Evangelical statement, and must sever any relationship with any church or body which holds membership in the National Council of Churches of Christ in the U.S.A. Constituent members are missionaries to the Navajos, members of Navajo mission boards who live in the region, Navajo Christian workers and one duly appointed delegate from each local Navajo church. Meetings are held once each quarter.

FAR EASTERN GOSPEL CRUSADE

P. O. Box 513, Farmington, Michigan 48024   *(313)477-4210*
Rev. Philip E. Armstrong, General Director

See Central Alaskan Missions, Inc.

FLAGSTAFF MISSION TO THE NAVAJOS

6 West Cherry Avenue, P. O. Box AA, Flagstaff, Arizona 86002
Field Directors: Miss Katherine Beard   *(602)774-2802*
                   Miss Imo Wardlow   1949
                   Rev. David Patterson
Chairman, Board of Directors: Mr. Harold Harper, 3735 N. Grand-
view, Flagstaff, Arizona 86002

Mission Personnel, including Field Directors - total 29; Navajo 13, w. 16. Full time - 22; 9 Navajo including 5 ord. men, 13 w. including 3 ord. and 1 lic. persons. Part time — 7; 4 Navajo including 1 lic. man, 3 w. including 1 medical doctor. Also volunteer workers.

Black Falls Station. 1963. *Black Falls Bible Church.* Arnold Begay, pastor, Navajo, part time. Resides and studies at Southwestern School of Missions, 2918 North Aris, Flagstaff, Arizona 86001. School phone *(602)774-3890.* Other missionaries serving Black Falls from Flagstaff: Mrs. Marion Newton (white) and Mrs. Ardith Curley (Navajo). Total fellowship approximately 62. Services in Navajo, some classes in English. SS and morning worship 35. Twice a month lunch and Bible classes or business meeting in afternoon. Wednesday Bible class, Wupatki, 9. Friday evening prayer meeting 14. Saturday workday about once a month 10. VBS, average 94. 2 Christmas programs, attendance 292. Saved 11, baptized 8, in Bible school 1.

Flagstaff Indian Bible Church. 1953. Scott Franklin, pastor, ord., Navajo. 317 North Sitgreaves Street, Flagstaff, Arizona 86001. *(602)774-4927* or Headquarters phone *(602)774-2802.* Pastor coordinates Radio Ministry for the area. Other assisting missionaries: Mrs. Ardith Curley (Navajo), Miss Helen Yazzie (Navajo), and white personnel - Miss Edith Henderson, Miss Mary Nemire, Rev. and Mrs. Dave Patterson, Miss Lenita Vetter. Total fellowship of approximately 148. Services and classes in Navajo and English. SS 72. Morning worship 94. Evening service 82. Tuesday: 2 school Bible classes 15 and 11; choir 16. Wednesday: jail ministry; school Bible class 25; evening service 58. Thursday: Girl Scouts 54. Friday: youth fun night 25. VBS, average 125. 8 Christmas programs, total attendance 633. Saved 24, baptized 10, in Bible school 3.

Grand Falls Mission. June 1976. Without pastor. Alvin Gon, a Navajo student at Southwestern School of Missions visits on Tuesday evenings. Other missionaries serving the area: Navajo - Mrs. Ardith Curley; white - Mrs. Helen Hilgeman, Mrs. Marion Newton. No membership. Tuesday evening Navajo Bible study 5. Wednesday morning Bible study in English and Navajo 6. VBS, average 62. Christmas program 214. Saved 7, baptized 2.

Gray Mountain Bible Church. March 1959. Leslie Cody, pastor, ord., Navajo. Gray Mountain, Arizona 86016. *(602)679-2394.* Station phone *(602)679-2366.* Other missionaries serving area: Navajo - Mrs. Rosemary Cody, Miss Gloria Singer, Miss Helen Yazzie; white - Mrs. Helen Hilgeman. Navajo assistant at Happy Playmates School - Mrs. Mary Posey. Dr. Walter Taylor, M.D. serves the Clinic on Clinic days. Total fellowship of approximately 132. Services in Navajo, some classes in English. SS and morning worship 95. Sunday evening service 51. Happy Playmates School, Monday to Friday, 10 a.m. to 2 p.m., 12 enrolled. Tuesday: literacy class 8. Wednesday: evening service 45. Thursday: Bible study at Buck Rogers, 15. Friday: prayer meetings in homes, 40 total. Saturday: young people 30. VBS, average 115. 4 Christmas programs 422. Saved 31, baptized 6, in Bible school 1.

Hidden Springs. December 1971. Wayne Benally, part time, pastor, Navajo. 6 West Cherry Avenue, P. O. Box AA, Flagstaff Arizona 86002. *(602)774-2802.* Mrs. Elsie Benally, Navajo, assists her husband. Potential fellowship about 65. Sunday worship and SS in Navajo, attendance 10. VBS 73. 3 Christmas programs 1,013. Saved 78, baptized 2.

Kayenta Bible Church. October 1963. Pastors: Chee Bedonie, ord., full time; Kayenta, Arizona 86033; *(602)697-3671;*

white - Harold Taggart, ord., full time; also directs the work in the area; P. O. Box 332, Kayenta, Arizona 86033; *(602)697-3485.* Other missionaries serving in the area: Mrs. Betty Gon and Mrs. Alice Largo, both Navajo, full time. Church organized with elders and trustees, but no formal membership. Total fellowship approximately 110. Services and classes in Navajo and English. SS 58. Sunday morning worship 78. Young people's meeting 9. Evening service 47. Monday: God and Family class 6; literacy class 14. Tuesday: Ladies' Bible class 7; Dorm Bible classes, Kayenta, 45. Wednesday: Dorm Bible classes, Dinnehotso, 35; prayer meeting 46. Thursday: school personnel prayer meeting 6; Cub Scouts 12; Boy Scouts 12. Friday: Narrow Canyon Bible study 9. VBS, average 190. 11 Christmas programs 3,079. Saved 196, baptized 3, in Bible school 5.

GOOD NEWS MISSION TO THE NAVAJO INDIANS, INC.

Houck, Arizona 85605 *(602)685-2626, 2656*
Rev. Harrison Lauber, Director

1927/1936. Three mission stations. 1 ord. w. minister; 1 w. lay woman worker; 2 Navajo layworkers. Church membership about 60. Sunday School. Prayer letter.

NAVAJO BIBLE SCHOOL AND MISSION, INC.

P. O. Box F, Window Rock, Arizona 86515
Dr. David H. Clark, General Director

Major ministry is training Navajo for the ministry in any church or mission.

3 churches, 6 chapels:

Window Rock Church, Bob Hilderman
Crystal Church, Daniel Taylor
Ft. Defiance Church, Louis McCabe
Mannelito, Tony Meyers

Average size of local church 30. Total communicant membership approximately 200. Total community about 500. Ord. Ind. ministers. Converts in 1976 - 32. Ab. 27. SS 3 - membership about 200. Adult education school 1. Adult correspondence course.

One elementary day school with 55 students. Teachers: 1 Ind. woman, 2 w. men, 3 w. women.

Radio Station.

Archives at Window Rock open to scholars. *The Navajo* - 1937.

The Native American Christian Community

NAVAJO GOSPEL CRUSADE

Route 1, Box 7, Cortez, Colorado 81321   *(303)565-3290*
Rev. Arthur S. Norris, Director; 1002 East Carpenter, Route 1,
Cortez, Colorado 81321

Administrative staff 4.   Indian pastors 2.   Indian workers 1.
White missionary staff 12.

   Aneth Outstation.   1959.   Aneth, Utah 84510.   Average Sunday
   attendance 40.   VBS.

   Montezuma Creek Station.   1964.   Montezuma Creek, Utah 84534.
   Tuesday and Wednesday evenings, attendance 15-40.   VBS.

   Bluff Outstation.   1965.   Bluff, Utah 84512.   New missionaries
   not yet holding regular services.   VBS.

   Navajo Bible Institute.   Route 1, Box 7, Cortez, Colorado
   81321.   *(303)565-3290.*   Administrative staff 4.   Teachers 7.
   Students in 1977-78 - 14.

NAVAJO GOSPEL MISSION, INC.

P. O. Box 41, Oraibi, Arizona 86039   *(602)725-3263*
Mr. Carlton Lucas, Field Director
Rev. Thomas Dolaghan, Administrator

1930.   Originally Navajo Indian Evangelization Movement, Inc.,
founded by Berlyn H. and Edith M. Stokely.   On Navajo Reservation.   10 churches, 8 chapels.   Total community 425.   35
converts in 1976.   15 adult baptisms.   Whites ordained 2,
Indian men layworkers 10, (5 employed by mission and 5 elders
in churches), white men layworkers 9, Indian women layworkers 4,
white women layworkers 12.   Average size of local churches 30,
Pinon largest.

   Navajo Bible Academy.   Oraibi.   Day and boarding.   5 w. women
   teachers.   Kindergarden to 8th grade.   35 day students, 40
   boarding.   SS 2 - enrollment 250.   2 weekday religious
   schools.   Bible training school for lay people in Fall and
   Spring.

The Mission maintains a campground in Flagstaff which is used
for Navajo pastors' conferences, family conferences,
children's camps and housing for Indian students attending
the Bible Training School in Flagstaff.

Annual report since 1934.   *Navajo Prayer Challenge* since 1940.
Early name *Other Sheep*.

Archives at Oraibi open to scholars.

Directory - Nondenominational Missionary Societies

Navajo Gospel Mission Church, Oraibi. 1930. Albert Johnson, lic., Navajo, and Carlton Lucas, ord., w., pastors. Oraibi, Arizona 86510. *(602)725-3263.* Membership 15 Navajo, 25 white, plus 60 school children. Ib. in 1977 - 4. SS 25. Close association with the Navajo Bible Academy and the Mission activities. 3 VBS. Services to community, etc.

Finger Point Navajo Gospel Mission. 15 years in this location. Box 41, Oraibi, Arizona 86039. *(602)725-3263.* Goy Begay, pastor, lic., Navajo. Attendance 20, increase of 6 in 1977. VBS. Camp meeting.

Sand Springs Navajo Gospel Church. 20 years in this location. Black Falls, Wupatki, Arizona. John McCabe, pastor, lic., Navajo. Attendance 10 (loss of 15 due to land disputes). VBS.

Cactus Valley Navajo Bible Church. 7 years in this location. Box 41, Oraibi, Arizona 86039. Clarence Blackrock and James Johnson, pastors, unordained, Navajos. Attendance 40-50, increase of 5. VBS.

Whitegrass Mountain Navajo Gospel Church. c.1968. Box 301, Kayenta, Arizona 86033. Paul Johnson, pastor, lic., Navajo. Attendance 40. Ib. in 1970 - 2. SS 10-12. VBS. Camp meetings.

Forest Lake Navajo Gospel Church. Meeting about 8 years. P. O. Box 301, Kayenta, Arizona 86033. Paul Johnson, pastor, lic., Navajo. Attendance 35. SS 12-15. VBS. Camp meetings.

Black Mesa Navajo Gospel Church. Meeting about 9 years. P. O. Box 301, Kayenta, Arizona 86033. Paul Johnson, pastor, lic., Navajo. Attendance 40-45, increase of 5. Ab. in 1977 - 5. SS 15. VBS. Choir. Camp meetings.

Burnt Corn Navajo Gospel Church. Meeting 4 years. Box 446, Pinon, Arizona 86510. *(602)725-3214.* Jackson Williams, pastor, unordained, Navajo. Attendance 15. VBS.

Pinon Navajo Gospel Church. Meeting about 10 years. P. O. Box 446, Pinon, Arizona 85610. *(602)725-3214.* Timothy Begay, pastor, unordained, Navajo. 4 Navajo elders also preach. Thomas Dolaghan, ord., w. minister also resides here. Attendance 140, increase of 50. Ab. in 1977 - 18. SS 55. Religious instruction classes 100+ on Wednesdays. Pastor's classes. Choir. VBS. Evangelistic crusades.

Whippoorwill Navajo Gospel Church. Meeting for 15 years, organized in 1977. P. O. Box 446, Pinon, Arizona 86510.

(602)725-3214. Jackson Williams, pastor, unordained, Navajo. Attendance 25 - 30. Ab. in 1977 - 1. SS 10. VBS.

Indian Church Ministries. P. O. Box 446, Pinon, Arizona 86510. Thomas A. Dolaghan, Director. A special ministry of Navajo Gospel Mission concerned with urban ministries, Navajo evangelistic teams, theological education by extension, missionary orientation, cross-cultural training, conferences and workshops, church support ministry, research and publication.

NAVAJO MISSIONS, INC.

P. O. Box 1230, 2103 West Main Street, Farmington, New Mexico 87401   *(505)325-0255*
R. Jack Drake, President and Director

Staff: 7 houseparents, evangelist (Rev. Jack Wheat), 19 others.

Child Care Ministry. Children attend Apache Elementary School, Tibbatts Junior High School and Farmington High School. One handicapped child attends a special school. Two girls are away in college. Most children with their house- parents attend Emmanuel Baptist Church. Ten made a profession of faith in Christ in 1976. There is a work program and an arts and crafts program.

Christian Bookstore. Sales of $11,000 in 1976.

Print Shop. Prints Navajo language literature. 370,170 impressions in 1976.

Cassette Lending Library.

Telephone Dial-A-Blessing Ministry.

Airplane Ministry. Over the Navajo Reservation.

OKLAHOMA INDIAN EVANGELISM

See Christian Indian Ministries

SANDERS BIBLE MISSION

P. O. Box 105, Sanders, Arizona 86512   *(602)688-2526*
Charles Row, Director   1941 c.1976
Ms. Florence Wagner, Secretary-Treasurer
Mission Board Members: 2 Navajo and 3 white.

Sanders Bible Church. 1976. P. O. Box 105, Sanders, Arizona 86512. *(602)688-2526.* Thomas Woods, pastor, Navajo. Mem. 19 adults. Baptisms in 1977 - 9. SS 40. YS 12. Daily noon hour classes with school children. VBS.

SLAVIC GOSPEL ASSOCIATION

P. O. Box 1122, Wheaton, Illinois 60187   *(312)690-8900*
Mr. Peter Deyneka, Jr., Director

Alaska Mission
9031 Noble Circle, Anchorage, Alaska 99502   *(907)243-4067*
Mr. Walter J. Covich, Field Chairman

King Cove Bible Chapel. Box 45, King Cove, Alaska 99612.
Aleut. Jim Ellsmore, pastor, w. SS. YS. WS.

Ivanof Bible Chapel. Ivanof Bay, Alaska 99502. Aleut.
The Misses Myrtle Lamond and Betty Kirsch, missionaries.
SS. Youth and adult activities.

Chignik Bible Chapel. Chignik, Alaska 99564. Aleut. Ron
Wilson, pastor. SS. YS. WS.

Port Lions Bible Church. P. O. Box 296. Port Lions,
Alaska 99550. Aleut/white. Bob Crane, pastor, w.

Kenai Bible Church. P. O. Box 176, Kenai, Alaska 99611.
Aleut/white. Vincent Rosheger, pastor, w. SS. YS. WS.

Kodiak Bible Church. P. O. Box 1245, Kodiak, Alaska 99615.
Aleut/white. Vacant. All church activities for children,
youth and adults.

SOUTHWEST INDIAN SCHOOL

See World Gospel Mission.

SUMMER SCHOOL OF LINGUISTICS AND WYCLIFFE BIBLE TRANSLATORS, North American Branch

P. O. Box 68, Eastlake, Colorado 80614   *(303)452-4349*
Mr. Alan R. Pence, Director

"Our overall aim is to see the Scriptures in use among North
American Indians. To do this we make linguistic studies as
appropriate, translate the Scriptures into the mother tongue,
encourage local involvement in the preparation of various
materials in the language, provide consultant help in the preparation of these materials, encourage the preservation of the
cultural heritage of the Indian and provide assistance with
learning to read and use the Scriptures. We work only with
groups that are still using their language as a major means of
communication."

Translation Projects and Workers:

Barbara Allen/Donna Gardiner - Isleta Pueblo; Route 1, Box 1360, Albuquerque, New Mexico 87532.
John Anderson - North Paiute; Box 69, McDermitt, Nevada 89421.
Rod Bartletts - East Cree; Baie du Poste, Mistassini Lake, Quebec, Canada GOW 1C0.
Curtis Bunneys - West Apache; Box 51, San Carlos, Arizona 85550.
Gene Burrhams - Alabama-Coushatta; 202 4th Street N.W., Springhill, Louisiana 71075.
Ray Collins - Upper Kuskokwim; Box 75, McGrath, Arkansas 99627.
Curtis Cooks - Zuni-Pueblo; 402 Canoncito, Gallup, New Mexico 87001.
Russ Daniels - Dakota Sioux; Star Route #174C, Hot Springs, South Dakota 57747.
Jonathan Ekstroms - Hopi; 15363 Goldenwest B-28, Huntington Beach, California 42647.
Don Frantzes - Blackfoot; Box 24, Arrowwood, Alberta, Canada TOL 0B0.
David Wests - Mikasuki Seminole; 3409 S.W. 12th Street, Fort Lauderdale, Florida 33312.
Roger Gilstraps - Algonquin; 15 rue Quay, Val d'Or, Quebec, Canada J9P 4Z8.
Fred Miskas - Crow; Box 75, Pryor, Montana 59066.
Jack Greens - Ute; 50 Route, Cortez, Colorado 81321.
Don Hekmons - Montaignais; 692 Avenue, Cartier, Sept Iles, Quebec, Canada G4R 2V1.
David Henrys - Koyukon; Box 1028, Fairbanks, Alaska 99707.
Hank Hildebrandt - Babine Carrier; Box 586, Burns Lake, British Columbia, Canada V0J 1E0.
Marshall Holdstocks - Beaver; Goodlow, British Columbia, Canada V0C 1S0.
David Hulls - Tiwa-Pueblo; Box 1141, Taos, New Mexico 87571.
Wayne Lemans - Cheyenne; Box 127, Busby, Montana 59016.
Paul Milonowskis - Upper Tanana; Mile 1284, Alaska Highway, Tok, Alaska 99780.
Vic Monuses - Slavey; Box 222, Fort Simpson, Northwest Territories, Canada X0E 0N0.
Dick Mueller - Kutchin; Box 329, Fort Yukon, Alaska 99740.
Constance Naish/Gilliam Story - Tlingit; Goodlow, British Columbia, Canada V0C 1S0.
Tom Nevers - Cocopa; Box 430, Somerton, Arizona 85350.
Dean Saxton - Papago; 5342 W. Bar 5 Street, Tucson, Arizona 85713.
Wolf Seilers - Kobuk R. Eskimo; Wycliff Bibeluebersetzer, Siegenweg 32, D-5909 Burbach-Holzhausen, West Germany (at present).
Dave Shinen - Yupik Eskimo; Box 629, Nome, Alaska 99762.
Hazel Shorey - Towa Pueblo; Box 126, San Ysidro, New Mexico 87053.

Tim Stimes - Atikamek; Sanmaur, Co Laviolette, Quebec, Canada
GOA 4MO.
Dick Walkers - Stuart L. Carrier; Box 365, Ft. St. James,
British Columbia, Canada VOJ 1PO.
Watson Williams - Micmac; 23 Dufferin Street, Campbellton, New
Brunswick, Canada E3N 2N3.
Herb Zimmerman - Dogrib; Box 551, Yellowknife, Northwest
Territories, Canada XOE 1HO.
Randy Speirs - Tewa Peublo; Route 2, Box 60, Espanola, New
Mexico 87532.

New Testaments have been finished in Navajo, Apache, Papago and
Inupiat. Some books in others.

Cooperative Work:

1. Bilingual education programs in cooperation with Bureau of
    Indian Affairs or local schools in Inupiat Eskimo, Upper
    Kuskokwim, Kutchin, Upper Tanana, Beaver, Carrier, Babine,
    Stoney, Blackfoot, Tiwa, Ute, Papago, Seminole, Zuni, Hopi,
    Apache, Mescalero Apache and a few others.
2. Consultant help given to missionaries mainly of NCEM but
    others also.
3. Publishing Scriptures through organizations like American
    Bible Society and World Home Bible League.
4. The development of the Summer Institute of Linguistics for
    Native Americans was a cooperative effort with the
    Univeristy of Albuquerque (later dropped out) and BIA
    officials.

Archives at Thornton, Colorado.

In Other Words, since 1945, formerly *Translation Magazine.*

UNITED INDIAN MISSIONS, INC.

P. O. Box U, Flagstaff, Arizona 86002   *(602)774-0651*
Mr. Donald G. Fredericks, General Director

Navajo Bible Church. Fort Defiance, Arizona 86504. Thomas
Kontz, pastor, ord., Navajo. Kenneth Foster, associate
pastor, Navajo. Attendance 75-100.

Hualapai Bible Church. Peach Springs, Arizona 86434.
Ruppert Parker and Grant Topaija, leaders, unordained,
Hualapai. Attendance 40-50.

Havasupai Bible Church. Supai, Arizona 86435. Daniel Kaska,
leader, unordained, Supai. Attendance 15-20.

Oakview Navajo Bible Church. Vander Wagen, New Mexico 87326.

Sam Arthur, leader, unordained, Navajo.   Attendance 20-25.

United Indian Missions also carries on evangelism among Indians in Canada at Burns Lake, Fort St. James, Tachie and Prince George, British Columbia and among the Carrier people (in B.C.) where *Moricetown Bible Chapel,* under Missionary Ken Miller, has an attendance of 20.   In Mexico there are missionaries at Hermosillo, Guaymas, and Navajoa in the State of Sonora, and two new village churches at Nuri and Cuba (attendance 25-30 each) under the leadership of Pastor Orona of Guaymas Evangelical Baptist Church (attendance 125-150).

WORLD GOSPEL MISSIONS

P. O. Box 948, Marion, Indiana 46952   *(317)664-7331*
Hollis F. Abbott, President

Southwest Indian School.   14202 North 73rd Avenue, Peoria, Arizona 85345.   *(602)979-6008.*   Rev. Doug Carter, Superintendant.

A service mission to other missions.   Children from many tribes.   Boarding school - grades 2-12.   Indian teachers: men 1, women 3.   White teachers: men 6, women 7.   Students 180.   *Call To Prayer.*

General Goals: 1.   To provide an interdenominational mean
whereby the Indian people may be reached
with the message and experience of
scriptural holiness.
2.   To contribute significantly to the
development and strengthening of the
church in the Indian community

WORLD—WIDE MISSIONS

1593 East Colorado Blvd., Box G, Pasadena, California 91109

Twin Wells Indian School.   Sun Valley, Arizona 86029.   1962. *(602)524-3792.*   Jerry Doolittle, Director.   Ron Roncase, Principal.   Teaching staff: 6 women, 7 men - all white. Students: 103 girls, 83 boys.

WYCLIFFE BIBLE TRANSLATORS

See Summer School of Linguistics.

B INDEPENDENT CHURCHES

Independent congregations are numerous but difficult to discover. They appear to be most numerous in Navajoland, and Thomas Dolaghan and David Scates have listed them in their *The Navajo Are Coming To Jesus*. Very few pastors to whom questionnaires were sent returned them.

Brighter Day Indian Church. 11153 South Broadway, Los Angeles, California 90061.

Calvary Indian Church. 933 South Perry Street, Denver, Colorado 80219. Al Smith, pastor.

First American Indian Church, Inc. 2218 Hancock Street, Los Angeles, California 90031.

Indian Bible Church. 590 South Logan Street, Denver, Colorado 80209. *(303)733-0732.* B. Byron Wilson, pastor. 1531 Coring Place, Northglenn, Colorado 80233. *(303)452-2136.* About 40 tribes have been represented in the past 8 years, Navajo and Sioux in the majority. The church is an outgrowth of American Indian Crusade of Phoenix. SS (attendance about 25) at 10 a.m., morning worship at 11 a.m., and evening service at 7 p.m. Midweek service, Thursday, 7:30 p.m. YS Sunday at 6 p.m.

Indian Revival Center. 5602 East Gage, South Gate, California 90280.

Mekusukey Baptist Church. Seminole. West Hollywood, Florida 33024. Jimmie Osceola, pastor, Seminole. There are 3 other

Independent Baptist Seminole churches. The 4 have resulted from the work of a missionary sent by the Baptist Seminoles of Oklahoma.

Mohegan Congregational Church. 1831. Mohegan and white. Uncasville, Connecticut 06382. Charles Duncan, pastor, ord., w. Danielson, Connecticut 06239. Mrs. Edith Crosby, clerk. 112 Dunham Street, Norwich, Connecticut 06320. Mem. 40. SS 20. This church belonged to the United Church of Christ until recently, but is now independent.

William Duncan Memorial Church. Metlakatla, Alaska 99926. This is the church which Duncan founded in the old Metlakatla in British Columbia and transferred with 600 of his Tsimshian followers to new Metlakatla in 1887. After his death the church was renamed in his honor.

There are independent Baptist churches among the Alabama-Coushatta in Texas. There are also 5 among the Haliwa in Halifax and Warren Counties, North Carolina, 2 of them Baptist, 1 Church of God.

INDEPENDENT CHURCH IN NAVAJOLAND

Aneth Navajo Church. c.1957. Aneth, Utah 84510. George Tohtsoni, pastor. Montezuma Creek, Utah 84534. Attendance 20. SS 30. YS 10. Prayer meeting 25.

Berean Baptist Church. 1956. Mixed tribes and non-Indians. 201 East California, Holbrook, Arizona 86025. *(602)524-6503.* DeWit Prichard, pastor, ord., w. P. O. Box 731, 233 West Florida Street, Holbrook, Arizona 86025. Mem. 43. Ab. in 1977 - 17. SS 33. WS 10. VBS. Camp.

Bible Baptist Shepherd Navajo Church. Box 1616, 507 North 5th Street, Gallup, New Mexico 87301. *(505)722-5269.* Edward E. Hannig, pastor, ord., w. Ab. in 1977 - 2. Special alcoholism ministry to transient Indians.

Bird Springs Navajo Baptist Church. 1967. Navajo. c/o Emma Yazzie, Box 847, Navajo Station, Ganado, Arizona 86505. No pastor. Mem. 20. SS. WS.

Cedar Ridge Baptist Church. 1960. Navajo. Cedar Ridge T.P., Cameron, Arizona 86020. Harry Sloan, Sr., pastor, ord., Navajo. Mem. 25, increase of 5 in 1977. Ab. in 1977 - 3. SS 15. WS 5. Wednesday prayer meeting. VBS.

Church of Christ. 1966. Navajo. Box 220, Montezuma Creek, Utah 84534. *(801)651-3461.* P. B. Middlebrook, Jr., lay pas., w. Mem. 28, increase of 5 in 1977. Ab. in 1977 - 5. SS 39. 2 VBS.

Hogback Church of Christ-Navajo Mission. 1965. P. O. Box 196, Waterflow, New Mexico 87421. *(505)598-5691.* C. C. (Skip) Knox, preacher-missionary, w. Mem. 41, increase of 12 in 1977. Ab. in 1977 - 10. SS 35. Youth Bible class 30. Ladies' Bible class 8. Wednesday evening meeting. 2 VBS.

Mexican Water Baptist Church. 1977. Navajo. Mexican Water, Arizona, Box 2117, Farmington, New Mexico 87401. David Gillwood, pastor, unordained, Ind. Mem. 26. SS 40-50. YS 20. Wednesday evening Bible study and prayer meeting. Monthly youth club. VBS.

Navajo Church of Christ. c.1970. P. O. Box 556, Ft. Defiance, Arizona 86504. *(602)729-5206.* Omar L. Bixler, missionary, w. Mem. 17, increase of 3 in 1977. Ab. in 1977 - 1. SS 25. 2 VBS 80.

Navajo Christian Church. 1966, organized 1969. Box 1049, Teec Nos Pos, Arizona 86514. *(303)882-4213.* David R. Scates and Vernon Hollett, missionaries, ord., w. 2 ord. Ind. pastors, 5 unordained, see below. 5 congregations, mem. 130, increase of 20 in 1977. Ab. in 1977 - 5. 3 SS 40, 20, 10. Men's group 10. Summer youth camps 60. Family camp 40. The 5 congregations are self-governing, self-supporting, self-determining, self-propagating.

Red Mesa. Jim Charley, pastor. Larry Johnson, assistant pastor. Attendance 55.

Sweet Water. Jim Charley, pastor. Albert Nargo, assistant pastor. Irregular.

Beclahbito, New Mexico. Harvey Yazzie, pastor. Richard Watchmen, assistant pastor. Attendance 25.

Cudei, New Mexico. Loy Harrison, pastor. Fred Juin, assistant pastor. Attendance 35.

Borrego Pass, New Mexico. Kee Tapaha, pastor. Attendance 12.

Navajo Christian Church. Dilkon, Arizona (not a post office). Related to the churches next above (Teec Nos Pos). Ernest Creamer, missionary. Winslow, Arizona 86047. Raymond Joey, Navajo pastor.

Navajoland Church of Christ. c.1972. Box 411, Many Farms, Arizona 86503. *(602)781-6326.* J. Ben Johnson, pastor, ord., Navajo. Mem. 50, increase of 12 in 1977. Ab. in 1977 - 13. SS 40. YS 26. Men's group 15. 2 VBS. 2 camps for children.

Thoreau Community Bible Church. 1950, names 1967. Navajo.

Unorganized. Box 700, Thoreau, New Mexico 87323. *(505)862-7545.*
Glenn E. Marshall, missionary pastor. Mem. 10. SS 30. Religious
instruction class at BIA school.

INDEPENDENT CONGREGATIONS REPORTS BY DOLAGHAN AND
SCATES ON WHICH NO OTHER INFORMATION IS AVAILABLE
(Questionnaires were sent.)

REPORTED AS CONSERVATIVE BAPTIST, BUT NOT REPORTED BY THE C.B.H.M.S.:

Black Mesa Camp Church. Tonalea, Arizona. Dick Begay, pastor.

Coalmine Baptist Church. Oraibi, Arizona 86039. Kii Littleman,
pastor.

Porcupine Ridge Church. Tuba City, Arizona 86045. Jimmy
Mexicano, pastor.

Red Mesa Baptist Church. Tonalea, Arizona 86044. Alex Morez,
pastor.

REPORTED AS GENERAL ASSOCIATION OF REGULAR BAPTISTS, BUT NOT LISTED BY DENOMINATION:

Cedar Baptist Church. Jones Ranch, Gallup, New Mexico 86301.
Rev. Mr. Gaston.

Indian Baptist Church. Winslow, Arizona 86047.

Rainbow Baptist Mission. Box 565, Chinle, Arizona 86503. Bill
Anderson, pastor.

REPORTED AS INDEPENDENT BAPTIST CHURCHES:

Bethel Navajo Baptist Church. Steamboat, Ganado, Arizona 86505.
Harold Noble, pastor.

Bible Baptist Church. Ganado, Arizona 86505. Pat Natoni,
pastor.

Burnham Baptist Church. P. O. Box 292, Fruitland, New Mexico
87416. Roger D. Deal, pastor.

Canyon Diabolo Baptist Church. Route 1, Box 43, Flagstaff,
Arizona 86001. Harry Russell, pastor.

Dok View Baptist Church. Chilchilto, Vander Wagen, New Mexico
87326. Jimmy Sector, pastor.

Faith Navajo Baptist Church. Thoreau, New Mexico 87323. John Bacora, pastor.

First Navajo Baptist Church. 308 Crownpoint, New Mexico 87313. Jimmy A. Ettsitty.

> *Coyotte Canyon Baptist Church.*
> *Smith Lake Baptist Church.*
> *Lake Powell Baptist Church.*

Ganado Baptist Church. Ganado, Arizona 86505. Rev. Mr. Godoby.

Memorial Baptist Church. Chinle, Arizona 86503. Lee Pearson, pastor.

Mt. Powell Mission. Box 686, Thoreau, New Mexico 87323. Frank Booker, pastor.

Pine Haven Navajo Baptist Church. Box 686, Gallup, New Mexico 87301. Charles Girton, pastor.

Round Rock Baptist Church. Round Rock Trading Post, Chinle, Arizona 86503. Elliott Hogue, pastor.

Shiprock Baptist Temple. Shiprock, New Mexico 87420. (Meets in DNA Building.) Rev. Mr. Walker, pastor.

REPORTED AS SOUTHERN BAPTIST CONVENTION, BUT NOT ON STATE CONVENTION ROLE:

Standing Rock Bible Baptist Shepherd Church. Box 1257, Crownpoint, New Mexico 87313. Neil Foerster, pastor.

REPORTED AS BRETHREN CHURCHES:

Community Navajo Grace Brethren Church. Counselor, New Mexico 87018. John Trujillo, pastor.

Grace Brethren. Box 17, Tonalea, Arizona 86044. Nelson Betoni, pastor.

Torreon Navajo Brethren Mission. Box 188, Cuba, New Mexico 87013. David Seiler, pastor.

CHURCH OF CHRIST (Not otherwise identified: Three above also with data.)

Kayenta Church of Christ. Box 844, Kayenta, Arizona 86033. Fred Austin, pastor.

Shiprock Church of Christ. Box 188, Shiprock, New Mexico 87420.
A. B. McPherson, pastor.

Tuba City Church of Christ. Box 1008, Tuba City, Arizona 86045.
Don Tullis, pastor.

FREE METHODIST (but the General Missionary Board of the
F.M.C. states that only the Farmington, N.M. Church of the
American Indian Bible Mission is affiliated.)

American Indian Mission. Shiprock, New Mexico 87420. Leo
Bennally, pastor.

Free Methodist Church. Whitehorse Lake, Cuba, New Mexico 87013.

"MISSION CHURCHES"

Alcoholic Rehabilitation Center. Box 172, Ganado, Arizona
86505. Alan Hill, Director, ord., Navajo.

American Indian Mission. 2826 North Petterson, Flagstaff,
Arizona 86001. George Baxter, pastor.

Crosslands Mission. Star Route 3, Box 10, Thoreau, New Mexico
87323. Rev. Mr. McBride, pastor.

Elim Haven. Box 66, Continental Divide, New Mexico 87312. Mrs.
Keist.

Ft. Defiance Bible Church. Ft. Defiance, Arizona 86504. Tom
Kuntz, pastor.

Immanuel Mission. Box 218, Sweetwater, Teec Nos Pos, Arizona
86514.

Inscription House Navajo Mission. Box 50, Tonalea, Arizona
86044. Bernard Reimer, pastor.

Christian Catholic Church. Shonto, Arizona 86054. Amos
Grass.

Ministry of John 3:16, Inc. Box 159, Holbrook, Arizona 86025.
Robert Kevin, pastor.

Navajo Bible Mission. Box 1655, Farmington, New Mexico 87401.
Chester Dean, pastor.

Navajo Evangelical Mission. Hunters Point, St. Michaels,
Arizona 86511. Tom Siedler, pastor.

Sand Springs Church. Wapatki National Monument, Flagstaff, Arizona 86001. John McCabe, pastor.

Star Lake Bible Mission. Star Route, Cuba, New Mexico 87013. Claude Fondaw, pastor.

Tsaile Home Church. Round Rock Trading Post, Chinle, Arizona 86503. Elliott Hogue, pastor.

Whitewater Gospel Mission. Whitewater, New Mexico (not a post office). Nora Rady, pastor.

Calvary Hogan Mission. Box 945, Chinle, Arizona 86503. Warren Smith, pastor.

FULL GOSPEL PENTECOSTAL CHURCHES (Not connected with Full Gospel Evangelistic Association of Katy, Texas)

Beclabito Full-Gospel Church. Beclabito, Teec Nos Pos, Arizona 86514. Helen Begay.

Bird Springs Full-Gospel Church. Star Route, Box 250, Winslow, Arizona 86047. Leonard Curtis.

Borrego Pass Full-Gospel Church. Borrego Pass, Crownpoint, New Mexico 87313. Dan and Amos Barleone.

Cameron Full-Gospel Church. Cameron, Arizona 86021. Thomas Hoover.

Castle Butte House Church. Castle Butte, Arizona. Gary Taha.

Chinle Full-Gospel Church. Chinle, Arizona 86503. Jerry Tom.

Church Rock Full-Gospel Church. Church Rock, New Mexico 87311. Sister Harvey.

Cottonwood Full-Gospel Church. Cottonwood, Chinle, Arizona 86503. Bobby Charlie.

Dennibito Full-Gospel Church. Johnny Begodi.

Ganado Pentecostal Church. Ganado, Arizona 86505. Tom White.

Gallegos Full-Gospel Church. Gallegos, New Mexico. Charley Shield.

Kaibito Full-Gospel Church. Kaibito, Arizona 86044. Eugene Bennett.

The Native American Christian Community

Lukachukai Full-Gospel Church. Box 1311, Lukachukai, Arizona 86507. George Davis.

Lukachukai Full-Gospel Church. Lukachukai, Arizona 86507. Margaret Buckingclien.

Lupton Camp Church. Lupton, Arizona 86508. Willard Stevens.

Mariano Lake Full-Gospel Church. Thoreau, New Mexico 87323. Sam Grey.

Mexican Springs Full-Gospel Church. Mexican Springs, New Mexico 87320. Emerson Ettsitty.

Navajo Full-Gospel Church. Shiprock, New Mexico 87420. Haswood Brown.

Navajo Nation Christian Center. Shiprock, New Mexico 87420. Scott Redhouse.

Oak Springs Church. Red Rock, Shiprock, New Mexico 87420. Russell Jackson.

Pinedale Full-Gospel Church. Thoreau, New Mexico 87323. Sam Grey.

Red Mesa Full-Gospel Church. Red Mesa, Teec Nos Pos, Arizona 86514. Jack Nakai.

Rock Point Pentecostal Church. Rock Point, Chinle, Arizona 86503. Johnson Bradly.

Sanostee Full Gospel Church. Sanostee, Shiprock, New Mexico 87420. George Sanderson.

Sheep Springs Full-Gospel Church. Tohatchi, New Mexico 87325. Alfred Leuppe.

Shiprock Full-Gospel Church. Shiprock, New Mexico 87420. Joe Nez.

Sunflower Butte Full-Gospel Church. Indian Wells, Arizona 86031. Albert Charley.

Tseyatoh Camp Church-Phillip Cove. Louis McCabe.

Teec Nos Pos Full-Gospel Church. Teec Nos Pos, Arizona 86514. Paul Todacheenie.

Tinian Full-Gospel Church. Cuba, New Mexico 87013. Eddie

Castillo.

Tonalea Full-Gospel Church.   Tonalea, Arizona 86044.   Homer
Bryant.

Tuba City Full-Gospel Church.   Tuba City, Arizona 86045.

Twin Lakes Full-Gospel Church.   Twin Lakes, New Mexico.   Charley
Johnson.

Twin Pines Full-Gospel Church.   Box 53, Counselor, New Mexico
87013.   Bahe Ettsitty.

INDEPENDENT PENTECOSTAL CHURCHES:

All Nations Mission.   1102 W. Wilson, Gallup, New Mexico 87301.
Mother Renolds.

Aneth Pentecostal Church.   Aneth, Utah 84510.   Johnny Billie.

Bisti Pentecostal Church.   Farmington, New Mexico 87401.
Charley Shield.

Bisti Home Church.   Farmington, New Mexico 87401.   Harvey K'aai.

Castle Butte Navajo Indian Mission.   Box 296, Holbrook, Arizona
86025.   Ross Vernon Mericle.

Christian Revival Fellowship.   Box 362, Cortez, Colorado 81321.
M. G. Wooten.

De Deez Ahi Church.   White Cone, Indian Wells, Arizona 86031.
Carlos Moore.

Defiance Pentecostal Church.   Defiance, Manuelito, New Mexico.
Sam Joe Spenser.

Desert View Mission.   Box 1814, Farmington, New Mexico 87401.
Sister Janson.

Gallup Independent Pentecostal Church.   700 N. Russian Street,
Gallup, New Mexico 87301.   Doris Alger.

Greasewood Pentecostal Church.   Greasewood, Arizona 86505.   Ben
James.

Harvest-Time Mission.   Sun Valley Station, Holbrook, Arizona
86025.

Holiness Indian Mission.   Church Rock, New Mexico 87311.   Blue

Water Outstation. Brother Poppelwells.

Many Farms House Church. Many Farms, Arizona 86503. Kii Begay.

Miracle Church. Blanco, New Mexico 87412.

Miracle Revival Church. Red Rock, Shiprock, New Mexico 87420.
Don Ellison.

Navajo Mission Pentecostal Holiness Church. Greasewood Boarding
School, Ganado, Arizona 86505. McElvie Purifoy.

Navajo Trails Tabernacle. Box 743, Flagstaff, Arizona 86001.
George Hanson.

New Testament Church. Red Rock, Shiprock, New Mexico 87420.
Joe Nakai.

Ninety & Nine Indian Mission. Hwy. 99, Star Route, Winslow,
Arizona 86041. Eddie Garver.

Oljeto Pentecostal Church. Oljeto, Monument Valley, Utah 84536.
Harry Sanders.

Oral Roberts Church. Black Hat, Window Rock, Arizona 86515.
Tom Nelson.

Red Rock Pentecostal Church. 612 S. 7th, Gallup, New Mexico
87301. Terry Goodwin.

Smith Lake Pentecostal Church. Thoreau, New Mexico 87323.
Sister Tate.

The Door (Four-Square). 400 N. 2nd Street, Gallup, New Mexico
87301. Ernie Lister.

Thoreau Revival Center. Manuelito, New Mexico 87318. Russell
P. Barker.

Tinian Pentecostal Church. Cuba, New Mexico 87013. James
Toledo.

Tohlakai Pentecostal Church. Tohlakai, Gallup, New Mexico
87301. Joseph Curman.

Waterflow Pentecostal Mission. Waterflow, New Mexico 87421.

PENTECOSTAL CHURCHES OF GOD (Not Pentecostal Church of God, Joplin, Missouri)

Bread Springs Pentecostal Church of God. Bread Springs, Gallup, New Mexico 87301. Harry John.

Church of God Indian Mission. Box 757. Gallup, New Mexico 87301. Denzel Teague.

Gallup Pentecostal Church of God. 34 N. 11th, Gallup, New Mexico 87301. John Hubbard.

Houck Pentecostal Church of God. Houck, Arizona 86506. Hoskie Joe.

Kit Carson Cave Pentecostal Church of God. Church Rock, New Mexico 87311. Sister Whitman.

Kit Carson Cave Pentecostal Church of God. Church Rock, New Mexico 87311. Sam Giegos.

Klagatoh Pentecostal Church of God. Klagatoh, Chambers, Arizona 86502. Bahe Woodman.

Mountain View Pentecostal Church of God. Ramah, New Mexico 87321. Pauline Rafilita.

Neesjaa Pentecostal Church of God. Ramah, New Mexico 87321. Shep D. Martine.

Pinedale Pentecostal Church of God. Church Rock, New Mexico 87311. Kenneth Begay.

Red Lake Pentecostal Church of God. Box 713, Winslow, Arizona 86047. Carol Irwin/Marcell Kennedy.

Rocky Point Pentecostal Church of God. Box 215, Mentmore, New Mexico 87319. Tom Chischilli.

Sand Mountain Pentecostal Church of God. Ramah, New Mexico 87321. Shep D. Martine.

Valley View Pentecostal Church of God. Valley View, Gallup, New Mexico 87301. Harry Begay.

WORD OF GOD CHURCHES

Lighthouse Mission. Star Lake, Cuba, New Mexico 87013. Isabel and Joe Salazar.

Word of God Church - Rincon Marquis. Cuba, New Mexico 87013. Philip Apatchito.

Word of God Church - Sanostee Full-Gospel. Sanostee, Shiprock, New Mexico 87420. Edith Smiley.

Word of God Church - Sweetwater. Teec Nos Pos, Arizona 86514. Willis George.

Word of God Church - White Horse Lake. Cuba, New Mexico 87013. Betty and Earl Betone.

V
NATIVE AMERICAN
URBAN CHURCHES
(IN CITIES OVER 30,000)

V
NATIVE AMERICAN URBAN CHURCHES
(IN CITIES OVER 30,000)

ALASKA

   Anchorage – 161,018

     Anchorage Friends Church.
     First Evangelical Covenant Church
     Holy Family Cathedral. Partial.
     Salvation Army.
     St. Innocent Orthodox Church.

ARIZONA

   Flagstaff – 31,370

     Flagstaff Indian Bible Church. Flagstaff Mission to the
     Navajos.

   Mesa – 100,763

     Ferguson Memorial Southern Baptist Church.

   Phoenix – 699,005   U. S. Census 1970 – Ind. pop. 10,127

     All Tribes Assemblies of God.
     Hillside Chapel. Assembly of God.
     Phoenix First Indian Baptist Church. (Southern)
     Valley Lutheran Indian Mission (Wisconsin Synod)

Tucson - 296,683   U. S. Census 1970 - Ind. pop. 8,704

> *Cristo Rey Church.* (Yaqui)
> *St. Anthony Mission.*
> *St. Nicholas Center.* (Church Services) (Papago, Yaqui)
> *St. Rosa.* (Yaqui)
> *San Martin de Porres.*
> *Pueblo Assembly of God*
> *Tucson Church of the Nazarene*

> Large Indian minorities in:
> *St. Augustine's Cathedral.*
> *Santa Cruz Church.*
> *Holy Family Church.*
> *St. John the Evangelist Church.*
> *Our Lady of Guadalupe Church.*

FLORIDA

Ft. Lauderdale - 152,959

> *First Seminole Baptist Church.* (Southern)

CALIFORNIA

El Cajon - 60,404

> *American Indian Baptist Church.*

Los Angeles - 2,727,399   U. S. Census 1970 - Ind. pop. 23,908

> *Brighter Day Indian Baptist Church.* Independent.
> *First American Indian Church.* Independent.
> *United Methodist Indian Mission.*
> *Bell Gardens,* Los Angeles Area: *First Southern Baptist*
>   *Church.*

San Francisco - 664,520.   U. S. Census 1970 - Ind. pop. 12,041

> *American Indian Baptist Church.* Creek.

San Jose - 555,707   U. S. Census 1970 - Ind. pop. 4,407

> *San Jose American Indian Baptist Church.*

Southgate - 56,560

> *Indian Revival Center.* Independent.

COLORADO

Denver – 484,531   U. S. Census 1970 – Ind. pop. 4,104

Calvary Indian Church. Independent.
Denver Christian Indian Center and Church. Christian Reformed.

ILLINOIS

Chicago – 3,009,391   U. S. Census 1970 – Ind. pop. 8,203

American Indian Church. Christian Reformed.
St. Augustine's Center and Chapel. Episcopal.

IOWA

Des Moines – 194,168

St. Paul's Indian Mission. Episcopal.

KANSAS

Lawrence – 50,887

Lawrence Mission. United Methodist.
Haskell Indian Mission. Southern Baptist.

Topeka – 119,203

Sullivan Chapel. United Methodist. Pottawatomie.

Wichita – 264,901   (Indian population said to be 4,673)

Holy Savior Church. Partial.
Wichita Mission. United Methodist.

MINNESOTA

Minneapolis – 398,112   U. S. Census 1970 – Ind. pop. 9,911
with St. Paul

Ascension Church. Partial. Roman Catholic.
St. Stephen's Church. Partial.
Holy Rosary Church. Partial.
All Saints' Church. Episcopal.

St. Paul – 279,535

Mazakute Memorial Mission. Episcopal.

NEW MEXICO

Albuquerque - 279,401   U. S. Census 1970 - Ind. pop. 2,822

> *Albuquerque Indian Mission.* Southern Baptist.
> *First Indian Church of the Nazarene.*
> *Queen of Angels Chapel.* (Catholic Chapel at Albuquerque
>   Indian School)

NORTH CAROLINA

No Indian congregations have been noted in the large cities of
North Carolina. There are three Urban Indian Associations:
The Cumberland County Association for about 4,000 Indians who
have come to Fayetteville and Cumberland Country; Guilford
Native American Association for about 3,000 Indians of Greens-
boro and Guilford County; and Metrolina Native American
Association for more than 4,000 Indians of Charlotte and
surrounding counties. No churches have been noted expecting -

Fayetteville - 65,915   U. S. Census 1970 - Ind. pop. 1,995

> *Fayetteville Assembly of God.* Lumbee, Tuscarora.

OKLAHOMA

Enid - 48,030

> *First Indian Church.* Southern Baptist.

Lawton - 76,421   U. S. Census 1970 - Ind. pop. 3,436

> *Lawton Mission.* Pentecostal Church of God.

Oklahoma City - 365,916   U. S. Census 1970 - Ind. pop. 12,951

> *American Indian Baptist Church.* Southern.
> *Billy Hooten Memorial Church.* United Methodist.
> *Central Indian Church.* Southern Baptist
> *Gethsemene Mission.* Southern Baptist.
> *Glorieta Indian Baptist Church.* Southern
> *Little Springs Church.* Southern Baptist
> *Mary Clark Lee United Methodist Church.*
> *New Trinity Baptist Mission.* Southern.
> *Oklahoma City Mission.* Pentecostal Church of God.
> *Westwood Indian Church.* Southern Baptist.

Tulsa - 331,726   U. S. Census 1970 - Ind. pop. 15,183

> *Boden Place Indian Chapel.* Southern Baptist.

Community Baptist Church. Southern.
New Life Baptist Church. Southern.
United Indian Methodist Church.
Witt Memorial United Methodist Church.

OREGON

Portland - 356,732   U. S. Census 1970 - Ind. pop. 4,059

Indian Baptist Church. Southern.

SOUTH DAKOTA

Rapid City - 48,156

Saint Isaac Joques.
Northside Indian Assembly of God.
St. Matthew's Church. Episcopal.

TEXAS

Dallas - 812,797   U. S. Census 1970 - Ind. pop. 5,500

Dallas Indian Revival Center. Assemblies of God.
First Indian Baptist Church. Southern.
Some Indians in *Cliff Temple* and *James Avenue Southern Baptist*
  Churches.

UTAH

Salt Lake City - 169,917

Salt Lake City Christian Indian Center. Church services.
  Christian Reformed.

WASHINGTON

Yakima - 49,264

All Tribes Christian Life Center. Assemblies of God.

WISCONSIN

Milwaukee - 669,002   U. S. Census 1970 - Ind. pop. 3,835

Milwaukee All Tribes Assembly of God.

Ten Catholic Churches have some Indian members:
St. Anne, St. Charles Borromeo, St. Florian, Gesu, Holy
Trinity-Guadalupe, St. Leo, St. Michael, St. Patrick, St.

Thomas Aquinas. About 2,000 Catholic Indians in the city.

Superior - 30,038

St. Louis Church.

Urban Churches 66 plus 19 partial.

Some other 1970 Urban Indian Statistics:

Anaheim-Santa Ana-Garden Gove, California 3,664
Baltimore 2,392
Buffalo 5,606
Detroit 5,203
New York City 9,984
Philadelphia 3,719
Sacramento 3,548
San Diego 6,007
Seattle-Everett 8,814
Washington, D.C. 2,686

VI
COUNCILS,
SERVICE AGENCIES
AND EDUCATIONAL
MINISTRIES

A.
COUNCILS OF CHURCHES
AND
COOPERATIVE MINISTRIES

NATIONAL COUNCIL OF CHURCH OF CHRIST IN THE UNITED STATES OF AMERICA

475 Riverside Drive, New York, N.Y. 10027   *(212)870-2200*
General Secretary, Ms. Clare Randall

Division of Church and Society
Associate for Indian Ministries, Mr. James West (Indian)
See Joint Native American Staff

IFCO: INTERRELIGIOUS FOUNDATION FOR COMMUNITY ORGANIZATION

475 Riverside Drive, New York, N.Y. 10027   *(212)870-3151*
Director: Lucius Walker
Native American Affairs: James West, Box 39, Tijeras, New
   Mexico 87059

Formed by constituent denominations with additional representa-
tion by ethnic and social minorities - Blacks, Native Americans,
Hispanics, Appalachians, etc. - to assist community organizations. IFCO offers technical assistance and finds support and
resources for the needs of minority people.

JSAC: JOINT STRATEGY AND ACTION COMMITTEE

475 Riverside Drive, New York, N.Y. 10027   *(212)870-3105*
Rev. John C. DeBoer, Executive Director
Ms. Sheila Collins, Associate for Publications

Full Members: American Baptist Churches, Episcopal Church,
Presbyterian Church in the U.S., Southern Baptist Convention,

United Church of Christ, United Methodist Church, United Presbyterian Church in the U.S.A., Lutheran Council in the U.S.A. (American Lutheran Church, Lutheran Church in America and Lutheran Church - Missouri Synod).

Associate Members: Church of the Brethren, Reformed Church in America. Other churches participate in the several task forces.

"JSAC is a coalition of denominational national mission agencies, which have decided to work collaboratively in areas of mutual concern ... work cooperatively on mutal agendas." Thus churches avoid unnecessary duplication and those who want to move together on any given issue or project are free to do so without waiting for all to join. JSAC maintains working relationship with various units in the National Council of Churches, the World Council of Churches and other ecumenical agencies.

TASK FORCE ON NATIVE AMERICAN MINISTRIES
    Staff person: Mr. James West. See Joint Native American
    Staff.

JOINT NATIVE AMERICAN STAFF

For JSAC Indian Task Force, National Council of Churches Division of Church and Society, and Interreligious Foundation for Community Organization.
    Mr. James West, Zamora, Box 39, Tijeras, New Mexico

NATIONAL FELLOWSHIP OF INDIAN WORKERS

c.1930. A nationwide interdenominational association of Native American and white ministers, missionaries and layworkers for study and consideration of matters of mutual interest and concern. Conferences are help every two years at the YMCA Conference ground at Association Camp, Colorado 90511 (Estes Park). Officers are all Native American. Mr. Larry Long, Secretary, 3025 Fir Street, San Diego, California 92102; Ms. Carolyn Ray, Treasurer, Cook Christian Training School, 708 S. Lindon Lane, Tempe, Arizona 85281.

ALASKAN NATIVE BROTHERHOOD: ANB

Grand Camp President: Mr. Frank O. Williams, Jr., c/o Mt.
    Edgecumbe Hospital, Sitka, Alaska 99839

The ANB and its sister organization were founded in Sitka in the 1920's with the help of the staff of Sheldon Jackson College for political action and preservation and development of the cultural heritage of the Tlingit, Haida and Tsimsian people of southeast Alaska. The Brotherhood is Christian in its charter and purpose and has always kept in close relationship to the churches. There are local camps in most villages and in

Anchorage and Seattle. They play a key role in the burial of village people. The annual meeting of the Grand Camp is a significant Alaskan political event. Some achievements of the ANB: gained recognition of citizenship rights of Alaskan Natives, including the vote, integrated public schools, secured workman's compensation for Natives, also aid to dependent children and direct relief for the aged, secured more adequate hospital services, got the Alaska equal rights law passed, and initiated the Tlingit and Haida land suits.

ALASKA CHRISTIAN CONFERENCE

813 West Third Avenue, Anchorage, Alaska 99501
Mrs. Mary Jane Landstom, President

The Conference has a Task Force seeking to coordinate efforts and to provide mutual learning among the units with Native Alaskan ministries. Rev. William Trudeau, Chairman. 3300 West Northern Lights Blvd., Anchorage, Alaska 99503.

CALIFORNIA

THE NORTHERN CALIFORNIA ECUMENICAL COUNCIL

944 Market Street, Fourth Floor, San Francisco, California
94102   *(415)433-3024*

The arm of this Council for ministry to Native Americans is the American Indian Ministry. Contact person: Rev. Andy Reinap, 250 Touchstone Place, #16, West Sacramento, California 95691.

INDIAN MINISTRY OF SAN DIEGO COUNTY   1971

3025 Fir Street at 30th, San Diego, California 92102
Mr. Larry Long, Director (Muskogee Creek)   *(714)239-9973*

Joint agency of the United Presbyterian Church in the U.S.A., The United Methodist Church, The Episcopal Diocese of San Diego, The United Church of Christ, The American Lutheran Church and The Christian Church (Disciples of Christ). Ministers to reservation and urban Indians. An advocacy ministry which seeks to enable the churches to respond more effectively to the priorities of the Native American community. Counseling, alcoholic rehabilitation, educational services to families, help in emergency needs (food, clothing, housing, travel, school affairs), resources such as material for repairing houses on reservation, transportation for elderly, presentations and seminars at non-Indian churches, coordinating work for projects by church groups on reservations.

COLORADO

NATIVE AMERICAN URBAN TRANSITION PROGRAM
548 South Lincoln, Denver, Colorado 80209   1975
Ms. Mary A. Pioche, Director (Indian)
Ms. Beverly Joeger, Assistant

A Christian institution funded by some denominations on the
national level. It attempts to assist and aid Indians in the
change from reservation to city life in Denver. It provides
Christian hospitality to newcomers, guidance, assistance in
finding employment, food and transportation when needed.
Wholesome Christian social life is introduced. Short-term
(2 week) housing is provided to one family at a time and there
is a long-term housing for single women.

KANSAS: THE WICHITA COUNCIL OF CHURCHES
216 East Second Street, Wichita, Kansas 67202   *(316)264-9303*
Thomas G.VanDerBloemen, Executive Minister
INDIAN SOCIAL MINISTRY: Mrs. Leo Heinze, Coordinator

This service is located in the Mid-American All Indian Center
and associated with it. 650 North Seneca, Wichita, Kansas
67203. *(316)262-5221.*

1977 Report: 191 familes or individuals received clothing; 86
received food; hospital visits 31, outreach 23; housing
assistance 52; financial assistance 50. Transportation given
to 18 individuals; household assistance 8; legal referrals 4;
medical referrals 6; al-anon 2 and A.A. 6. Telephone calls over
500. Holiday food baskets 10. Contributions of clothing 261,
of food 11 and of household 3. Group activities.

THE MINNESOTA COUNCIL OF CHURCHES
122 West Franklin Avenue, Room 230, Minneapolis, Minnesota 55404
Rev. Albert C. Lehman, Jr., Executive Director   *(612)870-3604*

INDIAN ADVOCATE MINISTRY
Supported financially by the Council "for and by Indians."
Three Areas:
Northeast/Northwest: Ms. Mary Ann Walt (Chippewa), 217 N.
   4th Avenue, West Duluth, Minnesota 55806. *(218)727-3011.*
Minneapolis and West: Department of Indian Work of the
   Greater Minneapolis Council of Churches, Ms. Vernell Wabasha
   (Indian), 2045 Park Avenue, South, Minneapolis, Minnesota
   55407.
St. Paul, South and Southwest: Ms. Sheila White Eagle
   (Indian), 1671 Summitt Avenue, St. Paul, Minnesota 55105.

"The Work of the Council centers in an *Advocate-Social Concerns*

ministry. This simply means that an attempt is made to help
establish Native American leadership whose chief task is to
assist and relate their people to those issues and services
which will help them achieve their rightful and selfdetermined
place in American society." There is an Indian Board, made up
of Native Americans, for each area. Each Board sets its own
budget, raises its own money (except that given by member
churches of the Council), and hires its own Native American
coordinator. Each regional Board appoints three members to the
Indian State Advisory Board.

An area coordinator is a liaison person between church and
Indian people seeking to develop understanding on both sides.
The coordinator continues the old task of securing funding for
Indian group activities and programs, but also sponsors workshops and seminars, involving clergy and congregations in Indian
concerns, helping the church to assume a positive role in
influencing legislation needed or supported by Indians and
stimulating the congregations to engage in non-tradional forms
of ministry and service to Indian people and to join in worship
and fellowship getherings.

GREATER MINNEAPOLIS COUNCIL OF CHURCHES

122 West Franklin Avenue, Room 208, Minneapolis, Minnesota 55404
Rev. David E. Witheridge, Executive Director   *(612)870-3660*

DIVISION OF INDIAN WORK

3045 Park Avenue, Minneapolis, Minnesota 55407
Mrs. Vernell Wabasha, Director   *(612)827-1795*

The Division continues the ministry and program organized in
1953 as the United Church Committee on Indian work in the Twin
Cities. It is the coordinating agency that served the Indian
population through a program of human services supported by
congregations and denominations. The service program
ministers to the special needs of Indians, using community
resources whenever appropriate. Services: counseling Indian
families in adjusting to urban life; providing aid in areas
of health, welfare, housing, education or recreation and when
necessary working with other agencies to provide these
services; acquainting Indians with programs and services
available to them in churches and community; explaining
Indian conditions and programs to churches; working with
social agencies concerned about Indian people; maintaining
liaison with reservation governments so that they will be
aware of DIW services. Emergency aid is given in food,
clothing, housing, medical, educational, spiritual, legal and
transportation situations. Cooperation with other Indian
agencies in planning and providing recreation and in
strategy formation and advocacy respecting needed legislation.

The DIW cooperates with The Minneapolis Regional Native
American Center.

During 1976 total persons served 1,628; total in household
5,219; total received food 993; total financial assistance
139; total received gas 97; total referred to other agencies
399.

MONTANA ASSOCIATION OF CHURCHES

Rocky Mountain College, Kimball Hall, 1511 Poly Drive, Billings,
Montana 59102   *(406)252-5138*
Rev. Cecil E. Gubser, Executive Director

The Association does not maintain a specific ministry to Indians
but acts in specific needs such as assistance to the Northern
Cheyenne Landowners Association in their efforts to secure
adequate consideration of their rights in connection with
permits and leases for coal strip mining and the holding of an
Impact Seminar in Billings in April 1976 on the people problems
and potential solutions in the search for and development of
energy, particularly coal. There is in process of formation an
ECUMENICAL CLERGY MUTUAL OBSERVER CORPS intended to be available
at demonstrations or in civil unrest "to assist in defusing
tension and potential turmoil."

INTERCHURCH MINISTRIES OF NEBRASKA

215 Centennial Mall South, Suite 303, Lincoln, Nebraska 86508
Rev. Robert W. Jeambey, Executive Secretary   *(402)432-3391*

INTERCHURCH MINISTRY TO NEBRASKA INDIANS   1972
A funding coalition formed under the auspices of Interchurch
Ministries of Nebraska by the Christian Churches in Nebraska
(Disciples), Nebraska Conference of the United Church of
Christ, The Nebraska Conference of the United Methodist
Church, The Synod of Lakes and Prairies of the United
Presbyterian Church in the U.S.A., and Nebraska Church Women
United. It channels its combined resources into UNITED
INDIANS OF NEBRASKA. The church funds provide organizational
support and staff leadership for UIN; and in turn, UIN seeks
national church funds, federal and state grants to develop
and conduct needed programs in Nebraska.

UNITED INDIANS OF NEBRASKA   1973
11924 Poppleton Plaza, Omaha, Nebraska 68114
Ms. Janice R. Searcey, Executive Director *(402)334-9477, 9478*

A coalition of 28 Indian organizations. Supported almost
entirely by contributions by religious organizations.

In 1975 it was named prime sponsor for a $175,000

Comprehensive Employment and Training Act program for Indian employment opportunities in Nebraska. This has led to greatly enlarged services of assistance to qualified Indian organizations seeking funds by validating their projects, funding them or referring them to other sources of funding, or validating them without funding or referral. UIN has a "Jobs for Indians" employment service, has funded a hot lunch program, has given scholarships, provided vehicles for transportation to several organizations and given emergency aid to individuals. In 1976 UIN generated more than $300,000 in additional funds for programs. It engages in public relations and legislative activy.

OKLAHOMA INDIAN MINISTRIES, INC.

701 N.W. 8th Street, Oklahoma City, OK 73102
Rev. Robert Pinezaddleby, Director   *(405) 232-3695*

An Ecumenical Christian Indian program begun in 1972 in which are represented the United Methodists, the Southern Baptists, American Baptists, Lutheran Church in America, Lutheran Church-Missouri Synod, Reformed Church in America, the Roman Catholic Church, Church of the Brethren, Christian Church (Disciples), Cumberland Presbyterian Church, Presbyterian Church in the U. S., United Presbyterian Church, the Episcopal Church, the Church of the Nazarene, and the Mennonites.

The GOALS: 1. To set up ministries in geographic areas of great Indian Impact; 2. to provide Chaplains at each Government Indian school in the state; 3. to involve young adults of 18-35 years in all areas of community and church life; 4. to help identify the concerns and problems in Church and community; 5. to provide spiritual foundations and experiences in helping the Indian's quest for spiritual growth; 6. to provide approaches and find solutions to Indian issues and problems; 7. to develop an ecumenical process that would express concern by many groups and organizations; 8. to be in a continuous process of developing ways to make the ministries more effective; 9. to help the non-Indian understand Indian life-style, values, and his whole heritage; 10. Indian Ministries would provide various kinds of resources (personnel, books, slides, arts and crafts, etc.) in fulfilling the above.

WASHINGTON: ASSOCIATED MINISTRIES OF TACOMA-PIERCE COUNTY

2520 Sixth Avenue, Tacoma, Washington 98406   *(206)383-3056*
Rev. E. Bruce Foreman, Metropolitan Minister

The Metropolitan Minister works on a consultative basis with various Native American groups from time to time.

WISCONSIN COUNCIL OF CHURCHES

818 West Badger Road, Suite 201, Madison, Wisconsin 53713
Rev. Willis J. Marriman, Executive Director   *(608)257-0541*

The initiative of the Wisconsin Council of Churches brought into being in 1972 the

WISCONSIN INDIAN RESOURCE COUNCIL (WIRC)

Room 142, Old Main Building, University of Wisconsin at Stevens Point, Stevens Point, Wisconsin 54481   *(715)346-2746*
Mr. Floyd E. Powless, Jr., Executive Director

Members are eleven tribal councils and eighteen other Indian organizations. It is supported financially by the Moravian Church, The American Lutheran Church, The Lutheran Church in American, The United Presbyterian Church, The United Church of Christ, The United Methodist Church, Church Women United, The Reformed Church in American, The Roman Catholic Church, The Episcopal Church, The Wisconsin Council of Churches and a dozen foundations.

The purposes are:
1. The Council is to set criteria and priorities for the distribution of monies contributed by religious bodies, foundations, various private and public groups and agencies for the benefit of Wisconsin Indians.
2. The Council is to be an instrument of advocacy for Indian concerns, inviting the support of religious organizations in such fields as legislation.
3. The Council is to make available to the Indians of Wisconsin seminars, training and education in fields such as proposal writing, resource development and administrative skills.

B.
SERVICE AGENCIES AND MINISTRIES

NATIONAL AGENCIES

AMERICAN BIBLE SOCIETY

1865 Broadway, New York, N.Y. 10023   *(212)581-7400*
Dr. Laton E. Holmgren, General Secretary

The ABS has been publishing the scriptures in Indian languages
since 1818, when a Delaware-English edition of the Johannine
Epistles was published. Parts of the Bible have been published
in approximately 35 Indian languages spoken in the United
States. Some are out-dated. Others are republishied as needed.

The most important translation project at present is the Navajo
Old Testament. The New Testament was published in 1956 and in
a revised translation in 1975.

The following are carred in stock:

			Order No.
Cherokee	New Testament	$1.25	46120
Cheyenne	New Testament	.07	46150
Choctaw	Psalms	.83	47910
Hopi	New Testament with English		
	Diglot	5.00	42940

Eskimo-Inupiaq	New Testament with English		
	Diglot	$4.24	45150
Muskogee	New Testament	1.26	74671
Navajo	New Testament with Psalms		
	and Proverbs	2.61	74709
	Genesis, Exodux, Joshua,		
	Ruth, Psalms, Jonah	3.41	74781

AMERICAN FRIENDS' SERVICE COMMITTEE, INC.

1501 Cherry Street, Philadelphia, Pennsylvania 19102
Louis W. Schneider, Executive Secretary
Native American Affairs: Ed Nakawatase; Karel Kilimnik

Advocacy and service ministries including Native Americans. No
report of specifics, although requested.

CAMPAIGN FOR HUMAN DEVELOPMENT

See under Roman Catholic Church in Section III.

FRIENDS COMMITTEE ON NATIONAL LEGISLATION: FCNL

245 Second Street, N.E., Washington, D.C. 20002   *(202)547-4343*
Edward F. Snyder, Executive Secretary
Nick Block, Administrative Secretary
Frances E. Neely and Don Reeves, Legislative Secretaries
George I. Bliss, Field Secretary

The Friends Committee on National Legistlation is a registered
lobbying group which attempts to influence public policy toward
peace, justice, and equity - by laying before Congress (and the
Administration) the concerns of like-minded Friends (Quakers)
and friends, by working for passage of pertinent legislation,
and by keeping FCNL constituents educated on the issues and
informed of opportunities to act.

American Indian Affairs is one of six priority areas in which
FCNL is active.

In addition to regular publication of update and background
articles in the monthly *FCNL Washington Newsletter*, FCNL
publishes an occasional *Indian Report*, with more detailed information. The *Newsletter* is availabe for a $10 contribution
($5 for those on limited income); the *Indian Report* is sent to
those who express a particular interest in Native American
affairs.

As American Indian issues surface in Congress, FCNL pays special
attention to those which set precedents for general policy in
U.S. Indian relations and to those which effect living
conditions for Native Americans. The right to Indian

self-determination, both of their lives and of the use of their resources, is a predominant concern.

FCNL works closely with Washington-based Indian groups and is often in close touch with Indian leadership beyond Washington. FCNL also relates to the religious community on Capitol Hill and helps provide leadership in ecumenical attention to Native American issues.

LUCHIP: LUTHERAN CHURCH AND INDIAN PEOPLE

See under Lutheran Church in Section III.

MENNONITE CENTRAL COMMITTEE

See Section III.

MENNONITE VOLUNTARY SERVICE

See Section III.

NATIONAL FELLOWSHIP OF INDIAN WORKERS

See under Section VI-A; Councils and Cooperative Ministries

NATIONAL INDIAN LUTHERAN BOARD

See Section III.

REGIONAL, STATE, LOCAL SERVICE AGENCIES AND MINISTRIES

AKWASASNE COMMUNITY CENTER. Mohawk. Hogansburg, New York 13655. Diocese of Ogdensburg, Roman Catholic Church. Senior Citizens program.

ANADARKO CHRISTIAN CENTER. 1953. P. O. Box 785, Anadarko, Oklahoma 73005. American Baptist Church. Rev. James G. Denny, Executive Director. Miss Barbara Johnson, Program Supervisor.

ARCHDIOCESE OF ANCHORAGE, ALASKA. Roman Catholic Church. Anchorage, Alaska 99501. Food and clothing service. 1000 Indians and Eskimos participate.

DENVER CHRISTIAN INDIAN CENTER. Christian Reformed Church. 501 South Pearl Street, Denver, Colorado 80209. *(303)733-3693.* Rev. Harry VanDam, Director. A Friendship House-Church combination. Services to individuals, mostly Navajos.

DIVISION OF INDIAN SERVICES, DIOCESE OF PORTLAND. Roman Catholic Church. 510 Ocean Avenue, Portland, Maine 04103. Services, advocacy, leadership, social planning, education, interpreting for Penebscot, Passamaquoddy and Micmac Tribes.

DIVISION OF INDIAN WORK, GREATER MINNEAPOLIS COUNCIL OF CHURCHES. 3045 Park Avenue, Minneapolis, Minnesota 55407. *(612)827-1795.* Mrs. Vernell Wabasha, Director. A coordinating agency of Protestant churches that serves the Indian population through a program of human services: counseling families in adjustment to urban life; aid·in the area of health, welfare, housing, education and recreation; acquainting Indians with programs available in churches and community; representing the Indians before the congregations; working with concerned social agencies; maintaining liaison with reservation governments so that they will be aware of DIW services; emergency aid in food, clothing, housing, medical, educational, spiritual, legal and transportation situations. Cooperates with the Minneapolis Regional Native American Center. Cooperates with other Indian agencies in planning and providing recreation aid in strategy formation and advocacy respecting needed legislation.

DULAC COMMUNITY CENTER. Houma. United Methodist Church. P. O. Box 100, Dulac, Louisiana 70353. Spiller Milton, Executive Director. Purpose is to preserve the heritage of the Houma Tribe; to secure ready acceptance into the total community life; to secure adequate education and to develop the spiritual life. Day care for 3-4 year old children; adult education school; homebound program; Scouting; recreation; women's society; youth society; personal and family counseling.

EPISCOPAL COMMUNITY SERVICES, DENVER, COLORADO. Emergency feeding and counseling service for Indians.

FRIENDSHIP HOUSE OF CHRISTIAN SERVICE. 3123 Eighth Avenue, South, Billings, Montana 59101. *(406)259-5569.* Paul J. Reeder, Director. An American Baptist, but ecumenically related, neighborhood house, receiving United Way support. Served in 1977 some 160 families, of whom 33 are Indian. Program: Kindergarden through 6th grade, after school groups, teen group, recreation, adult groups for sewing, crafts, nutrition, etc. Various community groups use the Center's building. Clothing distribution. Referral service. Works with South Park Task Force in community development and neighborhood improvement. Staff: 3 full time paid, 2 part time paid workers, 35 volunteers. 1 Crow woman in child care.

FRANCISCAN CENTER. P. O. Box 7339, Las Vegas, Nevada 89101. Fr. Louis Vitale, OFM, Director. Sr. Evelyn Montez, OP, community action.

YMCA'S, GENERAL CONVENTION OF SIOUX INDIAN
(A member of the National Council of YMCA's)
P. O. Box 218, Dupree, South Dakota 57623   *(605)365-3520*
Dwight W. Call, Director
Nathan Little Wounded, Associate Director

Bear Creek YMCA. Cheyenne River. Bear Creek, South Dakota. Mail to Lantry, South Dakota 57836. Verne Howard, vice-chairman. Mem. 12. Others served 60.

Cherry Creek YMCA. Cheyenne River. Cherry Creek, South Dakota 57622. Jerome White Horse, Sr., Chairman. Mem. 30. Others served 150.

Dupree Lakota YMCA. Cheyenne River. Dupree, South Dakota 57623. Leon Hale, Chairman. Mem. 50. Others served 150.

Frazier-Red Scaffold YMCA. Red Scaffold, South Dakota. Mail to Red Scaffold Route, Faith, South Dakota 57626. Kenneth War Bonnet, Chairman. Mem. 70. Others served 100.

Greenwood YMCA. Greenwood, South Dakota. Yankton. Mail to Route 3, Wagner, South Dakota 57380. Joe Lesly, Chairman. Mem. 23. Others served 50.

Okciya YMCA. Yankton, South Dakota 57078. Nelson Dragg, Chairman. General Delivery, Yankton, South Dakota 57078. Mem. 10. Other served 60.

Pejito YMCA. Cheyenne River. Green Grass, South Dakota. Mail to Eagle Butte, South Dakota 57625. David Dupris, Chairman. Mem. 25. Other served 60.

Takini YMCA. Cheyenne River. Bridger, South Dakota. Mail to Howes, South Dakota 57748. Bernard Littleton, Chairman. Mem. 30. Others served 70.

Thunder Butte YMCA. Cheyenne River. Thunder Butte, South Dakota. Mail to Dupree, South Dakota 57623. Lyle Elk Nation, Chairman. Mem. 25. Others served 70.

Tatanka Mani YMCA. Pine Ridge. Sharp's Corner, South Dakota. Mail to Sharp's Corner, Porcupine, South Dakota 57772. Regina Cotter, Chairman. Mem. 20. Others served 30.

Virgin Creek YMCA. Cheyenne River. Mail to Ridgeview, South Dakota 57652. Earl Deer With Horns, Chairman. P. O. Box 967, Eagle Butte, South Dakota 57625. Mem. 40. Other served 80.

Wakinyan Maza YMCA. Cheyenne River. Iron Lightning, South

Dakota. Mail to Dupree, South Dakota 57623. Gordon Condon, Chairman. Mem. 19. Others served 5.

Wanbli Paha YMCA. Cheyenne River. Eagle Butte, South Dakota 57625. Delma Iron Moccasin, Chairman. Mem. 60. Other served 100.

White Horse YMCA. Cheyenne River. White Horse, South Dakota 57661. Carl Makes Him First, Chairman. Mem. 75. Others served 50.

Wounded Knee YMCA. Pine Ridge. Wounded Knee, South Dakota 57794. Albert Hollow Horn, Chairman. Mem. 10. Others served 10.

INDIAN ADVOCATE MINISTRY OF THE MINNESOTA COUNCIL OF CHURCHES. Three areas: (1) Northeast/Northwest, Ms. Mary Ann Walt, (Chippewa), 217 North 4th Avenue, West Duluth, Minnesota 55806. *(218)727-3011*. (2) Minneapolis and West, The Department of Indian Work of the Greater Minneapolis Council of Churches (see). (3) St. Paul, South and Southwest, Ms. Sheila White Eagle, (Indian), 1671 Summitt Avenue, St. Paul, Minnesota 55105. An advocate-social concerns ministry. See entry under Councils of Churches and Cooperative Ministries.

INDIAN MINISTRY OF SAN DIEGO COUNTY. 1971. 3025 Fir Street at 30th, San Diego, California 92192. *(714)239-9773*. Mr. Harry Long, Director (Muskogee Creek). A joint agency of the United Presbyterian Church, the United Methodist Church, the Episcopal Diocese of San Diego, the United Church of Christ, the American Lutheran Church and the Christian Church (Disciples of Christ). Ministers to both reservation and urban Indians. An advocacy ministry seeking to stimulate the churches to respond more effectively to the priorities of the Native American community. Counseling, alcoholic rehabilitation, educational service to families, help in emergency needs (food, clothing, housing, travel, school affairs), finding resources such as material for repairing homes on reservation, transportation for elderly, presentations at non-Indian churches, coordinating work projects by church groups on reservations.

INDIAN SOCIAL MINISTRY of the Wichita Council of Churches. At the Mid-American All Indian Center. 650 North Seneca, Wichita, Kansas 67203. *(316)262-5221*. Mrs. Leo Heinze, Coordinator. Associated with the Center. Services: clothing, food, hospital visitation, outreach, housing assistance, financial help, transportation, household assistance, legal referrals, medical referrals, alcoholism counseling and referrals. See figures in entry under Councils of Churches.

INTERCHURCH MINISTRY TO NEBRASKA INDIANS. 1972. A
funding coalition formed under the auspices of Interchurch
Ministries of Nebraska by the Christian Church (Disciples of
Christ) in Nebraska, the Nebraska Conference of the United
Church of Christ, the Nebraska Conference of the United
Methodist Church, the Synod of Lakes and Prairies of the United
Presbyterian Church and Nebraska Church Women United. It
channels all its funds into UNITED INDIANS OF NEBRASKA for staff
leadership and organizational support.
> UNITED INDIANS OF NEBRASKA. 1973
> 11924 Poppleton Plaza, Omaha, Nebraska 68114
> *(402)334-9477, 9478*
> Ms. Janice R. Searcy, Executive Director

A coalition of 28 Indian organizations funded almost entirely by
contributions of religious organizations.

INTER-LUTHERAN REGIONAL COORDINATION AND SERVICE
DIRECTORS. See under Denominational Churches, The Lutheran
Churches.

MENOMINEE MINISTRY, THE UNITED METHODIST CHURCH. 1968.
Menominee. 626 South Franklin Street, Shawano, Wisconsin 54166.
(715)526-6297. Rev. James Feay. A chaplaincy-type ministry:
spiritual advisor-at-large, jail missionary, senior citizens'
aid, counseling, juvenile detention work, work service projects.

MENNONITE VOLUNTEER SERVICE PROGRAMS. Administered by:
Mennonite Board of Missions, P. O. Box 370, Elkhart, Indiana
46512. Mr. John W. Eby, Secretary for Relief and Service. The
several Mennonite Churches in the U.S.A. and Canada participate.
See entry under the Denominational Churches.

> Mennonite Service Unit. Hopi. Hopi Indian School, Oraibi,
> Arizona 86039. *(602)734-2453*. Two volunteers teach and serve
> at the School.

> Mennonite Service Unit. Northern Cheyenne. General Delivery,
> Lame Deer, Montana 59043. Contact persons: David and Diane
> Klaus. Advocacy work with Northern Cheyenne Tribe.

> Mennonite Service Unit. Choctaw. Route 7, Box 273,
> Philadelphia, Mississippi 39350. *(601)656-1836*. Five
> volunteers work in adult education and consumer education.

> Mennonite Service Unit. Blackfeet. Box 328, Browning,
> Montana 59417. *(406)338-7479*. John Schmid, Program Director.
> Five volunteers work in a nursing home, in youth recreation,
> in special education, in a woodcutting project and in ONHE
> (winterizing homes).

Mennonite Service Unit. Houma. Box 100, Dulac, Louisiana 70353. *(504)563-4501*. Day care and research service to the Dulac Community Center.

Mennonite Service Unit. Tunica. Route 3, Box 85-D, Marksville, Louisiana 71351. A couple assists the Tunica Tribe in construction and development of a community center, working on Federal recognition, proposal writing and adult education.

Mennonite Service Unit. Hoopa. Box 606, Hoopa, California 95546. *(916)625-4166*. Three volunteers work with the Hoopa Indians in recreation, tutoring and other types of assistance with the Tribal Council.

Voluntary Service Unit. 552 Paha Sapa, Rapid City, South Dakota 57701. *(605)348-4425*. Three permanent staff and college student summer volunteers work with youth in recreation, camping, vocational training, Bible study, etc.

LEGAL AID PROGRAM. P. O. Box 268, Okeene, Oklahoma 73736. Rev. Joe Burger. A program of the Roman Catholic Archdiocese of Oklahoma City.

MINNEAPOLIS CATHOLIC NEIGHBORHOOD SOCIAL SERVICE CENTERS I and II. Archdiocesan Catholic Charities. Branch I: 1308 East Franklin, Minneapolis, Minnesota 55404. Sister Joan Connors and 6 lay persons. 7,000 Indians participate. Branch II: 901 Hennepin Avenue, Minneapolis, Minnesota 55414. Staff: 15 lay persons. 1,500 Indians participate.

MOTHER BUTLER CENTER. Rapid City, South Dakota 57701. Fr. Richard G. Pates, S.J., Director. Brother Paul Rosonke, CSC. Comprehensive program. The pioneer Roman Catholic urban center. Closely affiliated with St. Isaac Joques Church.

NATIVE AMERICAN URBAN TRANSITION PROGRAM. 1975. 548 South Lincoln, Denver, Colorado 80209. Ms. Mary A. Pioche, Director (Indian). Ms. Beverly Joeger, Assistant. A Christian agency funded by some denominations on the national level. It assists and aids Indians in the change from reservation to city life in Denver. It provides Christian hospitality to newcomers, food and transportation when needed. Wholesome Christian social life. Short-term (2 weeks) housing is provided to one family at a time and long-term housing for single women. *Newsletter.*

ST. AUGUSTINE'S CENTER FOR AMERICAN INDIANS. 4512 North Sheridan Road, Chicago, Illinois 60640. *(312)784-1050*. Mrs. Amy Skenadore, Executive Director. Fr. Peter John Powell, Spiritual Director and Chaplain. Daily mass in St. Augustine's

Chapel. Case work counseling. Family assistance. Alcoholism
program. Family assistance. About 3,000 families served per
year, 8,000 persons benefited.

ST. NICHOLAS CENTER. Papago, Yaqui and others. 314 West 31st
Street, Tucson, Arizona 85713. *(602)622-5363.* Fr. Edward
Schultz, OFM, Director. Sisters (OFS) Ange Mayers, Janice
Weniger, Louise Bauer. Other Staff: 5 Ind. catechists, 2
whites, 2 Ind. men, 1 Ind. lay woman worker, 8 white men lay-
workers. Learning center, emergency services, referrals, week-
day religious education, social service, parish ministry.
Serves 3,500 yearly.

ST. PAUL'S INDIAN MISSION. Episcopal Diocese of Iowa. 524
Center Street, P. O. Box 895, Sioux City, Iowa 51103.
(712)233-2940. Rev. James D. Marrs, Sr. Both parish ministry
and community services: housing, health, education, welfare,
services to youth and elderly, referrals, alcoholism counseling.
Community program is funded by the Episcopal Diocese of Iowa.

ST. VALERIAN CATHOLIC INDIAN CENTER. SISTERS OF THE
BLESSED SACRAMENT. 506 West 66th Avenue, Gallup, New Mexico
87301. A learning center to assist Native Americans,
predominantly Navajos, to make the transition from BIA boarding
schools to Diocesan and public schools. Special classes give
students the basic courses which will enable them to feel secure
and not become dropouts. Material assistance is given to
approximately 280 persons per month in food, clothing, housing,
hospitalization, counseling, employment and child care.
Referrals.

SAN FRANCISCO FRIENDSHIP HOUSE. Christian Reformed Church.
Alcoholism Rehabilitation Program at 1340 Golden Gate Avenue,
San Francisco, California 94115. *(415)922-3866.* Al Walcott,
Interim Director. Friendship House at 89 Turquois Way, San
Francisco, California 94131. Rev. Donald Klompeen, pastor.

SALT LAKE CITY CHRISTIAN INDIAN CENTER. Christian
Reformed Church. 2514 South 1500 East, Salt Lake City, Utah
84109. *(801)466-1566.* Norman Jonkman, Director.

SALVATION ARMY CORPS COMMUNITY CENTER. Rapid City, South
Dakota. Welfare assistance is about 85% to Indian persons:
lodging, meals, grocery orders, Salvage Store goods, gasoline
and bus transportation to five reservations in the surrounding
area.

TOM SEAY SERVICE CENTER. Salvation Army. 1025 West Sunnyside at Broadway, Chicago, Illinois 60640. *(312)271-6182.*
Directors: Capt. and Mrs. David Dalberg, Located in Chicago's

Uptown District where there is a large Indian population. Services: alcoholic treatment residence, crisis counseling center, daily free nutrition program, food pantry, therapy programs, daily religious services, New Life House for runaway teenage girls, summer day camp.

YAKIMA INDIAN CHRISTIAN MISSION. (Disciples) Yakima. Two Friendship Houses: A-7 South Toppenish Avenue, Toppenish, Washington 98948. 217 South Wapato Avenue, Wapato, Washington 98951. Both staffed by Indians. These Houses offer information, referral services, limited material aid, light recreation and counseling.

CHURCH-SPONSORED HEALTH SERVICES

ALCOHOLISM COUNSELING and in some cases treatment are offered at: Alcoholism Counseling Service, Archdiocese of Anchorage, Alaska.

Alcoholism ministry, especially to transient Indians, Bible Baptist Shepherd Navajo Church, 507 North 5th Street, Gallup, New Mexico 87301. *(505)722-5269.* Rev. Edward H. Hanning.

Alcoholism service, Salvation Army, Anchorage, Alaska 99509. Capt. David Boyd, Box 4992, Anchorage, Alaska 99509.

Alcoholic Rehabilitation Center. P. O. Box 172, Ganado, Arizona 86505. Rev. Alan Hill (Navajo). Mr. Hill maintains his ministry by operating a funeral casket manufacturing shop, which provides an important service to Indians.

Brethren in Christ Mission. Bloomfield, New Mexico 87413.

Kateri Alcohol Center, St. Catherine's Church, Squaw Lake, Minnesota 56681.

Outreach Counseling in Alcoholism. Roman Catholic Church, Diocese of Fairbanks, Fairbanks, Alaska. Sister Dorothy, Counselor.

St. Augustine's Center. Episcopal Church, 4512 North Sheridan Road, Chicago, Illinois 60640. *(323)784-1050.*

Tekawitha Alcohol Center. St. Stephen's Indian Mission. Catholic Church. Arapaho. Wind River Reservation. P. O. Box 294, St. Stephen's, Wyoming 82524.

Tom Seay Service Center. Salvation Army, 1025 West Sunnyside at Broadway, Chicago, Illinois 60640. *(312)271-6181.* Capt. and Mrs. David Dalberg.

DENTAL AND MEDICAL CLINIC. United Presbyterian Church. Wright City. Wright City, Oklahoma 74766.

FAITH HOSPITAL AND CLINIC. Central Alaskan Mission, Inc. Glennallen, Alaska 99588. 1 physician, 4 nurses, 4 other staff. Patients per year 10,000.

MONUMENT VALLEY SEVENTH DAY ADVENTIST HOSPITAL.   1961.
Navajo. P. O. Box 6, Monument Valley, Utah 84536. Tom
Cummings, Medical Director. Staff 33. Beds 27.

ROCK POINT OUTPATIENT CLINIC.   Rock Point, Chinle, Arizona
85603. A ministry of the Navajo Evangelical Lutheran Mission.
Nurse Elsie Benson and Ms. Clara Tohtsani (Navajo).

URBAN CENTERS PUBLICALLY FUNDED

These Centers are not church ministries. Some were brought into
being by churches and churches and members contribute to many of
them. There is close cooperation between the churches and some
Centers. These are listed for reference only.

ARIZONA

AMERICAN INDIAN ASSOCIATION OF TUCSON, INC. 2512 South 6th
Avenue, Tucson, Arizona 85713. *(602)884-7131.* Grover Banks,
Director.

PHOENIX INDIAN CENTER. 4025 N. 2nd Street, Phoenix, Arizona
85012. *(602)279-4116.* Syd Beane, Director.

NATIVE AMERICANS FOR COMMUNITY ACTION, INC. 15 North San
Francisco, P. O. Box 472, Flagstaff, Arizona 86001.
(602)779-1838. Joe Washington, Director.

CALIFORNIA

INTER-TRIBAL FRIENDSHIP HOUSE. 523 E. 14th Street, Oakland,
California 94606. *(415)452-1235.* Felix Spencer, Director.

FRESNO AMERICAN INDIAN COUNCIL. 703 North Fulton, Fresno,
California 93721. *(209)268-6177.* Jeff Davis, Director.

INDIAN ACTION COUNCIL OF NORTHWESTERN CALIFORNIA. P. O. Box
3108, Eureka, California 95501. *(707)443-8401.* Paul Puzz,
Director.

INDIAN CENTER OF SAN JOSE, INC. 3485 East Hills Drive, San
Jose, California 95127. *(408)259-9722.* Gus Adams, Director.

LOS ANGELES INDIAN CENTER, INC. 1127 W. Washington Blvd., Los
Angeles, California 90015. *(215)747-9521.*

SACRAMENTO INDIAN CENTER. P. O. Box 16094, 2007 O Street,
Sacramento, California 95816. *(916)446-4096.*

COMMUNITY ACTION FOR THE URBANIZED AMERICAN INDIAN. 225 Valencia

Street, San Francisco, California 94102. *(415)552-1070*.

SOUTH BAY INDIAN SERVICES. 3646 Long Beach Blvd., Long Beach, California 90807. *(213)424-0941*. Ms. Wee Cie Ford, Director.

SAN BERNARDINO INDIAN CENTER. 441 W. 8th Street, San Bernardino, California 92401. *(714)889-8516*. Don Cornelius, Director.

SANTA ROSA INDIAN CENTER. 1305 Cleveland Avenue, Santa Rosa, California 95406. *(707)527-8711*. Ed Harris, Director.

COLORADO

DENVER NATIVE AMERICANS UNITED, INC. 1525 Josephine Street, Denver, Colorado 80206. *(303)339-6450*. Kent Scott, Director.

ILLINOIS

NATIVE AMERICAN COMMITTEE. 4546 North Hermitage, Chicago, Illinois 60640. *(312)728-1477*. Matt Pilcher, Director.

KANSAS

INDIAN CENTER OF TOPEKA, INC. 407 W. Lyman Road, Topeka, Kansas 66608. *(913)357-1811*. Mrs. Connie Lewis, Director.

MID-AMERICAN ALL INDIAN CENTER. 650 North Seneca, Wichita, Kansas 67203. *(316)262-5211*. Jay Hunter, Director.

MASSACHUSETTS

BOSTON INDIAN COUNCIL. 105 S. Huntington Avenue, Jamica Plain, Boston, Massachusetts 02103. *(617)232-0343*. Cliff Saunders, Director.

MICHIGAN

GRAND RAPIDS INTER-TRIBAL COUNCIL. 756 Bridge, N.W., Grand Rapids, Michigan 49504. *(616)774-8331*. Wagnor J. Wheeler, Director.

NORTH AMERICAN INDIAN ASSOCIATION OF DETROIT. 360 John R. Street, Detroit, Michigan 48226. *(313)963-1710*. Hank Bonga, Director.

LANSING NORTH AMERICAN INDIAN CENTER. 1427 E. Michigan Street, Lansing, Michigan 48912. *(517)487-5409*. Ms. Janice Beckhorn, Director.

MINNESOTA

MINNEAPOLIS REGIONAL NATIVE AMERICAN CENTER. 1530 E. Franklin,
Minneapolis, Minnesota 55404. *(612)348-5612.*

ST. PAUL AMERICAN INDIAN CENTER. 1001 Payne Avenue, St. Paul,
Minnesota 55106. *(612)776-8592.* Artley Skenandore, Director.

MISSOURI

AMERICAN INDIAN CULTURAL CENTER OF MID-AMERICA. 3524-26 Gravios
Street, St. Louis, Missouri 63110. *(314)773-7422.* Gregory
Roberts, Director.

HEART OF AMERICAN INDIAN CENTER. 3220 Independence Avenue,
Kansas City, Missouri 64124. *(816)231-4736.* Robert Lieb,
Director.

MONTANA

MONTANA UNITED INDIAN ASSOCIATION. P. O. Box 786, Helena,
Montana 59601. *(406)443-5350.* George Henkel, Director.

NEBRASKA

THE INDIAN CENTER, INC. 243 South 20th Street, Lincoln,
Nebraska 68508. *(402)477-5231.* Marshall Prichard, Director.

OMAHA AMERICAN INDIAN CENTER. 613 S. 16th Street, Omaha,
Nebraska 68102. *(402)344-0111.* Fred Buckles, Director.

NEW MEXICO

ALBUQUERQUE COALITION OF INDIAN ORGANIZATIONS. 510 2nd N.W.,
Room 224, Albuquerque, New Mexico 87102. *(505)243-2253.* Nate
Parker, Director.

GALLUP INDIAN COMMUNITY CENTER. 200 West Maxwell Avenue,
Gallup, New Mexico 87301. *(505)722-4388.* Ms. Pauline Sice,
Director.

NEW YORK

AMERICAN INDIAN COMMUNITY HOUSE. 10 East 38th Street, New York,
N.Y. 10016. *(212)532-4897.* Michael Bush, Director.

NORTH DAKOTA

DAKOTA ASSOCIATION OF NATIVE AMERICANS, INC. 309½ East Main
Bismark, North Dakota 58501. *(701)663-4271.* Ms. Elizabeth

Hallmark, Director.

OHIO

CLEVELAND AMERICAN INDIAN CENTER. 5500 Lorain Avenue, Cleveland, Ohio 44102. *(216)961-3490.* Jerome War Cloud, Director.

OKLAHOMA

NATIVE AMERICAN COALITION. P. O. Box 2646, Tulsa, Oklahoma 74102. *(918)583-3643.*

NATIVE AMERICAN CENTER. 1214 N. Hudson, Oklahoma City, Oklahoma 73106. *(405)232-1512.* Ms. Millie Giago, Director.

SOUTHERN PLAINS INTER-TRIBAL CENTER. 120 Northeast Rogers Lane, Lawton, Oklahoma 73501. Jimmy Ray Gaddo, Director.

PENNSYLVANIA

COUNCIL OF THREE RIVERS. 803 North Homewood Avenue, Pittsburg, Pennsylvania 15208. *(412)782-4457.* Russell Simms, Director.

UNITED AMERICAN INDIANS OF DELAWARE VALLEY. 225 Chestnut, Philadelphia, Pennsylvania 19106. *(215)574-9020.* William Lynch, Director.

SOUTH DAKOTA

RAPID CITY INDIAN SERVICE COUNCIL. P. O. Box 2029, 502 Omaha Street, Rapid City, South Dakota 57701. *(605)342-4772.* Frank Gangone, Director.

TEXAS

AMERICAN INDIAN CENTER OF DALLAS. 1314 Munger Blvd., P. O. Box 22334, Dallas, Texas 75222. *(214)826-8856.* Ms. Juanita Elder, Director.

UTAH

UTAH NATIVE AMERICAN CONSORTIUM, INC. 120 West 1300 South, Salt Lake City, Utah 84115. *(801)485-9204.* Reynolds Harrison, Director.

WASHINGTON

SEATTLE INDIAN CENTER. 121 Stewart Street, Seattle, Washington 98104. *(206)624-8700.*

AMERICAN INDIAN COMMUNITY CENTER. 1007 North Columbus, Spokane, Washington 99202. *(509)489-2370.* Ms. Celina Goalsby, Director.

TACOMA INDIAN CENTER. 519 E. 28th Street, Tacoma, Washington 98421. *(206)383-3063.* Ms. Faye LaPointe, Director.

WISCONSIN

MILWAUKEE INDIAN URBAN AFFAIRS COUNCIL. 1410 North 27th Street, Milwaukee, Wisconsin 53208. *(414)342-4171.* Sheila Williams, Director.

CHILD CARE CENTERS AND HOMES

CHARLES HALL YOUTH SERVICES   1965
P. O. Box 1995, 219 North 7th Street, Bismarck, North Dakota
58501   *(701)255-2773*

A children's home for Mandan, Arikara and Hidatsa young people. Hall Home and Good Bird Home (1970) each accommodate eight. Houseparents and alternate houseparents, tutors and counselor. A field worker visits the parents on the Fort Berthold Reservation. Nondenominational. Established by the North Dakota Conference of the United Church of Christ and named in memory of pioneer Congregationalist missionary at Ft. Berhold, Dr. Charles L. Hall.

CHRISTIAN CHILD CARE HOME
220 West Jefferson Street, Gallup, New Mexico 87301
                                                       (505)863-6046

A ministry of the Church of God in Christ, Mennonite. Volunteer workers 6.

DULAC COMMUNITY CENTER
P. O. Box 100, Dulac, Louisiana 70353   *(504)563-4501*
Rev. Spiller Milton, Executive Director.

Serves Houma Tribe. Offers day care for 3 and 4 year olds. 23 children. United Methodist Church.

EAST FORK LUTHERAN NURSERY
P. O. Box 55, Whiteriver, Arizona 85941
Dr. H. E. Hartzell, Superintendent
Mrs. Virginia Burgess, Matron

Apache. A ministry of the Evangelical Lutheran Mission of the Wisconsin Evangelical Lutheran Mission. Staff: 14 full time. Both full care and day care. In October 1977 - 31 children for varying periods of time.

GOODLAND PRESBYTERIAN CHILDREN'S HOME AND FAMILY SERVICE AGENCY
Goodland Route, Hugo, Oklahoma 74743
Ralyn C. Parkhill, Executive Director

An agency of the Presbyterian Church in the United States. Founded in 1850 as Goodland Mission School, to which an Orphanage was added in 1894. The School has been replaced by a public school which operates on the campus. The name was changed to the present form in 1972.

Services: a residential, group-living program for 40 children aged 11 to 18 in four coed cottages under group parents; emergency care for children in need of shelter in Choctaw County; individual care in foster homes; an adoption service; family counseling at St. Andrew's Presbyterian Church in Oklahoma City. Twelve buildings on campus. Now open to all ethnic groups in addition to Choctaws.

1977 - 30 Indian families served and 11 children in care. Oklahoma City Office: 32 intakes in 6 months; counseling 19 families per month; 27 children in foster homes in May 1978; adoptive families 5 per month; advice and referral 150 calls per month.

HOGAN HOZHONI CHRISTIAN CHILD CARE SERVICE
P. O. Box 645, Window Rock, ARizona 86515   *(602)871-4021*

Navajo. A ministry of the Church of God in Christ, Mennonite. Volunteer workers 10.

HOME FOR EMOTIONALLY DISTURBED ESKIMO CHILDREN
Bethel, Alaska 99559.

Operated by Jesuit Volunteers. Staff of 4 professionals. Patients 10-30 annually.

HOPE RANCH
P. O. Box 1136, Poplar, Montana 59255   *(406)768-3973*
Ted Shining Warior, Director

Fort Peck Tribes.

HOUSE OF SAMUEL, INC.
11777 S. Old Nogales Highway, Tucson, Arizona 85706
Gary Woods, Director   *(602)294-1997*

Apache and Navajo. An independent service agency, the purpose of which is "to provide solid Christ-centered family love to neglected, abused or delinquent children." A group home for 10

children, placement service for 50 children and an Accelerated
Christian Education School, 1-8 grades. Counseling for families.
Receives children in genuine need from birth to 18 years, all
races, some handicapped. 6 children resident in 1978, 30 in
foster homes, 40 receiving some form of care. Dependent on free
will gifts of individuals and churches. *Newsletter.*

KODIAK BAPTIST MISSION   1893
P. O. Box 785, Kodiak, Alaska 99615
Rev. Robert L. Childs, Superintendent

Aleut, Athabascan, Eskimo. A ministry of the American Baptist
churches begun on Woody Island in 1893 and moved to Kodiak in
1939. A three-fold child care program: a receiving home for
temporary care, a group home for intermediate term aid
especially to teenagers, and long term care. Staff: 12 white
workers. 81% of children are Native Americans.

MURROW INDIAN CHILDREN'S HOME
Box 38, Bacone Station, Muskogee, Oklahoma 74401 *(918)687-4711*
Mrs. Mary Horsechief, Executive Director

Tribes represented: Creek (largest), Cheyenne, Kiowa, Pawnee,
Winnebago, Sac and Fox. Many are urban children. Independent
board of Trustees, self-perpetuating. Related to American
Baptist Churches, Division of Homeland Ministries, which holds
title to the property.
Staff: 11 paid workers, 4 cottage fathers - not paid, given room
and board.
Capacity: 40 beds, number usually at 30.
Eligibility: Indian children 6-14 years, but may stay through
high school. Children from broken homes. Placed by courts,
social workers and ministers.
Support: Individuals and local churches.
History: Rev. and Mrs. J. S. Murrow, Southern Baptist mission-
aries, began to take Indian orphans into their home at the end
of the Civil War. In 1902 it became officially a "Christian
Home for Indian Orphans" at Atoka, and the Choctaw and Chickasaw
Tribes contributed land for it. The two American Baptist Home
Mission Societies in 1910 took up sponsorship, purchased land
near Muskogee and renamed the institution The Murrow Indian
Children's Home. Creek families in 1922-23 donated funds to
build dormitories, now used by Bacone College. This property
was exchanged with Bacone College in 1956 for a tract bordering
on State Route 16 and four cottages were erected.
Periodical: *The Papoose.*

NAVAJO MISSIONS, INC. CHILD CARE MINISTRY
P. O. Box 1230, 2103 West Main Street, Farmington, New Mexico
87401   *(505)325-0255*
R. Jack Drake, President and Director.

Staff: 7 houseparents, evangelist (Rev. Jack Wheat), 19 others.
Children attend public schools and 2 are in college. Most
children attend Emmanual Baptist Church and 10 made a profession
of faith in Christ in 1976. A work program and arts and crafts.

THE OAKS INDIAN MISSION HOME   1927
P. O. Box 10, Oaks, Oklahoma 74357   *(918)868-2196*
Rev. Elwin Bergstroesser, Director   Cherokee

A ministry of the American Lutheran Church. Accepts children
grades 1 through 12 if stable and emotionally functional.
Children are usually placed by parents, sometimes referred by
court order. Orphans 5%. Children attend public school which
was formaly the Mission School.

TEKAKWITHA INDIAN CHILDREN'S HOME
Sisseton, South Dakota 57262   *(605)698-7518*
Rev. Robert Reitmeier, O.M.I., Superintendent

Brothers 2. Children 64.

C.
EDUCATIONAL MINISTRIES

THEOLOGICAL SEMINARIES, TRAINING FOR MINISTRY

ALLIANCE CENTERS FOR THEOLOGICAL STUDY. 1948. (Formerly
Mokahun Indian Bible School.) Christian and Missionary
Alliance. Route 2, Box 129, Cass Lake, Minnesota 56633.
(218)335-6734. Daniel R. Wetzel, Coordinator. Primarily for
Native Americans, but open to others. Statement of Purpose:
Alliance Centers for Theological Study is a program of
theological training which places an emphasis upon the practical
skills necessary to minister effectively with American Indian
congregations. It has been designed to fulfill the educational
requirements for an ordained ministry in the Christian and
Missionary Alliance. This course of study has been set to:
(1) provide a Biblical and Theological basis for pastoral
ministry; (2) encourage self-discipline and Christian maturity;
(3) promote church planting and evangelism; (4) stimulate active
involvement in the world wide ministries of the Christian and
Missionary Alliance.

ACTS operates entirely through Theological Education by
Extention. Regional representatives are being appointed as
also the center-leaders. The regions are:

Minnesota, Wisconsin, Lake-of-the-Woods area of Ontario,
Turtle Mountain, North Dakota

(Male; non-Indian. This individual is a linguist and is
working in conjunction with the Bible Societies as coordinator
for an Ojibwa translation.)

Navajo Reservation:
(Male; Navajo)

South Dakota, North Dakota (other than Turtle Mtn.) and
Montana:
(this position is not yet filled)

Canadian Midwest: Western Ontario, Manitoba, Saskatchewan

(The congregations involved in this area are nearly all
urban. The Canadian C&MA must submit a name for the
position.)

Western Canadian: Peace River area of northern Alberta

(no one has been appointed as yet)

In addition to these areas one congregation in North Carolina
which is part of the C&MA is handled out of the central office
in Cass Lake. The pastor, who is Indian, handles the discussion
sessions.

Levels of Instruction: ACTS operates on two basic levels of
instruction. These levels have been given arbitrary level
names in order to avoid stratification of the students who
enroll and create a "class" structure within the program.

Level H. Students must be able to read and write the English
language well enough to handle the materials provided. They
are written at the 5th to 6th grade reading level. This
level is recognized by the society as sufficient training for
ministry. Students who wish to continue their studies and who
achieve at acceptable levels (approx. 80%) may enroll in
further studies at an advanced level.

Level Q. Level Q requires a high school diploma or GED.
Students who have a minimum 8th grade education but do not
have a diploma may be admitted on a probationary basis. This
status can be changed to a permanent one after demonstrating
their ability to handle the materials.

NOTE: All students are examined on the same basis for the
receipt of a Pastoral Studies Diploma. They must serve a
minimum one year period of ministry as a pastor, church
planter, or similar position. During this year they are
subject to evaluation by the educational program's staff. It
is strongly recommended that this minimum requirement be
fulfilled while they are studying, not subsequent to their
studies.

Entrance Requirements:

1. All students must be in active fellowship with a Christian congregation. The approval of the congregational leaders is required before any student may begin studies.
2. All applicants must be at least 17 years old.
3. Students will be admitted to the appropriate educational programs based upon previous educational experiences.

Students enrolled: 67.

COOK CHRISTIAN TRAINING SCHOOL. 1911, restructured 1940. A resource center for church leadership development. 708 South Lindon Lane, Tempe, Arizona 85281. Dr. Cecil Corbett, Executive Director. Rev. Gary Gush. Cook is governed by an independent Borad of Trustees, the majority of members being nominated by participating denominations, with some trustees-at-large. Churches represented: American Baptist Churches, Association of Congregational Christian Churches, Christian Reformed Churches, United Church of Christ, United Methodist Church, United Presbyterian Church. Cook School is fully open to persons of all churches and races. It is a member of NATA - The Native American Theological Association. The resources of the School are directed towards the development and training of church leadership to all levels.

Administrative staff 3. Campus teaching staff 7. Extension teachers 50, 30 of them active in spring 1978. On campus students in 1978 - 19. Extension students: 137 new students in 1977-78, and a total of 568 have been enrolled.

Admission Requirements for Resident Studies Program:

The level of studies, expected participation, and the campus community require one to have the strength, interest and endorsement discussed above. The more specific requirements for application to residency study are that a person must:

1. Be 18 years of age or older.
2. Have necessary basic academic skills (such as reading and writing, preferably at 8th grade level), to benefit from the campus program and meet future employment or service.
3. Have been active in a local parish for six months or longer.
4. Have the endorsement of a majority of the elected officers of the person's local congregations where the person has been active for six months or longer.
5. Have submitted a study plan for desired studies, and projection of educational goals.

6. Be in adequate health to pursue a course of study.
7. Have identified financial resources, in consultation with Cook School, for the costs of education.
8. Submit all application materials.

Admission Requirements for Extension Studies:

For persons who wish to attend Cook School courses offered in the person's community, the requirements for admission are that a person must:

1. Be 15 years of age or older.
2. Be approved by the extension class teacher.
3. Be in adequate health to pursue a course of study.
4. Have identified financial resources, in consultation with the extension class teacher, to pay for the costs of the course.
5. Submit an application to the extension class teacher, who will send the application to Cook School.

All students who are applying for admission to Cook School, whether to participate in campus or extension classes, are advised to check denominational requirements. Cook School will help identify the process or the individuals to contact.

Financial Information:

Resident Tuition 14--18 Credits, per term (fall or spring) $225.00

Resident Tuition per credit (for those taking less than 14 or more than 18 semester hours)   18.00

Extension Tuition per credit (There will be an additional charge for texts)   18.00

There is a possibility of the above extension tuition costs being reduced in areas where the extension teacher will be in a position to donate his salary.

Resource Fees, per term (fall or spring)   50.00

Apartment Fee (married students) including furnishings and utilities, per term (fall and spring)
   Efficiency apartment   405.00
   2-bedroom apartment   495.00
   3-bedroom apartment   562.50

Apartment fee (single students) (minimum of two students per apartment) including furnishings and utilities, per student, per term   250.00

Students should add the cost of food, transportation and personal expenses which may run on an average of $35.00 a week for a single student, up to as much as $75.00 a week for married families with children.

Scholarship assistance is possible when needed.

Cook School offers three certificate programs. For lay leaders who seek to serve in the Church as teachers, Cook School offers a Certificate of Church Education. For other lay leaders, especially church officers, Cook School offers a Certificate of Lay Leadership. A Lay Pastoral Skills Certificate is available for those who seek to serve the church as lay pastors.

Many of the courses in the certificate programs can be completed by extension either before coming to the resident program or after. It also should be noted that many of the certificate courses can be transferred to the Native American Theological Association member colleges and seminaries.

Certificate of Church Education, Certificate of Lay Leadership, and Certificate of Lay Pastoral Skills.

The Developmental Learning Lab and Individualized Learning Center were begun in 1972. The *Midwinter Workshops* on campus are similar workshops arranged in other communities are important resources for continuing education.

Theological Education by Extension--TEE. Cook Christian Training School has been the leader in the development of Theological Education by Extension for all forms of church ministries and leadership. It inaugurated the program in 1975. By February 1978, 568 persons, belonging to 14 denominations, have enrolled for 99 seminars in 47 extension sites in 17 states and Canadian provinces taught by 50 different seminar leaders. During 1977-78, 137 new students were enrolled, 17 new extension sites were established, and 21 new seminar leaders were enlisted. 52% or 184 of these persons are eligible for Track #3 of NATA, 183 for Tract #2, and 31 for Tract #1.

NATA: NATIVE AMERICAN THEOLOGICAL ASSOCIATION. 122 West Franklin Avenue, Minneapolis, Minnesota 55404. *(612)870-3685.* Howard Anderson, Executive Director. A consortium intended to promote education and training for Native American Church ministers of all levels in the perspective of the needs of the Native American Christian community rather than conformity to the traditional standard American seminary pattern. Member institutions: Cook Christian Training School,

Huron College, Northland College, Dakota Leadership Program, Dubuque Theological Seminary, United Theological Seminary of the Twin Cities, and Luther-Northwestern Theological Seminary. Denominational members: Episcopal Church, United Church of Christ, United Methodist Church, United Presbyterian Church, and church in a consultation relationship: American Baptist Church, American Lutheran Church and the Roman Catholic Church. Alternative curricula are offered through the member schools: Track #1 consists of three years of college and two of seminary; Track #2 is the "standard" four years of college and three of seminary; and Track #3 requires three years. The last is open to mature Indians and Eskimos, at least 32 years of age, high school graduate or GED certificate holder, with at least one year of experience as a church officer or lay pastor. It leads to a NATA Certificate. Enquire of the Executive Secretary, the member schools or of officers of participating denominations.

ST. HERMAN'S THEOLOGICAL SEMINARY. 1973. Aleuts, Indians, Eskimos. Orthodox Church in America. P. O. Box 65, Kodiak, Alaska 99615. The Very Rev. Joseph P. Kreta, Dean. The Rt. Rev. Gregory, Bishop of Sitka and Alaska, is President. A four year course leads to the B.D. degree. Two have graduated and been ordained priests. A one year "Reader's Program" trains men and women to conduct services in the absence of ordained clergy. 27 have graduated from this program.

DIACONATE AND SACRAMENTALIST TRAINING PROGRAMS

DAKOTA LEADERSHIP TRAINING PROGRAM. Box 506, Mobridge, South Dakota 57601. *(605)845-7322.* Rev. George Harris, Director. A joint project of the Episcopal Dioceses of North and South Dakota. Open to persons of other denominations also. Deacon's Training Program in South Dakota involved 7 deacons completing the course in 1977-78. Conferences on Ministry with local parishes. Extension Program in 1978 - 18: 8 centers, 15 courses, 121 students, 11 Field Associates.

DAKOTA CATHOLIC LEADERSHIP PROGRAM. St. Paul's Mission, Marty, South Dakota 57361. Fr. Hugh Smith, Director. Diaconate and other training.

DIOCESE OF ALASKA. Episcopal Church. *Sacramentalists Training Program.* P. O. Box 441, Fairbanks, Alaska 99707. Rev. Andrew Fairfield, Coordinator. 15 Sacramentalists have been educated and ordained: 6 Athabascan men, 1 woman; 7 Eskimo men, 1 woman.

DIOCESE OF FAIRBANKS. Roman Catholic Church. *Jesuit Permanent Diaconate Program.* Rev. Rene Astruc, S.J., Director. 1316 Peger Road, Fairbanks, Alaska 99701. Rev. Charles J.

Peterson, S.J., Diocesan Director of Vocations. Parish Council
selects candidates for the Permanent Diaconate. When their
training has been completed, the Deacons are involved in
pastoral ministry in their villages. 13 have completed the
training and 19 are in training in 1977-78.

DIOCESE OF RAPID CITY. Roman Catholic Church. *Diaconate
Training Program. Sioux Spiritual Center.* Plainview, South
Dakota 57771. Staff: Revs. John Hatcher, S.J.; Pat McCorkell,
S.J.; Damien O'Connell, S.J.; James Steh, S.J. Permanent
Deacons in service 4.

DIOCESE OF WESTERN NORTH CAROLINA. Episcopal Church. *St.
Bede's House of Studies.* Rev. William Paul Austin, Director.
Box 275, Route 2, Whittier, North Carolina 28789. Near
Cherokee. For the training of Indians and others under Canon 8.
All students at present are white.

COLLEGES

ALASKA BIBLE COLLEGE. 1966. P. O. Box 289, Glennallen,
Alaska 99588. *(907)322-3201.* Central Alaska Missions, Inc.
Bob Lee, President. Entrance requirements: high school graduation, born-again believer, open admission for academics –
4 year course leads to B.A.; 3 years to A.A.; 2 years to Bible
certificate. Teaching staff: 6 full time, 6 part time.
Tuition $25.00 per credit hour. Students: 20 men, 20 women,
including Indians, Eskimos, Aleuts, whites and others.
Graduated in 1976 – 7, in 1977 – 7, from 1967 to 1977 – 33.
95% of graduates are in pastorate or other church related
ministries.

BACONE COLLEGE. 1880. Muskogee, Oklahoma 74401.
(918)683-4581. Dr. Wesley N. Harres, President. An independent junior college, American Baptist related, with a
"personalized system of instruciton" and a "care program"
available where needed. 2 year course, A.A. degree. Tuition
$40.00 per credit hour. Tuition, room and board $1,200 per
year. Administrative staff 6. Faculty: 4 Indians, 34 others.
Students: 154 men, 383 women, including 317 Indians. 99
graduated in 1976, 126 in 1977 and 571 in last five years.
Smoke Signales, quarterly.

THE COLLEGE OF GANADO. 1970 (1901). Ganado, Arizona 86505.
(602)755-3442. Dr. Thomas Carson Jackson, President. A
United Presbyterian related junior community college on the
campus of the former Ganado High School. It operates under a
covenant relationship with Grand Canyon Presbytery. The Church
provides some personnel and financial support, but direct
grants will end in June 1979. Board of Regents: 21, of whom

16 are Navajos; chairman, Roger C. Davis, Director of Natural
Resources of Recreation for the Navajo Nation. 11 full time
faculty members, 6 administrators, 25 support staff. 250
students, mostly Navajo but also 12 other tribes. Three
Divisions: Humanities and Social Sciences, Business and Natural
Science, Mathematics. Degrees: A.A., A.S., and A.A.S. Career
studies program, Navajo advocates training program, Navajo
Alcoholism Training program. The Navajo Academy, a college
preparatory school is on the campus.

CONCORDIA COLLEGE CENTER FOR INDIAN MINISTRIES AND
STUDIES. Concordia Teachers College, 800 North Columbia
Avenue, Seward, Nebraska 68434. Professor James Nelesen,
Director; Ron L. Wagoner, Field Coordinator. Supported by the
College and three Districts of the Lutheran Church - Missouri
Synod. Program objectives are thus stated:
1. To foster greater intercultural awareness, understanding
   and appreciation between Anglos and Native Americans.
2. To provide needed skills for people in the church who work
   within and/or near Indian communities.
3. To develop programs of teacher education and pre-professional training with Indian people.
4. To develop new and existing resource services for Indian
   ministry with congregations and Districts.
5. To provide counseling and support services to individual
   Anglos, Native Americans, teachers, students and
   administrators.

It is stated: "The essence of the organization is maintenance
of the supportive contacts with people and the offering of
human, spiritual and material resources to those in need."

A curriculum/program for Indian students will be worked out in
the 1978-79 academic year. The program is fluid. There is an
Inter-Disciplinary Course on Anglo culture for Indian students
which is designed to facilitate their understanding of their
environment. There is an option of six hours of independent
study per semester for Indian students if desired or warranted.

HURON COLLEGE. 1883. Huron, South Dakota 57305. Dr. W. L.
Jahnke, President. *(605)352-8721*. A United Presbyterian
related Liberal Arts college. Interracial with special concern
for Native Americans. 3 staff members are Native Americans.
Students: Fall term 77-78 - 27 on campus, 19 in Extension;
Spring term 77-78 - 23 on campus, 7 at Ft. Thompson Extension.
Counselor to Indian students. Cooperates with Cook Christian
Training School and Dubuque Seminary in Native American
education, and is a founding member and participant in the
Native American Theological Association. The Extension program
at Ft. Thompson leads to the A.A. degree.

SHELDON JACKSON COLLEGE. 1878. P. O. Box 479, Sitka, Alaska 99835. *(907)747-5222.* Independent, but United Presbyterian related. Open admission. Tuition and expenses $2,100. Degrees: A.A., A.S., B.A. in Elementary Education, DA Certificate and Fishery Certificate. Eight extension centers. Administrative staff 6. Campus teaching staff 17. Extension staff 5. Students on campus: 91 men, 80 women. Extension students: 6 men, 68 women. Graduated in 1976 - 48; 1977 - 33.

BIBLE SCHOOLS AND INSTITUTES

AMERICAN INDIAN BIBLE INSTITUTE, INC. 1956. Many tribes. 10020 North 15th Avenue, Phoenix, Arizona 85021. *(602)944-3335.* Assemblies of God. Rev. Don R. Ramsey, President; Alma Thomas, Academic Dean; Rev. Eugene Herd, Vice-President and Business Manager. Teachers: John Chisnell, Marion Herd, Eugene Hunter, David Moore. Administrative staff 4. Extension staff 4. 1 Indian on staff. A 3-year course leading to a diploma in Christian Education. Admission requirements: must be over 18 years of age, able to handle oral and written English, have his/her minister's recommendation, show evidence of conversion experience, and have a vocation to Christian ministry. Normally expected to have completed high school. Students: 26 men, 23 women, total 49. Graduated 72 between 1967 and 1977, 11 in 1976 and 9 in 1977. Newspaper: *The AIBI Thunderer,* 4 to 6 times a year.

ARCTIC BIBLE INSTITUTE. 1968. Athabascan. Arctic Mission, Inc. Palmer, Alaska 99645. A four years post high school course.

BRAINERD INDIAN SCHOOL. 1946. Dakota. Star Route, Box 167, Hot Springs, South Dakota 57747. *(605)745-3733.* Wesleyan Church. J. Franklin Heer, President. Bible School: a four year course beyond high school. See under HIGH SCHOOLS.

EASTERN INDIAN BIBLE INSTITUTE. 1969. Route 1, Box 760, Shannon, North Carolina 28386. North Carolina District Council of the Assemblies of God. Rodger Cree, President. Teachers: Rodger Cree, Charles Hadden, Hubert Boese, Esther Cree, Jeannette Duber, Judy McKnight, Joan Morris. Two semesters: Diploma at completion of courses. Admission requirements: applicant should show evidence of conversion and a desire to serve the American Indians. Pastor's recommendation required.

FRIENDS BIBLE TRAINING SCHOOL. 1930. Eskimo. California Yearly Meeting of Friends. P. O. Box 687, Kotzebue, Alaska 99752. Mark L. Ocker, Administrator. Administrative staff 9, including 7 Inuit (Eskimos). Teachers: 2 Inuit men part time, 2 Inuit women full time, 2 white men full time and 4 part time,

2 white women part time. An intinerating extension program.
The Kotzebue facility is operated full time. The itinerant
ministry seeks to reach all the village churches with one or
two week classes. The itinerant program has enrolled over 200
students, mostly older men and women. A programmed learning
course is now in the planning.

MT. ECHO BIBLE INSTITUTE, INC. 1953. Iroquois and others.
Pumpkin Hollow Road, Great Valley, New York 14741. Rev. W. Dale
Welch, Director. Purpose is to train Indian Christian leadership for the reservations. Course: three years post high
school. Entrance requirements: high school graduation or
equivalent, membership in a local church. Expenses about $600
per year. Teachers: 2 white men, 1 white woman. Students in
1975-76: 5 men, 6 women. 4 graduated in previous year.
Graduates become pastors, pastors' wives, Christian education
teachers. Tribes represented: Blackfoot, Seneca, Seminole,
Tuscarora, Cayuga.

NAVAJO BIBLE INSTITUTE. 1953. Navajo Gospel Crusade,
Route 1, Box 7, Cortez, Colorado 81321. *(303)565-3290.* Rev.
Arthur S. Norris, Principal. Applicants must be 18 years and
above. High school graduation is desired but not required.
Applicants must be born again and sign agreement to abide by
rules. 4 year course leading to diploma. Certificate is
awarded to non-English speaking students. Tuition: $100 per
year. Boarding. Administrative staff 4. Teachers 7. Students
in 1977-78: 6 men, 8 women. 13 graduated between 1967-77.
Listen, published 11 months of the year.

NAZARENE INDIAN BIBLE SCHOOL. 2315 Markham Road, S.W.,
Albuquerque, New Mexico 87105. *(505)877-0240.* Rev. Merle Gray,
Superintendent. Wayne Stark, Acting Superintendent. Four year
course in theology and practice, four year course for Director
of Christian Education. 6 teachers. 3 couples graduated in
1977.

SOUTHWEST PENTECOSTAL INDIAN BIBLE SCHOOL. Pentecostal
Church of God. 2000 West Buckeye Road, Phoenix, Arizona 85009.
Will open in 1978.

CONTINUING PASTORAL AND MISSIONARY EDUCATION

INDIAN CHURCH MINISTRIES. P. O. Box 41, Oraibi, Arizona
86039. *(602)725-3263.* Thomas A. Dolaghan, Director. Navajo
Gospel Mission. Short term training for urban ministries,
Navajo evangelistic teams, theological education by extension,
missionary orientation, cross-cultural factors, conferences and
workshops, church support ministry, research and publication.

LEARNING CENTERS

ST. VALERIAN CATHOLIC INDIAN CENTER. 506 West 66th Avenue,
Gallup, New Mexico 87301. *(505)863-9261.* Sister M. Daniel
Ignatius, SBS, Director. Staff: 4 Sisters of the Blessed
Sacrament. The Center assists Native Americans, chiefly Navajo,
in transition from BIA boarding schools to Diocesan or public
day schools, offering students basic courses which will enable
them to feel secure when they become part of an integrated
situation and prevent them from becoming dropouts.

HIGH SCHOOLS

BISHOP KELLEY HIGH SCHOOL. 1960. 3905 South Hudson, Tulsa,
Oklahoma 74135. *(918)627-3390.* Sister Ida Marie Deville,
Principal. Day School. Grades 9-12. Administrative staff 37,
including Indians. 1 Indian man teacher. Indian boys 51,
Indian girls 56, total 106. *Perspective*, every four weeks.

BRAINERD INDIAN SCHOOL. 1946. Star Route, Box 167, Hot
Springs, South Dakota 57747. *(605)745-3733.* Wesleyan Church.
J. Franklin Heer, President and Principal. Grades 7-12.
Administrative staff 2. Teachers: 6 white men, 5 white women.
Other staff: 6 white men, 13 white women. Students: 9 Indian
boys, 21 Indian girls, total 30.

COVENANT HIGH SCHOOL. 1954. P. O. Box 184, Unalakeet, Alaska
99684. *(907)624-3282.* Alfred S. White, Principal. Evangelical
Covenant Church of America. Day and boarding. Grades 9-12.
Administrative staff 5. Teachers: 3 white men, 4 white women,
1 Inuit woman. Students: 32 Inuit boys, 42 Inuit girls,
total 74.

EAST FORK LUTHERAN HIGH SCHOOL. Apache. P. O. Box 128,
East Fork, Arizona 85943. James R. Opitz, Principal. Wisconsin
Evangelical Lutheran Synod. Day and boarding. Grades 9-12.
Teachers: Reginal Riesop, Eugene Caruss, Deborah Eaton, Nelson
Zimmermann, Margo Semon, Roxanne Farrell, Peter Bauer.
Students 99.

LABRE INDIAN HIGH SCHOOL. Ashland, Montana 59003.
(406)784-2347. Ray Streeter, Superintendent. Fred Mesteth,
Principal. School sisters of St. Francis 3. Lay teachers 25.
Students 107 boys, 89 girls, total 196.

MARTY INDIAN SCHOOL. See under ELEMENTARY SCHOOLS.

MENAUL SCHOOL. 1881. 301 Menaul Blvd., N.E., Albuquerque, New Mexico 87107. Edmundo Vasquez, President. United Presbyterian Church in the U.S.A. Open to all ethnic groups now. Grades 9-12. Administrative staff 4. Teachers: 10 white men, 11 white women. Students: 3 Indian boys, 5 girls, total 8.

NAVAJO METHODIST MISSION SCHOOL. Navajo Reservation. United Methodist Church. 1200 West Apache, Farmington, New Mexico 87401. *(505)325-7578.* Rev. Hector M. Navas, Director. Boarding. Grades 7-12. Administrative staff 3. Teachers: 7 white men, 2 Navajo women. Students: 39 boys, 53 girls, total 92.

RED CLOUD INDIAN HIGH SCHOOL. Pine Ridge, South Dakota 57770. Fr. William Stolz, S.J., Principal. Teachers: 9 religious, 31 lay. Students 231.

REHOBETH CHRISTIAN SCHOOL. 1903. Navajo. Navajo Reservation. Christian Reformed Church. Box 41, Rehobeth, New Mexico 87332. *(505)863-6091.* Keith Kupers, Superintendent. Day school 140, boarding 180. Grades 1-12. Administrative staff 2. Teachers: 2 Indian men, 7 white men, 7 Indian women, 2 white women. Students: 120 boys, 132 girls, total 252.

ST. CATHERINE INDIAN SCHOOL. Pueblo. P. O. Box 1883, Santa Fe, New Mexico 87501. *(505)982-1889.* Sister Katherine, Director. Sisters of the Blessed Sacrament. Day and boarding. Grades 7-12. Administrative staff 4. Teachers: 10 Sisters of the Blessed Sacrament, 1 of them Indian. 6 lay women, 6 lay men, 2 Brothers, 1 Priest. Day students 32, boarders 206. Indian boys 109, Indian girls 98.

ST. MARY'S HIGH SCHOOL. Yupik Eskimo. St. Mary's, Alaska 99658. Rev. James R. Landwein, S.J., Administrator. Sister Francis X. Porter, OSU, Principal. Diocese of Fairbanks, Society of Jesus, Order of St. Ursula. Day and boarding. Jesuit Brothers 3. Ursuline Sisters 9. Sister of St. Ann 1. Jesuit lay volunteers 21. Day students 40, boarders 120, total 160.

ST. MARY'S SCHOOL FOR INDIAN GIRLS. Sioux. Springfield, South Dakota 57062. Kenyon Gull, Headmaster. Episcopal Church. Grades 5 through high school.

ST. MICHAEL'S HIGH SCHOOL. St. Michael's, Arizona 85611. Sister Anne Regina, Principal. Sisters of the Blessed Sacrament. SBS Sisters 13, lay women teachers 2, lay men 2, Priests 2. Indian girls 110.

SOUTHWEST INDIAN SCHOOL. World Gospel Mission, 14202 North
73rd Street, Peoria, Arizona 85345. Rev. Doug Carter, Superintendent. Boarding school. Grades 2-12. Indian teachers:
1 man, 3 women. White teachers: 6 men, 7 women. Students 180.

VICTORY HIGH SCHOOL. Palmer, Alaska 99645. Boarding school
operated by Arctic Missions, Inc. Boarding students in this
school and Arctic Bible Institute number 80-90.

Summary for High Schools: Schools 15. Students about 1,761.
Teaching staff 260.

ELEMENTARY SCHOOLS

ROMAN CATHOLIC

HOLY CHILDHOOD INDIAN BOARDING SCHOOL. 150 West Main
Street, Harbor Springs, Michigan 49740. Sisters of Notre Dame.
Sr. Helen Setterston, Principal. 12 Sisters, 1 Brother.
Pupils 81.

HOLY FAMILY - ST. FRANCIS CONSOLIDATED SCHOOL. P. O.
Box 689, 232 North First Street, Bayfield, Wisconsin 59814.
(715)779-3342. John H. Diehl, Administrator. Day school.
Grades 1-8. Administrative staff: 1 man. Teachers: 1 white
man, 2 Sisters of St. Francis of Mary Immaculate, 3 lay women.
Students: 24 Indian boys, 47 girls, total 71.

HOLY NAME SCHOOL. 433 Jackson, Ketchikan, Alaska 99901.
(907)225-2400. Sister Andrea Nenzel, Principal/Superintendent.
Day school. Grades 1-6. Administrative staff: 6. Teachers:
2 white men, 3 Sisters of St. Joseph of Peace, 2 lay women.
Pupils: 6 Indian boys, 8 Indian girls, 1 Aleut boy, 2 Aleut
girls.

HOLY ROSARY SCHOOL. 2430 18th Avenue, South, Minneapolis,
Minnesota 55404. Sr. Kathleen Hayes, Principal. Sisters 6,
lay teachers 5. Pupils 160, Indians 95.

LABRE INDIAN SCHOOL. 1887. Northern Cheyenne. Ashland,
Montana 59003. *(406)784-2347.* School Sisters of St. Francis,
Capuchin Order. Day and boarding. Grades K-12. See LABRE
HIGH SCHOOL.

MARTY INDIAN SCHOOL. (Dakota Institute of Learning).
Yankton Sioux. Marty, South Dakota 57361. Sisters of the
Blessed Sacrament. Day and boarding. K to 8 grades. SBS
Sisters 4, OSBS 1, women lay teachers 6, lay men teachers 1.
Pupils 150.

OUR LADY OF LOURDES ELEMENTARY SCHOOL. Box 2, Porcupine, South Dakota 57772. Religious 4, lay teachers 6. Pupils 174.

RED CLOUD INDIAN GRADE SCHOOL. Pine Ridge, South Dakota 57770. Staff: Religious 4, lay teachers 37. Students 274.

SACRED HEART SCHOOL. Navajo. Farmington, New Mexico 87401. Ursuline Sisters. Sr. Charles Marie, Superintendent. Sisters 6, lay teachers 6. Pupils 265.

ST. ANN'S SCHOOL. Penobscot. Indian Island, Old Town, Maine 04468. Sr. Helen McKeogh, RSM, Principal. Teachers: Srs. Mary Florence and Gheresa R., RSM. A school supported by the State.

ST. ANN'S SCHOOL. Passamaquoddy. Peter Dana Point, Indian Township, Princeton, Maine 04668. *(207)796-2359.* Sisters of Charity: Janet Campbell, Prinicpal; Anne Marie Kiah, Carol Letourneau, Janet Spelman. School supported by the State.

ST. ANN'S SCHOOL. Passamaquoddy-Micmac. Pleasant Point, Perry, Maine 04667. Sisters of Charity: Anselma Colford, Principal; Mary Kelley, Maureen Wallace. School is supported by the State.

ST. ANTHONY SCHOOL. Menominee. Neopit, Wisconsin 54150. Sister Karen Krahenbuhl, Principal. Franciscan Sisters of Christian Charity of Manitowoc, Wisconsin. Grades 1-6. Sisters teaching 3½, lay women teachers 3½. Teacher aides: 5 Indian women, 2 Indian men. 1 Indian woman clerical aide. Pupils: boys 55, girls 57, total 112.

ST. ANTHONY MISSION SCHOOL. 1923. Zuni. P. O. Box 486, Zuni, New Mexico 87327. *(505)782-4477.* Rev. Meldon Hickey, Director. Day school. Grades K-8. Administrative staff 2. Teachers: 1 Indian man, 2 white men, 8 white women, 10 Zuni teacher aides. Pupils: boys 122, girls 118, total 240.

ST. AUGUSTINE'S SCHOOL. Winnebago, Nebraska 68071. Teachers 7. Pupils 101.

ST. FRANCIS ELEMENTARY SCHOOL. P. O. Box 96, Lumberton, New Mexico 87547. *(505)759-3252.* Sister Michele Mick, Prinicpal. St. Francis Parish School. Mixed. Grades 1-8. Poor Sisters of St. Francis Seraph of the Perpetual Adoration. Administrative staff 2. Teachers: Sisters 2, lay teacher 1. Pupils: 96 in all, 27 Indian girls, 32 Indian boys, total Indians 59.

ST. FRANCIS SOLANUS ELEMENTARY SCHOOL. Route 2, Stone Lake, Wisconsin 54876. Sister M. Felissa Zander, OSF,

Principal. Sr. Mary Rose Theobold, OSF, Sister Polykarp
Haseidle, OSF. Pupils 98.

ST. IGNATIUS SCHOOL. Chippewa. New Post, Route 2, Stone
Lake, Wisconsin 54876. 1 Sister, 4 lay teachers. Pupils 120.

ST. JOHN'S INDIAN SCHOOL. 1900. Pima, Maricopa. Route 1,
Box 751, Laveen, Arizona 85339. *(602)243-4303.* Rev. Walter
Holly, OFM, Superintendent. Sister Patricia Ellen Owens,
Principal. Franciscan Sisters of Christian Charity. Grades
1-8. Teachers: Sisters 3, lay teacher 1, teacher aides
(Indian) 2. Pupils: boys 25, girls 35, total 60. The high
school and boarding school closed in May 1977.

ST. JOSEPH INDIAN SCHOOL. Chamberlain, South Dakota 57325.
(605)734-5509. Rev. Thomas J. Cassidy, SCJ, Superintendent.
Deacon Joseph DiVenuto, Principal. Boarding school. 6
Brothers, 17 lay teachers. Pupils 210.

ST. JOSEPH SCHOOL. 1873. Menominee. P. O. Box 488, Keshena,
Wisconsin 54135. Fr. Joseph Hagan, OFM, pastor. Sister Mary
Cornelius, CSJ, Principal. Sisters of St. Joseph of Carondelet.
Originally a boarding high school for Indians only, now the
parish day elementary school for all children. Grades 1-8.
Administrative staff 8, including 6 Indians. Teachers: 5
Sisters, 2 lay teachers. Students: Indian boys 42, girls 42.

ST. MARY'S SCHOOL. P. O. Box 2455, Kodiak, Alaska 99615.
(907)486-3513. Sister Diane Bardol, GNSH, Principal. Grey Nuns
of the Sacred Heart. Sisters 3, lay teachers 3. Pupils 123.

ST. MARY'S MISSION SCHOOL. 1889. Red Lake Reservation.
Red Lake, Minnesota 56671. *(218)679-3388.* Sister Elizabeth
Theis, OSB, Principal. Grades 1-6. Benedictine Sisters (of
St. Joseph, Minnesota) 4. Title I teachers, 4 white women,
4 Indian women aides. Pupils: Indian boys 66, Indian girls
76, total 142.

ST. MICHAEL'S INDIAN SCHOOL. 1902. Navajo. P. O. Box 130,
St. Michaels, Arizona 86511. Sister M. Theodore, Director.
Sister Anne Regina, Principal. Sisters of the Blessed
Sacrament. Teachers: Sisters 10, 3 are Indians; lay teachers
10. Three of the Sisters in the elementary and high schools
are Indians. Pupils: boys 173, girls 193, total 366.

ST. PAUL'S MISSION GRADE SCHOOL. 1885. Hays, Montana
59527. *(406)673-4231.* Sister M. Griswalda, OSF, Principal.
Sisters of St. Francis. Grades 1-8. Administrative staff 2.
Teachers: 2 men, Sisters 5, lay teachers 3. Pupils: boys 23,
girls 33, total 56.

ST. PETER'S MISSION SCHOOL. Pima. P. O. Box 886, Bapchule,
Arizona 85221. Sister Mary Casey, OSF, Principal. Teachers:
Sr. Jennifer Hansen, OSF; Sr. Pamela Biehl, OSF. 1 Indian
teacher aide. Pupils 88.

ST. STEPHEN'S SCHOOL. 2211 Clinton Avenue, South,
Minneapolis, Minnesota 55404. Sr. Jean Funk, Principal. Srs.
Jackie Lawson, Carol Ann Richter, Margaret Brown. 8 lay
teachers. 38% of pupils are Indian, i.e. 64.

ST. STEPHEN'S SCHOOL. Arapaho. P. O. Box 294, St. Stephen's,
Wyoming 82524. 10 Sisters of St. Francis of Philadelphia, 6
Servants of the Immaculate Heart of Mary. 1 Sister of St.
Joseph.

SAN DIEGO MISSION SCHOOL. 1907. Pueblo. Jemez Pueblo, New
Mexico 87024. *(505)834-7300.* Sister Alberta Wieser, Principal.
Poor Sisters of St. Francis Seraph of the Perpetual Adoration.
Sisters 6, Priests 2, lay teachers 6, including 1 Indian,
teachers aides 9, including 1 Indian. Pupils: boys 83, girls
82, total 165.

SAN ANTONIO DE PALA SCHOOL. Mission Indians. Pala
Reservation. P. O. Box 80, Pala, California 92059. Sisters of
the Blessed Sacrament 7, lay teachers 2. Grades K-8. Pupils
162.

SAN CARLOS MISSION SCHOOL. Apache. San Carlos Reservation.
P. O. Box 338, San Carlos, Arizona 85550. Sister Alice Carmel
Reynolds, Principal. Sisters of the Blessed Sacrament 4: Sr.
Patricia Murray, 2nd grade; Sr. Maureen Hynes, 1st grade; Sr.
Regina Douglas, 3rd grade. Lay teachers 3. Pupils 108.
Religious education (CCD). 75 Indians participate.

SAN XAVIER MISSION SCHOOL. Papago. San Xavier Reservation.
Route 11, Tucson, Arizona 85706. Sisters of St. Francis.
Pupils 200.

Summary of Elementary Schools: Schools 32. Pupils 3,905+.
Teachers: Sisters 133 (including
4 Indians), lay women 194 (1
Indian), teachers aides 23 Indian
women, 8 white women. 1 Brother.
2 Priests. 7 white men, 5 Indian
men, 17 laymen not differentiated.
Total teaching staff 195.

PROTESTANT

ALL SAINTS' SCHOOL. Sioux Falls, South Dakota 57101.

Episcopal Church. Mrs. Mary Lou Kelley, Headmistress. Nursery, kindergarden, grades 1-6.

BRETHREN IN CHRIST SCHOOL. Navajo. Route 4, Box 6000, Bloomfield, New Mexico 87413. *(505)325-2006.* Dr. Marion Heisey, Administrator. Day and boarding. Grades K-6. Administrative staff 6. Teachers: 1 white man, 5 white women. Pupils: boys 34, girls 3, total 37.

EAST FORK LUTHERAN ELEMENTARY SCHOOL. 1895. Apache. Fort Apache Reservation. Wisconsin Evangelical Lutheran Synod. Day and boarding. Grades K-8. Pupils 173. See EAST FORK HIGH SCHOOL.

GETHSEMANE LUTHERAN DAY SCHOOL. Apache. Fort Apache Reservation. Wisconsin Evangelical Lutheran Synod. Cibecue, Arizona 85901. Wayne Cole, Principal. Mrs. Beth Serve, teacher. Grades 1-8. Pupils 64.

HOPI MISSION SCHOOL. 1951. Hopi. Hopi Reservation. Under control of a Hopi Mission School Board appointed by 6 Hopi Protestant churches and supported financially by the General Conference Mennonite Church. Grades K-8. 1 teacher is Hopi, also the secretary-bookkeeper, cook, kitchen help and bus driver (i.e. 4 women, 1 man). 4 teachers are white Mennonite women, 1 man. Mennonite Voluntary Service assists. Tuition $100.

NAVAJO BIBLE ACADEMY. 1930. Navajo. Navajo Reservation. Navajo Gospel Mission. Oraibi, Arizona 86039. Walter McCully, Administrator. Day and boarding. Grades K-8. Administrative staff 1. Teachers: 5 white women. Dormitory and dining room personnel: Navajo women 2, white women 4, white men 1. Pupils: Indian boys 24, girls 34, total 58 (2 white children). Small school and dorm fees and for those who need help a sponsor is obtained.

NAVAJO BIBLE SCHOOL AND MISSION, INC. Elementary School. Navajo Reservation. Window Rock, Arizona 86515. Teachers: 1 Navajo woman, 3 white women, 2 white men. Pupils 55.

OUR SAVIOR LUTHERAN SCHOOL. 1926. Apache. San Carlos Reservation. Wisconsin Evangelical Lutheran Synod. General Delivery, Bylas, Arizona 85530. Willis Hadler, Principal. Day school. Grades K-8. Administrative staff 1. Teachers: 1 white man, 3 white women. Pupils 151.

REHOBETH CHRISTIAN SCHOOL. 1903. Navajo. Navajo Reservation. Christian Reformed Church. Box 41, Rehobeth, New Mexico 87332. See REHOBETH HIGH SCHOOL.

ROCK POINT LUTHERAN ELEMENTARY SCHOOL. Navajo. Navajo Reservation. Navajo Evangelical Lutheran Mission. Roger Rorback, Principal. Grades 1-6. Teachers: 1 Navajo, 4 white. Pupils: boys 21, girls 22, total 43.

SEVENTH DAY ADVENTIST MISSION SCHOOL. 1945. Navajo. P. O. Box 880, Holbrook, Arizona. Earl Spaulding, Principal. Pupils 44.

SEVENTH DAY ADVENTIST MISSION SCHOOL. Dakota. P. O. Box 380, Pine Ridge, South Dakota 57770. Guy L. Gatewood, Principal. Pupils 42.

SOUTHWEST INDIAN SCHOOL. Mixed tribes. World Gospel Mission, 14202 North 73rd Avenue, Peoria, Arizona 85345. *(602)979-6008.* Rev. Doug Carter, Superintendent. A service mission to other missions. Boarding school. Grades 2-12. See under HIGH SCHOOLS.

ZUNI CHRISTIAN REFORMED MISSION SCHOOL. Zuni. P. O. Box 445, Zuni Pueblo, New Mexico 87327. *(505)783-4546.* Miss Wanda VanKlompenberg, Principal. Day school. Grades 1-8. Administrative staff 5. Teachers: 2 white men, 3 white women. Students: boys 49, girls 39, total 88.

VII
CHRISTIAN
POPULATION
REPORTS

VII
CHRISTIAN POPULATION
REPORTS

TRIBES OR NATIONS

Note: The tribes are not always indicated. Inferences have been
        made from locations. Determination could not be made for
        many churches. BIA registration figures of 1973 are given
        when possible. Inclusive membership figures are given
        when provided.

ACOMA. Acoma Pueblo, New Mexico. Population 1,980.
            Pentecostal Church of God: 1 church, 40 members.
            Roman Catholic Church: 4 churches and chapels, about
            3,000 members.
            Southern Baptist Convention: 1 church, 105 members,
            250 community (Acoma-Laguna).

ALABAMA-COUSHATTA. Polk County, Texas. Reported population
    360.
            Assemblies of God: 1 church, 130 members.
            A few independent Baptist churches.

ALASKAN NATIVE PEOPLES. Population 61,026. Aleuts;
    Athabascan, Haida, Tlingit and Tsimshian Indians; Eskimos or
    Inuit. Total churches about 309. Inclusive membership about
    38,000

    Aleuts: Orthodox Church in America: 51+ churches.
             Slavic Gospel Mission: 6 churches.

Eskimos or Inuit:
> American Lutheran Church: 5 churches, 3,048 communicants, 3,600 inclusive membership.
> Central Alaska Mission: 3 churches, 118 members (Eskimos and Indians).
> Christian and Missionary Alliance: 1 church, 50 members.
> Episcopal Church: 4 churches plus 1 mixed, 1,500 members.
> Evangelical Covenant Church: 14 churches, 374 members.
> Friends Church: 12 churches, 630 members.
> Moravian Church: 22 churches, inclusive membership about 2,600.
> Orthodox Church: 27 churches.
> Southern Baptist Convention: 11 churches.
> United Presbyterian Church: 8 churches, 1,326 members.
> Roman Catholic Church: (Eskimos with Indians) 31 churches, 10,500 members.

Athabascans:
> Arctic Mission: 6 churches, 202 members.
> Episcopal Church: 18 churches, 2,985 members.
> Orthodox Church: 5 churches.
> Pentecostal Church of God: 2 churches (mixed), 120 members.
> Southern Baptist Convention: 3 churches.
> Roman Catholic Church:
> United Presbyterian Church: 9 churches, 719 members.

Tlingit: Orthodox Church: 5 churches.
> Salvation Army: 10 Corps.

Tsimshian:
> 1 Independent Church
> Salvation Army: 1 Corps.
> United Presbyterian Church: 1 church.

APACHE.
1. White Mountain Apaches. Fort Apache Reservation, Arizona. Population 7,200.
   > Assemblies of God: 2 churches, 120 members.
   > Roman Catholic Church: 1 church.
   > Southern Baptist Convention: 1 church, 131 members, 200 community.
   > Wisconsin Lutheran Church: 9 churches, 589 communicant members.

2. San Carlos Reservation, Arizona. Population 5,097.
   > Assemblies of God: 1 church, 40 members.
   > Roman Catholic Church: 1 church.

Southern Baptist Convention: 1 church, 47 members,
   60 community.
Wisconsin Lutheran: 4 churches, 624 communicant
   members.

3. Chiricahua Apaches, Oklahoma.
      American Baptist Churches: 1 church.
      Pentecostal Church of God: 1 church, 20 members
         (other tribes also).
      Reformed Church in America: 1 church, 77 members.

4. Jicarilla Apaches. Jicarilla Reservation, New Mexico.
      Population 1,963.
      Assemblies of God: 1 church, 35 members.
      Reformed Church in America: 1 church, 37 members.
      Southern Baptist Convention: 1 church, 32 members.

5. Mescalero Apaches. Mescalero Reservation. New Mexico.
      Population 1,987.
      Reformed Church in America: 1 church, 81 members.
      Roman Catholic Church: 1 church, 65 members.
      Southern Baptist Convention: 1 church, 43 members.

6. Kiowa-Apache or Prairie Apache. Oklahoma.
      Pentecostal Church of God: 3 churches.

ARAPAHO. Oklahoma.
      American Baptist Church: 1 church, 300 members.
      General Conference Mennonite Church: 1 church, 34
         members, 54 community.
      Pentecostal Church of God: 1 church (with Kiowas,
         etc.).
      Roman Catholic Church. 1 church.
      United Methodist Church: represented in some Cheyenne
         churches.

   Northern Arapaho. Wind River Reservation, Wyoming.
      Episcopal Church: 1 church, 360 members.
      Roman Catholic Church: 2 churches, 900 members.

ARIKARA. Fort Berthold Reservation, North Dakota.
      Episcopal Church: 1 church, 135 members (with Mandan
         and Gros Ventre).
      United Church of Christ: 8 churches, 355 members.
      Roman Catholic Church.

ASSINIBOINE. Fort Peck Reservation, Montana. Churches are
   Assiniboine-Sioux.
      Pentecostal Church of God: 1 church, 50 members.
      Roman Catholic Church: 5 churches, 1,268 members.

Southern Baptist Convention: 2 churches, 104 members.

BLACKFEET. Montana.
Roman Catholic Church:
Southern Baptist Convention: 1 church.
United Methodist Church: 1 church, 112 members.

BANNOCK. Shoshone-Bannock. Fort Hall Reservation, Idaho.
Population 2,782.
Episcopal Church: 1 church.
Roman Catholic Church: 1 church, 1 church partial.
Southern Baptist Convention: 1 church, 44 members.

CADDO. Oklahoma.
Southern Baptist Convention: 1 church.
United Methodist Church: 2 churches, 112 members.

CAWTABA TRIBE. South Carolina.
Church of Jesus Christ of Latter Day Saints: entire
tribe.

CAYUGA. Oklahoma.
Friends: 1 church (combined with Seneca).

CAYUSE. Oregon.
Roman Catholic Church: 1 church, 350 members (with
Umatilla and Walla Wala).

CENTRAL CALIFORNIA INDIANS.
Assemblies of God: 3 churches.
Roman Catholic Church: Fresno Diocese—4 churches,
2,500 members.
Sacramento Diocese—1 church, 250 members.
United Methodist Church: 1 church, 16 members.
United Presbyterian Church: 1 church, 42 members.

CHEMEHUEVI. Colorado River Reservation, Arizona-California.
Pentecostal Church of God: 1 church, 50 members (with
Mohave).
Roman Catholic Church: 1 church.
United Presbyterian Church: 1 church, 35 members
(with Mohave).

CHEROKEES, EASTERN. North Carolina and Tennessee.
Episcopal Church: 1 church, 15 members.
United Methodist Church: 1 church, 214 members.
Southern Baptist Convention: North Carolina - 9
churches, 1,167+ members. Tennessee - 1 church.

CHEROKEES, OKLAHOMA
American Lutheran Church: 1 church, 105 members.
United Methodist Church: 11 churches, 509 members.
Roman Catholic Church: 1 church partial.
Southern Baptist Convention: 45 churches, 4,716
members.

CHEYENNE, OKLAHOMA. Concho Agency – 4,200 Cheyenne and
Arapaho.
American Baptist Church: 2 churches, 600 members.
Episcopal Church: 1 church, 36 members.
General Conference Mennonite Church: 3 churches, 229
members.
Pentecostal Church of God: 3 churches, 140 members
(mixed).
Roman Catholic Church: 1 church.
Southern Baptist Convention: 2 churches, 288 members.

CHEYENNE, NORTHERN. Montana.
General Conference Mennonite Church: 4 churches, 96
members.
Pentecostal Church of God: 2 churches, 100 members.
Roman Catholic Church: 3 churches, 1,000 members.

CHICKAHOMINY. Virginia.
Southern Baptist Convention: 1 church, 41 members.

CHICKASAW. Oklahoma. Ardmore Agency. Population 6,050.
Pentecostal Church of God: 2 churches, 120+ members.
Presbyterian Church in the U.S.: 1 church, 78 members.
United Methodist Church: 4 churches, 200 members.
Southern Baptist Convention: 25 churches, 862 members
(Choctaw–Chickasaw Association). Others: 14
churches, 900 members.

CHIPPEWAS.
Michigan: Roman Catholic Church: 0 churches, 300 members.
United Methodist Church: 9 churches, 152+ members.

Wisconsin: Roman Catholic Church: 16 churches, 5,539 members.
United Methodist Church: 1 church, 29 members, (some
Ojibway).
United Presbyterian Church: 3 churches, 259 members.

Minnesota: American Lutheran Church: 3 churches, 160 members.
Christian and Missionary Alliance: 3 churches, 120
members.
Episcopal Church: 8 churches, 2,090 members.
Roman Catholic Church: 8 churches, 805 members.

CHITIMACHA. St. Mary's Parish, Louisiana. Population 270.
    Roman Catholic Church: 1 church partial, 55 members.

CHOCTAW, EASTERN. Mississippi. Population 3,379.
    Mennonite Church: 6 churches, 70 members, 75 community.
    Pentecostal Church of God: 1 church, 70 members.
    Roman Catholic Church: 3 churches, 1,020 members.
    Southern Baptist Convention: 14 churches, 1,096
      members. Tennessee: 1 church, 40 members.
    United Methodist Church: 2 churches, 182 members, 500
      community.

CHOCTAW, OKLAHOMA.
    Assemblies of God: 1 church, 17 members.
    Cumberland Presbyterian Church: 14 churches, 432
      members.
    Pentecostal Church of God: 1 church, 20 members.
    Presbyterian Church in the U.S.: 2 churches, 106
      members.
    Southern Baptist Convention: Choctaw-Chickasaw 39
      churches, 1,762 members.
    United Methodist Church: 40 churches, 1,324 members.
    United Presbyterian Church: 16 churches, 541 members.

COCOPAH. Arizona and California. (Yuma and Winterhaven)
    Assemblies of God: 1 church, Sunday School 40.
    Roman Catholic Church: 1 church, 450 members.
    United Methodist Church: 1 church, 96 members (with
      Quechan).

COLVILLE. Washington.
    United Methodist Church: 1 church, 36 members, 53
      community.

COMANCHE. Oklahoma.
    American Baptist Churches: 2 churches.
    Church of the Nazarene: 2 churches, 120 members.
    Pentecostal Church of God: 1 church, 80+ members.
    Reformed Church in America: 1 church, 72 members.
    United Methodist Church: 6 churches, 675 members.

COUER D'ALENE. Washington.
    Roman Catholic Church: 3 churches.

CREE. Montana.
    Lutheran Church in America: 1 church, 163 confirmed
      members, 347 baptized.

CREEKS, ALABAMA.
    Southern Baptist Convention: 1 church, 66 members.

The Citronella area churches: 10 churches, 1,220
members.

CREEKS, OKLAHOMA. Okmulgee Agency. Population 15,480.
Southern Baptist Convention: Muskogee-Seminole-Wichita
Association; 67 churches, 4,000 members.
San Francisco; 1 church, 68 members.
United Methodist Church: 17 churches, 596 members.

CROW. Montana. Reservation Population 4,344.
American Baptist Churches: 3 churches, 395 members,
595 community.
Pentecostal Church of God: 1 church, 40 members.
Roman Catholic Church: 5 churches and chapels. (Cree
and Sioux)

DAKOTAS OR SIOUX. North and South Dakota. Santee Reservation
in Nebraska
Protestant Churches:
Assemblies of God: 3 churches, 142 members.
Christian and Missionary Alliance: 3 churches, 65
members, 115 community.
Episcopal Church: 110 churches, 4,366 communicants,
8,501 baptized.
Mennonite Brethren Church: 2 churches, 37 members.
Seventh Day Adventist Church: 1 church, 45 members.
Southern Baptist Convention: 14 churches, 501 members.
United Church of Christ: 6 churches, 346 members.
United Presbyterian Church: 20 churches, 986 members.
Wesleyan Church:

Totals: 268 churches, 9,993 members.

Roman Catholic Church: 56 churches, 20,000 members.

Episcopal Church in Minnesota: 2 churches, 190
members. In Iowa: 1 church, 427 members.

Totals: 327 churches, 30,420 inclusive membership
or community.

DELAWARE. Oklahoma.
United Methodist Church: 1 church, 55 members.

EUCHA. Oklahoma.
United Methodist Church: 1 Eucha church, 87 members;
2 Eucha-Creek churches, 215 members.

GROS VENTRE. Fort Belknap, Montana.
Christian and Missionary Alliance: 1 church, 60 mem.

Roman Catholic Church: 14 churches, 1,000 members.

HALIWA TRIBE. North Carolina. Population 3,000.
Independent Churches: 5.

HIDATSA. Fort Berthold, North Dakota.

HOH. Western Washington. Population 53.
Southern Baptist Convention: summer Bible School.

HOOPA. Northern California.
Assemblies of God: 2 churches.
Roman Catholic Church: 1 church, 160 members.
Southern Baptist Convention: 1 church.
United Presbyterian Church: 1 church, 75 members.

HOPI. Arizona. Population 6,567.
American Baptist Churches: 3 churches, 41+ members.
General Conference Mennonite Church: 3 churches, 86 members.
Roman Catholic Church: 2 churches.
Widow's Mite Mission: 1 church.

HOUMA. Louisiana.
Roman Catholic Church: 5 churches, 6,420 members.
United Methodist Church: 1 church, 200 members.

HUALAPAI. Arizona.
United Indian Missions, Inc.: 1 church, 50 members.

IOWA. Kansas.

ISLETA. Isleta Pueblo, New Mexico. Population 2,681.
Roman Catholic Church: 1 church, 2,000 members.
Southern Baptist Convention: 1 church, 12 members.

JEMEZ. Jemez Pueblo, New Mexico. Population 1,953.
Assemblies of God: 1 church, 42 members.
Southern Baptist Convention: 1 church, 35 members.
Roman Catholic Church: 8 churches, 3,000 members.
United Presbyterian Church: 1 church, 24 members.

KICKAPOO. Oklahoma.
Friends: 1 church, 20 members.
Roman Catholic Church: 1 church mixed Pottawatomie and
white, 1,000 members.
United Methodist Church: 1 church, 65 members.

KIOWA. Oklahoma.
American Baptist Churches: 3 churches, 85 members in 1.

Pentecostal Church of God: 3 churches, mixed, about
90 members.
3 Kiowa-Apache churches.
United Methodist Church: 6 churches, 804 members.

KLALLAM.   Lower Elwha Reservation, Washington.   Population 224.
Assemblies of God: 1 church, 20 members.

KLAMATH.   Oregon.
Roman Catholic Church: 1 church partial, 129 members.
United Methodist Church: 2 churches (with Modoc), 129
members.

KOOTENAI.   Idaho.
Roman Catholic Church: 1 mission.

KUROC.   Round Valley Reservation, Central California.   Population
402.
Pentecostal Church of God: 1 church (with Yuroc).

LAGUNA.   Laguna Pueblo, New Mexico.   Population 4,883.
Church of the Nazarene: 1 church, 26 members.
Pentecostal Church of God: 1 church, 40 members.
Roman Catholic Church: 6 churches, about 4,000
members.
Southern Baptist Convention: 1 church, 105 members,
250 in community.
United Presbyterian Church: 1 church, 65 members.

LUMBEES.   North Carolina.   Population about 30,000.
Assemblies of God: 1 church, 20 members.
Christian and Missionary Alliance: 1 church, 125
members, 160 community
Seventh Day Adventists: 1 church.
Southern Baptist Convention: 48 churches, 6,147
members (adults).
United Methodist Church: 12 churches, 1,785 members.

MAKAH.   Washington.
Lutheran Church - Missouri Synod: 1 church, 10
members.

MANDAN.   North Dakota.
Mixed with others.

MARICOPA.   Arizona.   The Maricopa live with the Pima on the
Salt River and Gila River Reservations and the churches are
usually mixed.   See Pimas.   The Assemblies of God report one all
Maricopa church with 75 members and the Seventh Day Adventists
have one with 25 members.

MATTAPONI. Virginia.
>   Southern Baptist Convention: 1 church, 30 members.

MENOMINEE. Wisconsin.
>   Christian and Missionary Alliance: 1 church.
>   Orthodox Presbyterian Church: 1 church.
>   Roman Catholic Church: 2 churches, 1,800 members.
>   United Methodist Church: 1 ministry.

MICMAC. Maine.
>   Roman Catholic Church: 1 reservation church and 7
>   partial ones.

MODOC. Oregon.
>   United Methodist Church: 2 churches, 60 members (with
>   Klamath).

MOHAVE. Colorado River Reservation, Arizona and California.
>   Church of the Nazarene: 3 churches, 116 members (1
>   with Chemehuevi).
>   Pentecostal Church of God: 1 church, 50 members.
>   Roman Catholic Church: 1 church.

MOHAWK. St. Regis Reservation in New York on international
border. All churches at Hogansburg.
>   Assemblies of God: 1 church.
>   Roman Catholic Church: 1 church, reports 5,000
>   Catholic Indians in the diocese.
>   United Methodist Church: 1 church, 43 members.

MOHEGAN. Connecticut.
>   1 Independent congregational church at Uncasville.

NESPELEM. Washington.
>   Pentecostal Church of God: 1 church, 20 members.

MORONGO. Morongo Reservation, Southern California. Population
260.
>   Moravian Church: 1 church, 108 members, 186 community.

NAVAJO. Navajo Reservation and borders in Arizona, New Mexico,
Utah and Colorado. Population 136,386.

>   Churches and Missions:
>   American Indian Bible Mission: 4 churches, 90
>   communicants.
>   Assemblies of God: 13 churches, 1,224 communicants,
>   2,390 community
>   Berean Mission: 4 churches, 89 members.
>   Brethren in Christ: 2 churches, about 80 community.

Church of the Brethren: 1 church, 20 members, 40
community.
Church of God: 4 churches, 100 members, 400 community.
Church of the Nazarene: 17 churches, 922 members.
Conservative Baptist Home Mission Board: 5 churches,
68+ members.
Episcopal Church: 13 churches, 1,224 communicants,
2,390 baptized members.
Evangelical Church of N.A.: 8 churches, 233 members,
450 community.
Fellowship of Baptists for Home Missions: 4 churches,
30 members.
Flagstaff Mission to Navajos: 6 churches, 1,117
members.
Good News Mission: 3 churches, 60 members.
Independent Churches: 151 churches, 5,297 in
attendance.
Mennonite Church, General Conference: 2 churches, 65
members, 75 community.
Navajo Bible School and Mission: 9 churches, 200
members, 500 community.
Navajo Gospel Crusade: 2 churches, 70 members.
Navajo Gospel Mission: 18 churches, 425 members.
Navajo Missions: child care.
Pentecostal Church of God: 5 churches, 205 members.
Sanders Bible Mission: 1 church, 19 members.
Seventh Day Adventist Church: 3 churches, 428 members.
Southern Baptist Convention: 19 churches, 878 members.
United Indian Mission: 2 churches, 125 members.
United Methodist Church: 2 churches, 150 members,
250 community
TOTAL PROTESTANT CHURCHES - 309 churches, 16,398
community.

Roman Catholic Churches: 52 churches, 18,000 baptized
members. From 1873 to 1973 it is estimated that
there were 30,000 baptisms.

Mormon Church: number unknown. 8 are listed in the
Navajo telephone book. A large scale Mormon
evangelistic campaign was launched in the summer of
1978. 47 churches, 20,000 Mormons reported.

Fellowships: Navajo Evangelical Fellowship. See
Nondenominational Societies.
Western Navajo Bible Fellowship. A fellowship of
Navajo Christians in the Western third of the
reservation. Secretary: Rev. John Mexicano, P. O.
Box 254, Tuba City, Arizona 86045.

The Native American Christian Community

NEZ PERCE. Idaho.
> Church of God: 1 church, 40 members.
> Roman Catholic Church: 1 church.
> United Methodist Church: 1 church, 14 members, 85
> community.
> United Presbyterian Church: 5 churches, 146 members.

NOOSACK. Washington.
> United Methodist Church: 1 church, 72 members.

NORTHERN CALIFORNIA INDIANS, including Hoopa Valley. BIA
Hoopa Agency. Population 9,398.
> Assemblies of God: 4 churches.
> Roman Catholic Church: 7 churches, one reports 1,840
> members.
> Southern Baptist Convention: 1 church.

OMAHA. Nebraska.
> Reformed Church in America: 1 church, 81 communicant
> members.
> Roman Catholic Church: 1 mission, 280 members, Omaha
> and Winnebago.

ONEIDA. Wisconsin.
> Assemblies of God: 1 church, 75 members.
> Episcopal Church: 1 church, 800 members.
> United Methodist Church: 1 church, 235 communicant
> members, 348 community.

ONONDAGA. New York.
> Episcopal Church: 1 church, 65 members.
> United Methodist Church: 2 churches, 1 with 45
> members.

OSAGE. Oklahoma.
> Friends: 1 church, 20 members.
> Roman Catholic Church: 1 church, 750 members.
> Southern Baptist Convention: 1 church.

OTOE-MISSOURIA. Oklahoma.
> Pentecostal Church of God: 1 church mixed, 30 members.
> Southern Baptist Convention: 1 church, 184 members.

PAPAGO. Arizona. Population 8,435.
> Assemblies of God: 3 churches, 76 members.
> Church of the Nazarene: 2 churches, 87 members.
> Roman Catholic Church: 49 churches, 11,580 members.
> United Presbyterian Church: 3 churches, 199 members.

PAIUTE.   Nevada.
    Assemblies of God: 3 churches, 1 with 70 members.
    Pentecostal Church of God: 1 church.
    Southern Baptist Convention: 2 churches, 1 with 32
      members.
    United Methodist Church: 1 church, 24 members. Also
      1 Paiute-Modoc-Shoshone Church in Oregon, 26 members.
    United Presbyterian Church: 1 church, 103 members.

PAMUNKEY.   Virginia.
    Southern Baptist Convention: 2 churches, 123 members
      in 1.

PASSAMAQUODDY.   Maine.
    Roman Catholic Church: 2 churches, 1 with Micmac, on
      reservation and 5 partial off reservation churches.

PAWNEE.   Oklahoma.
    Roman Catholic Church: 1 church.
    United Methodist Church: 2 churches, 31 members in 1.

PENOBSCOT.   Maine.
    Roman Catholic Church: 1 reservation church, 5 partial
      Indian churches off the reservation.

PICURIS.   Picuris Pueblo, New Mexico. Population 173.
    Pentecostal Church of God: 1 church, 30 members.
    Roman Catholic Church: 1 church.

PIMA.   Arizona. Pima Agency. Population 8,597. Pima and
  Maricopa often in the same churches on the Salt River and Gila
  River Reservations.
    Assemblies of God: 1 church, 100 members.
    Church of the Nazarene: 1 church, 41 members.
    Roman Catholic Church: 3 churches, report that 25% of
      the Pima or about 2,000 are Catholic.
    United Presbyterian Church: 16 churches, 501 communi-
      cant members. The Pima are said to be 80-85%
      Presbyterian.

PONCA.   Oklahoma.
    Church of the Nazarene: 1 church, 39 members.
    United Methodist Church: 2 churches, 309 members.

POTAWATOMIE.
  Michigan: United Methodist Church: 3 churches, 38 members in 1.

  Oklahoma: Roman Catholic Church: 1 church, about 1,000
      members.
      United Methodist Church: 2 churches, 140 members.

PUEBLO PEOPLES. New Mexico

NORTHERN PUEBLO AGENCY

Nambe. Population 235.
Roman Catholic Church.

Picuris. Population 173.
Pentecostal Church of God: 1 church, 30 members.
Roman Catholic Church.

Pojoaque. Population 76.

San Ildefonso. Population 354.
Roman Catholic Church.

San Juan. Population 1,358.
Roman Catholic Church.

Santa Clara. Population 989.
Roman Catholic Church.
Southern Baptist Convention: 1 church, 32 members.

Taos. Population 1,494.
Pentecostal Church of God: 1 church, 40 members.
Roman Catholic Church: 1 church, about 1,000 members
   or 70% baptized. 200-250 attend Sunday Mass.
Southern Baptist Convention: 1 church, 82 members.

Tesuque. Population 249.
Roman Catholic Church. About 70 attend Sunday Mass.

SOUTHERN PUEBLO AGENCY.

Acoma. Population 1,980.
Pentecostal Church of God: 1 church, 40 members.
Roman Catholic Church: 4 churches, 3,000 members.
Southern Baptist Convention: 1 church (with Laguna),
   105 members, 250 community.

Cochiti. Population 488.

Isletta. Population 2,681.
Roman Catholic Church: 1 church, 2,000 members.
Southern Baptist Convention: 1 church, 12 members.

Jemez. Population 1,953.
Assemblies of God: 1 church, 42 members.
Roman Catholic Church: 8 churches, 3,000 members.
Southern Baptist Convention: 1 church, 35 members.

United Presbyterian Church: 1 church, 24 members.

Laguna. Population 4,883.
Pentecostal Church of God: 1 church (with Acoma),
40 members.
Roman Catholic Church: 6 churches, about 4,000
members.
United Presbyterian Church: 1 church, 65 members.
Laguna-Acoma Southern Baptist Church: 105 members,
250 communicants.

Sandia. Population 216.
Roman Catholic Church.

San Felipe. Population 1,645.
Roman Catholic Church.

Santa Anna. Population 392.
Roman Catholic Church.

Santo Domingo. Population 2,349.
Roman Catholic Church.

Zia. Population 508.
Roman Catholic Church.

ZUNI   Population 5,428.
Christian Reformed Church: 1 church, 35 members,
10 families.
Roman Catholic Church: 2 churches, about 30% or
1,600 baptized. About 250 attend Sunday Mass.
Southern Baptist Convention: 1 church, 31 members.

QUAPAW.   Oklahoma.
Southern Baptist Convention: 1 church, 260 members.

QUECHAN.   California (and Arizona).
Church of the Nazarene: 1 church, 61 members.
Roman Catholic Church: In Cocopah parish at Ft. Yuma.
United Methodist Church: 1 church, 96 members (Cocopah
and Quechan).

QUILEUTE. Washington.
Lutheran Church - Missouri Synod: 1 church, 25
members.

QUINALT.   Washington.
Southern Baptist Convention: a Bible Fellowship only.

RAPPAHANNOCK. Virginia.
Southern Baptist Convention: 1 church.

SAC and FOX, (SAUK). Iowa (575) and Kansas.
Some are a minority in certain Baptist and Methodist churches.

SEMINOLES. Everglades region in Florida. 4 Reservations.
Population 1,594.
Independent Baptist Churches 4.
Southern Baptist Convention: 6 churches and chapels, 515 members.
United Methodist Church: 1 church, 60 members.

SEMINOLES, Oklahoma. Wewoka Agency. Population 3,208.
Southern Baptist Convention: churches joined with Creeks and Wichita in the Muskogee-Seminole-Wichita Association: 67 churches, about 4,000 members.
United Methodist Church: 1 church, 280 members.
United Presbyterian Church: 4 churches, 175 members.

SENECA.
New York: United Presbyterian Church: 3 churches, 229 members.

Oklahoma: Friends: 2 churches mixed with Cayuga and Wyandot.

SHAWNEE. Oklahoma.
Southern Baptist Convention: 1 church.

SHINNECOOK. Long Island, New York.
United Presbyterian Church: 1 church, 198 members.

SHOSHONE.
Nevada: Pentecostal Church of God: 1 church, 20 members.
United Methodist Church: 1 church, 103 members.

Utah: Episcopal Church: 1 church.
Roman Catholic Church: 1 church.
Southern Baptist Convention: 1 Shoshone-Bannock church, 44 members.

Wyoming: Episcopal Church: 1 church, 957 members.
Roman Catholic Church: 1 church, 150 members.

SIOUX. See Dakota.

SOUTHERN CALIFORNIA INDIANS (MISSION INDIANS).
Roman Catholic Church: 7 churches on 7 reservations, 1,065 members.

STOCKBRIDGE-MUNSEE. Wisconsin.
Orthodox Presbyterian Church: 1 church.
Lutheran Church - Missouri Synod: 3 churches, 355
members.

TAOS. Taos Pueblo, New Mexico. Population 1,494.
Roman Catholic Church: 1 church, about 1,000 members.
Southern Baptist Convention: 1 church, 82 members.

TULALIP. Washington.
Church of God: 1 church, 55 communicant members, 100
community.

UMATILLA. Oregon.
Roman Catholic Church: 1 church (with Cayuse and
Walla Wala), 300 members.
United Presbyterian Church: 1 church, 42 members.

UTE. Colorado.
Episcopal Church: 2 churches, 300 members.
Roman Catholic Church: 2 churches, about 520 members.
Southern Baptist Convention: 2 churches, 191 members,
1 Bible Fellowship.
United Presbyterian Church: 1 church, 44 members.

WACCAMAW-SIOUAN. North Carolina.
Seventh Day Adventist Church: 1 group.

WAMPANOAG. Massachusetts.
American Baptist Church: 2 churches, 121 members, 1
church is Pawkumnawakutt.

WARM SPRINGS FEDERATED TRIBES. Oregon. Population 1,745.
Roman Catholic Church: 1 church, 40 members.
Southern Baptist Convention: 1 church, 100 members.
United Presbyterian Church: 1 church, 60 members.

WICHITA. Oklahóma.
American Baptist Church: 1 church.
Southern Baptist Churches: 67 churches in the
Muskogee-Seminole-Wichita Association, 4,000 members.
United Methodist Church: 1 church, 66 members.

WINNEBAGO.
Nebraska: Roman Catholic Church: 1 mission, 280 members (with
(Omaha).
Reformed Church in America: 1 church, 40 members.

Wisconsin: United Church of Christ: 1 church, 90 members.

WITCHEPEK. Northern California.
Southern Baptist Convention: 1 church with Hoopa.

WYANDOT. Oklahoma.
Friends: 1 church (mixed with Seneca).

YAKIMA. Population 6,300.
Assemblies of God: 1 church, 18 members.
Christian Church (Disciples): 2 churches, 75 members.
United Methodist Church: 1 church, 111 members, 222 community.

YAQUI. Three communities in southern Arizona.
Pentecostal Church of God: 1 church, 100 members.
Roman Catholic Church: 3 churches, 2 with 950 members.

YAVAPAI. Arizona.
United Indian Missions: 1 church, 20 members.
United Presbyterian Church: 1 church, 15 members.

ZUNI. Zuni Pueblo, New Mexico.
Christian Reformed Church: 1 church, 35 members.
Roman Catholic Church: 2 churches, 1,600 baptized members, 250 attend Sunday Mass.
Southern Baptist Convention: 1 church, 31 members.

U.S. CENSUS OF 1970 ON NATIVE AMERICAN POPULATION

STATE	GENERAL	URBAN	STATE	GENERAL	URBAN
Alabama	2,163	1,210	Montana	26,385	5,070
Alaska	61,080	4,696	Nebraska	6,671	3,332
Arizona	94,310	16,442	Nevada	7,476	2,832
Arkansas	2,088	1,225	New Hampshire	310	159
California	88,263	67,202	New Jersey	4,255	3,776
Colorado	8,002	5,421	New Mexico	71,582	13,405
Connecticut	2,322	1,859	New York	25,560	17,161
Delaware	479	180	North Carolina	44,195	6,194
Florida	6,392	4,275	North Dakota	13,565	1,810
Georgia	2,271	1,579	Ohio	6,181	5,079
Hawaii	1,168	1,034	Oklahoma	96,803	47,623
Idaho	6,646	1,990	Oregon	13,210	6,976
Illinois	10,304	9,542	Pennsylvania	5,543	4,412
Indiana	3,305	2,336	Rhode Island	1,417	1,224
Iowa	2,924	2,052	South Carolina	2,091	858
Kansas	8,261	6,130	South Dakota	31,043	9,115
Kentucky	1,322	934	Tennessee	1,432	1,095
Louisiana	4,519	1,543	Texas	16,921	14,567
Maine	1,872	856	Utah	10,551	3,689
Maryland	3,886	3,282	Vermont	204	15
Massachusetts	4,237	3,346	Virginia	4,862	3,055
Michigan	16,012	10,541	Washington	30,824	16,102
Minnesota	22,322	11,703	West Virginia	518	193
Mississippi	3,791	3,617	Wisconsin	18,776	7,439
Missouri	4,890	578	Wyoming	4,717	1,040
			U. S. Total	763,594	340,367

CHRISTIAN POPULATION BY STATES

Note: The Resident population figures are BIA estimates for March 1973. They are for reservations, but may include some still enrolled who have moved away. Christian population figures include urban church membership and Catholics unattached to city parishes but reported.

ALABAMA

Indian Population: 815 in communities, up to 10,000 Creek descendents.
Southern Baptist Convention: 11 churches, 1,330 members.

ALASKA

Total Eskimo, Aleut, Indian Population: 61,028

Orthodox Church: 83 churches, 20,000 members, 22,000 community.
Protestant Churches: 120 churches, 9,972 members, 10,940 community.
Roman Catholic Churches: 30 churches, 10,500 members.

Total Christian Community 43,440 (71%).

Missions: American Baptist (Child Care)
American Lutheran Church
Archdiocese of Anchorage, Roman Catholic Church
Arctic Missions, Inc.
Central Alaskan Missions, Inc.
Diocese of Alaska, Episcopal Church
Diocese of Fairbanks, Roman Catholic Church
Diocese of Juneau, Roman Catholic Church
Evangelical Covenant Church
Friends Church, California Yearly Meeting
Moravian Church in America
Pentecostal Church of God
Salvation Army   Slavic Gospel Mission
Southern Baptist Convention

ARIZONA

Resident Indian Population: 114,178

Protestant Churches: 255 churches, 12,238 members, 16,107 community.
Roman Catholic Church: 125 churches, 29,484 community.

Total 45,591

Churches and Missions:
American Baptist Churches
American Franciscan Missions, St. Barbara Province
American Franciscan Missions, St. John the Baptist Province
American Lutheran Church
Church of God
Church of God in Christ, Mennonite
Church of the Nazarene
Christian and Missionary Alliance
Conservative Baptist Home Missionary Society
Diocese of Arizona, Episcopal Church
Diocese of Gallup, Roman Catholic Church
Diocese of Phoenix, Roman Catholic Church
Diocese of Tucson, Roman Catholic Church
Evangelical Church of N.A.
Evangelical Lutheran Wisconsin Synod
Fellowship of Baptists for Home Missions

Flagstaff Mission to the Navajo Indians
Good News Mission to Navajo Indians
Lutheran Church - Missouri Synod
Mennonite Church
Mennonite Church, General Conference
Navajo Bible School and Mission
Navajo Evangelical Lutheran Mission
Navajo Gospel Mission
Pentecostal Church of God
Seventh Day Adventist Church
Sisters of the Blessed Sacrament
Southern Baptist Convention
United Indian Missions
United Methodist Church
United Presbyterian Church in U.S.A.
Independent Churches 68

CALIFORNIA

Resident Indian Population: 37,582

Protestant Churches: 23 churches, 871 members, 1,150 community.
Roman Catholic Church: 21 churches, 6,310 community.

Total 7,460

Churches and Missions:
Assemblies of God
Church of the Nazarene
Diocese of Fresno, Roman Catholic Church
Diocese of Sacramento, Roman Catholic Church
Diocese of San Diego, Roman Catholic Church
Moravian Church in America
Pentecostal Church of God
Southern Baptist Church
United Methodist Church
United Presbyterian Church in U.S.A.
Independent Churches

COLORADO

Resident Indian Population: 1,745

Protestant Churches: 8 churches, 118+ members, 180+ community.
Roman Catholic Church: 2,520 community.

Total 2,700

Churches and Missions:
Christian Reformed Church

> Diocese of Denver, Roman Catholic Church
> Diocese of Pueblo, Roman Catholic Church
> Fellowship of Baptists for Home Missions
> Pentecostal Church of God
> Southern Baptist Convention
> United Presbyterian Church

CONNECTICUT

Mohegan Congregational Church: 40 members.

FLORIDA

Resident Indian Population: 1,549

Protestant Churches: 11 churches, 570 members, 700 community.

Churches and Missions:
> United Methodist Church
> Southern Baptist Convention
> Independent Baptist Churches

IDAHO

Resident Indian Population: 5,105

Protestant Churches: 9 churches, 264 members, 676 community.
Roman Catholic Church: 6 churches, 840 members, 1,000 community.

> Total: 1,104 members, 1,676 community

Churches and Missions:
> Church of God
> Diocese of Boise, Roman Catholic Church
> Diocese of Idaho, Episcopal Church
> Southern Baptist Convention
> United Methodist Church
> United Presbyterian Church

IOWA

Resident Indian Population: 575

Protestant Churches: 2 churches, 101 members, 450 community.

Churches: Diocese of Iowa, Episcopal Church
> United Presbyterian Church

KANSAS

Resident Indian Population: 917

Protestant Churches: 6 churches, 304 members, 360 community.
Diocese of Wichita, Roman Catholic Church: 4,673 community.

LOUISIANA

Resident Indian Population: Chitimacha reservation 182 (The
parish priest says the Chitimachas number 250, of whom
55 are Catholics.)
Houma. Not reported by BIA.

Protestant Churches: 1 church, 174 members, 200 community.
Roman Catholic Church: 6 churches, 6,470 community.

Churches: Diocese of Houma-Thibodaux, Roman Catholic Church
Diocese of Lafayette
United Methodist Church

MAINE

Roman Catholic Diocese of Portland: 8 churches, 4,000 members.
Conservative Baptist Home Mission Society: 1 church, 40
members, 50 community.

Total 4,050

MASSACHUSETTS

American Baptist churches 2, members 121, community 200.

MICHIGAN

Resident Indian Population: 2,252

Roman Catholic Church: 15 churches, 6,870 community. (Dioceses
of Gaylord, Marquette, Saginaw)
United Methodist Church: 11 churches, 261 members, 326
community.

Total 7,196

MINNESOTA

Resident Indian Population: 11,273

Protestant Churches: 25 churches, 1,184 members, 2,327
community.

Roman Catholic Church: 30 churches, mostly partial, 11,976 community.

Total 14,303

Churches: American Lutheran Church
Archdiocese of St. Paul-Minneapolis
Christian and Missionary Alliance
Diocese of Crookston, Roman Catholic Church
Diocese of Duluth, Roman Catholic Church
Diocese of Minnesota, Episcopal Church
Diocese of St. Cloud, Roman Catholic Church
United Methodist Church
United Presbyterian Church

MISSISSIPPI

Resident Indian Population: 3,379

Protestant Churches: 22 churches, 1,418 members, 2,860 community.
Roman Catholic Church: 1,020 community.

Total 3,880

Churches: Mennonite Church
Pentecostal Church of God
Southern Baptist Convention
United Methodist Church

MISSOURI

Roman Catholic Church, Archdiocese of St. Louis 4,500

MONTANA

Resident Indian Population: 25,922

Protestant Churches: 23 churches, 1,269 members, 1,811 community.
Roman Catholic Church: 14,700 baptized membership

Total 16,511

Churches: American Baptist Church
American Lutheran Church
Christian and Missionary Alliance
Diocese of Great Falls, Roman Catholic Church
Diocese of Helena, Roman Catholic Church
Mennonite Church, General Conference

Pentecostal Church of God
Southern Baptist Convention
United Methodist Church
United Presbyterian Church

NEBRASKA

Resident Indian Population: 2,492

Protestant Churches: 9 churches, 242 members, 327 community.
Roman Catholic Church: 2 churches, 407 community.

Total 784

Churches: Diocese of Nebraska, Episcopal Church
Diocese of Omaha, Roman Catholic Church
Reformed Church in America
United Church of Christ

NEVADA

Resident Indian Population: 4,662

Protestant Churches: 9 churches, 362 members, 430 community.
Roman Catholic Church: 1 church, 400 community.

Total 730

Churches: Assemblies of God
Pentecostal Church of God
Southern Baptist Convention
United Presbyterian Church

NEW HAMPSHIRE

Roman Catholic Church, Diocese of Manchester: 100 community.

NEW MEXICO

Resident Indian Population: 92,963

Protestant Churches: 108 churches, 4,657 members, 6,266
community.
Roman Catholic Church: 71 churches, 29,760 community.

Total 30,426

Churches and Missions:
American Indian Bible Mission
Archdiocese of Santa Fe, Roman Catholic Church

Assemblies of God
Berean Mission, Inc.
Brethren in Christ
Church of the Brethren
Church of God
Church of the Nazarene
Christian Reformed Church
Diocese of El Paso (Apache church)
Diocese of Gallup, Roman Catholic Church
Diocese of the Rio Grande, Episcopal Church
  (Navajoland Episcopal Mission)
Evangelical Church of North America
Navajo Missions
Pentecostal Church of God
Reformed Church in America
Seventh Day Adventist Church
Southern Baptist Convention
United Methodist Church
United Presbyterian Church in U.S.A.
Independent Churches

NEW YORK

Protestant Churches: 8 churches, 756 members, 866 community.
Roman Catholic Church, Diocese of Ogdenburg: 1 church, 5,100
  community. (Report was 2,000 in 1976.)

  Total 5,966

Churches: Assemblies of God
          United Methodist Church
          United Presbyterian Church in U.S.A.

NORTH CAROLINA

Resident Indian Population: 4,940 (Lumbees not included)

Protestant Churches: 74 churches, 8,257 members, 10,624
  community.

Churches: Assemblies of God
          Christian and Missionary Alliance
          Diocese of Western North Carolina, Episcopal Church
          Seventh Day Adventist Church
          Southern Baptist Convention
          United Methodist Church

NORTH DAKOTA

Resident Indian Population: 14,881

Protestant Churches: 17 churches, 776 members, 1,225 community.
Roman Catholic Church: 12 churches, 19,222 community.

Total 20,847

Churches: Christian and Missionary Alliance
Diocese of Bismarck, Roman Catholic Church
Diocese of Fargo, Roman Catholic Church
Diocese of Montana, Episcopal Church
United Church of Christ
United Presbyterian Church

OKLAHOMA

Resident Indian Population: (former reservations and
Independent Nations) 85,228

Protestant Churches: 377 churches, 23,525 members, 27,700
community.
Roman Catholic Church: 12 churches, 3,650 community.

Total 31,350

Churches and Missions:
American Baptist Church
American Lutheran Church
Archdiocese of Oklahoma City, Roman Catholic Church
Assemblies of God
Church of the Nazarene
Cumberland Presbyterian Church
Diocese of Oklahoma, Episcopal Church
Diocese of Tulsa, Roman Catholic Church
Friends, Associated Committee of
Mennonite Brethren Church
Oklahoma Indian Evangelism
Pentecostal Church of God
Presbyterian Church in the U.S.
Reformed Church in America
Southern Baptist Convention
United Methodist Church
United Presbyterian Church in U.S.A.

OREGON

Resident Indian Population: 2,883

Protestant Churches: 6 churches, 220 members, 255 community.
Roman Catholic Church: 4 churches, 1,000 community.

Total 1,255

Churches: Diocese of Baker, Roman Catholic Church
Diocese of Portland, Roman Catholic Church
Southern Baptist Convention
United Methodist Church
United Presbyterian Church

SOUTH DAKOTA

Resident Indian Population: 31,579

Protestant Churches: 162 churches, 5,750 members, 10,044
community.
Roman Catholic Church: 16,760 community.

Total 26,804

Churches: Assemblies of God
Christian and Missionary Alliance
Church of God
Diocese of Rapid City, Roman Catholic Church
Diocese of Sioux Falls, Roman Catholic Church
Diocese of South Dakota, Episcopal Church
Fellowship of Baptists for Home Missions
Mennonite Brethren Church
Seventh Day Adventist Church
Southern Baptist Convention
United Church of Christ
United Presbyterian Church in U.S.A.
Wesleyan Church

TENNESSEE

Southern Baptist Convention: 2 churches, 40+ members, 45
community.

TEXAS

Protestant Churches: 7 churches, members c. 350, community c.
500.

Churches: Assemblies of God
Christian Indian Ministries
Southern Baptist Convention
United Indian Missions Inc.

UTAH

Resident Population: 7,391

Protestant Churches: 11 churches, 1,400 members, 1,800 community.

Roman Catholic Church: 2 churches, community c. 800.

Total 2,600

Churches: Episcopal Church
Navajo Gospel Crusade
Roman Catholic Church, Diocese of Salt Lake City

VIRGINIA

Southern Baptist Convention: 6 churches, 260 members, community c. 300.

WASHINGTON

Resident Population: 17,708

Protestant Churches: 15 churches, 625 members, 760 community.
Roman Catholic Church: 19 churches, 7,793 community.

Total 8,553

Churches: Archdiocese of Seattle, Roman Catholic Church
Assemblies of God
Church of God
Christian Church, Disciplies
Diocese of Spokane, Roman Catholic Church
Diocese of Yakima, Roman Catholic Church
Lutheran Church - Missouri Synod
Pentecostal Church of God
Southern Baptist Convention
United Methodist Church
United Presbyterian Church in U.S.A.

WISCONSIN

Resident Population: 7,952

Protestant Churches: 14 churches, 1,113 members, 1,430 community.
Roman Catholic Church: 22 churches, 7,255 community.

Total 8,685

Churches: Archdiocese of Milwaukee, Roman Catholic Church
Assemblies of God
Lutheran Church - Missouri Synod
Orthodox Presbyterian Church
Reformed Church in America
United Church of Christ

United Methodist Church
United Presbyterian Church in U.S.A.

WYOMING

Resident Indian Population: 4,538

Protestant Churches: 3 churches, 475 communicants, 1,600
community.
Roman Catholic Church: 3 churches, communicant members c. 600,
1,050 community.

Total 2,650

Churches: Diocese of Cheyenne, Roman Catholic Church
Diocese of Wyoming, Episcopal Church

VIII
STATISTICAL
TABLES

TABLE I – NATIVE AMERICAN PERSONNEL

CHURCH OR MISSION	ORDAINED MINISTERS PRIESTS M	W	SACRAMENTALISTS M	W	DEACONS M	W	LICENSED PASTORS M	W	LAY PASTORS M	W	RELIGIOUS S	B	LAY WORKERS M	W	TEACHERS M	W	SERVICE PERSONNEL M	W	MEDICAL STAFF M	W
American Baptist Churches	3	1							7					3						
Assemblies of God	5						1						2	3	4			1		
Brethren in Christ Church									2				6		1					
Christian & Missionary Alliance									14				2							
Christian Church, Disciples																				
Christian Reformed Church	4	1							7											
Church of God	4								1											
Church of God in Christ, Mennonite																				
Church of the Brethren	11	3							3	4			8	4						
Church of the Nazarene							19	1												
Churches of God, Gen'l Conf.	2																			
Conservative Baptist Home Mission Society									1				1	1						
Cumberland Presbyterian Church	10								1				121#							
Episcopal Church	36	13	2	3	2															
Evangelical Church of N.A.	1																			
Evangelical Covenant Church	6																			
Fellowship of Baptists for Home Missions							4									1				
Free Methodist Church									2											
Friends, Associated Committee	6	2																		
Friends, Calif. Yearly Meeting									2											
Friends, Rocky Mtn. Yrly. Mtg.																				
Lutheran: Nat'l Indian Luth. Bd.																				
Lutheran: American Luth. Church	1												1							
Lutheran Church in America	1																			
Lutheran Church-Missouri Synod																				

M–Men; W–Women; S–Sisters; B–Brothers; #–Total

TABLE I – NATIVE AMERICAN PERSONNEL, continued

CHURCH OR MISSION	ORDAINED MINISTERS PRIESTS M	ORDAINED MINISTERS PRIESTS W	SACRAMENTALISTS M	SACRAMENTALISTS W	DEACONS M	DEACONS W	LICENSED PASTORS M	LICENSED PASTORS W	LAY PASTORS M	LAY PASTORS W	RELIGIOUS S	RELIGIOUS B	LAY WORKERS M	LAY WORKERS W	TEACHERS M	TEACHERS W	SERVICE PERSONNEL M	SERVICE PERSONNEL W	MEDICAL STAFF M	MEDICAL STAFF W
Lutheran Mission, Navajo Evan.	1												4	2		1				1
Lutheran Synod, Wisconsin Evan	1															2				
Mennonite Brethren Church	3								3							5				
Mennonite Church	1																			
Mennonite Church, Gen'l Conf.									2											
Moravian Church in America	5				6		1													
Orthodox Church in America	10								17											
Orthodox Presbyterian Church																				
Pentecostal Church of god	1								4	1										
Presbyterian Church in US																				
Reformed Church in America	2																			
Roman Catholic Church	11				46						52	1	4	2	4	16				
Salvation Army	2						60		21				624#							
Seventh-day Adventist Church																				
Southern Baptist Convention	248																			
United Church of Christ	8	1											8	1						
United Methodist Church	79				2				5					15						
United Presbyterian Church	27																			
Wesleyan Church	35																			
American Indian Bible Mission	4	3							1				1			15				
Arctic Mission, INc.		1											1							
Berean Missions, Inc.																				
Central Alaskan Missions																				

M-Men; W-Women; S-Sisters; B-Brothers; #-Total

TABLE I – NATIVE AMERICAN PERSONNEL, concluded

Church or Mission	Ordained Ministers / Priests M	W	Sacramentalists M	W	Deacons M	W	Licensed Pastors M	W	Lay Pastors M	W	Religious S	B	Lay Workers M	W	Teachers M	W	Service Personnel M	W	Medical Staff M	W
Christian Indian Ministries	1	5					1						7	9						
Flagstaff Mission to Navajos													2	1						
Good News Mission to Navajos																				
Navajo Bible School & Mission													1		1					
Navajo Gospel Crusade							3	5	2				10	4						
Navajo Gospel Mission									1											
Sanders Bible Mission																				
Slavic Gospel Mission									5											
United Indian Mission	1																			
Southwest Indian School																3				
Cook Christian Training School	(2)	5																		
Independent Churches	1								61	2			3	5			2	5		
Councils & Cooperative Agency																(1)				
Service Agencies																				
Grand Totals	541	12	13	2	57	2	89	7	162	7	52	1	863#		10	44	2	6		1

M–Men; W–Women; S–Sisters; B–Brothers; #–Total

TABLE II – WHITE AND OTHER PERSONNELL

Church or Mission	Ordained Ministers / Priests M	W	Sacramentalists M	W	Deacons M	W	Licensed Pastors M	W	Lay Pastors M	W	Religious S	B	Lay Workers M	W	Teachers M	W	Service Personnel M	W	Medical Staff M	W
American Baptist Churches	6												2	1	10	8				
Assemblies of God	32	2					1	6	50	26					1	5				
Brethren in Christ Church	1	1																		
Christian & Missionary Alliance	4						1							6			2			
Christian Church, Disciples																				
Christian Reformed Church	9								4						10	11				
Church of God	1	3							3	3				18						
Church of God in Christ, Mennonite																				
Church of the Brethren	1																			
Church of the Nazarene	9								4											
Churches of God, Gen'l Conf.	1													5						
Conservative Baptist Home Mission Society															6#					
Cumberland Presbyterian Church	2												1	1						
Episcopal Church	36	1							2	1			1	5						
Evangelical Church of N.A.	4						5													
Evangelical Covenant Church	4														3	4				
Fellowship of Baptists for Home Missions													5	5						
Free Methodist Church	1								4	3			1							
Friends, Associated Committee	(3)								2				1	2				(3)		
Friends, Calif. Yearly Meeting																				
Friends, Rocky Mtn. Yrly. Mtg.																		(2)		
Lutheran: Nat'l Indian Luth. Bd.									2	1										
Lutheran: American Luth. Church	8														6	2				
Lutheran Church in America	1																			
Lutheran Church-Missouri Synod	5																(1)			

M–Men; W–Women; S–Sisters; B–Brothers; #–Total

TABLE II – WHITE AND OTHER PERSONNEL, continued

Church or Mission	Ordained Ministers / Priests (M)	Ordained Ministers / Priests (W)	Sacramentalists (M)	Sacramentalists (W)	Deacons (M)	Deacons (W)	Licensed Pastors (M)	Licensed Pastors (W)	Lay Pastors (M)	Lay Pastors (W)	Religious (S)	Religious (B)	Lay Workers (M)	Lay Workers (W)	Teachers (M)	Teachers (W)	Service Personnel (M)	Service Personnel (W)	Medical Staff (M)	Medical Staff (W)
Lutheran Mission, Navajo Evan.	(4) 9												3	1	8	10		14		2
Lutheran Synod, Wisconsin Evan	2																	3		
Mennonite Brethren Church	1						1											5#		
Mennonite Church	3																			
Mennonite Church, Gen'l Conf.																				
Moravian Church in America	3																			
Orthodox Church in America	10												28	2		16				
Orthodox Presbyterian Church	12								1	7				20						
Pentecostal Church of God	1	3							7	7				2						
Presbyterian Church in US																				
Reformed Church in America	7																			
Roman Catholic Church	339				1						480	38	2	10 / 569#	2	307# (192#) (3) 1		15# +(13)		34#
Salvation Army	13						12		12				2	1						
Seventh-day Adventist Church	5																			
Southern Baptist Convention	63																			
United Church of Christ	3								3											
United Methodist Church	25	2											21#		6	38#				
United Presbyterian Church	39	2																		
Wesleyan Church	2													12						
American Indian Bible Mission	14									8			1	2	5	20		15		1
Arctic Mission, Inc.	1								1											
Berean Missions, Inc.																				8
Central Alaskan Missions	4																			

M–Men; W–Women; S–Sisters; B–Brothers; #–Total

TABLE II – WHITE AND OTHER PERSONNEL, concluded

CHURCH OR MISSION	ORDAINED MINISTERS PRIESTS M	W	SACRAMENTALISTS M	W	DEACONS M	W	LICENSED PASTORS M	W	LAY PASTORS M	W	RELIGIOUS S	B	LAY WORKERS M	W	TEACHERS M	W	SERVICE PERSONNEL M	W	MEDICAL STAFF M	W
Christian Indian Ministries	3						–													
Flagstaff Mission to Navajos	3												–	9						
Good News Mission to Navajos	–																		–	
Navajo Bible School & Mission	–												–	15#	7#					
Navajo Gospel Crusade									5				9	12		5				
Navajo Gospel Mission	2																			
Sanders Bible Mission									1											
Slavic Gospel Mission																				
United Indian Mission									4	2										
Southwest Indian School	–												–	–						
Cook Christian Training School	(1)														6	7				
Independent Churches	10								58	13					7#					
Councils & Cooperative Agency													115#							
Service Agencies	(16)													5						
Mennonite Service Agencies													24	5	2	1	9	6		
Summer School of Linguistics/Wycliffe																	+39#			
Others																	68#			
Grand Totals	703	15					21	6	172	57	480	38	997#		515*		174**		46#	

M–Men; W–Women; S–Sisters; B–Brothers; #–Total
*plus 192 Religious tablulated elsewhere
**plus 13 Religious

TABLE III – CHURCH STATISTICS

Church or Mission Society	Churches/Chapels	Active Members (Communicants)	Total Community	Conversions (1977)	Adult Baptisms	Infant Baptisms	Sunday Schools	Women's Societies	Youth Societies	Vacation Bible Schools	Week-Day Religious Education/C.C.D.	Elementary Schools	High Schools	Colleges	Bible Schools & Seminaries
American Baptist Churches	18	1,000	1,200		15		8	6	18	10	2	1		1	3
Assemblies of God	72	2,980	3,300		145		33	20							1
Brethren in Christ Church	2	35	50												
Christian & Missionary Alliance	22	745	1,358	38		6	10	1	2	1					
Christian Church, Disciples	2	76	93						1						
Christian Reformed Church	25	942	2,206		20	22	14				-	2	1	-	1
Church of God	4	230	605				4	3							
Church of God in Christ, Mennonite	4	37	102				2								
Church of the Brethren	1	20	40				1								
Church of the Nazarene	32	1,557	2,652		62		27	23	21	14					
Churches of God, Gen'l Conf.	1	35	40					1							
Conservative Baptist Home Mission Society	3	108	135	56	12		2	1		1					
Cumberland Presbyterian Church	14	209	500		3	6	12	7	9	8					
Episcopal Church	180	10,364	19,674			629	42	4	2	1					
Evangelical Church of N.A.	8	233	450				2					2	1		4
Evangelical Covenant Church	14	315	950				2		2	1			1		
Fellowship of Baptists for Home Missions	6	130	150												
Free Methodist Church	1	(30)	(40)				1								
Friends, Associated Committee	4	70	100												
Friends, Calif. Yearly Meeting	12	725	775				9		4						
Friends, Rocky Mtn. Yrly. Mtg.	3	80	90												
Lutheran: Nat'l Indian Luth. Bd.	12														
Lutheran: American Luth. Church	1	163	1,758			17	3	4	4	1					
Lutheran Church in America			347				1		1	1					
Lutheran Church-Missouri Synod	6	385	505	10		10	3	1		1				-	-

TABLE III – CHURCH STATISTICS, continued

CHURCH OR MISSION SOCIETY	CHURCHES/CHAPELS	ACTIVE MEMBERS (COMMUNICANTS)	COMMUNITY TOTAL	CONVERSIONS (1977)	ADULT BAPTISMS	INFANT BAPTISMS	SUNDAY SCHOOLS	WOMEN'S SOCIETIES	YOUTH SOCIETIES	VACATION BIBLE SCHOOLS	WEEK-DAY RELIGIOUS EDUCATION/C.C.D.	ELEMENTARY SCHOOLS	HIGH SCHOOLS	COLLEGES	SEMINARIES & BIBLE SCHOOLS
Lutheran Mission, Navajo Evan.	(3)	(85)	(230)		12	149	(3)					—			
Lutheran Synod, Wisconsin Evan	16	1,160	3,095		16		9					3			
Mennonite Brethren Church	4	213	250				5								
Mennonite Church	6	156	195				9	5	5						
Mennonite Church, Gen'l Conf.	11	445	629					6	3	7		1	—		
Moravian Church in America	23	2,780	3,000	12	1	14	20	3	2						—
Orthodox Church in America	83	20,000	2,200	30	8	25									—
Orthodox Presbyterian Church	2	50	100	18											
Pentecostal Church of god	38	1,980	2,200		492		3	6	6						
Presbyterian Church in US	4	260	494				6	7	10						
Reformed Church in America	6	402	500							2					
Roman Catholic Church in America	454		177,651			3,665	4				76	32	7	2	
Salvation Army	13	180	210												
Seventh-day Adventist Church	6	634	750									2			
Southern Baptist Convention	381	28,444	36,000	43	491		227	150	27	77					3
United Church of Christ	25	1,083	1,350		2	6	8	5					—		
United Methodist Church	163	11,969	14,360	15	1	14	29	22	6	3			—	3	
United Presbyterian Church	105	6,826	8,190												
Wesleyan Church	30	500	500												
American Indian Bible Mission	4	90	105		26		3		2	2					
Arctic Mission, Inc.	11	225	500		100		1						—		
Berean Missions, Inc.	5	89	100				3						—	—	—
Central Alaskan Missions	3	118	130								3				—

TABLE III – CHURCH STATISTICS, concluded

Church or Mission Society	Churches/ Chapels	Active Members (Communicants)	Total Community	Conversions (1977)	Adult Baptisms	Infant Baptisms	Sunday Schools	Women's Societies	Youth Societies	Vacation Bible Schools	Week-day Religious Education/C.C.D.	Elementary Schools	High Schools	Colleges	Seminaries & Bible Schools
Christian Indian Ministries	1	376	25				5		3	6	3				
Flagstaff Mission to Navajos	6	60	450	141	28		1					1			1
Good News Mission to Navajos	3	200	75	32			3								
Navajo Bible School & Mission	9	80	500												
Navajo Gospel Crusade	3		90												1
Navajo Gospel Mission	1	425	500	35	15		8	4		12	1	1	1		1
Sanders Bible Mission	1	19	25						1	1		1			
Slavic Gospel Mission	–	60	75						5	2					
United Indian Mission	6	195	225				4								
Southwest Indian School	4														
Cook Christian Training School															
Independent Churches	164	6,950	8,000												
Others															
Grand Totals	2,048		320,199	430	1,449	4,563	544	275	114	152	86	47	17	9	21